••••• soltbank 4G 0:00 100%

< MEMO END

Magical Girl Site

VOLUME 16

D1075967

AUTHOR
KENTARO SATO

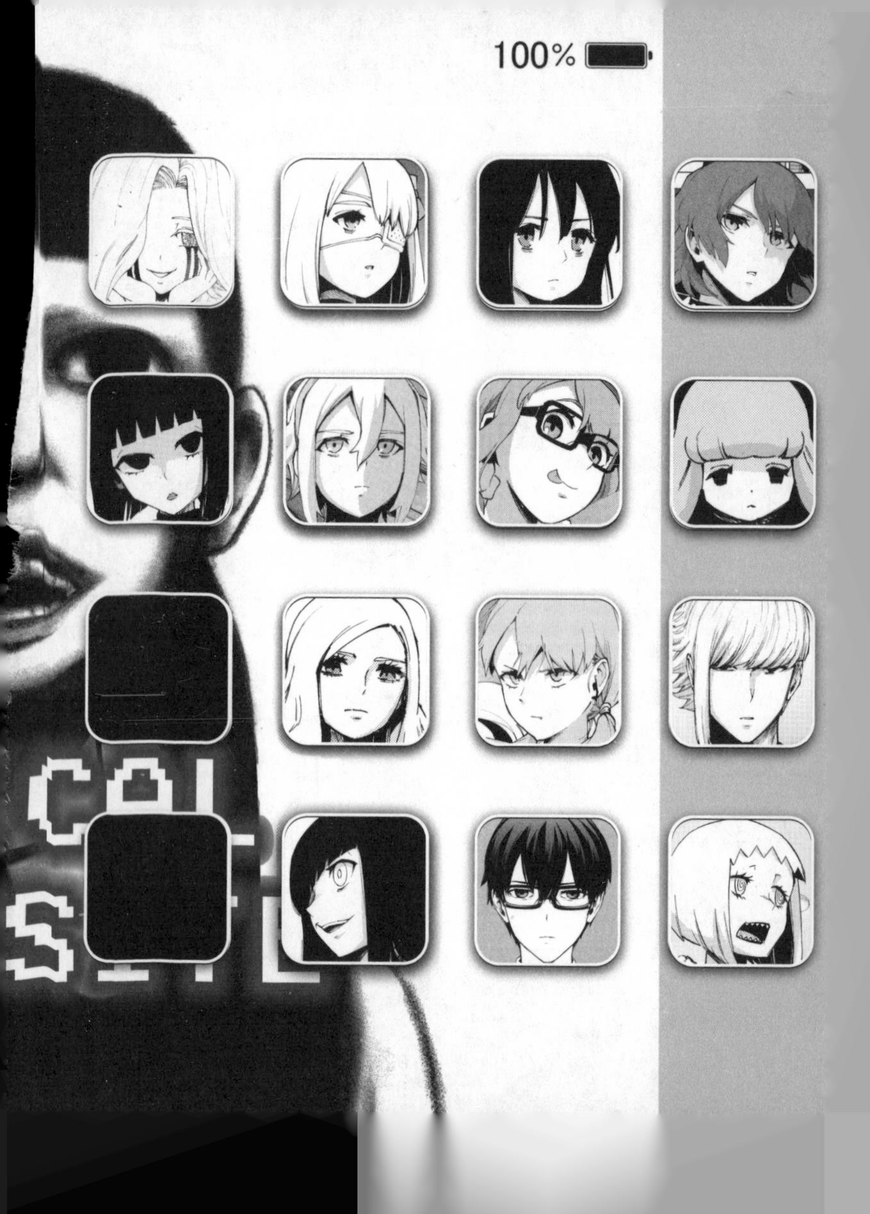
100%

●●●●● soltbank 4G 0:00

MEMO END

After Nana shared her regained memories, Aya and the others learned the whole story of Magical Girl Site, including the King's one weakness. The girls set off to stop the Tempest, only to be intercepted by a group of Site Managers!

When Manager Ni attempted to freeze the girls using the power of time, Asahi risked her life to bring the girls beyond the scope of time. In an attempt to save Yatsumura Tsuyuno, Aya and Sarina turned back to fight the Managers.

Meanwhile, the others split into two groups and began their plan to stop the Tempest. Kayo and her team set out to take care of the Palace of the Star. Misumi and Kaname, with Rina's support, were dispatched to take out the King from the outside. Unfortunately, the strongest of all the Managers, Ichi, showed up to protect the King, putting Kaname and Misumi in danger.

The battle between Aya, Sarina, and the Managers was a fierce and bloody one. Ultimately, Sarina sacrificed herself to protect Aya, who managed to extract Yatsumura Tsuyuno out of Manager Ni.

As Aya reflected on Sarina's death, a mysterious figure approached...but who could it be?! Can Aya save the world and her family from the grip of the King?!

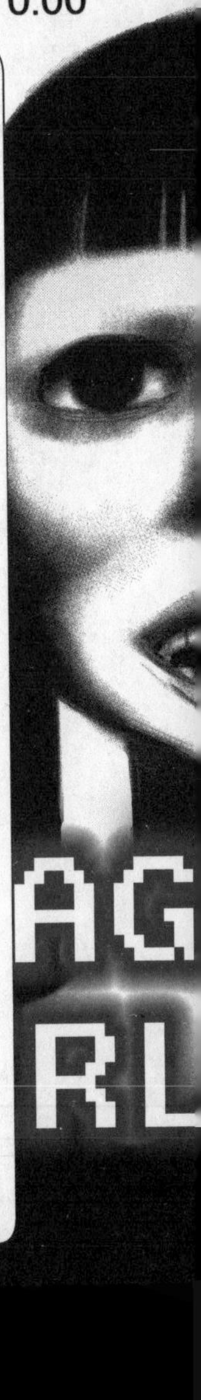

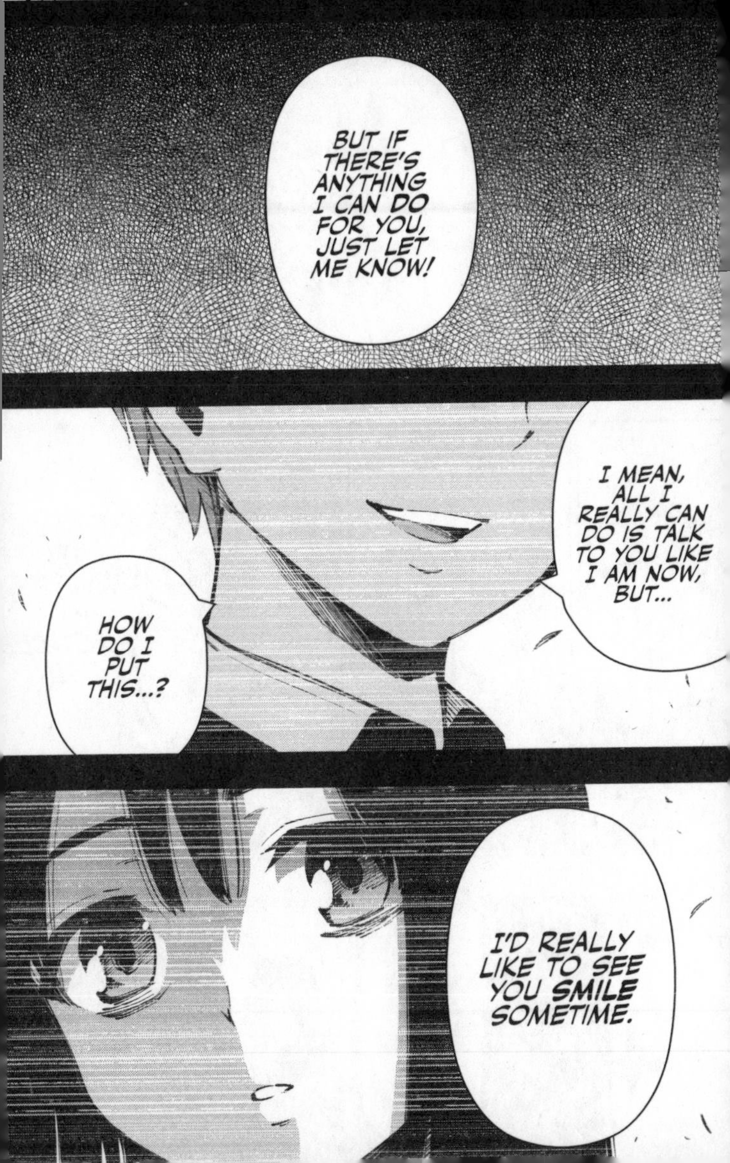
BUT IF THERE'S ANYTHING I CAN DO FOR YOU, JUST LET ME KNOW!
I MEAN, ALL I REALLY CAN DO IS TALK TO YOU LIKE I AM NOW, BUT...
HOW DO I PUT THIS...?
I'D REALLY LIKE TO SEE YOU SMILE SOMETIME.

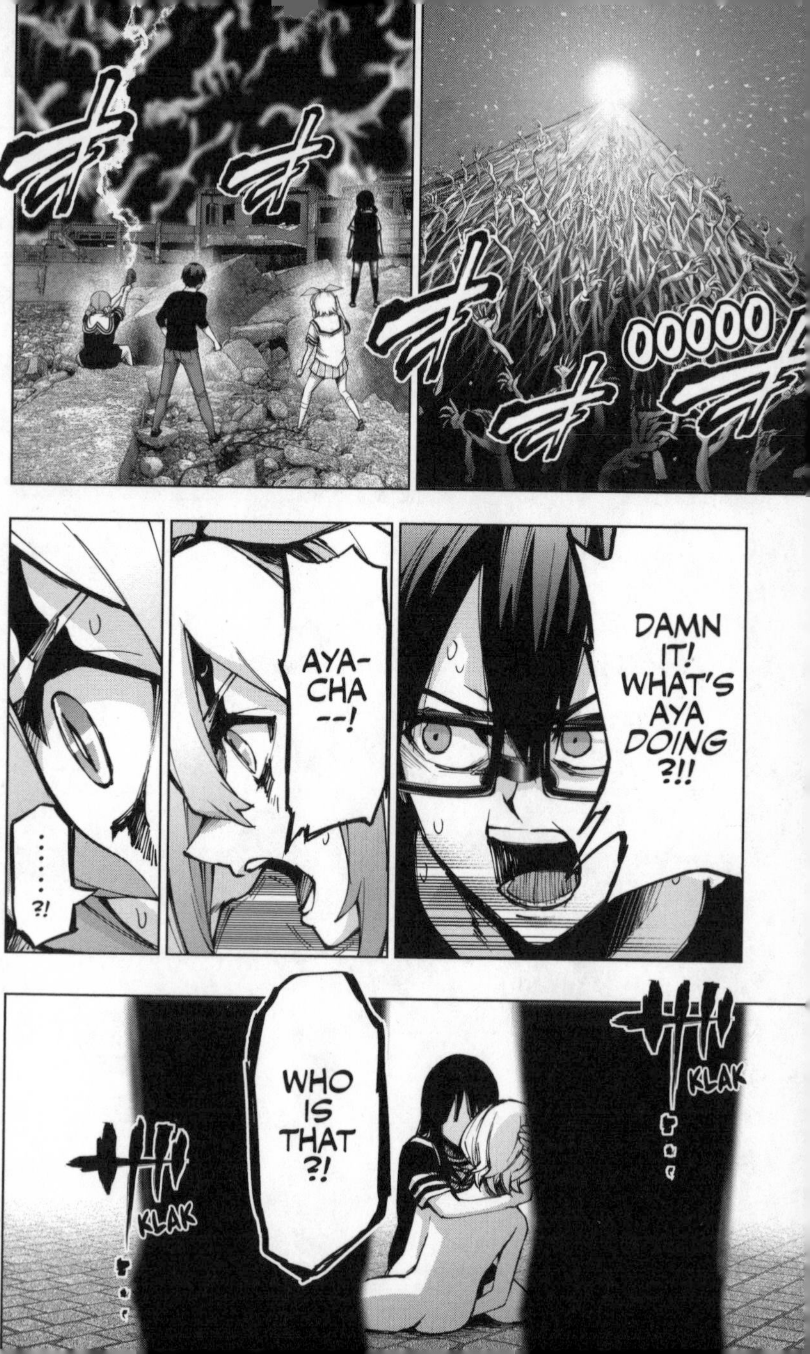
OOOOO
DAMN IT! WHAT'S AYA DOING?!!
AYA-CHA--!
......?!
KLAK
WHO IS THAT?!
KLAK

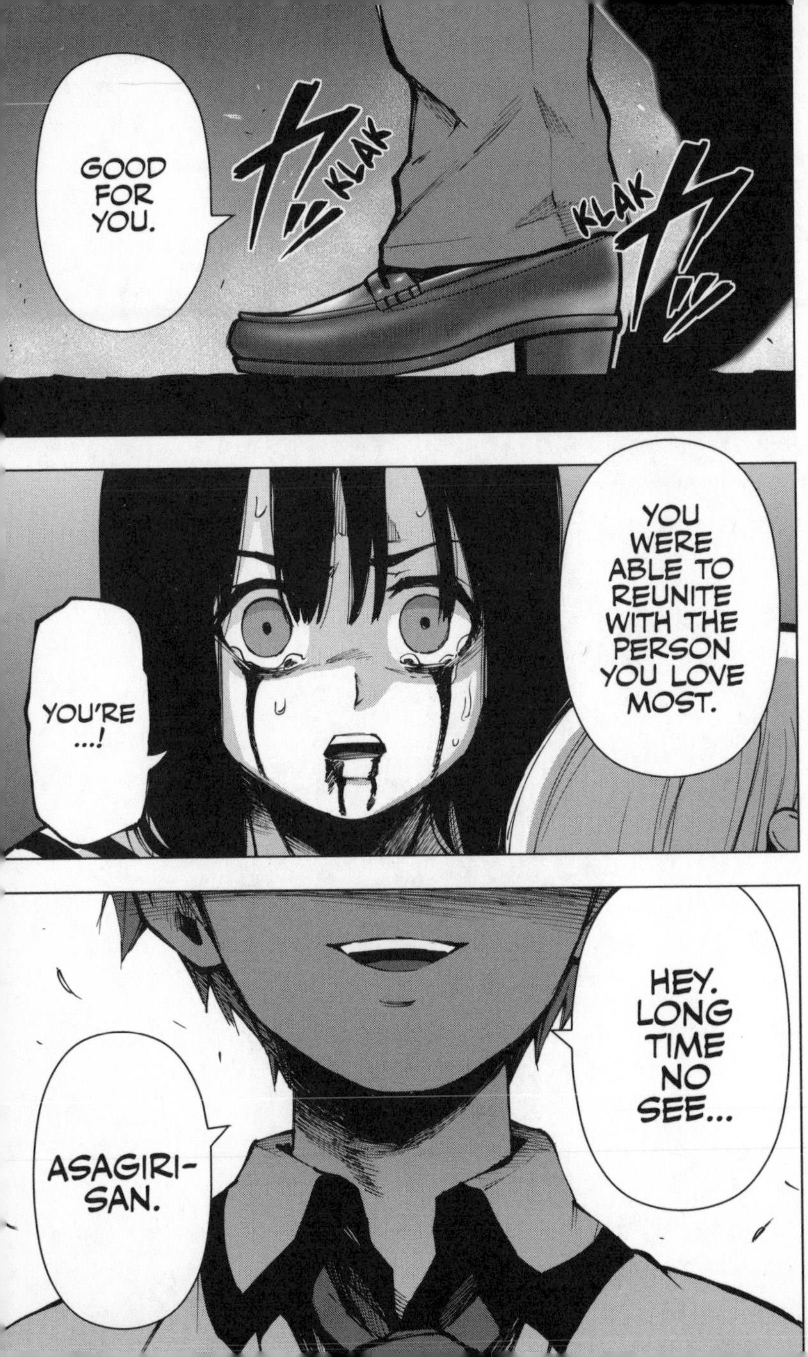
KLAK
KLAK
GOOD FOR YOU.
YOU WERE ABLE TO REUNITE WITH THE PERSON YOU LOVE MOST.
YOU'RE ...!
HEY. LONG TIME NO SEE...
ASAGIRI-SAN.

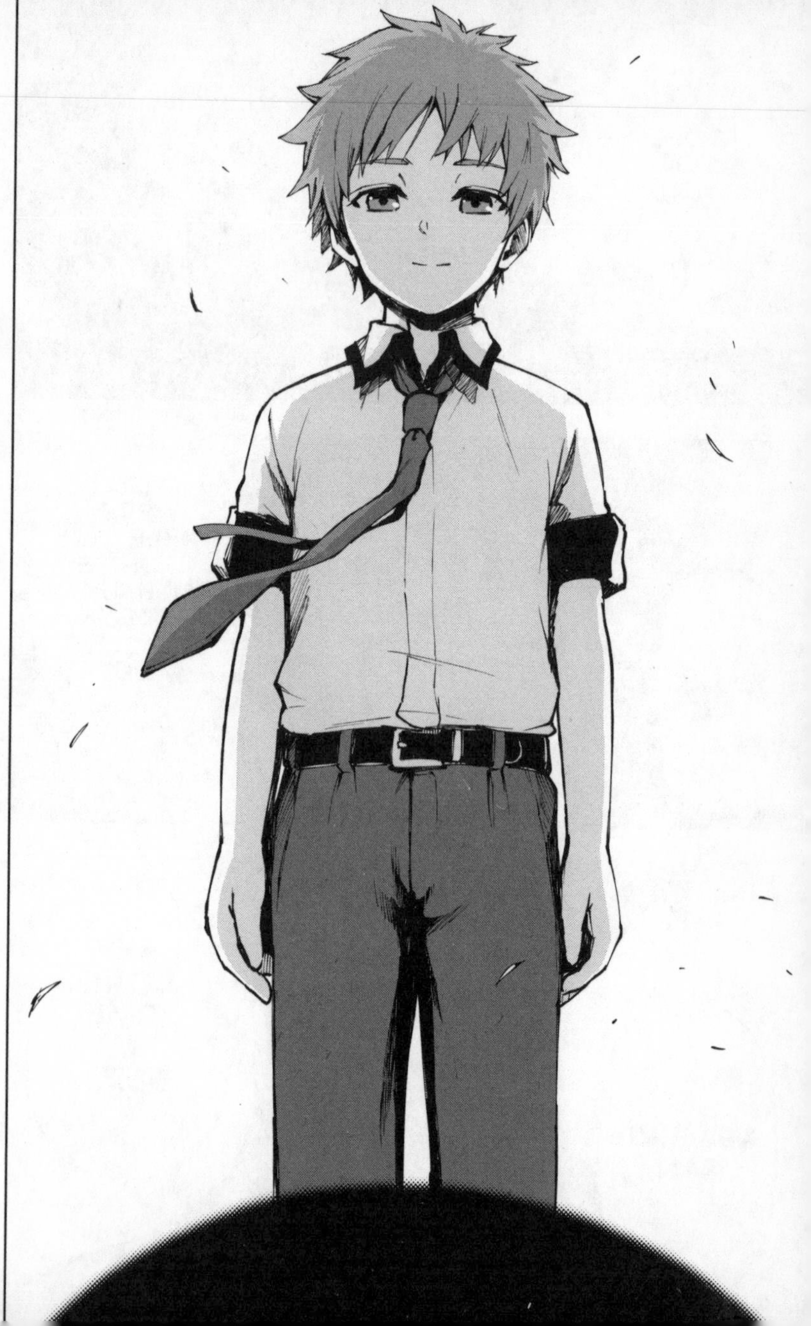

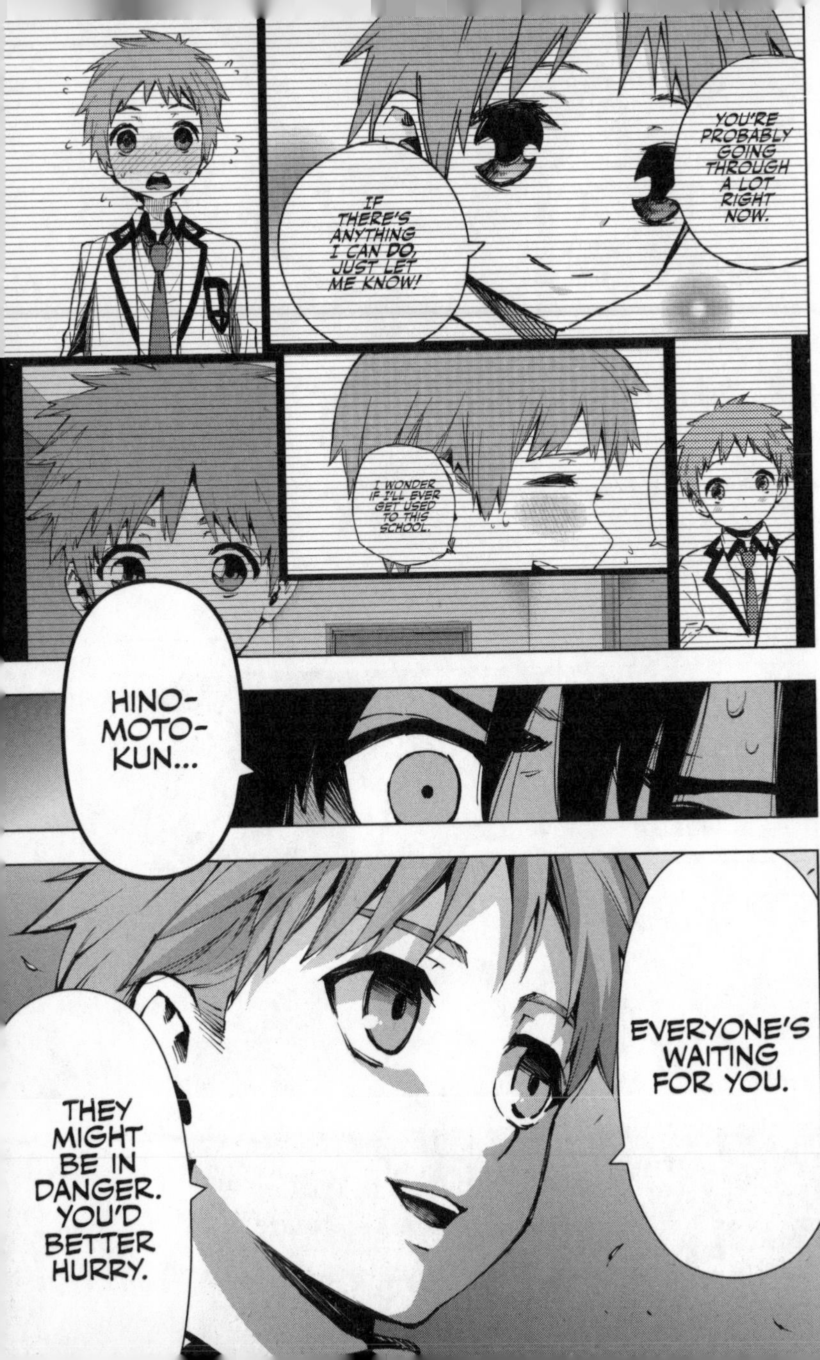
YOU'RE PROBABLY GOING THROUGH A LOT RIGHT NOW.
IF THERE'S ANYTHING I CAN DO, JUST LET ME KNOW!
I WONDER IF I'LL EVER GET USED TO THIS SCHOOL.
HINO-MOTO-KUN...
EVERYONE'S WAITING FOR YOU.
THEY MIGHT BE IN DANGER. YOU'D BETTER HURRY.

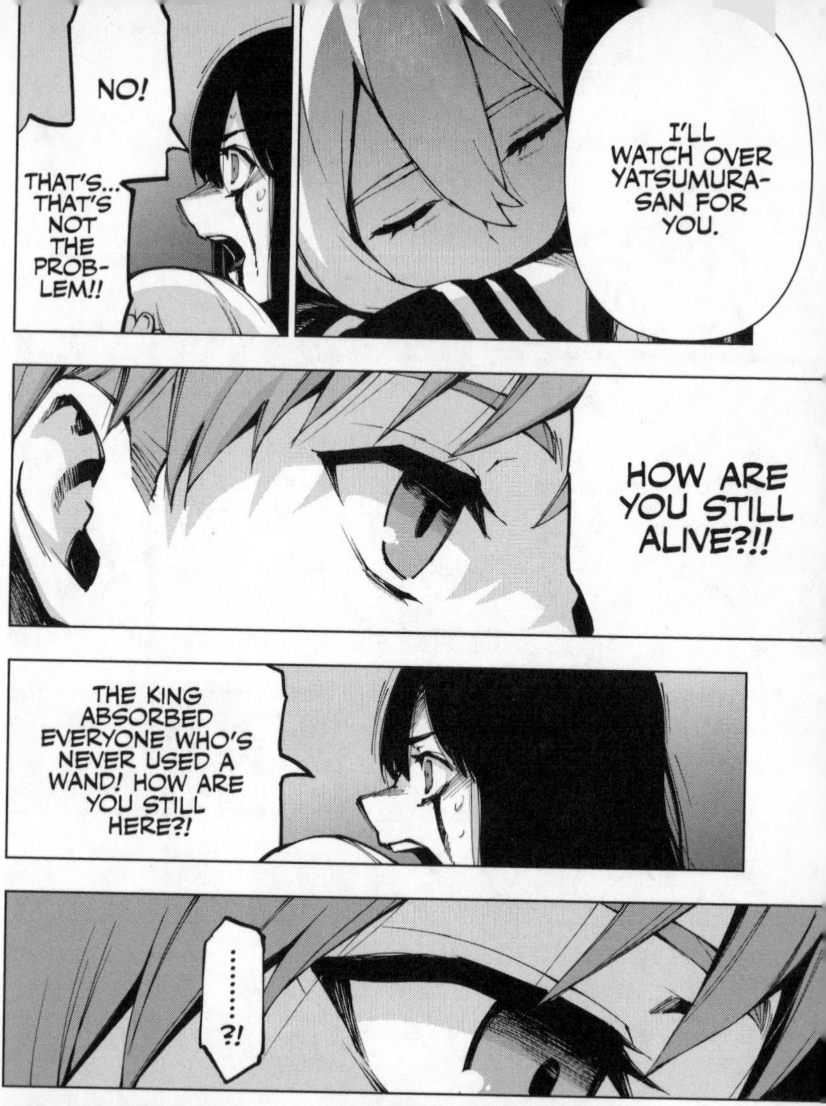
I'LL WATCH OVER YATSUMURA-SAN FOR YOU.
NO!
THAT'S... THAT'S NOT THE PROB-LEM!!
HOW ARE YOU STILL ALIVE?!!
THE KING ABSORBED EVERYONE WHO'S NEVER USED A WAND! HOW ARE YOU STILL HERE?!
........?!

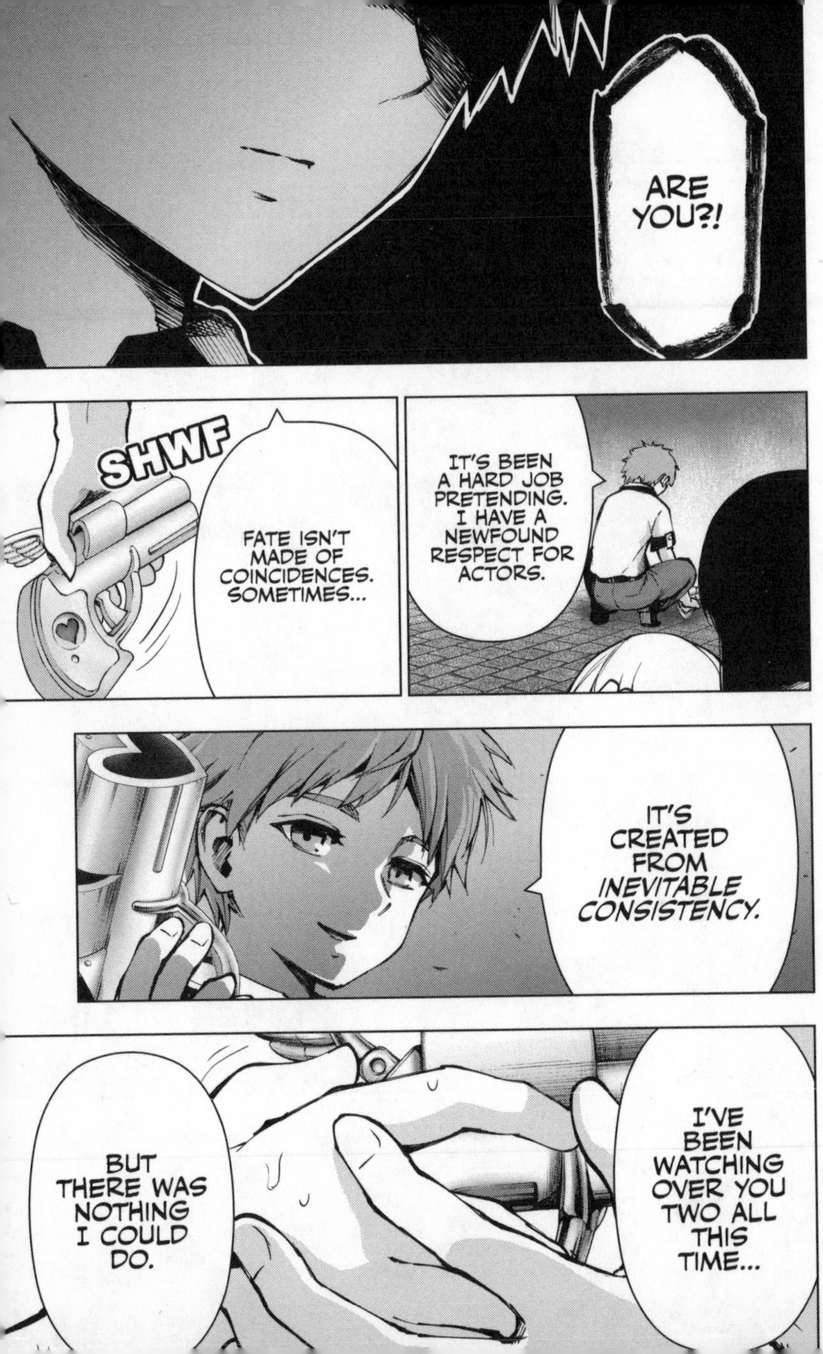

ARE YOU?!
IT'S BEEN A HARD JOB PRETENDING. I HAVE A NEWFOUND RESPECT FOR ACTORS.
SHWF
FATE ISN'T MADE OF COINCIDENCES. SOMETIMES...
IT'S CREATED FROM *INEVITABLE CONSISTENCY.*
I'VE BEEN WATCHING OVER YOU TWO ALL THIS TIME...
BUT THERE WAS NOTHING I COULD DO.

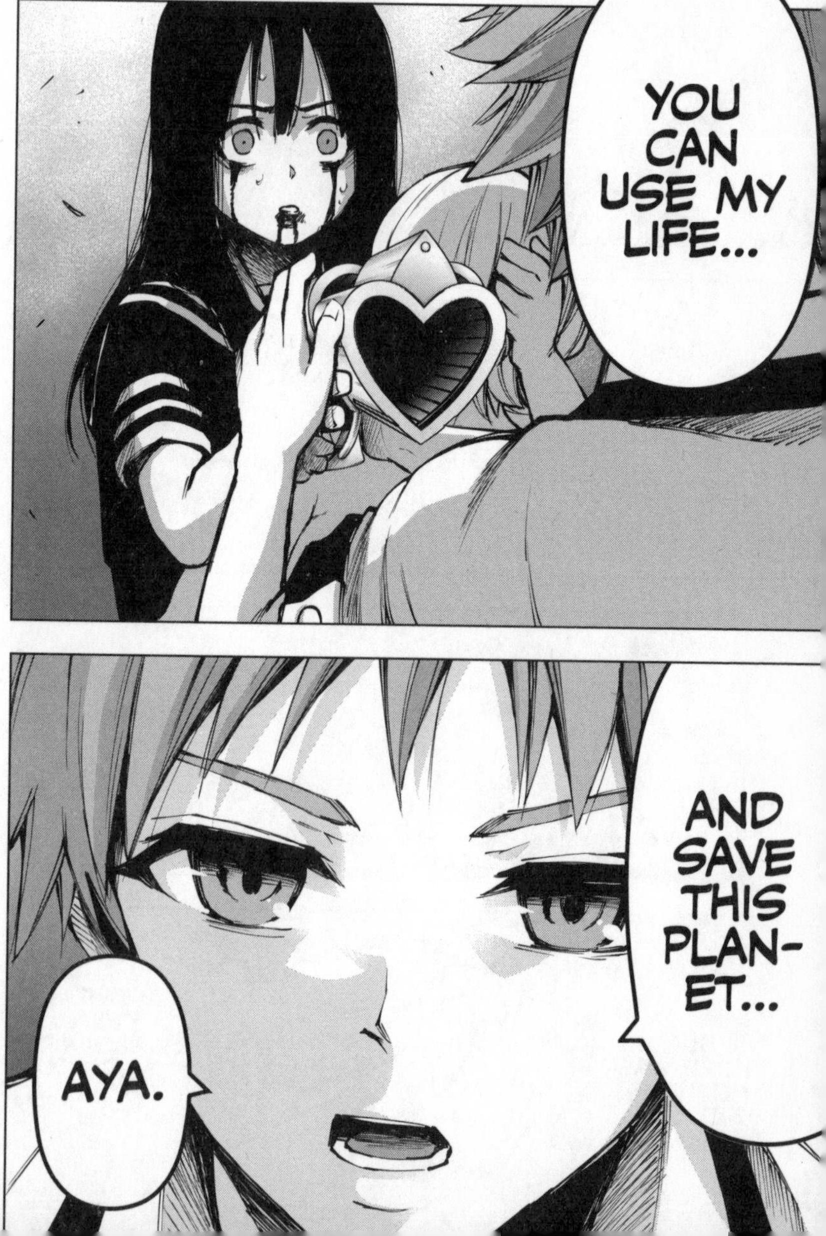
YOU CAN USE MY LIFE...
AND SAVE THIS PLAN-ET...
AYA.

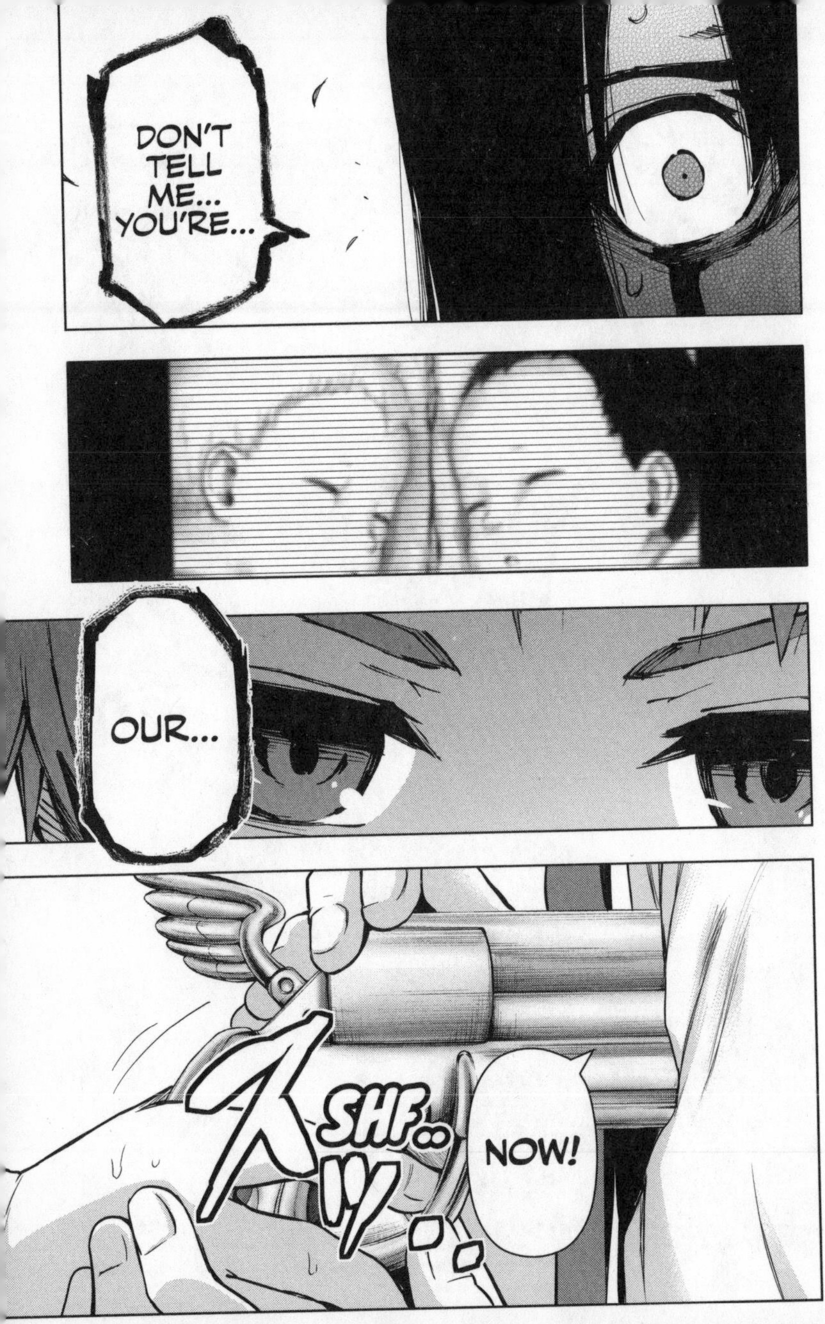
DON'T TELL ME... YOU'RE...
OUR...
NOW!
SHF..

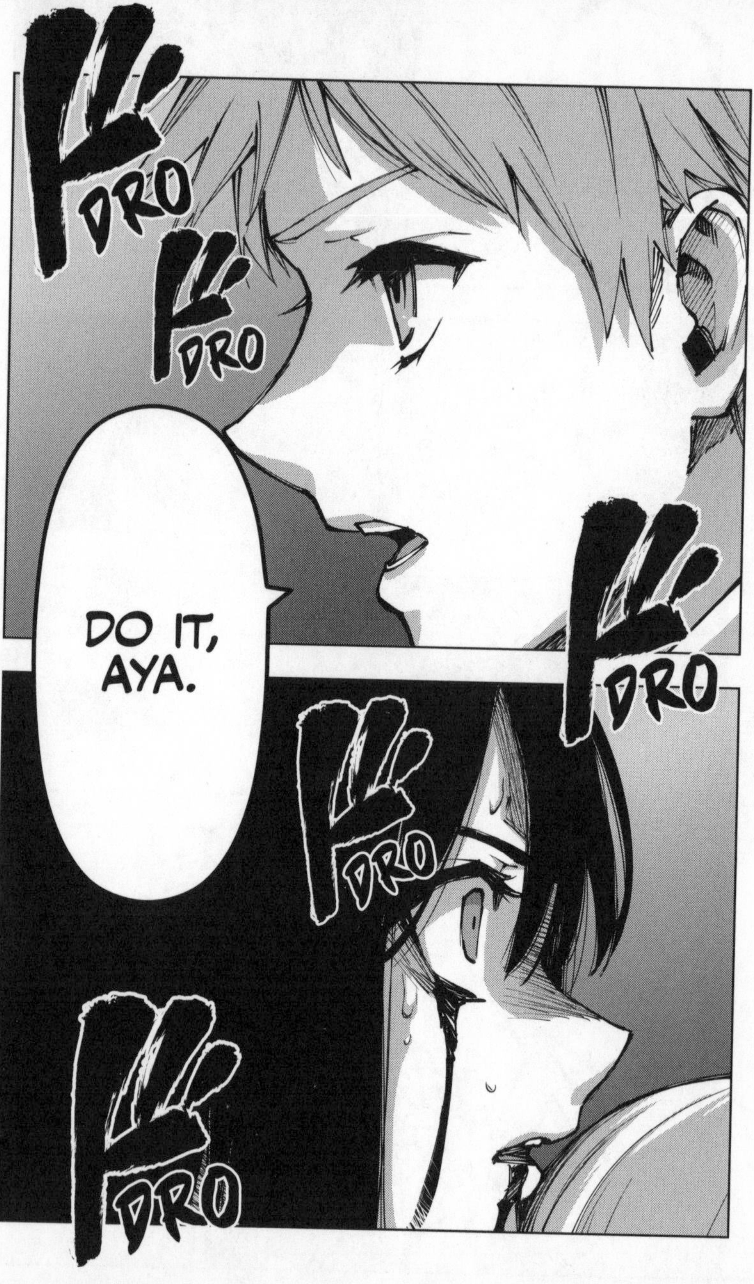
DRO
DRO
DO IT, AYA.
DRO
DRO
DRO

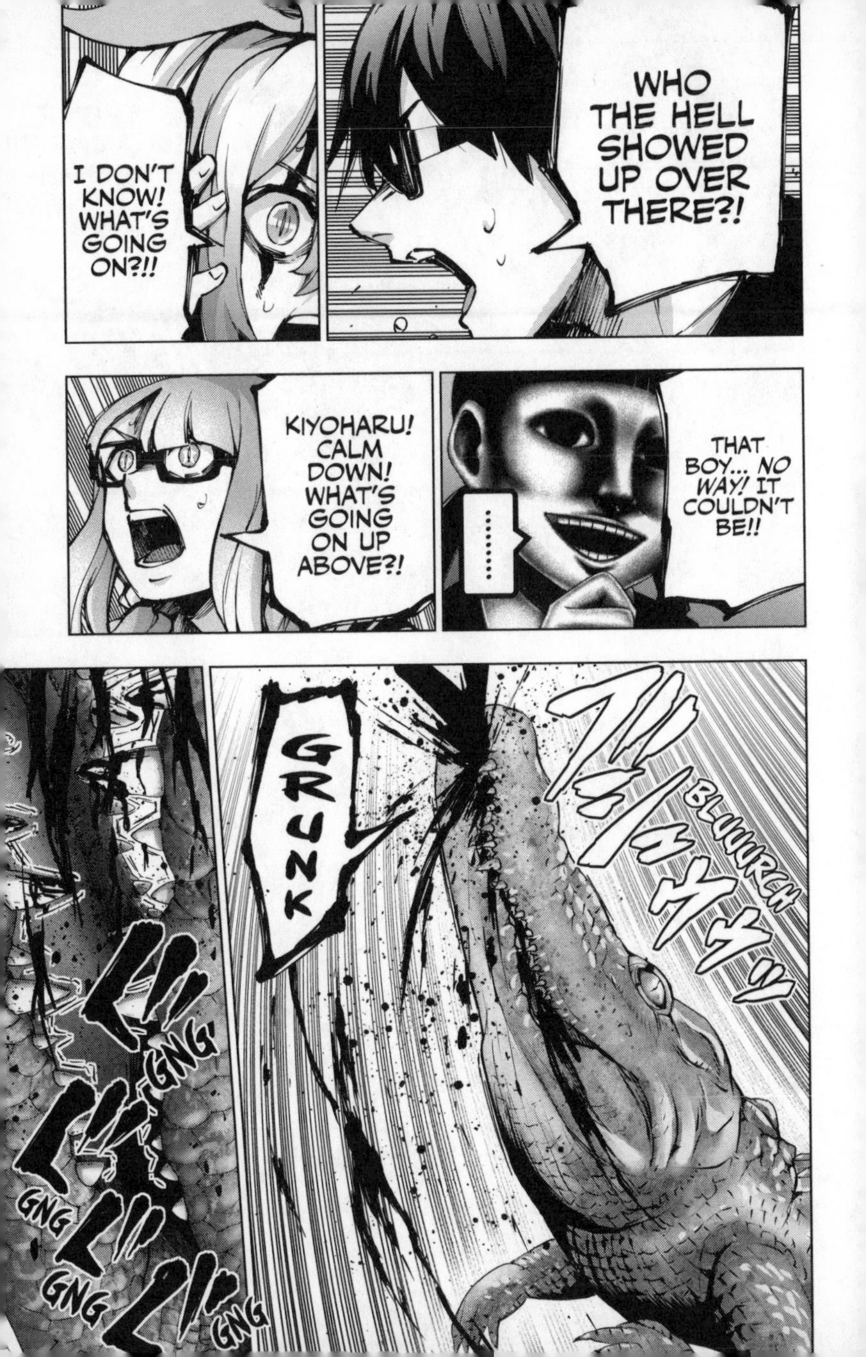
WHO THE HELL SHOWED UP OVER THERE?!
I DON'T KNOW! WHAT'S GOING ON?!!
THAT BOY... NO WAY! IT COULDN'T BE!!
......
KIYOHARU! CALM DOWN! WHAT'S GOING ON UP ABOVE?!
BLUUURCH
GRUNK
GNG
GNG
GNG
GNG

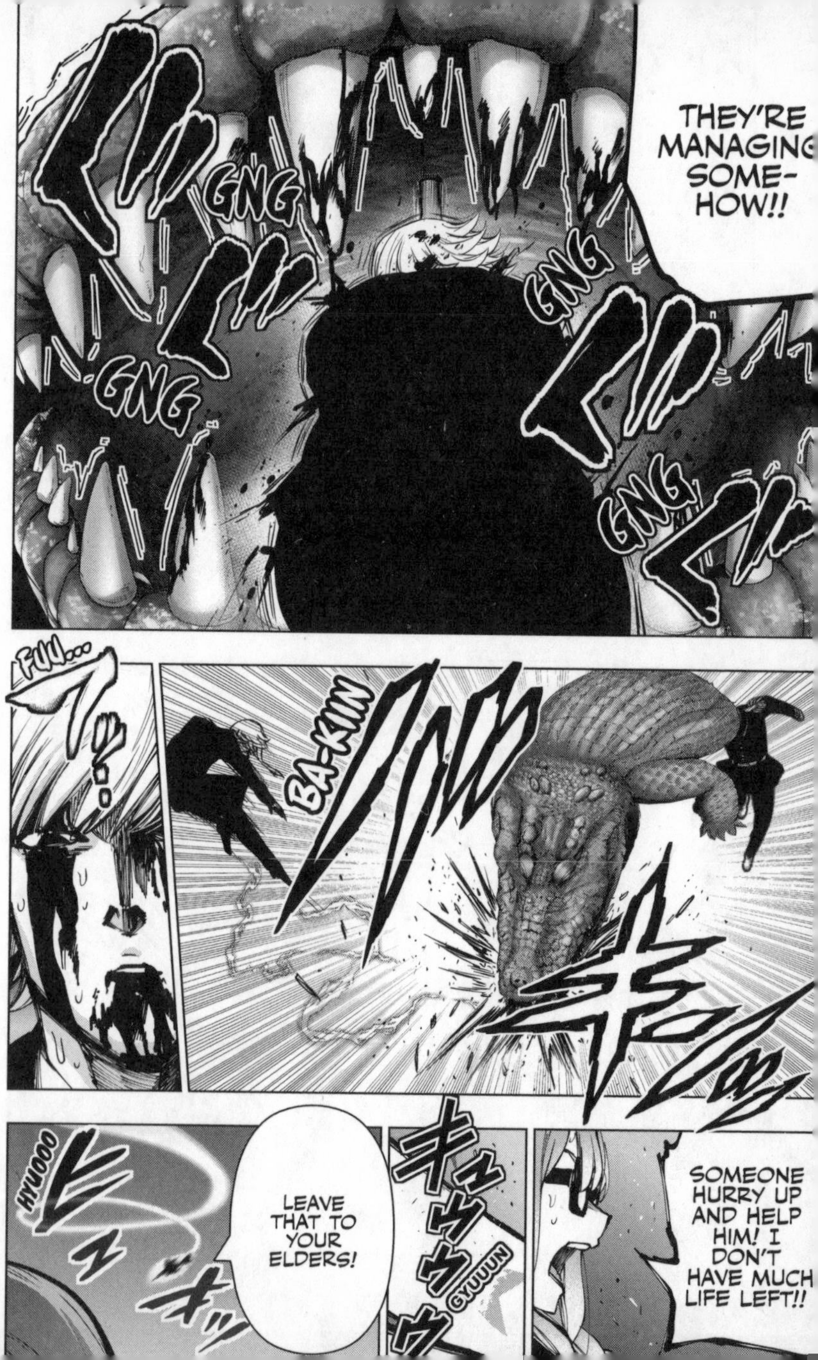
THEY'RE MANAGING SOME-HOW!!
GNG
GNG
GNG
GNG
BA-KIIN
FUU...
SOMEONE HURRY UP AND HELP HIM! I DON'T HAVE MUCH LIFE LEFT!!
GYUUUN
LEAVE THAT TO YOUR ELDERS!
HYUOOO

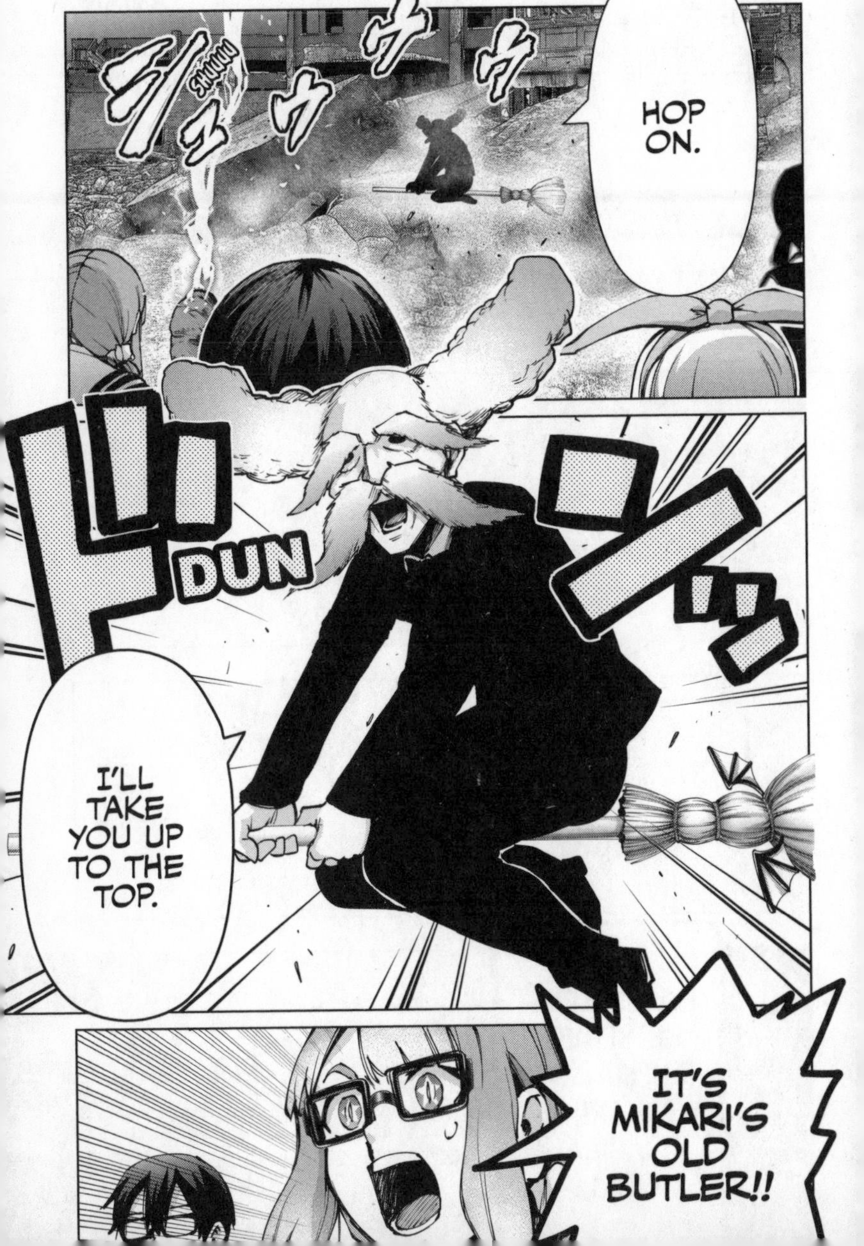
HOP ON.
SHUUUU
DUN
I'LL TAKE YOU UP TO THE TOP.
IT'S MIKARI'S OLD BUTLER!!

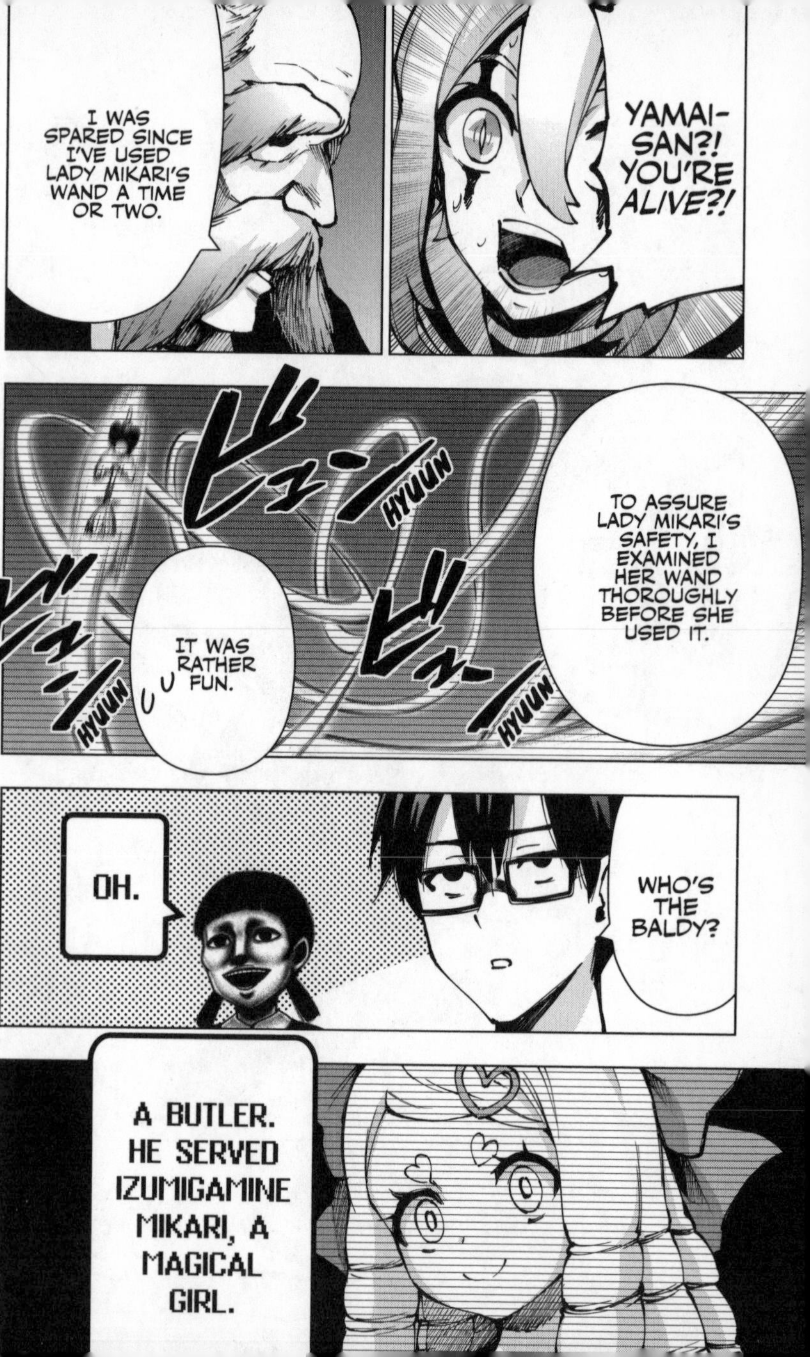

YAMAI-SAN?! YOU'RE ALIVE?!
I WAS SPARED SINCE I'VE USED LADY MIKARI'S WAND A TIME OR TWO.
TO ASSURE LADY MIKARI'S SAFETY, I EXAMINED HER WAND THOROUGHLY BEFORE SHE USED IT.
HYUUN
HYUUN
IT WAS RATHER FUN.
HYUUN
WHO'S THE BALDY?
OH.
A BUTLER. HE SERVED IZUMIGAMINE MIKARI, A MAGICAL GIRL.

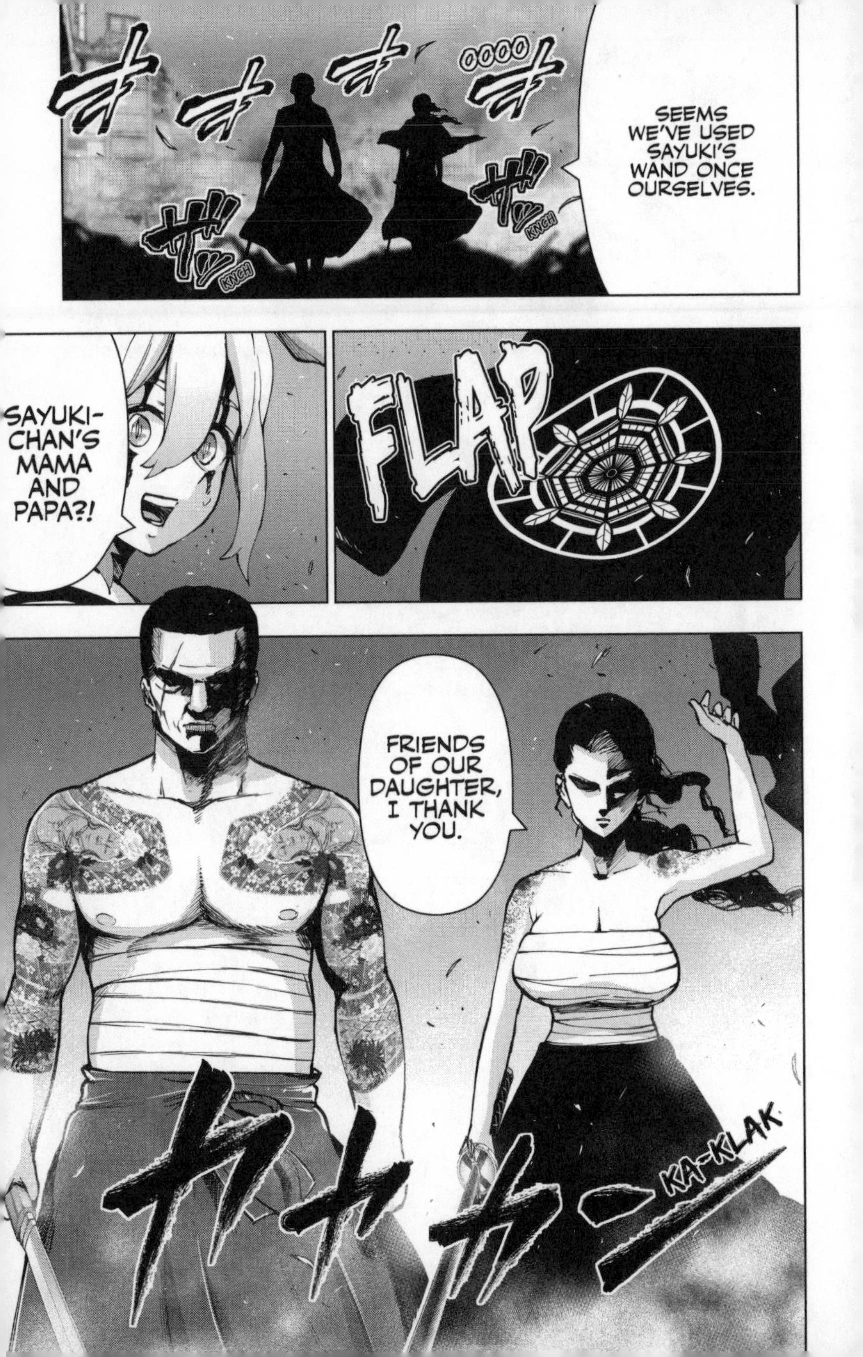
SEEMS WE'VE USED SAYUKI'S WAND ONCE OURSELVES.
OOOO
KNCH
KNCH
FLAP
SAYUKI-CHAN'S MAMA AND PAPA?!
FRIENDS OF OUR DAUGHTER, I THANK YOU.
KA-KLAK

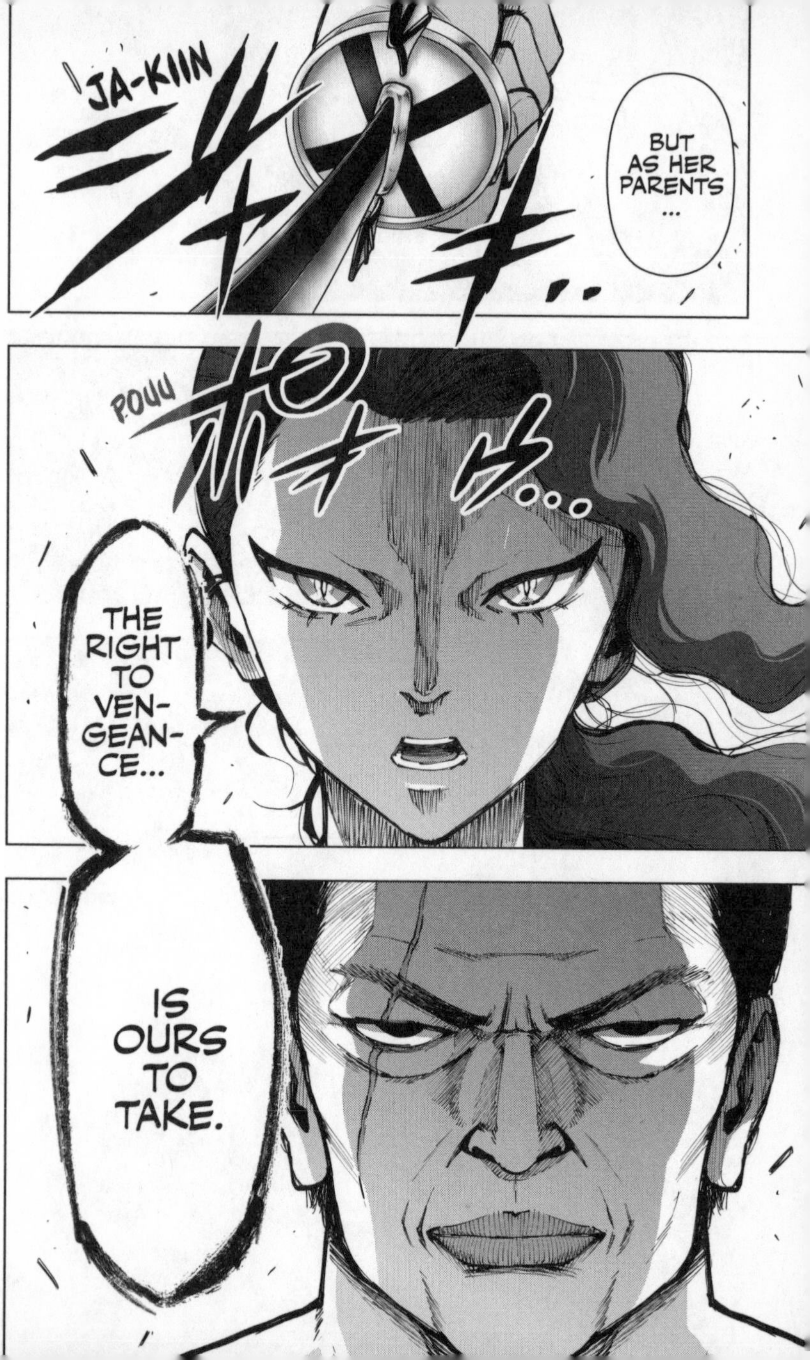
BUT AS HER PARENTS ...
JA-KIIN
POUU
THE RIGHT TO VEN-GEAN-CE...
IS OURS TO TAKE.

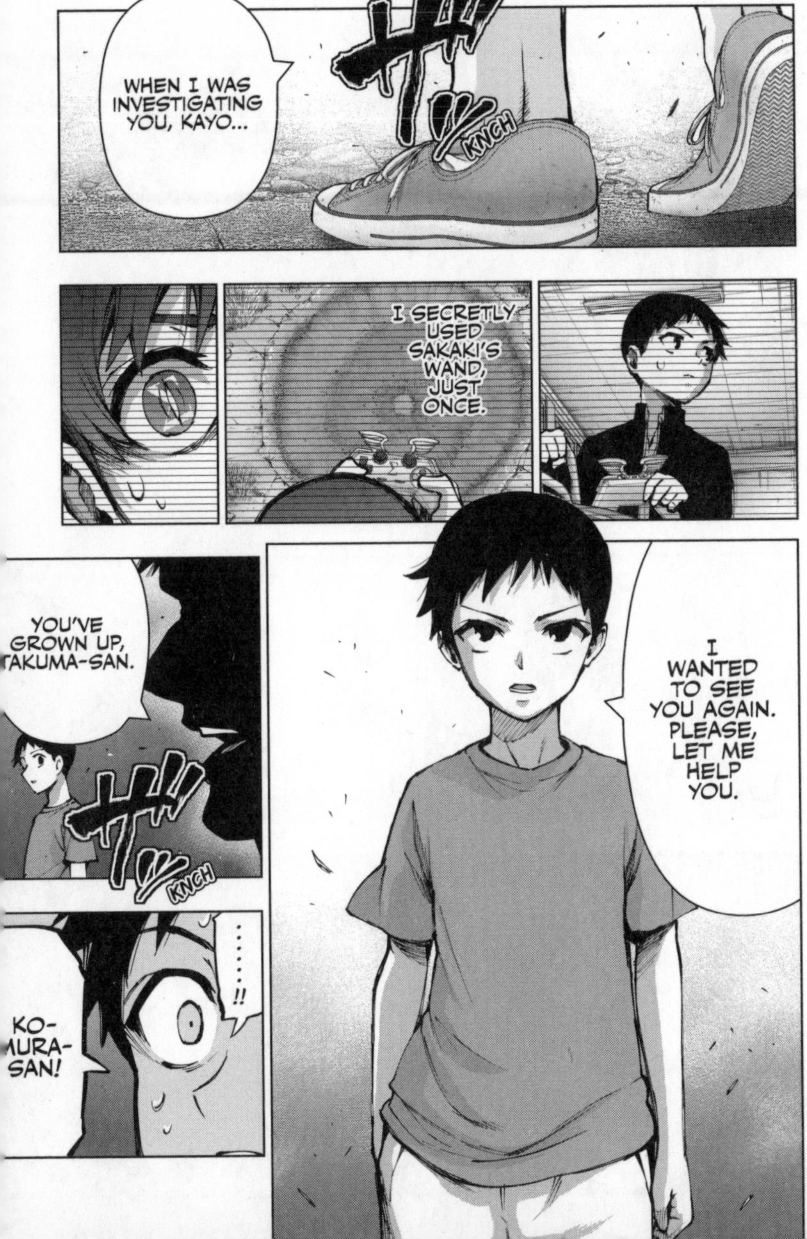
KNCH
WHEN I WAS INVESTIGATING YOU, KAYO...
I SECRETLY USED SAKAKI'S WAND, JUST ONCE.
I WANTED TO SEE YOU AGAIN. PLEASE, LET ME HELP YOU.
YOU'VE GROWN UP, TAKUMA-SAN.
KNCH
......!!
KO-MURA-SAN!

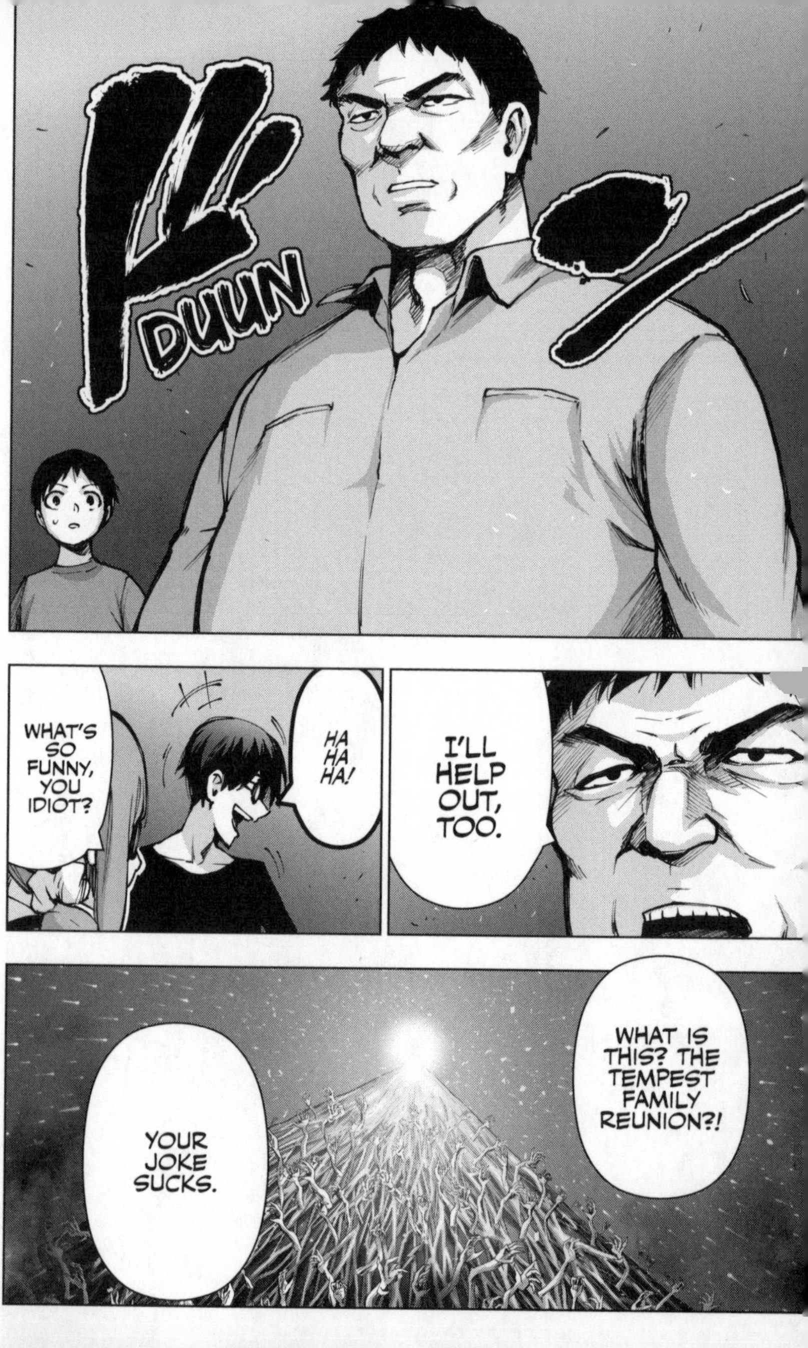
DUUN
I'LL HELP OUT, TOO.
HA HA HA!
WHAT'S SO FUNNY, YOU IDIOT?
WHAT IS THIS? THE TEMPEST FAMILY REUNION?!
YOUR JOKE SUCKS.

ENTER.130 WEAKNESS

GYUUUUUN
OOOO
I TOLD YOU BEFORE.
GNG
GNG
GNG
SHUBA

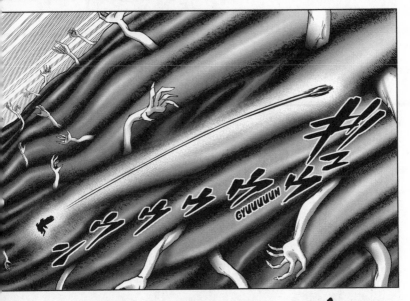

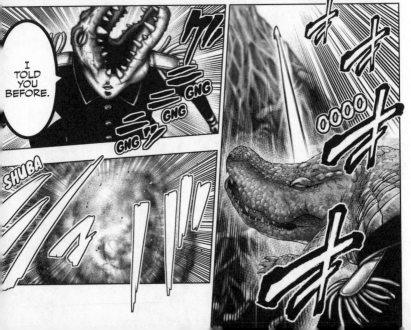

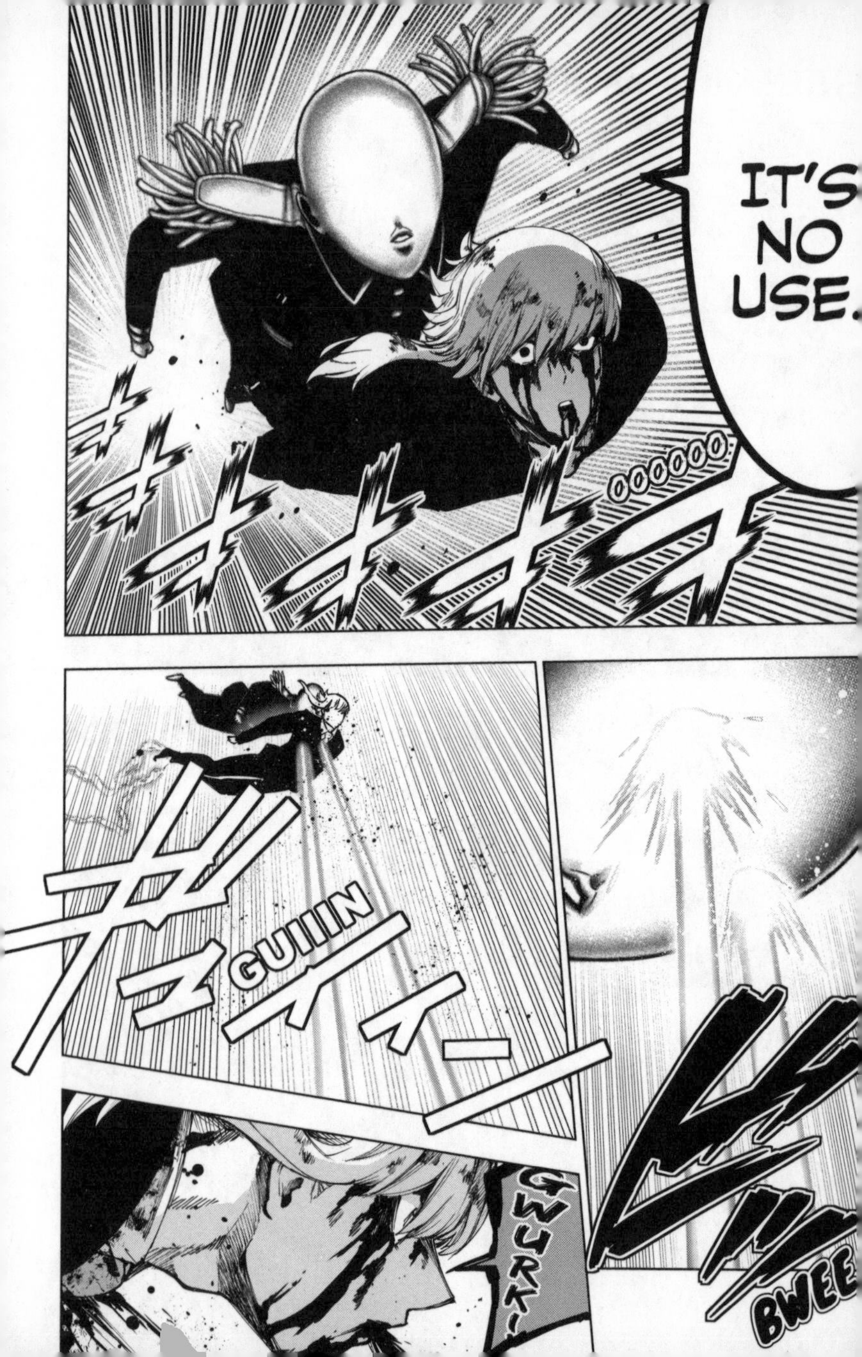
IT'S NO USE.
OOOOOO
BWEE
GUIIIN
GWURK!

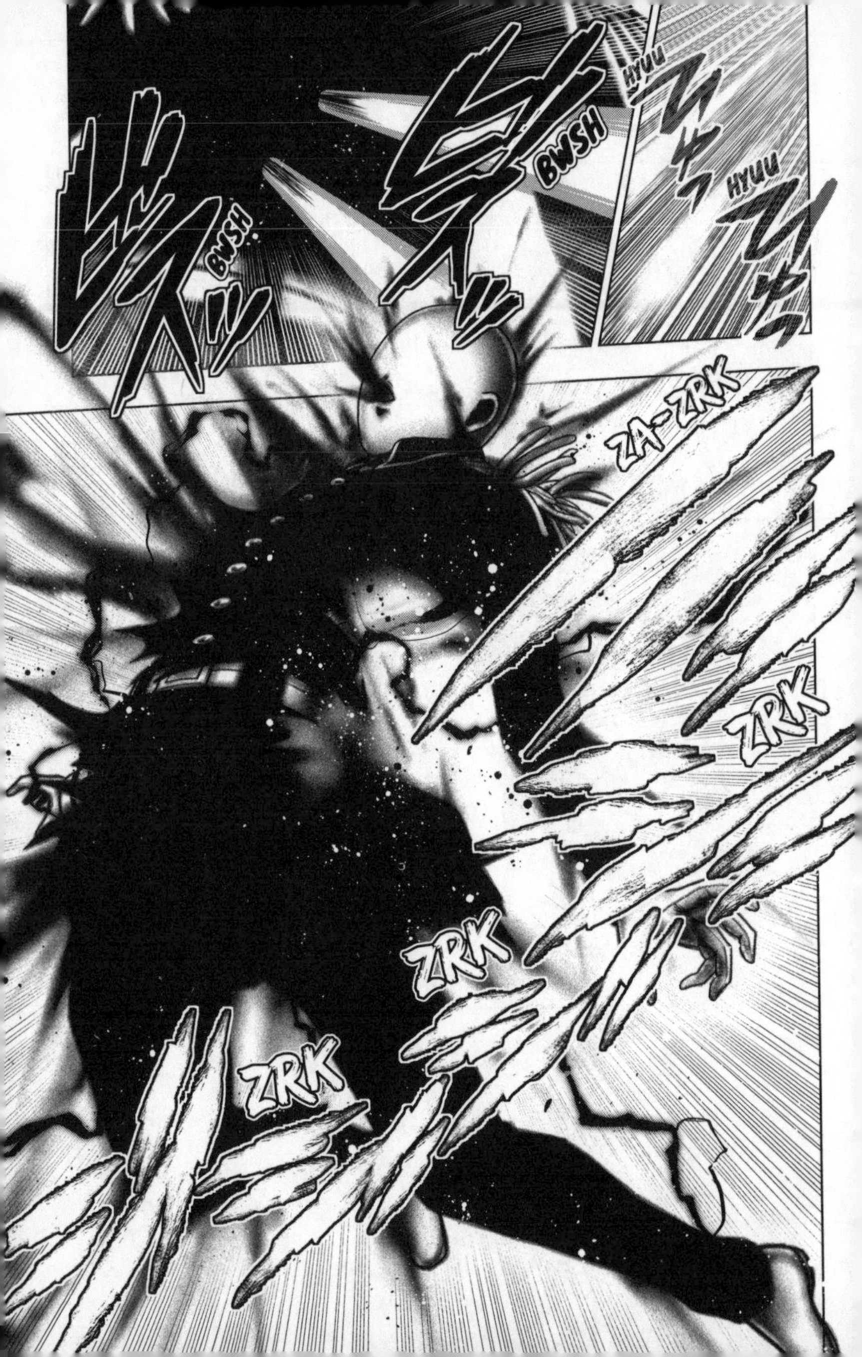
HYUU
HYUU
BWSH
BWSH
ZA-ZRK
ZRK
ZRK
ZRK

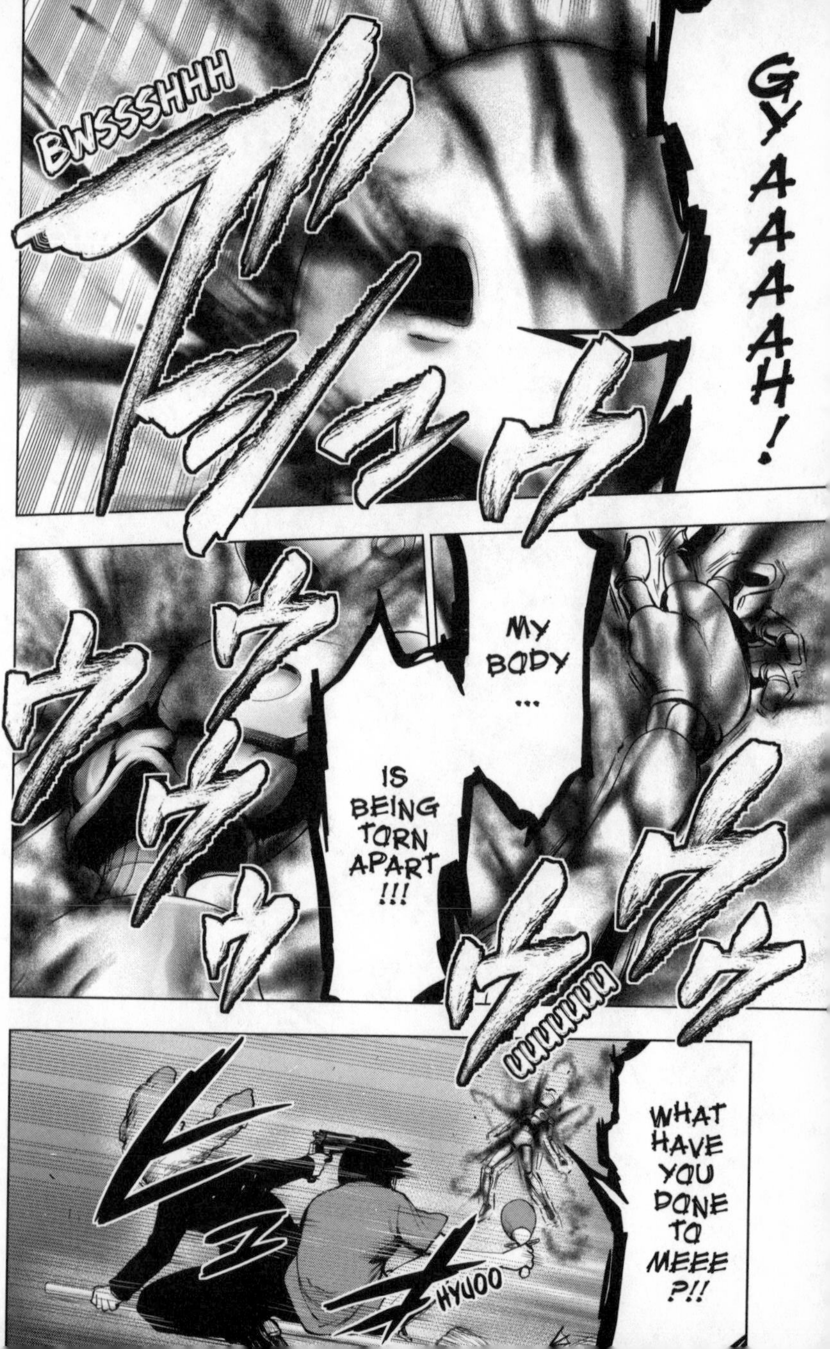
GYAAAAAH!
BWSSSHHH
MY BODY ...
IS BEING TORN APART!!!
WHAT HAVE YOU DONE TO MEEE?!!
HYUOO

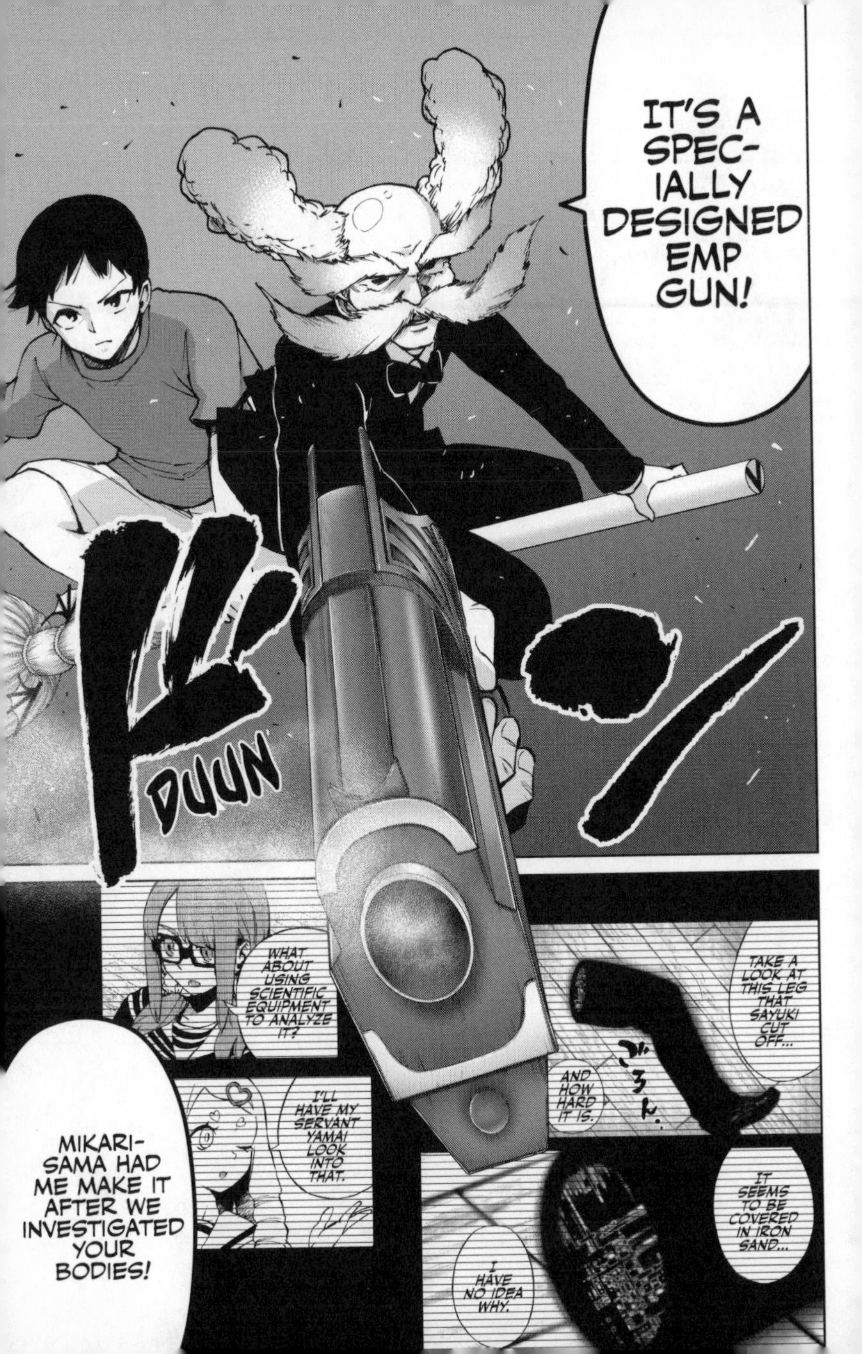
IT'S A SPECIALLY DESIGNED EMP GUN!
DUUN
MIKARI-SAMA HAD ME MAKE IT AFTER WE INVESTIGATED YOUR BODIES!
TAKE A LOOK AT THIS LEG THAT SAYUKI CUT OFF...
AND HOW HARD IT IS.
WHAT ABOUT USING SCIENTIFIC EQUIPMENT TO ANALYZE IT?
IT SEEMS TO BE COVERED IN IRON SAND...
I HAVE NO IDEA WHY.
I'LL HAVE MY SERVANT YAMAI LOOK INTO THAT.

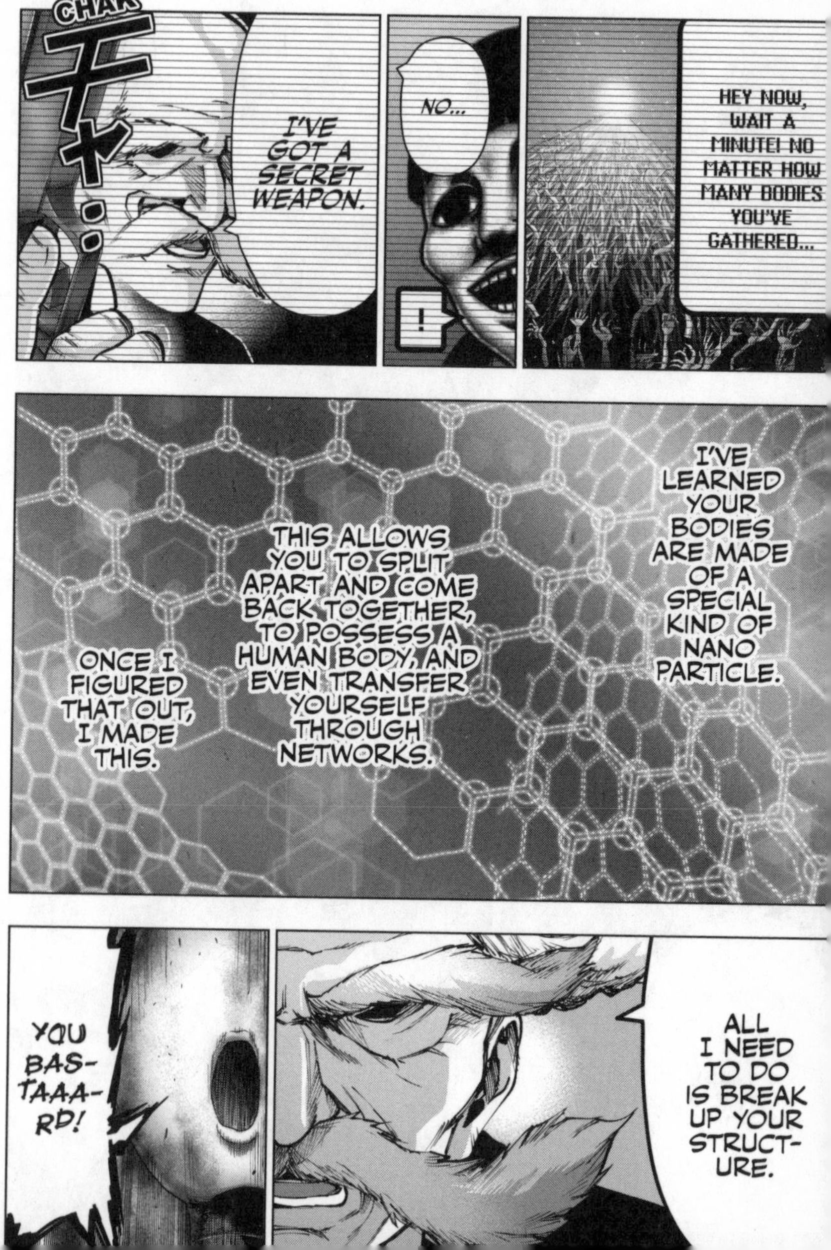
HEY NOW, WAIT A MINUTE! NO MATTER HOW MANY BODIES YOU'VE GATHERED...
NO...
!
I'VE GOT A SECRET WEAPON.
CHAK
I'VE LEARNED YOUR BODIES ARE MADE OF A SPECIAL KIND OF NANO PARTICLE.
THIS ALLOWS YOU TO SPLIT APART AND COME BACK TOGETHER, TO POSSESS A HUMAN BODY, AND EVEN TRANSFER YOURSELF THROUGH NETWORKS.
ONCE I FIGURED THAT OUT, I MADE THIS.
ALL I NEED TO DO IS BREAK UP YOUR STRUCTURE.
YOU BAS-TAAA-RD!

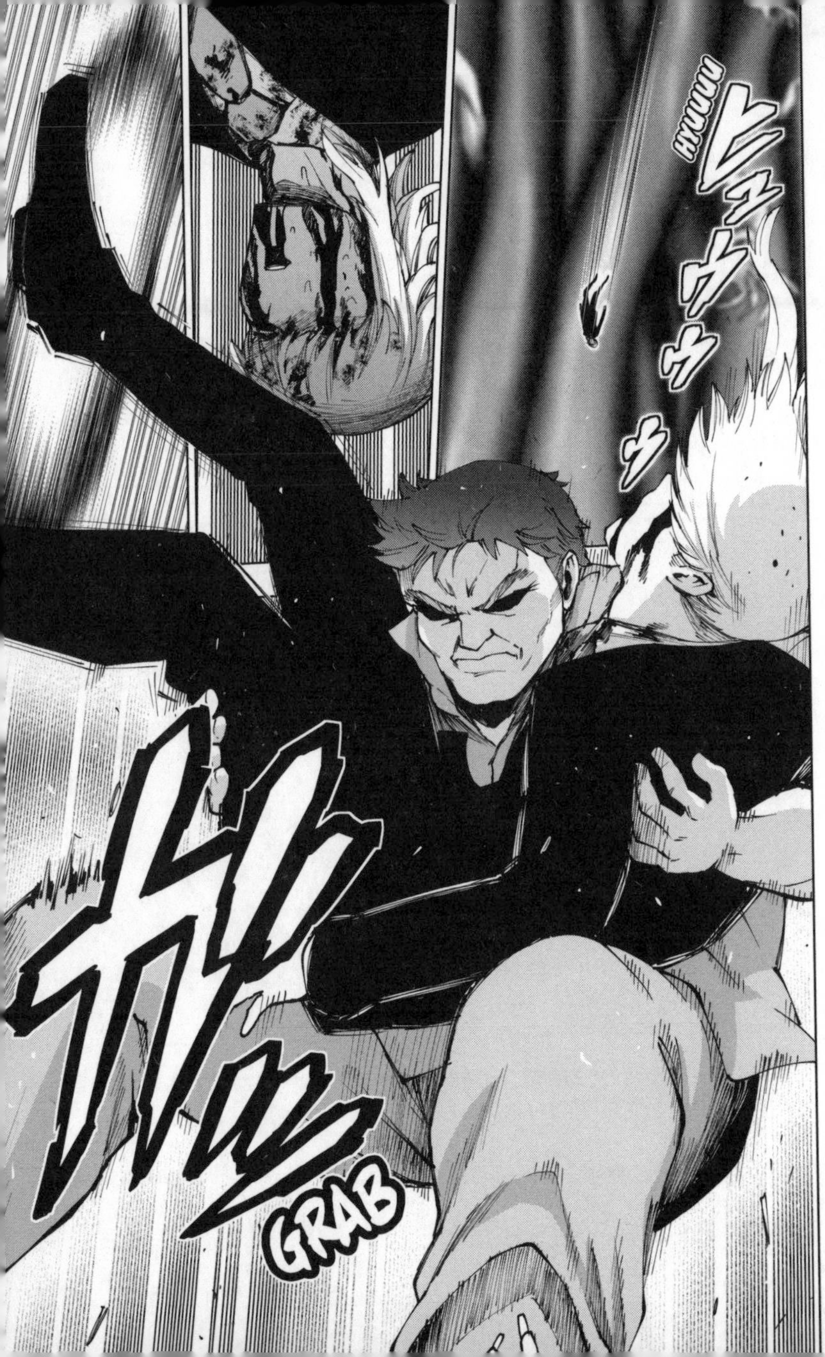
HYUUUN
GRAB

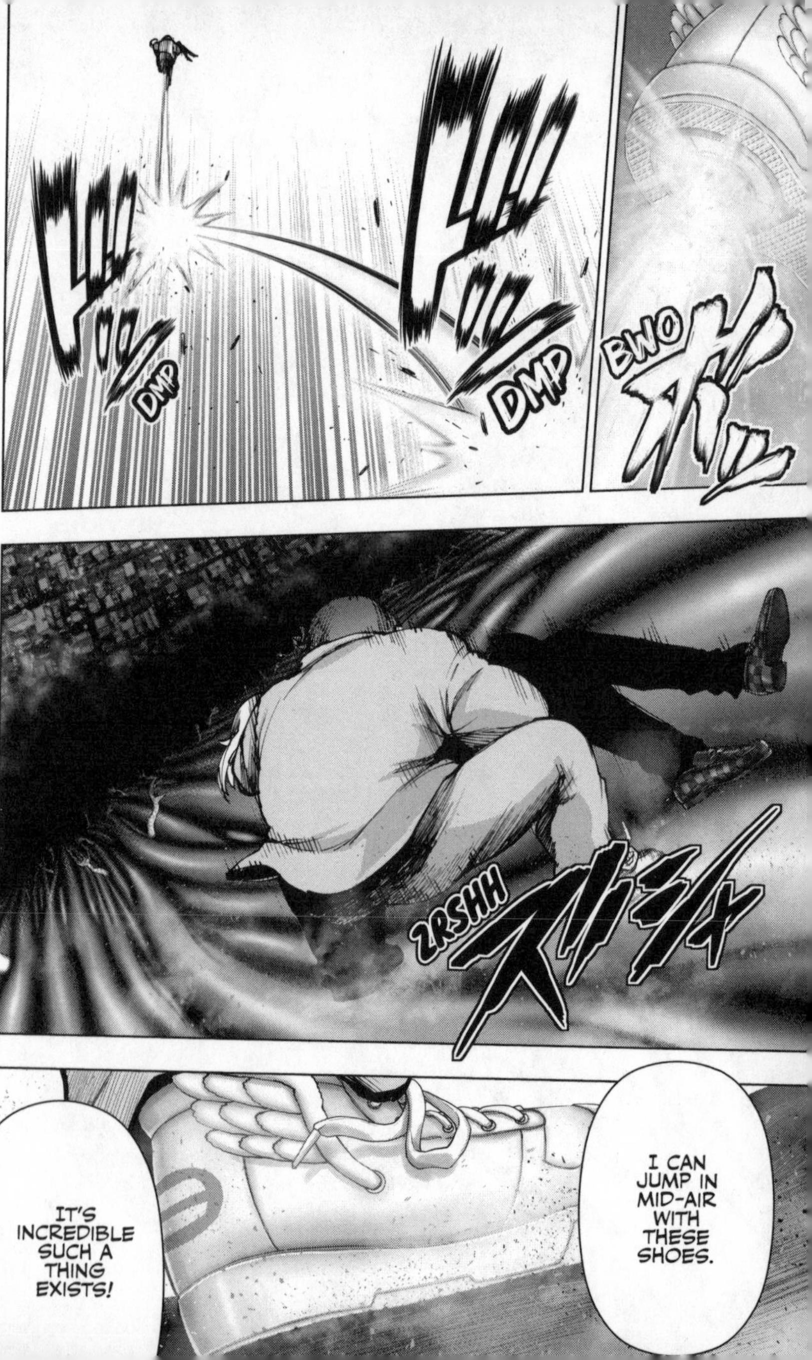
BWO
DMP
DMP
ZRSHH
I CAN JUMP IN MID-AIR WITH THESE SHOES.
IT'S INCREDIBLE SUCH A THING EXISTS!

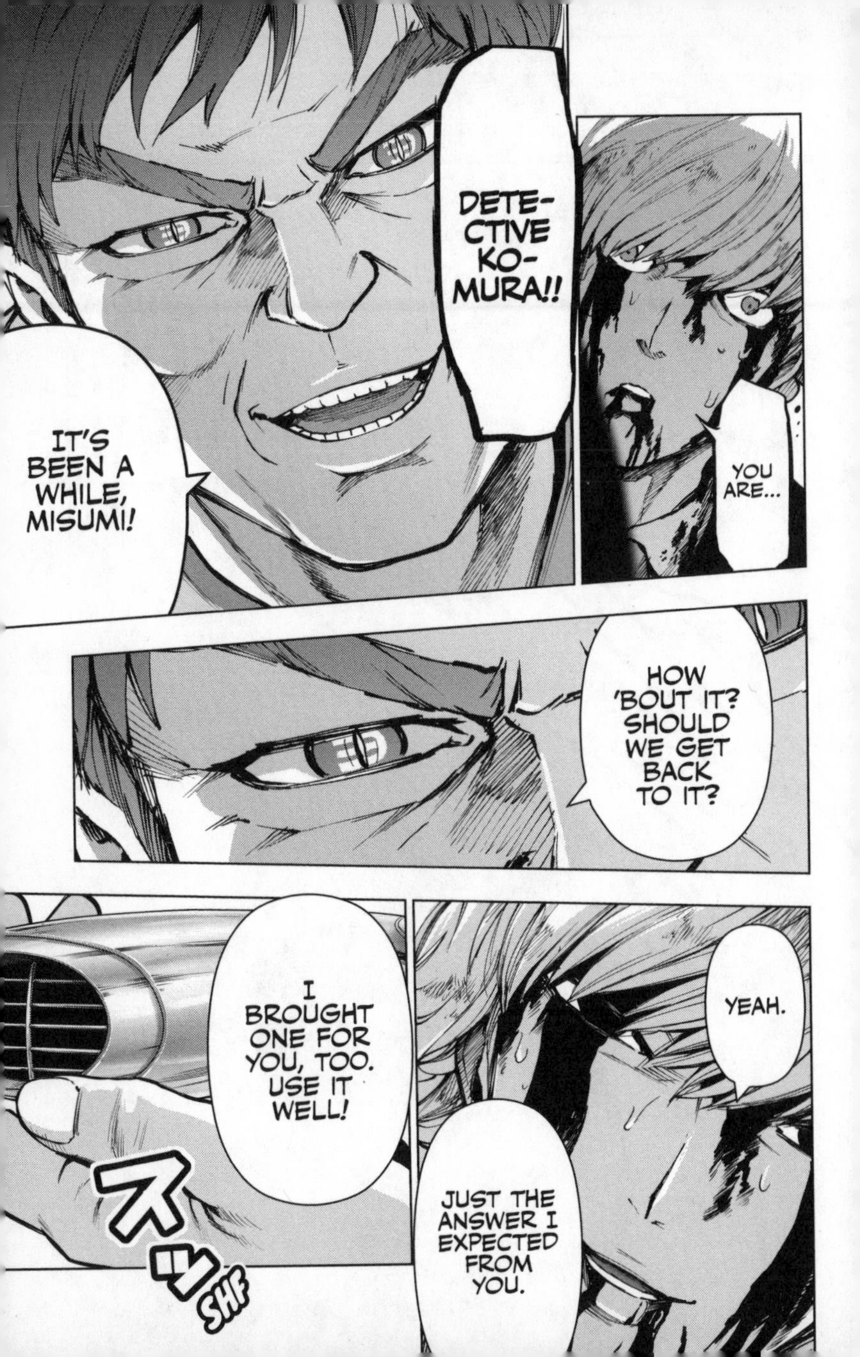
YOU ARE...
DETECTIVE KOMURA!!
IT'S BEEN A WHILE, MISUMI!
HOW 'BOUT IT? SHOULD WE GET BACK TO IT?
YEAH.
JUST THE ANSWER I EXPECTED FROM YOU.
I BROUGHT ONE FOR YOU, TOO. USE IT WELL!
スッ SHF

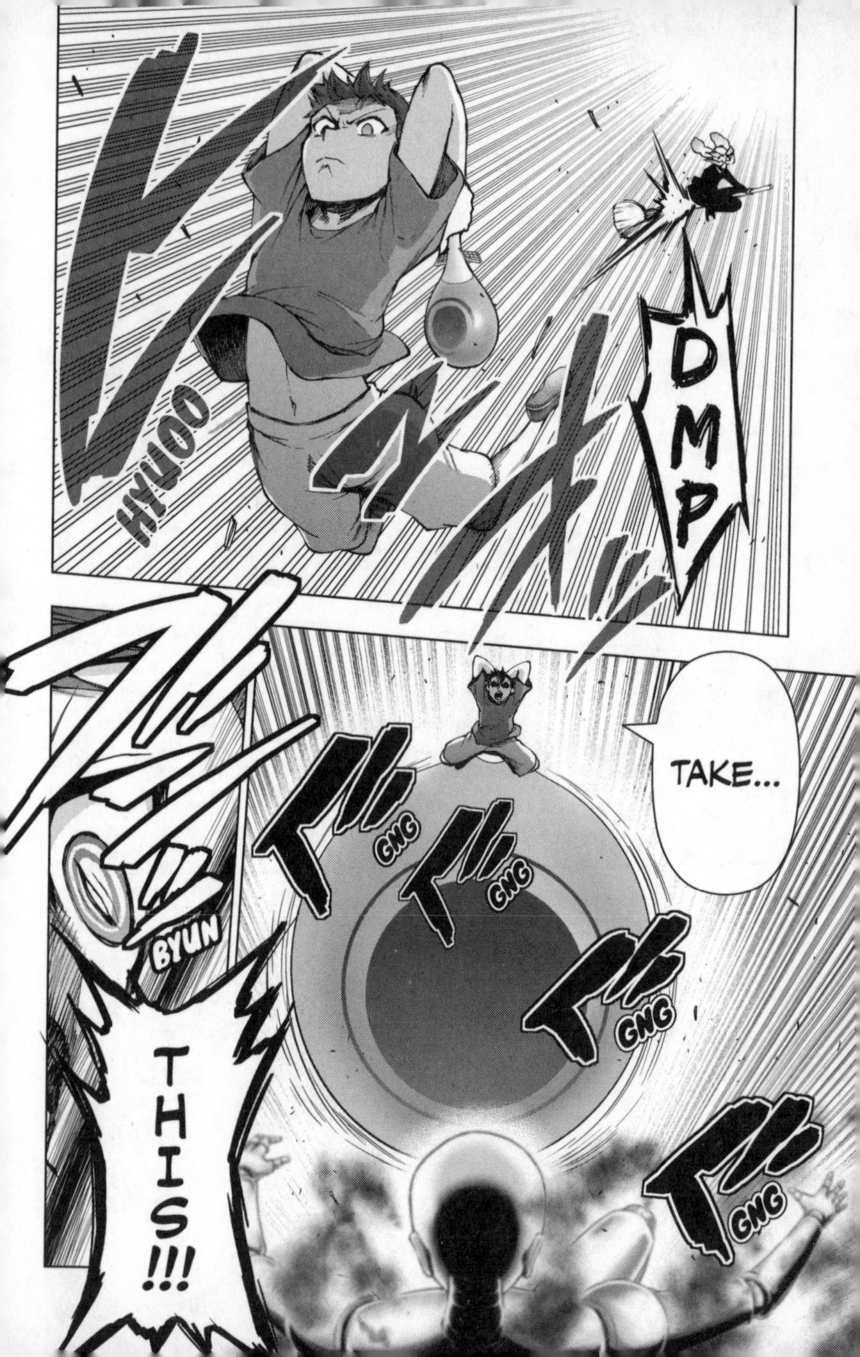
DMP
HYUOO
TAKE...
GNG
GNG
GNG
BYUN
THIS!!!
GNG

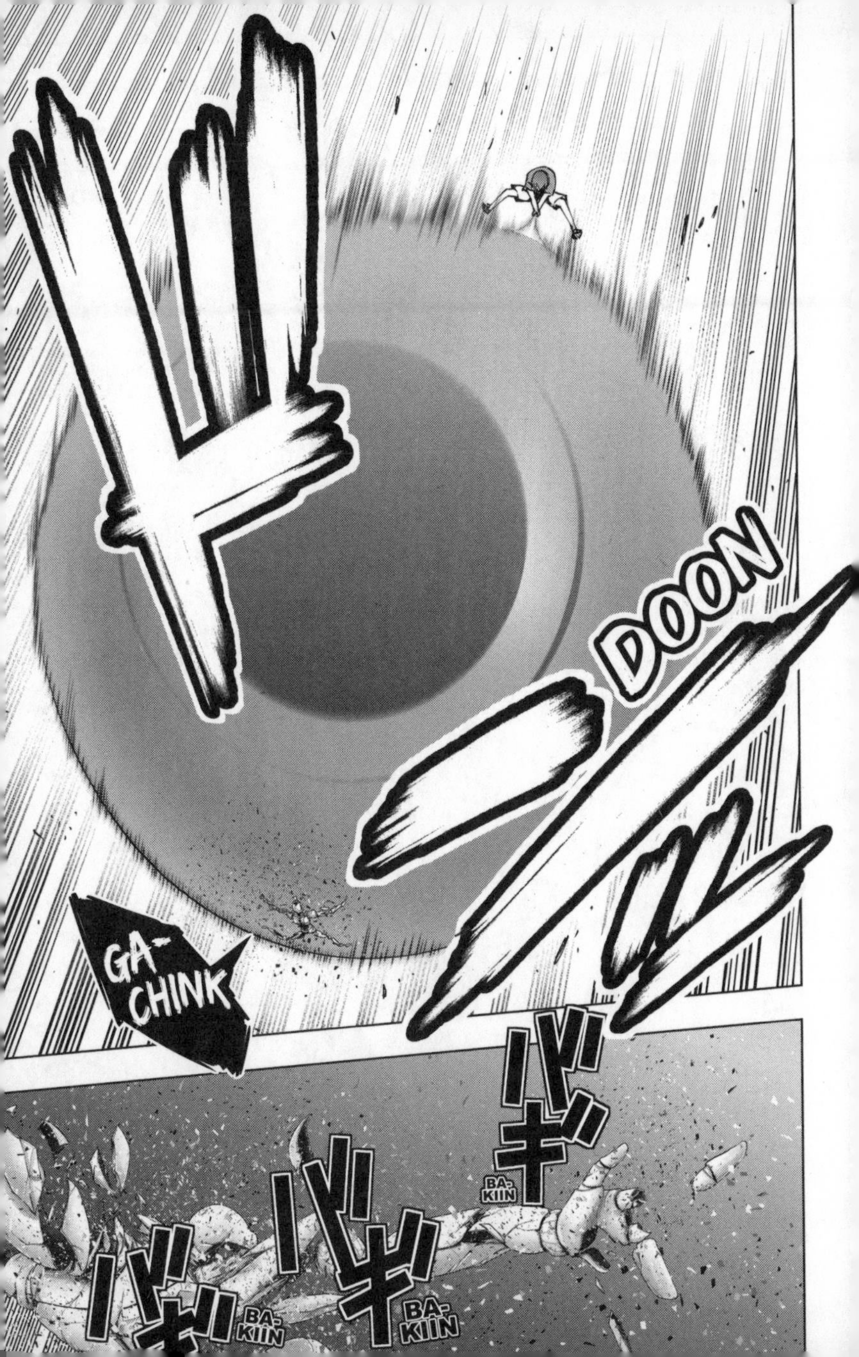

ドン
DOON
GA-CHINK
バギ
BA-KIIN
バキン
BA-KIIN
バキン
BA-KIIN

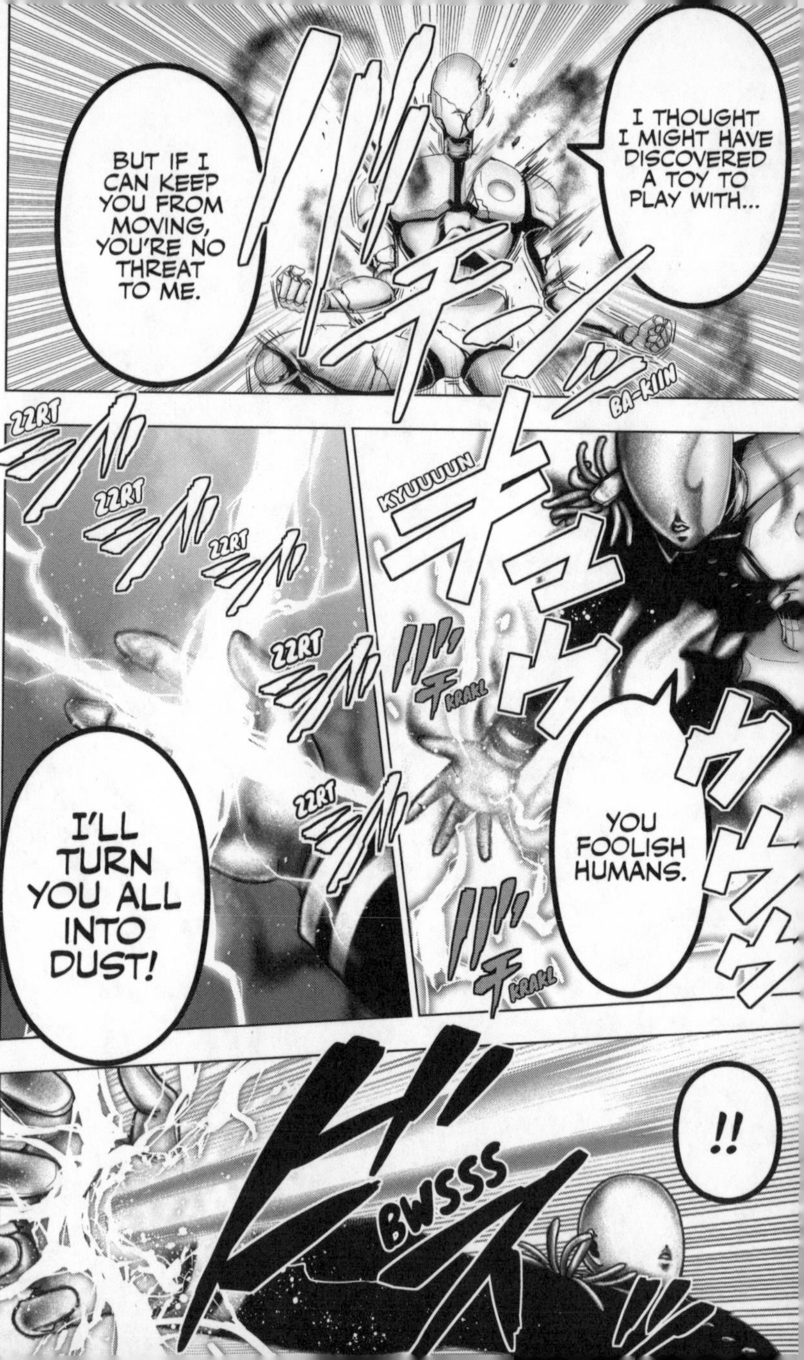

I THOUGHT I MIGHT HAVE DISCOVERED A TOY TO PLAY WITH...
BUT IF I CAN KEEP YOU FROM MOVING, YOU'RE NO THREAT TO ME.
BA-KIIN
KYUUUUN
KRAKL
YOU FOOLISH HUMANS.
KRAKL
ZZRT
ZZRT
ZZRT
ZZRT
ZZRT
I'LL TURN YOU ALL INTO DUST!
!!
BWSSS

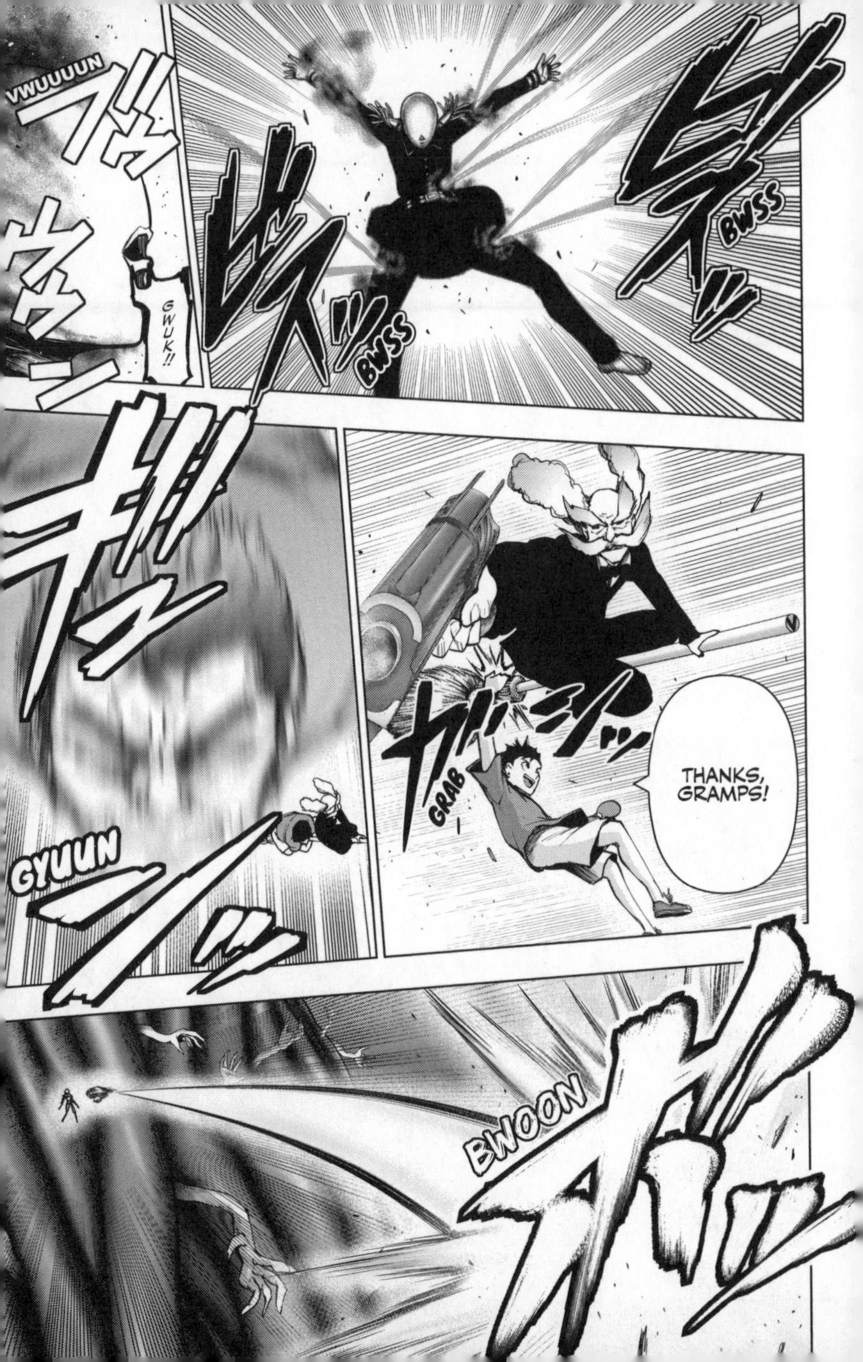
BWSS
BWSS
VWUUUUN
GWUK!!
GRAB
THANKS, GRAMPS!
GYUUN
BWOON

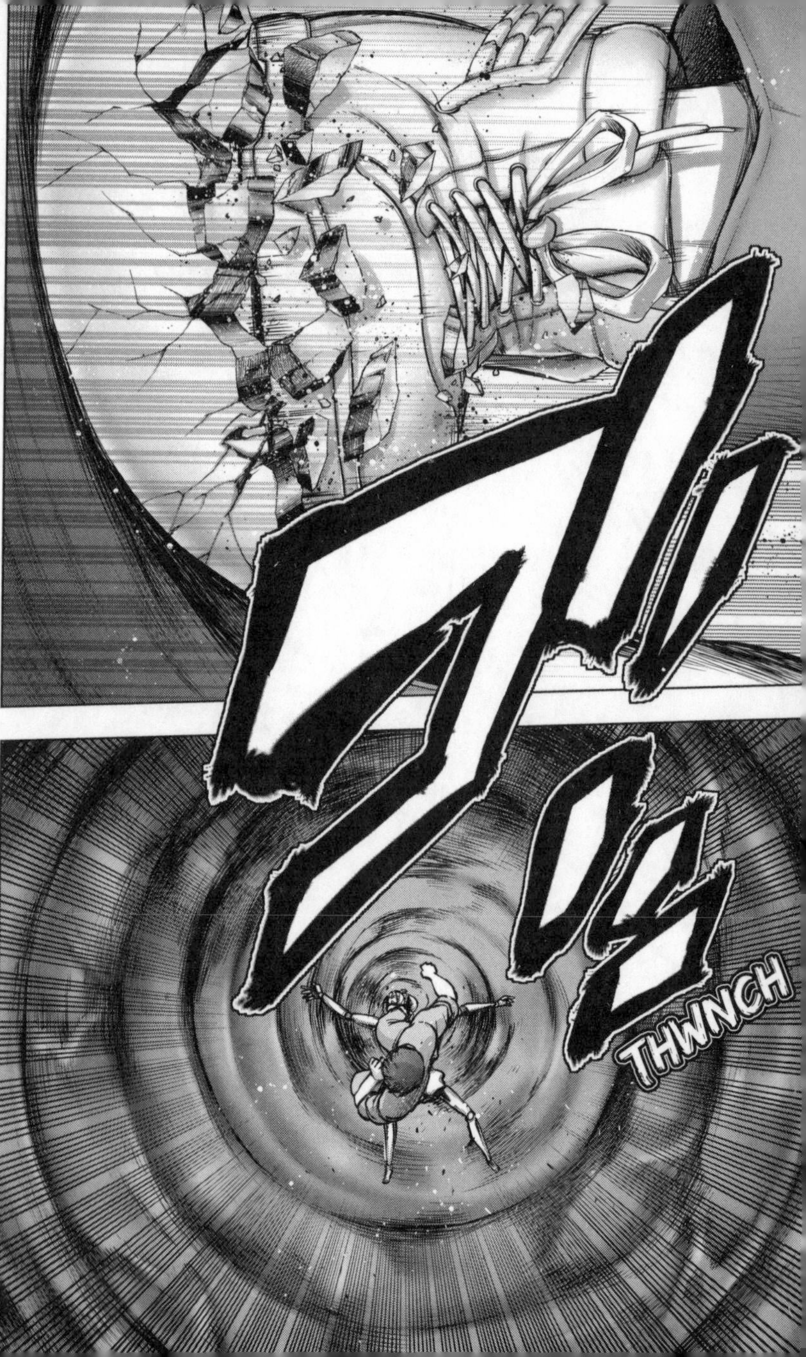
THWNCH

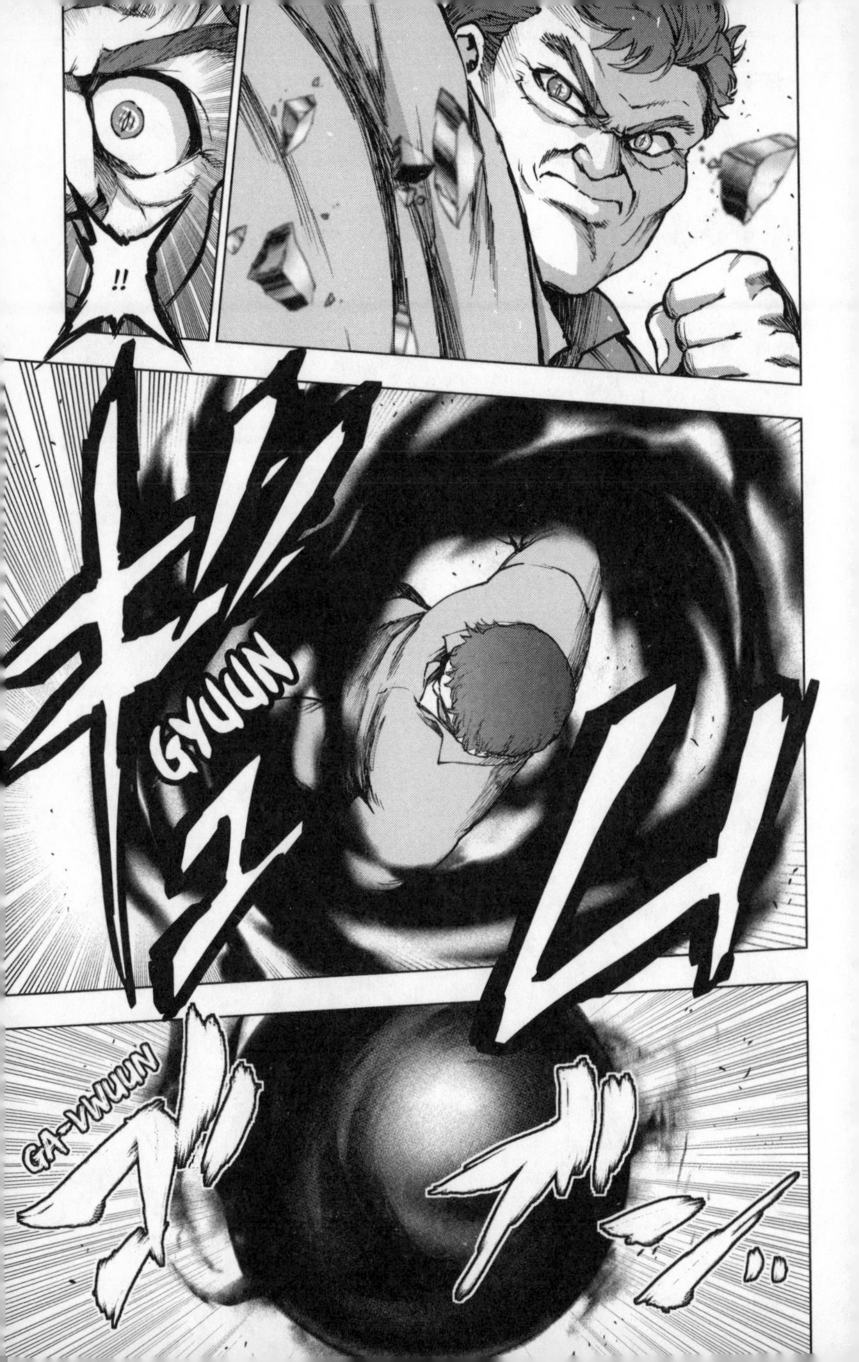
!!
GYUUN
DO
GA-VWUUN

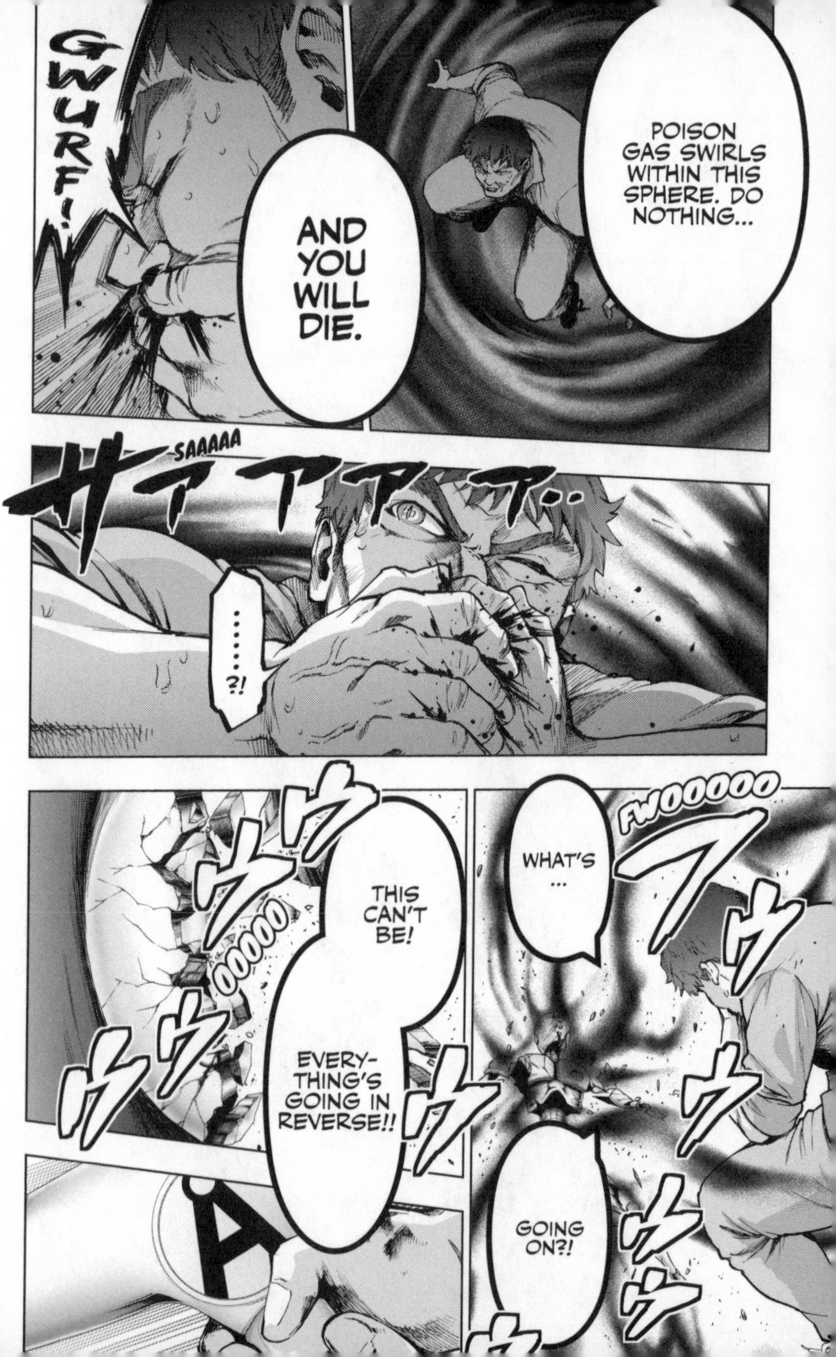
POISON GAS SWIRLS WITHIN THIS SPHERE. DO NOTHING...
AND YOU WILL DIE.
GWURF!
SAAAAA
......?!
FWOOOOO
WHAT'S ...
GOING ON?!
THIS CAN'T BE!
EVERYTHING'S GOING IN REVERSE!!
OOOOOO

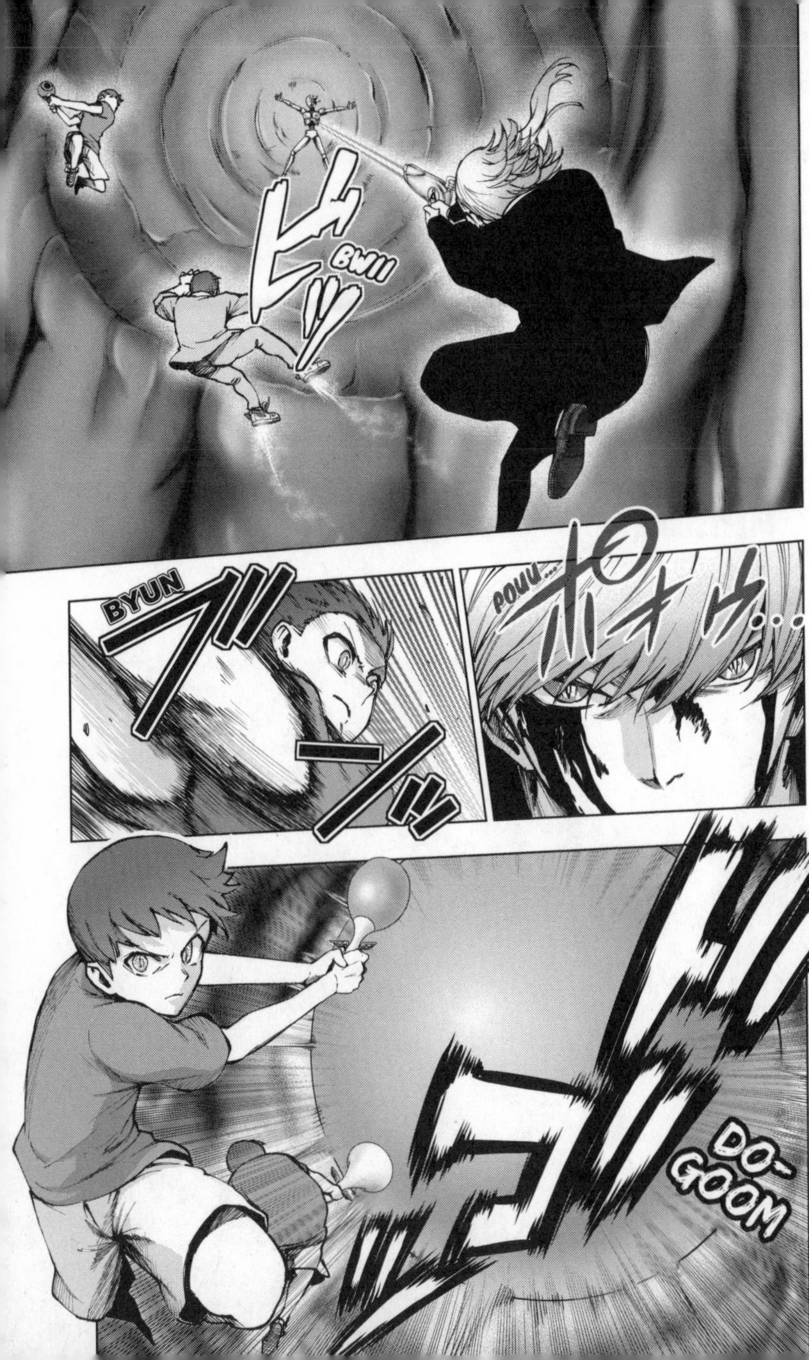
BWII
POUU...
BYUN
DO-
GOOM

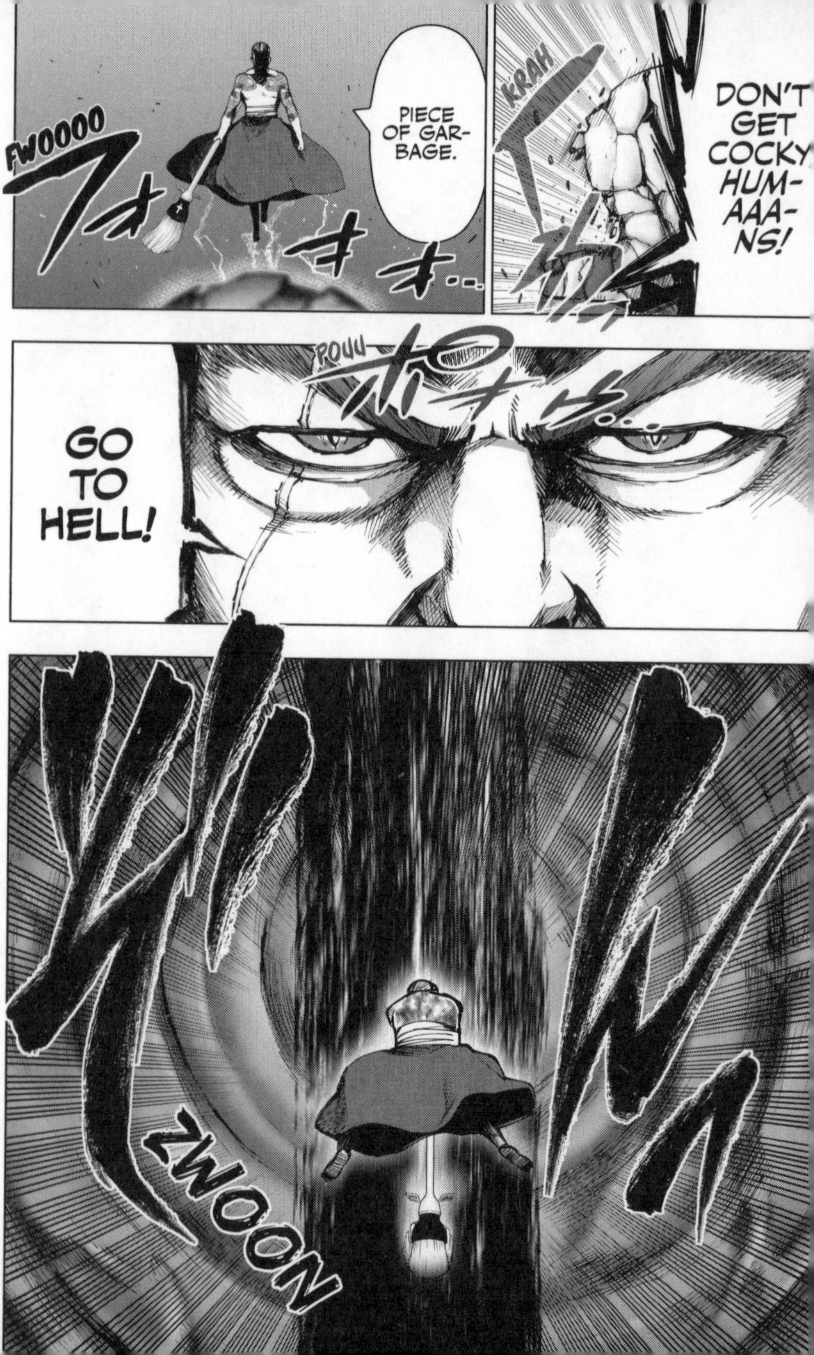
KRAH
DON'T GET COCKY HUM-AAA-NS!
FWOOOO
PIECE OF GAR-BAGE.
POUU
GO TO HELL!
ZWOON

ENTER.131 STOP

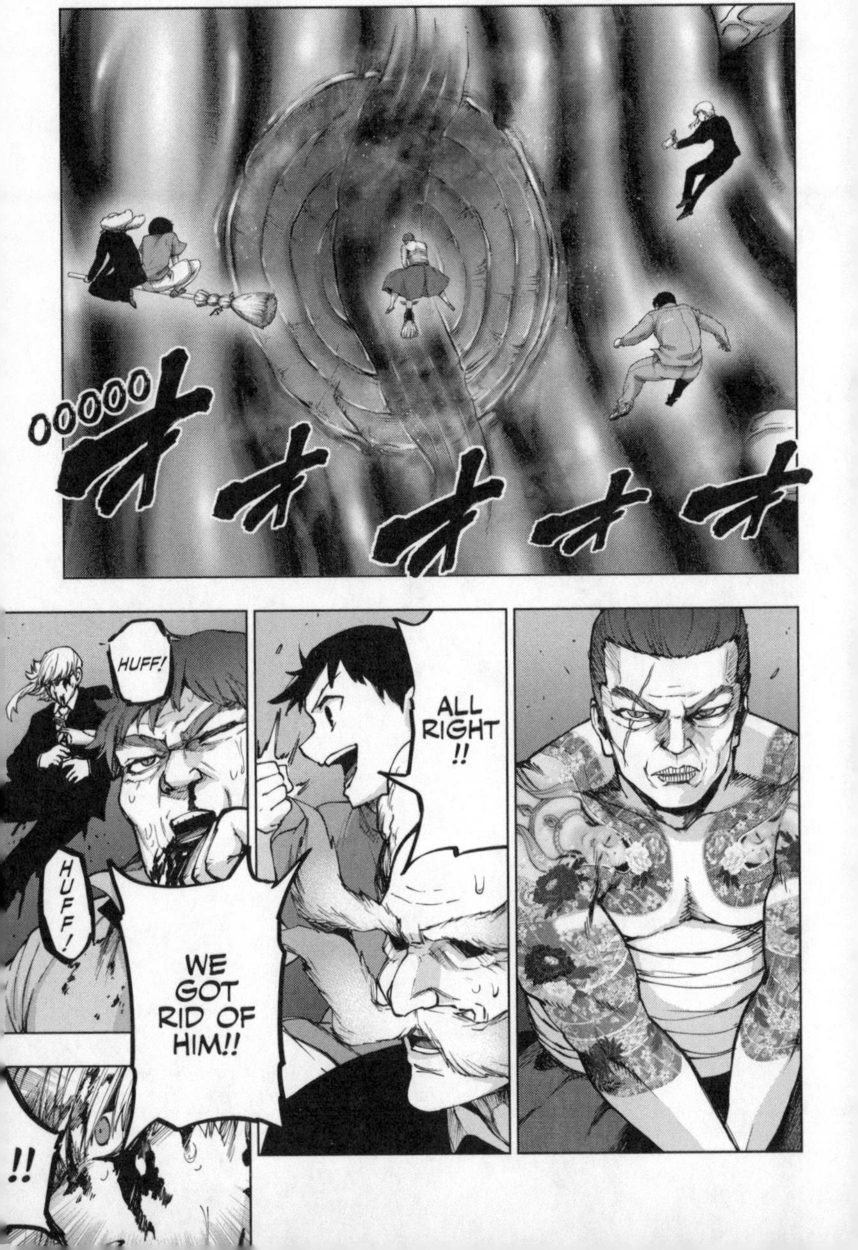
OOOOO
オオオオオ
ALL RIGHT !!
WE GOT RID OF HIM!!
HUFF!
HUFF!
!!

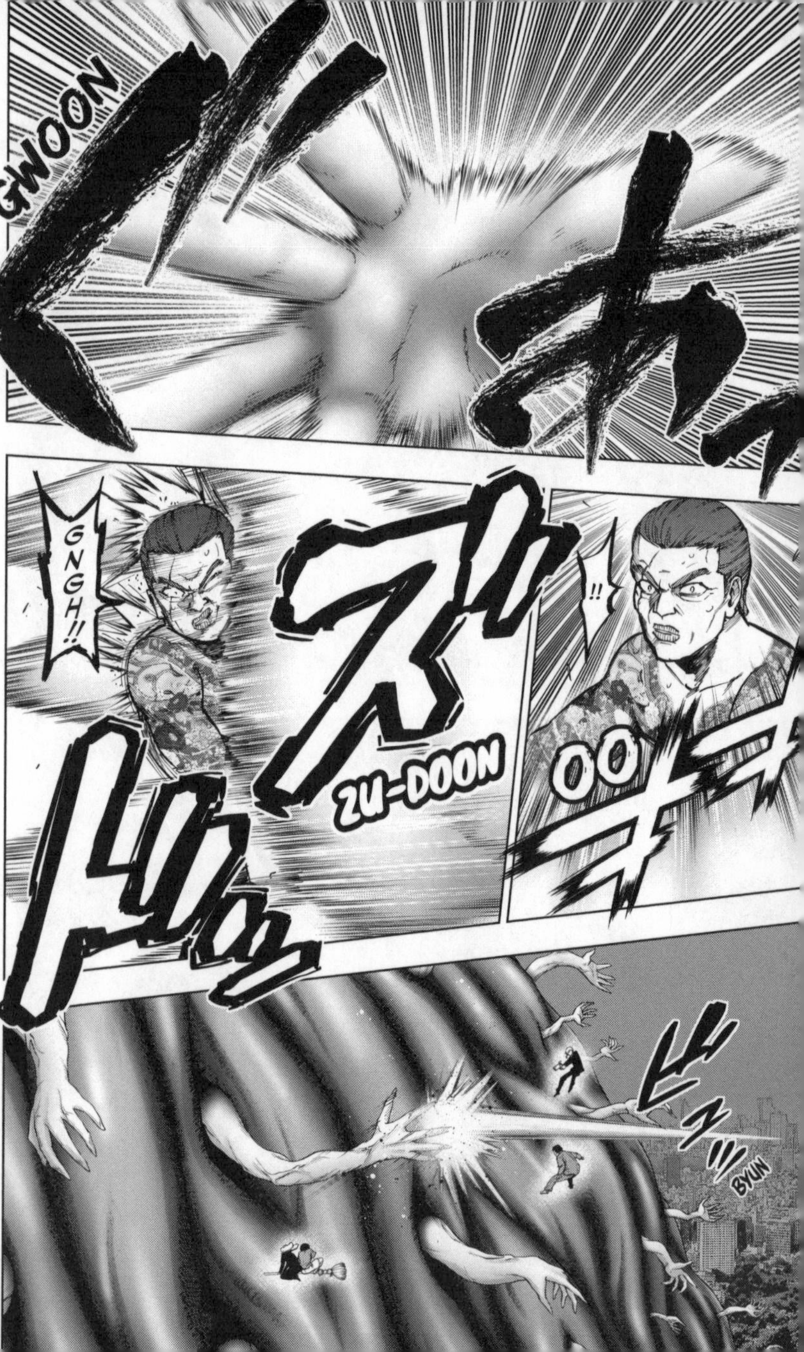
GWOON
!!
OO
GNGH!!
ZU-DOON
BYUN

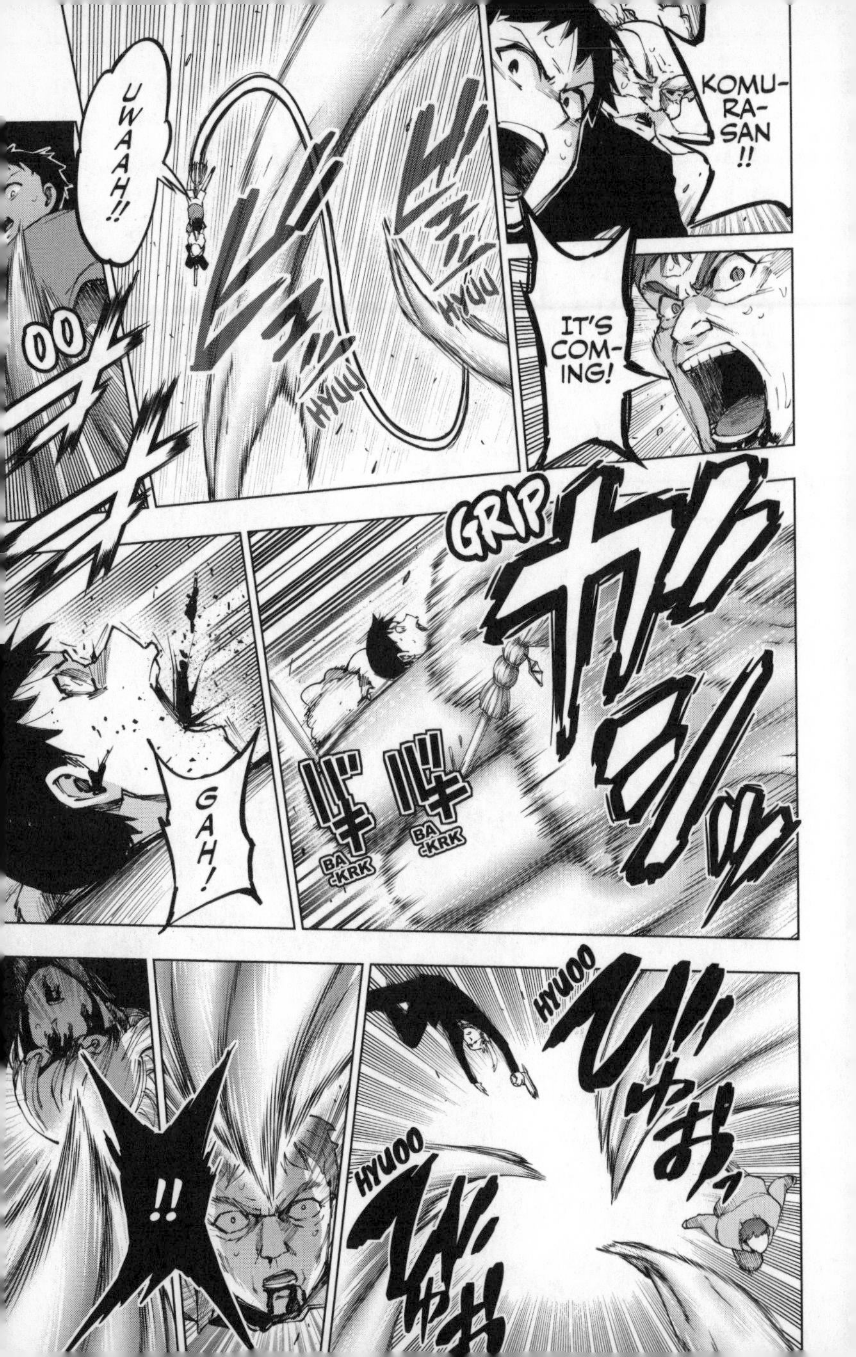
KOMURA-SAN!!
IT'S COMING!
HYUU
HYUU
UWAAH!!
OO
GRIP
BA-KRK
BA-KRK
GAH!
HYUOO
HYUOO
!!

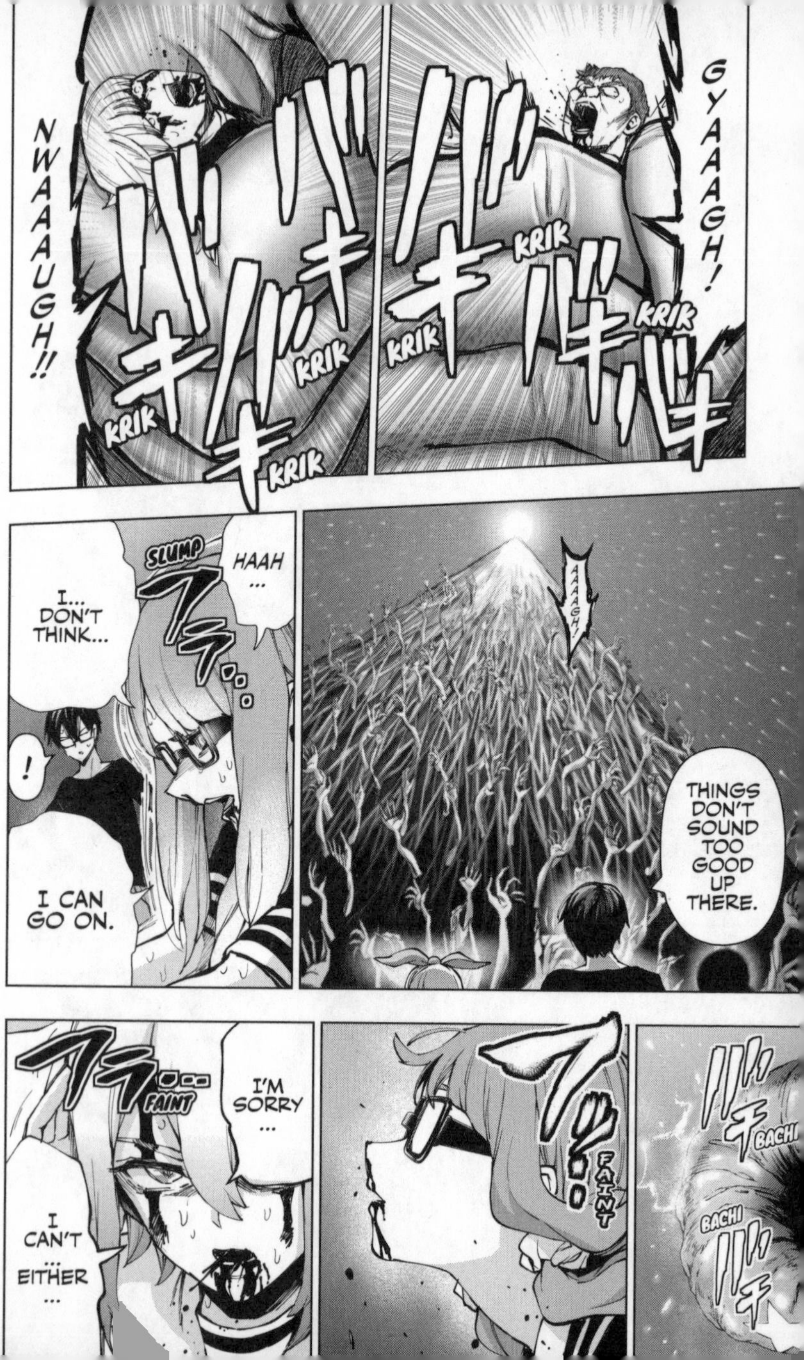
GYAAAAGH!
KRIK
KRIK
KRIK
NWAAAAUGH!!
KRIK
KRIK
KRIK
AAAAGH!
THINGS DON'T SOUND TOO GOOD UP THERE.
HAAH...
SLUMP
I... DON'T THINK...
I CAN GO ON.
!
BACHI
BACHI
FAINT
I'M SORRY...
FAINT
I CAN'T... EITHER...

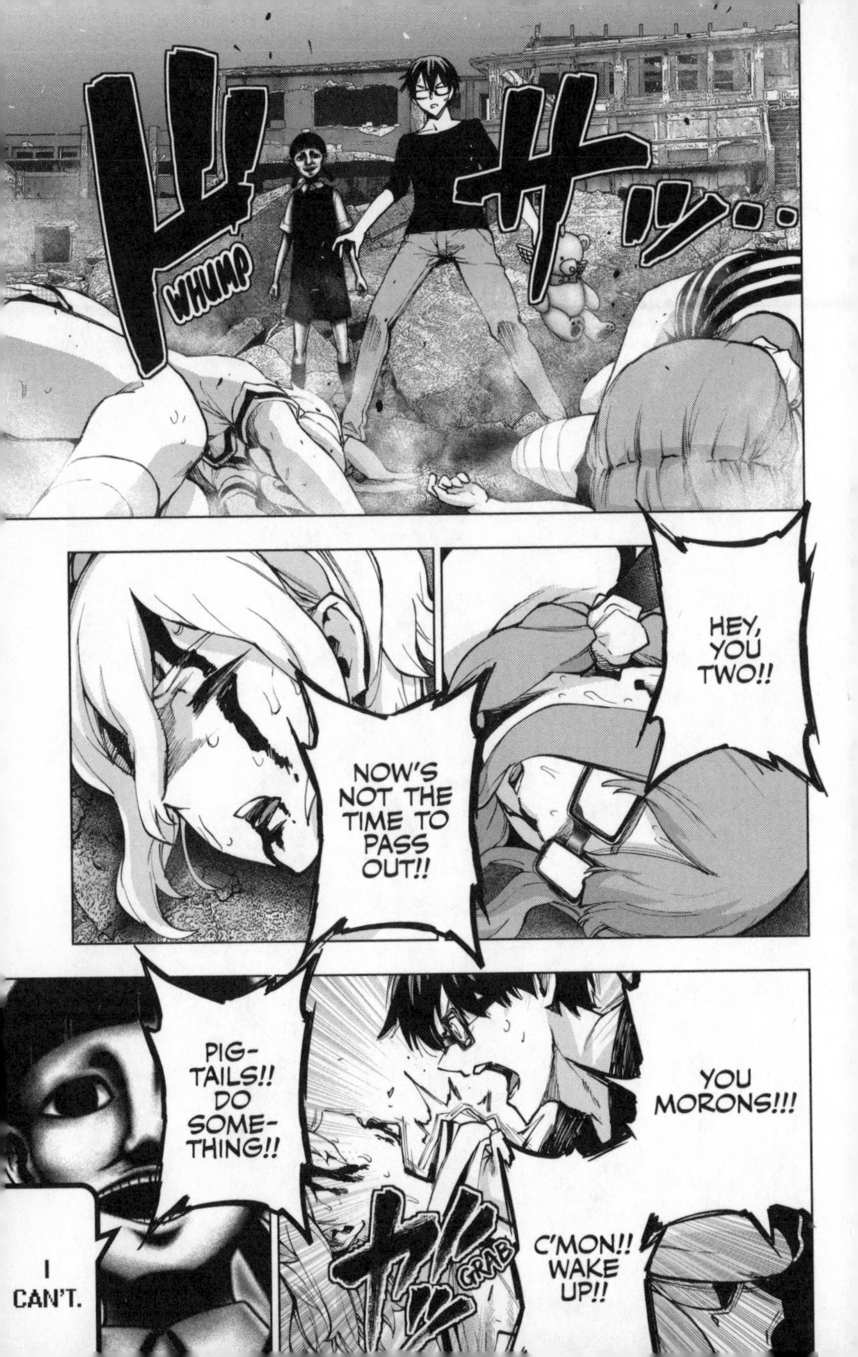
WHUMP
HEY, YOU TWO!!
NOW'S NOT THE TIME TO PASS OUT!!
YOU MORONS!!!
PIG-TAILS!! DO SOME-THING!!
C'MON!! WAKE UP!!
GRAB
I CAN'T.

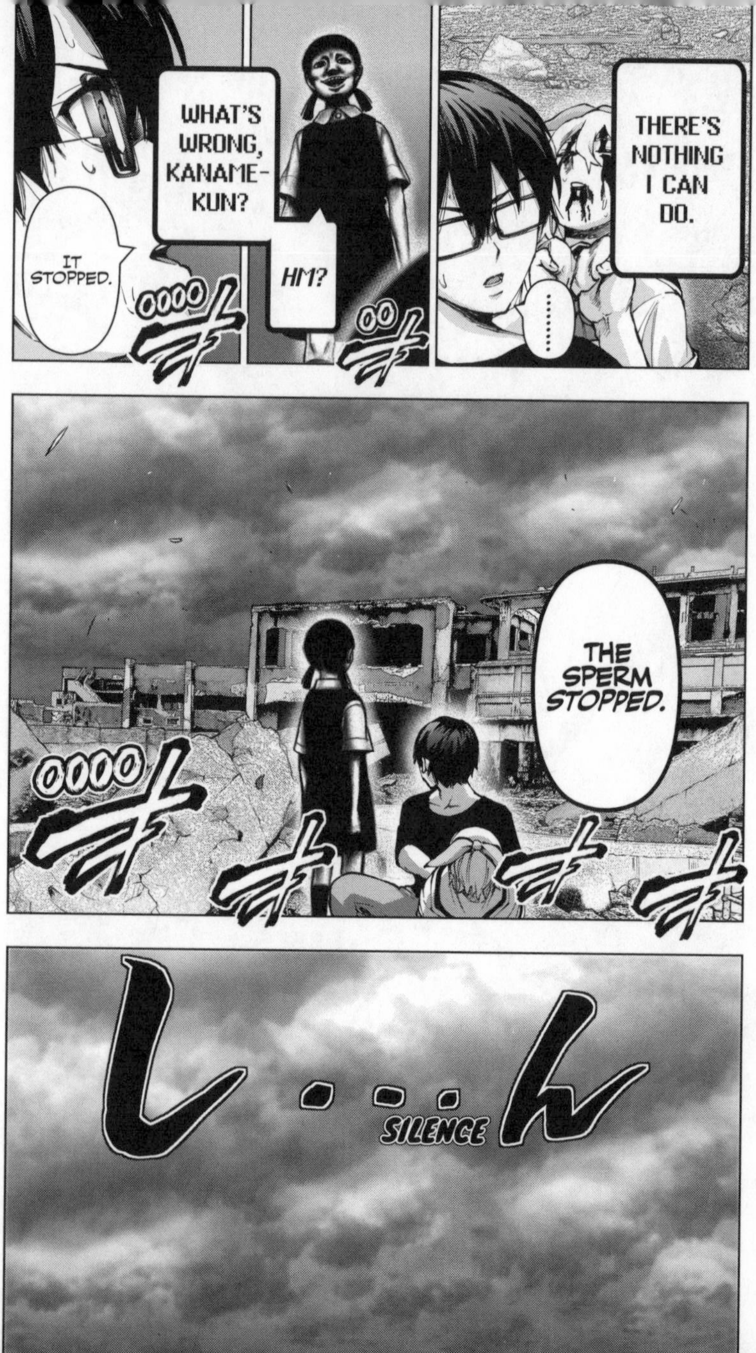
THERE'S NOTHING I CAN DO.
......
WHAT'S WRONG, KANAME-KUN?
HM?
OO
IT STOPPED.
OOOO
THE SPERM STOPPED.
OOOO
SILENCE

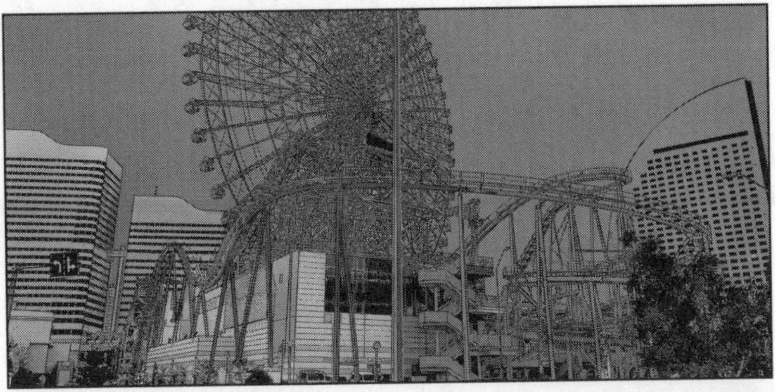

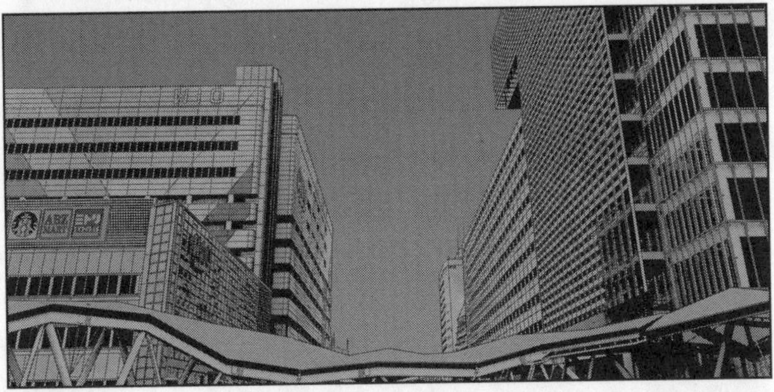

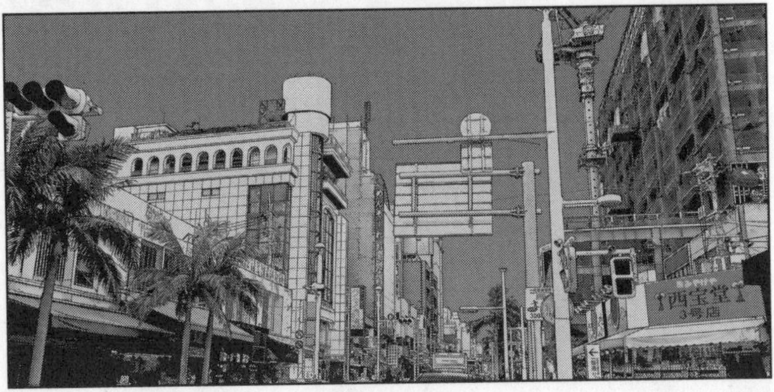
西宝堂
3号店

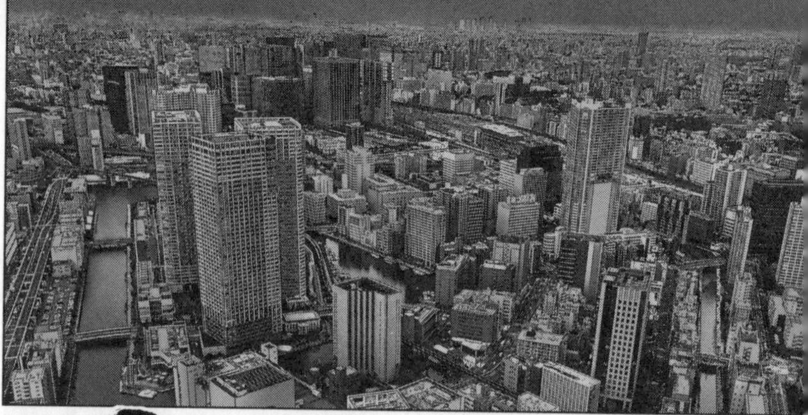

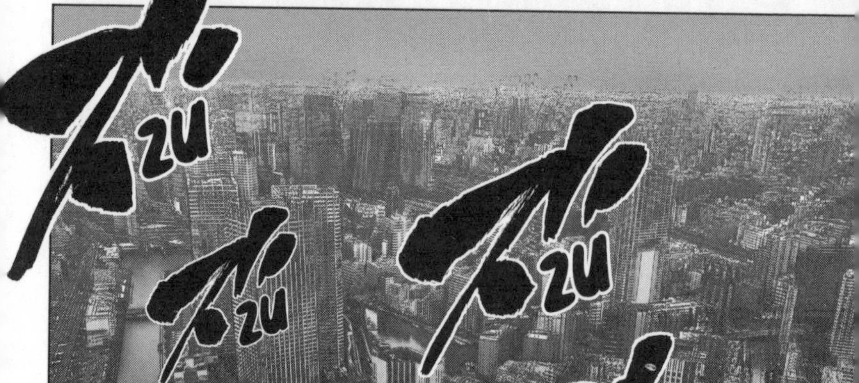
ZU
ZU
ZU
ZU

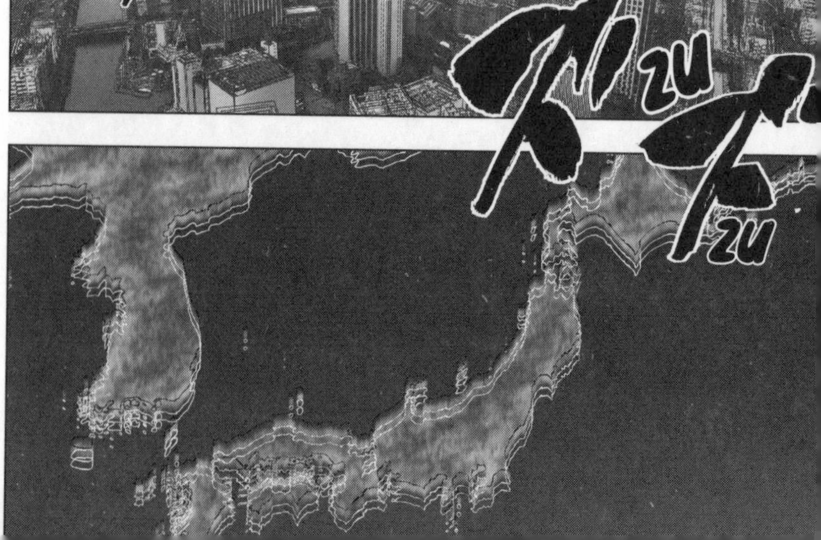
ZU

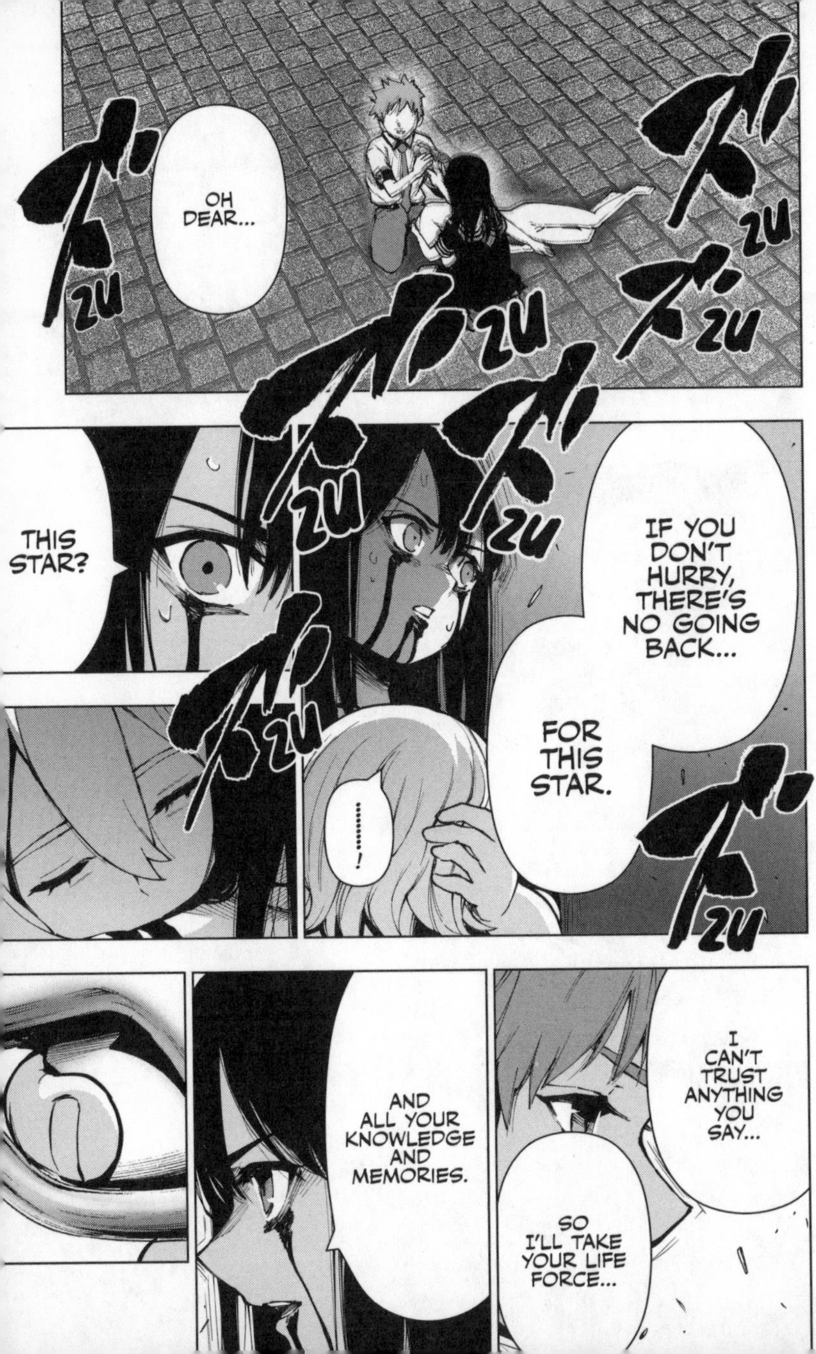
ZU
ZU
ZU
OH DEAR...
ZU
ZU
ZU
IF YOU DON'T HURRY, THERE'S NO GOING BACK...
FOR THIS STAR.
ZU
THIS STAR?
ZU
......!
I CAN'T TRUST ANYTHING YOU SAY...
SO I'LL TAKE YOUR LIFE FORCE...
AND ALL YOUR KNOWLEDGE AND MEMORIES.

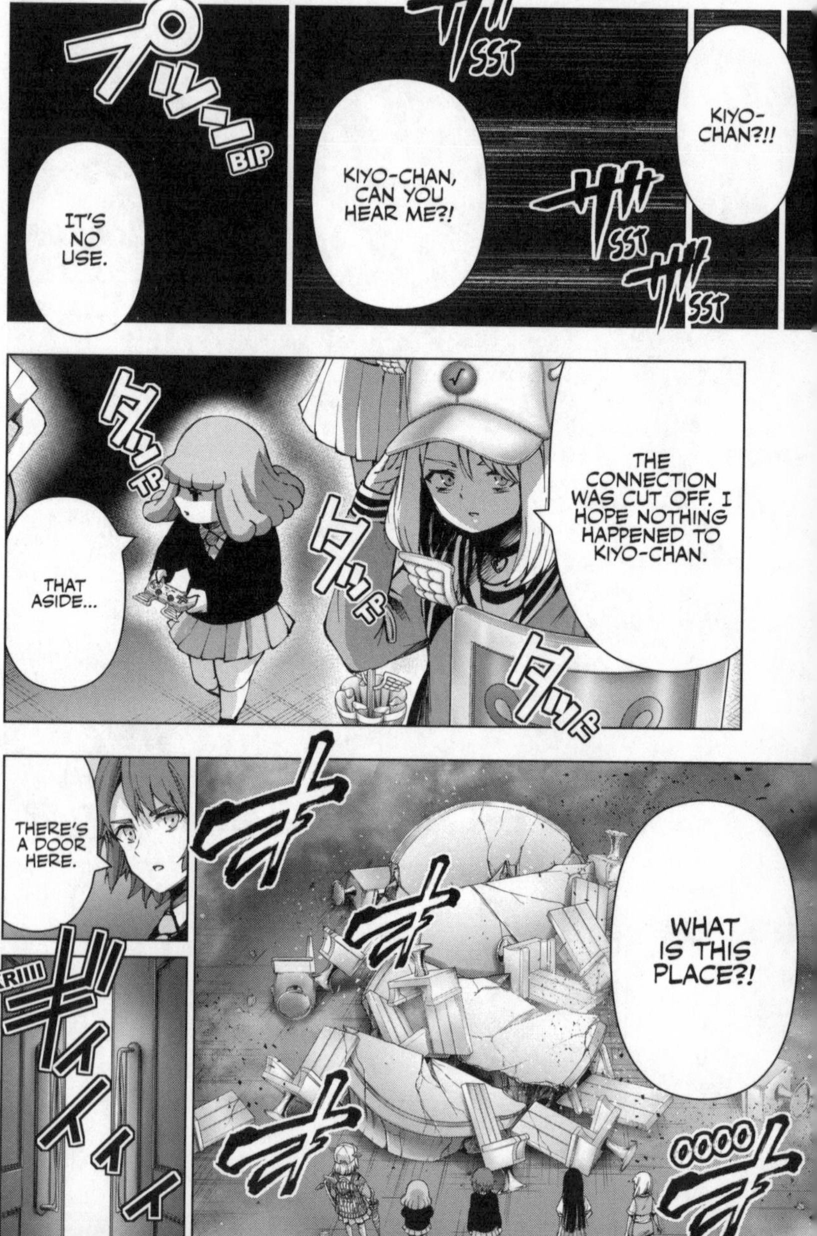
KIYO-CHAN?!!
SST
KIYO-CHAN, CAN YOU HEAR ME?!
SST
SST
BIP
IT'S NO USE.
THE CONNECTION WAS CUT OFF. I HOPE NOTHING HAPPENED TO KIYO-CHAN.
TP
TP
TP
TP
THAT ASIDE...
WHAT IS THIS PLACE?!
OOOO
THERE'S A DOOR HERE.
KRIIII

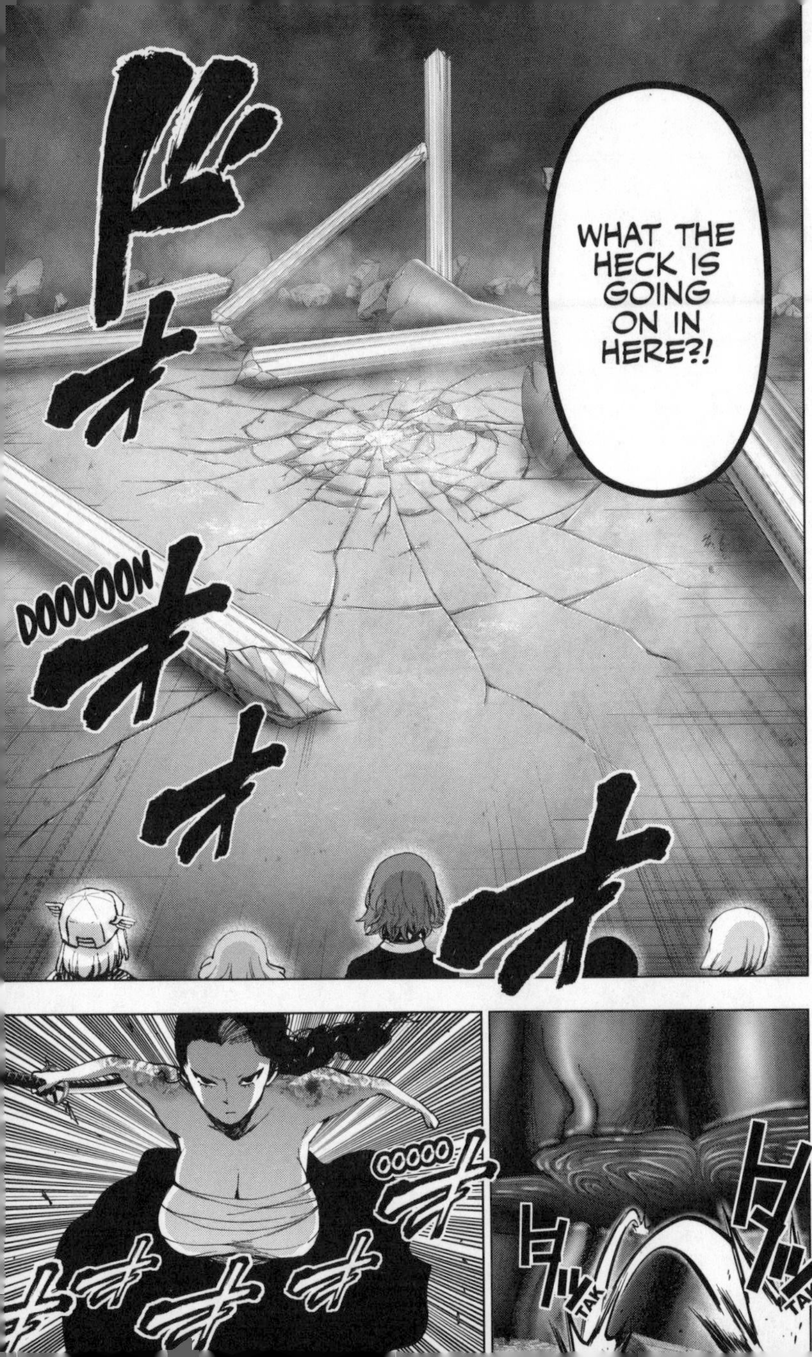
WHAT THE HECK IS GOING ON IN HERE?!
DOOOOON
TAK
TAK
OOOOO

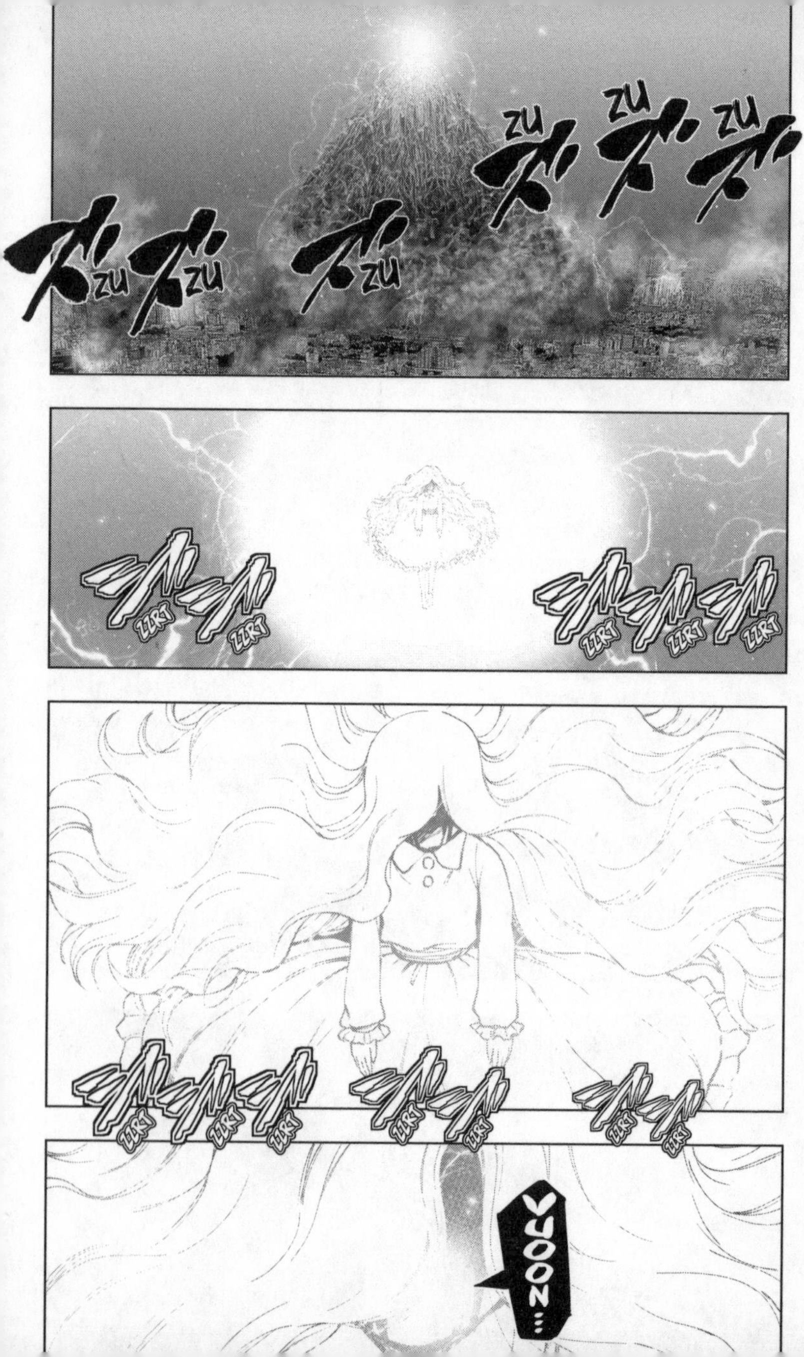
ZU
ZU
ZU
ZU
ZU
ZU
ZZRT
ZZRT
ZZRT
ZZRT
ZZRT
ZZRT
ZZRT
ZZRT
ZZRT
ZZRT
ZZRT
ZZRT
VUOON...

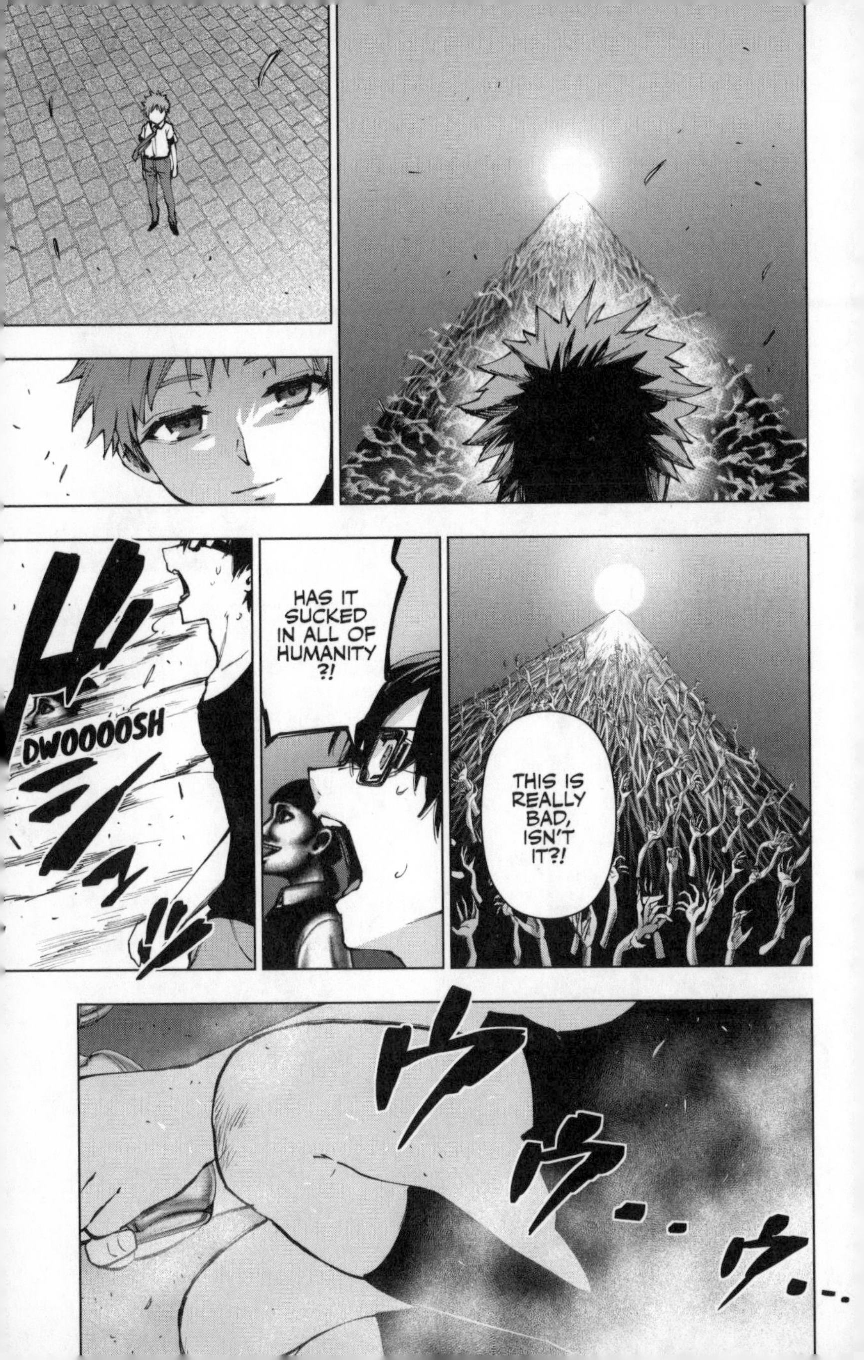
THIS IS REALLY BAD, ISN'T IT?!
HAS IT SUCKED IN ALL OF HUMANITY ?!
DWOOOOSH

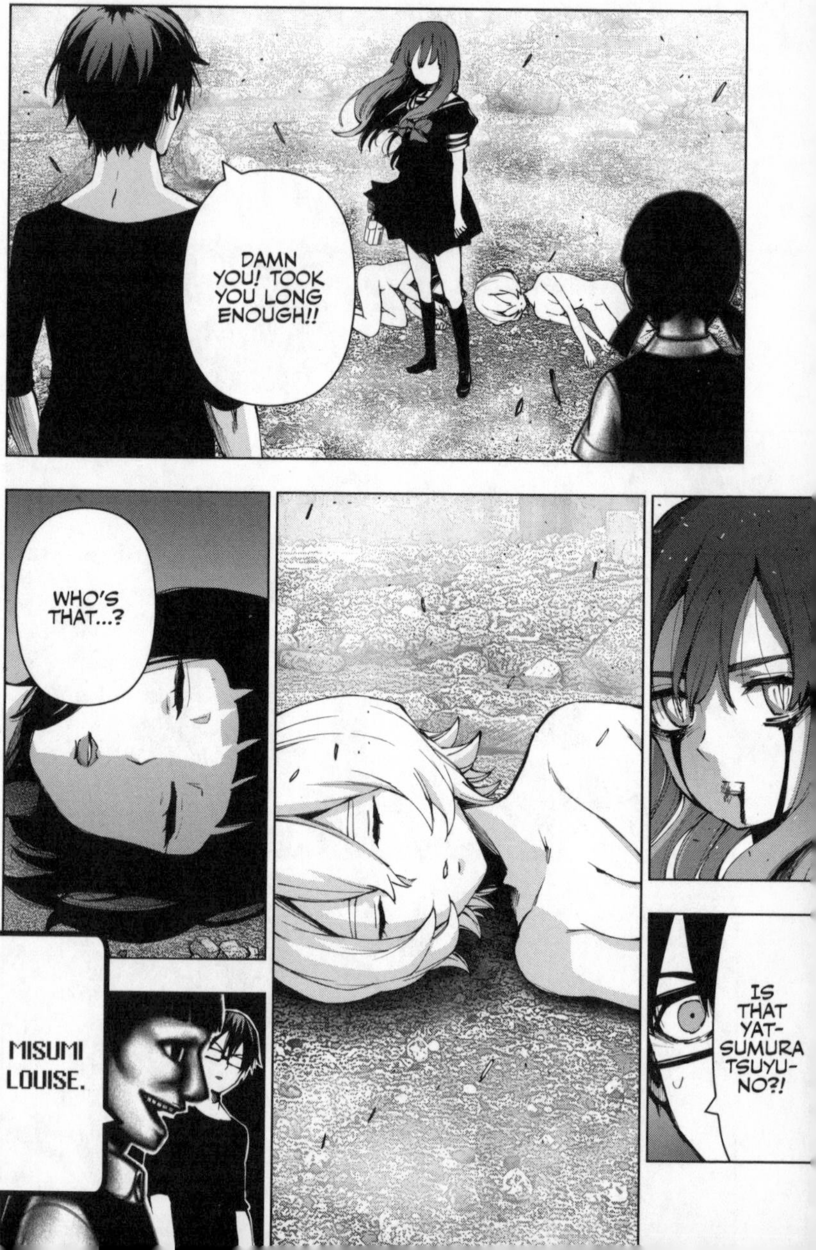
DAMN YOU! TOOK YOU LONG ENOUGH!!
IS THAT YAT-SUMURA TSUYU-NO?!
WHO'S THAT...?
MISUMI LOUISE.

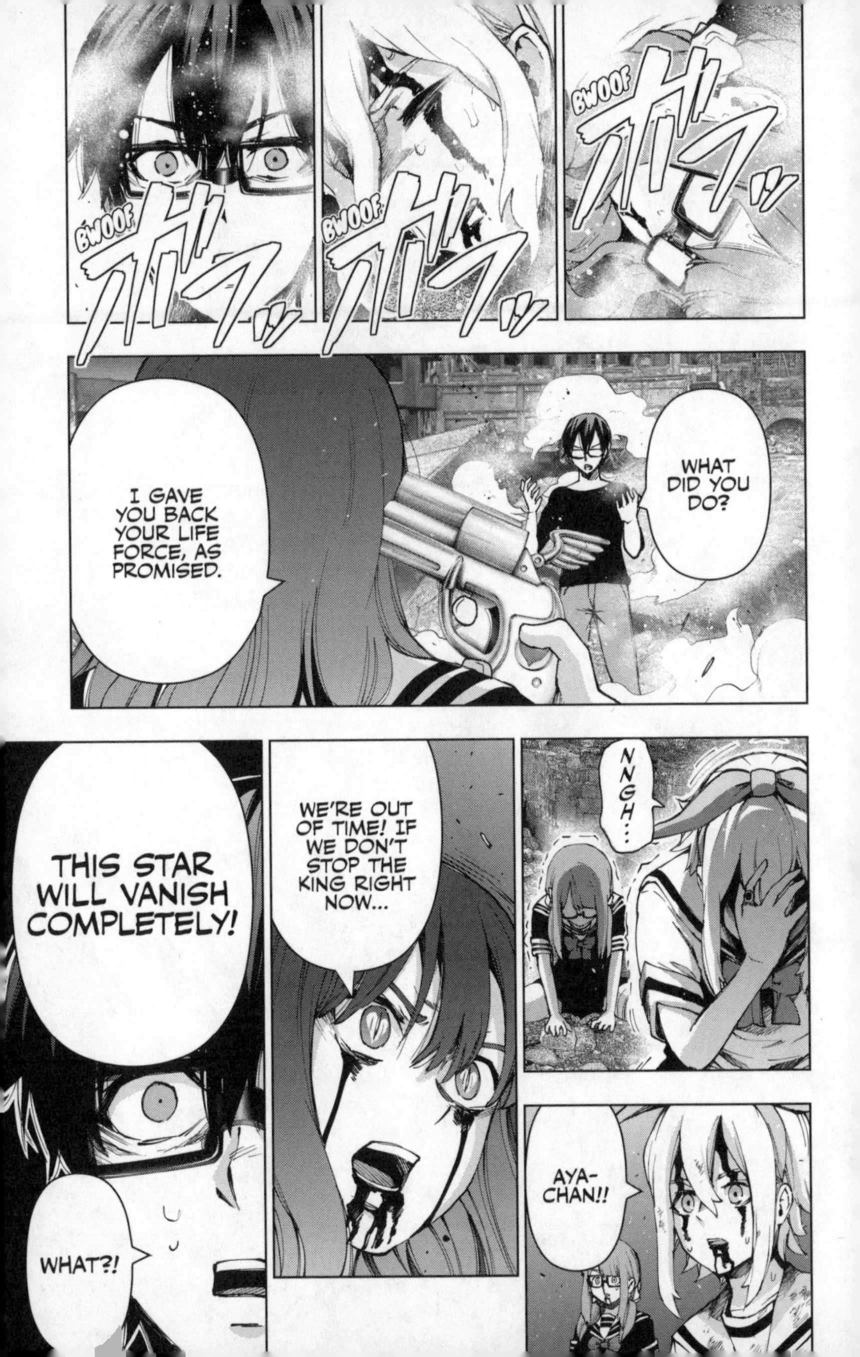
BWOOF
BWOOF
BWOOF
WHAT DID YOU DO?
I GAVE YOU BACK YOUR LIFE FORCE, AS PROMISED.
NNGH...
AYA-CHAN!!
WE'RE OUT OF TIME! IF WE DON'T STOP THE KING RIGHT NOW...
THIS STAR WILL VANISH COMPLETELY!
WHAT?!

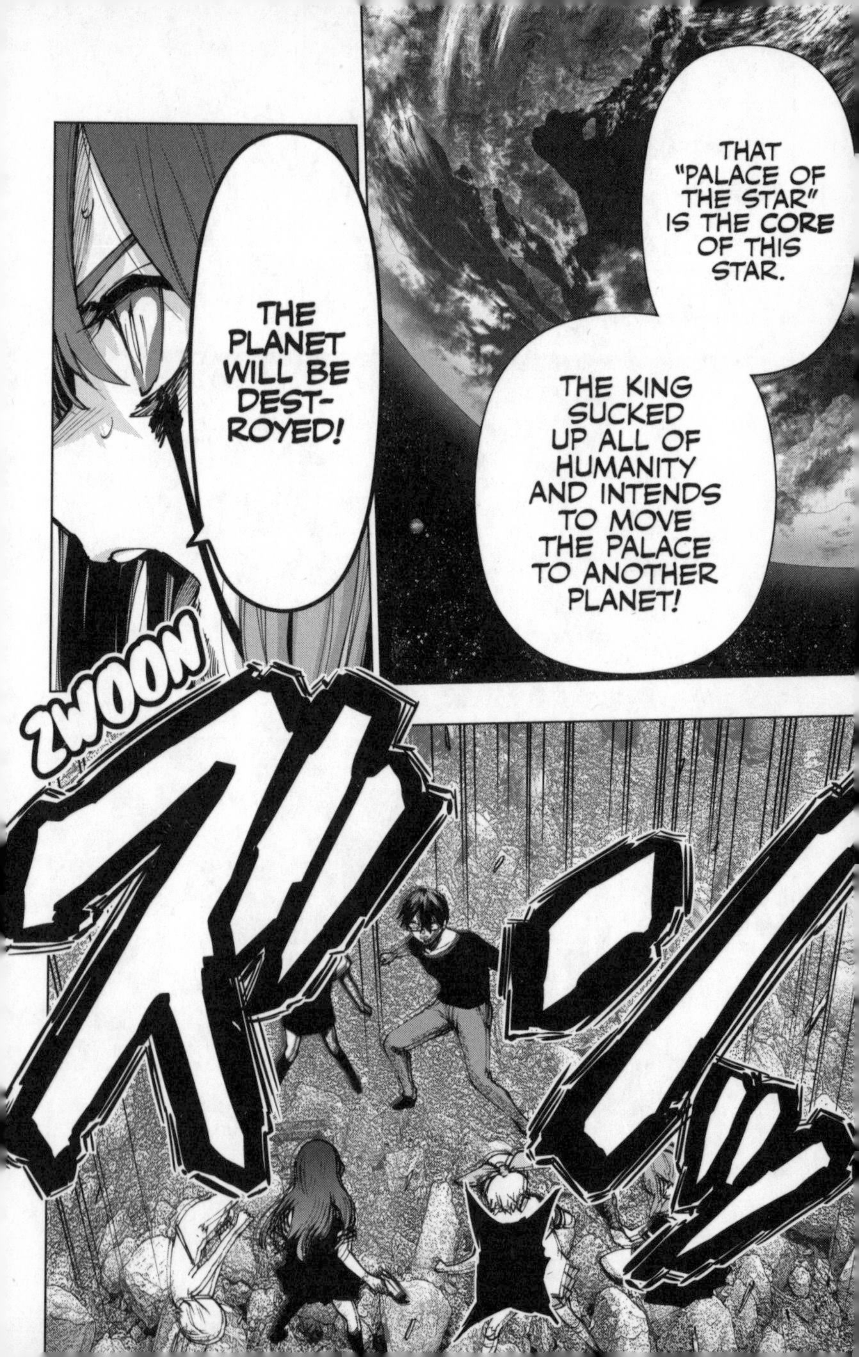
THAT "PALACE OF THE STAR" IS THE CORE OF THIS STAR.
THE KING SUCKED UP ALL OF HUMANITY AND INTENDS TO MOVE THE PALACE TO ANOTHER PLANET!
THE PLANET WILL BE DEST-ROYED!
ZWOON

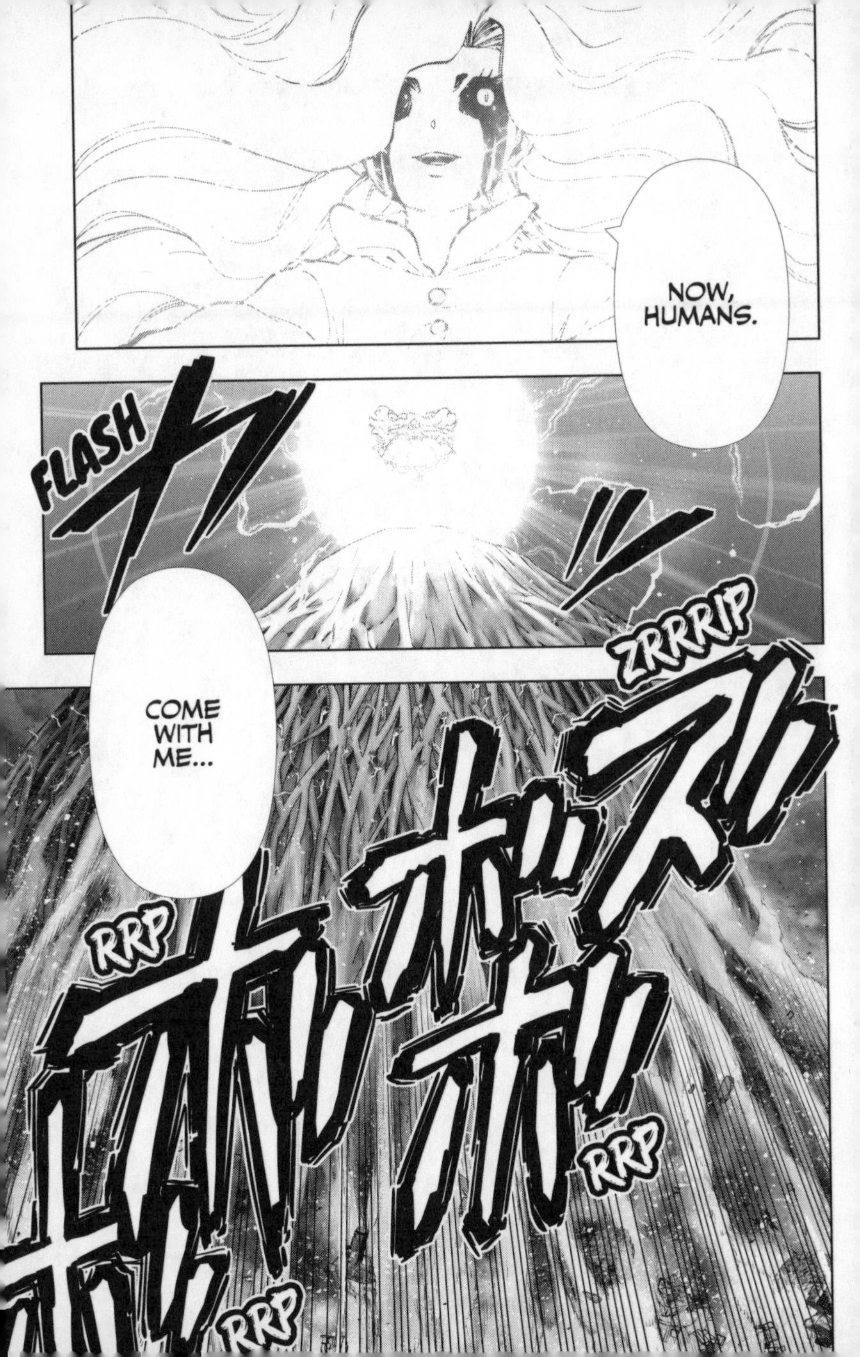
NOW, HUMANS.
FLASH
ZRRRIP
COME WITH ME...
RRP
RRP
RRP

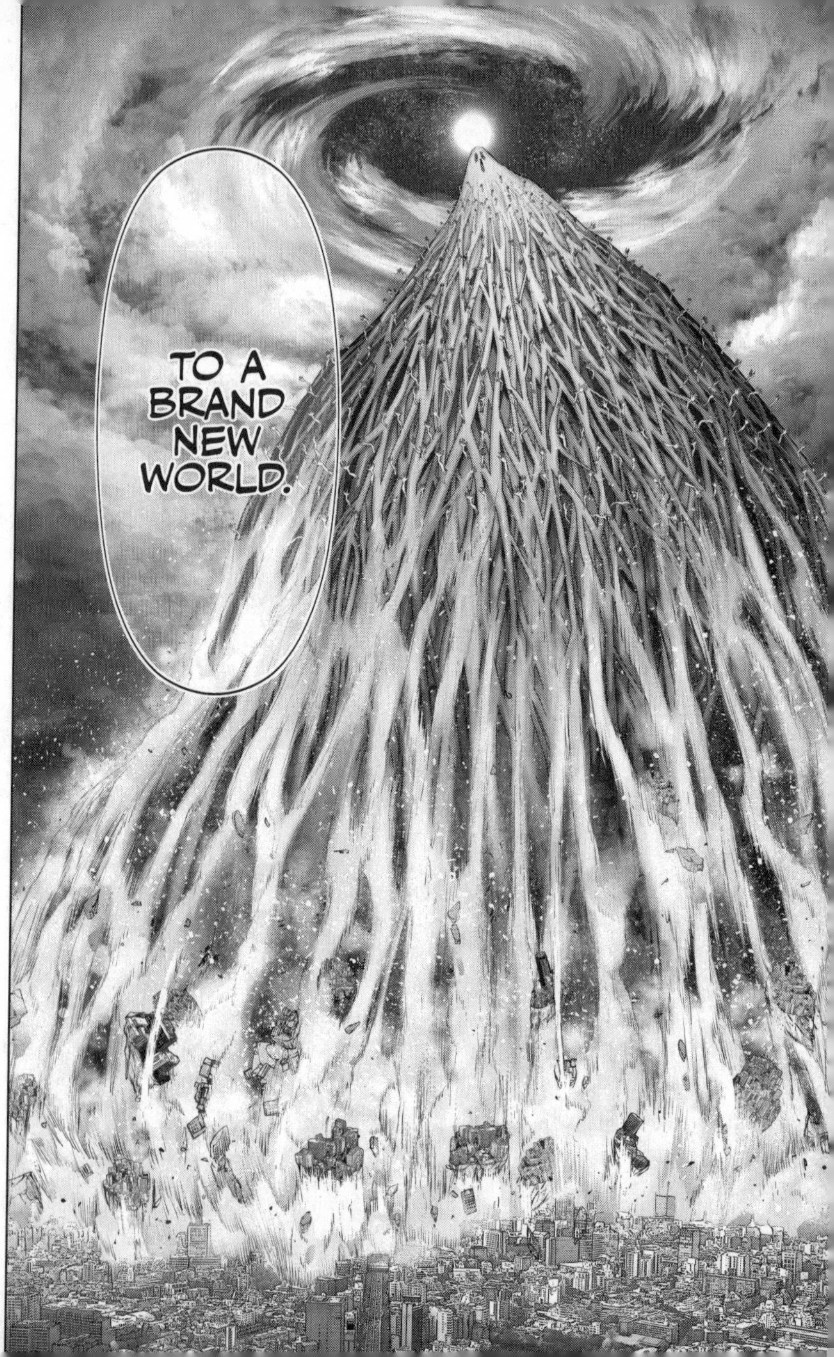
TO A BRAND NEW WORLD.

THE KING INTENDS TO TAKE ALL OF HUMANITY TO ANOTHER PLANET AND START A NEW RACE.

IT'LL NO LONGER BE OF USE.

ANOTHER PLANET? WHAT WILL HAPPEN TO EARTH?

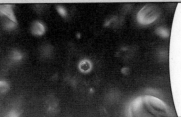

PLANETS ARE LIVING CREATURES. THE ROOTS OF THAT LIFE FORM, THE CORE, ARE CALLED THE "PALACE OF THE STAR."

IF THE CORE IS MOVED TO ANOTHER PLANET, THEN THE STAR IT LEAVES MUST BE THROWN AWAY.

ON THE NEW PLANET, HUMANITY WILL PROSPER, DEVELOP CULTURE...

AND THEN, THAT PLANET...

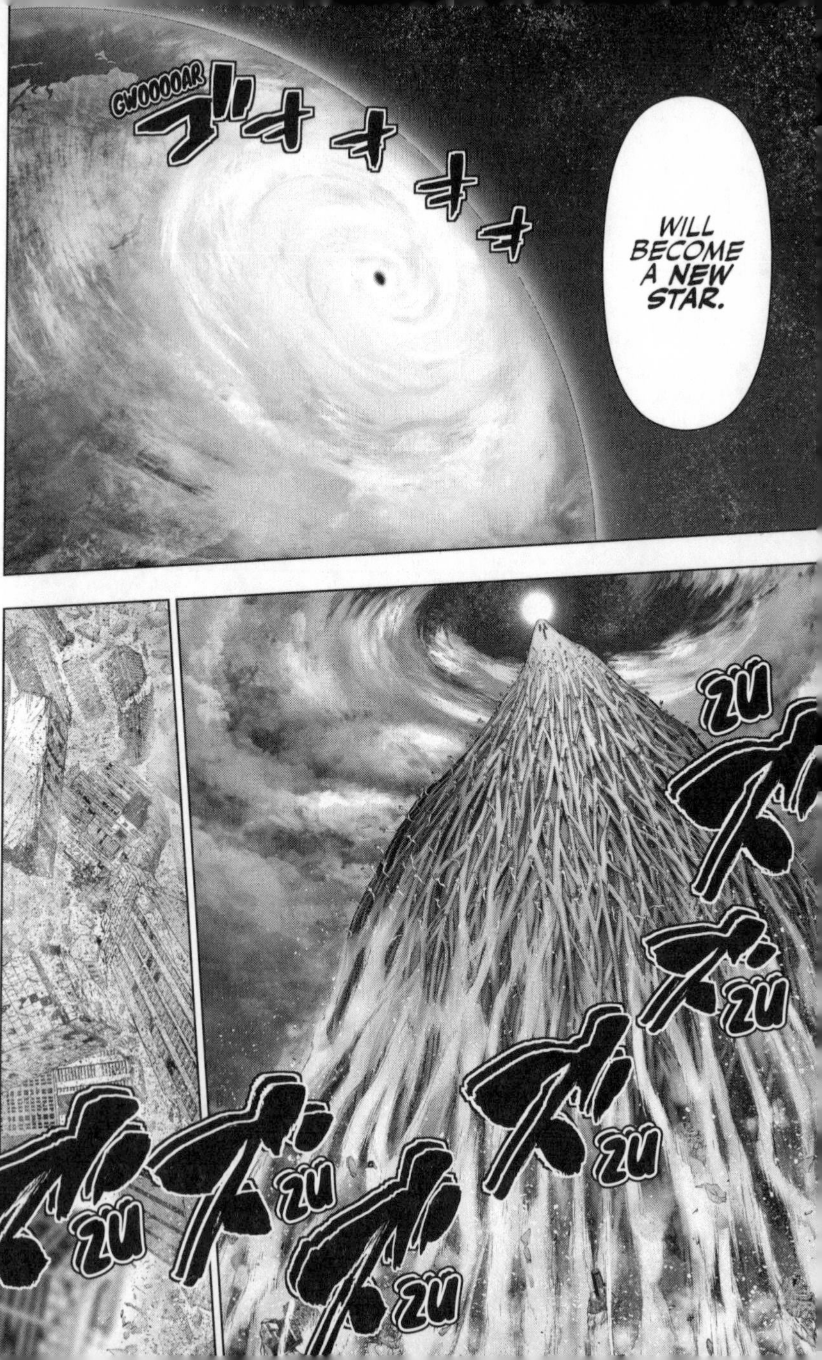
WILL BECOME A NEW STAR.
GWOOOOAR
ゴォォォォ
ZU
ZU
ZU
ZU
ZU
ZU
ZU

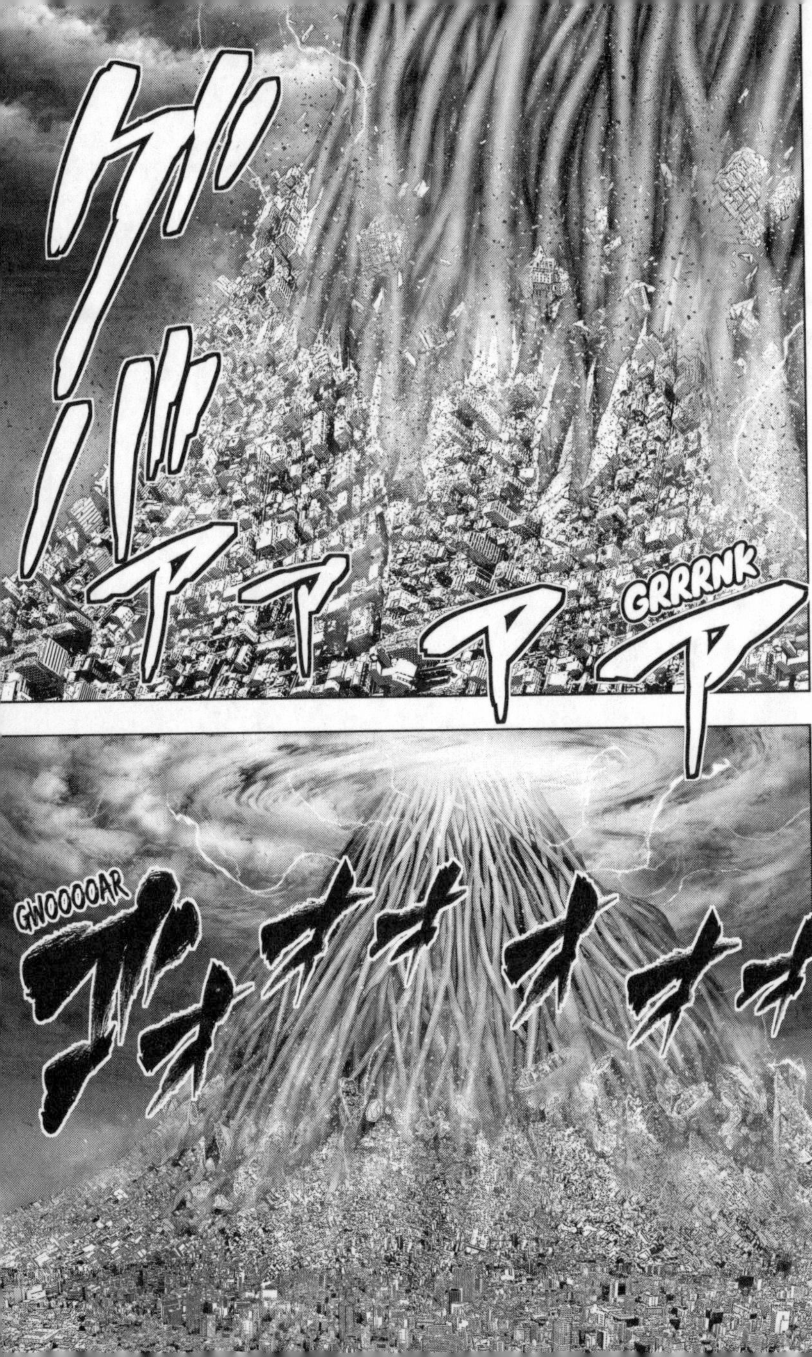
GRRRNK
GWOOOOAR
ゴオオオオオオ

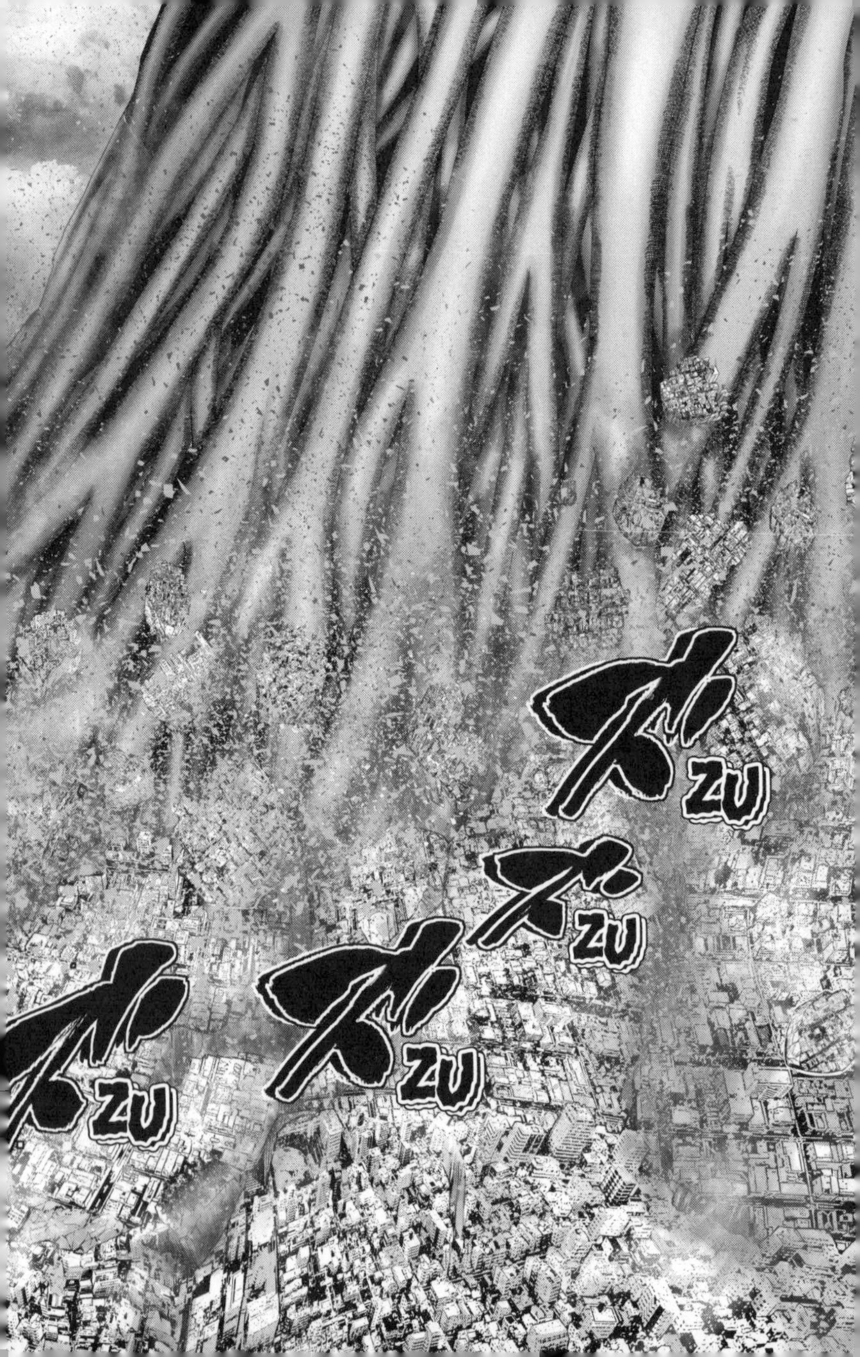
ズ ZU
ズ ZU
ズ ZU
ズ ZU

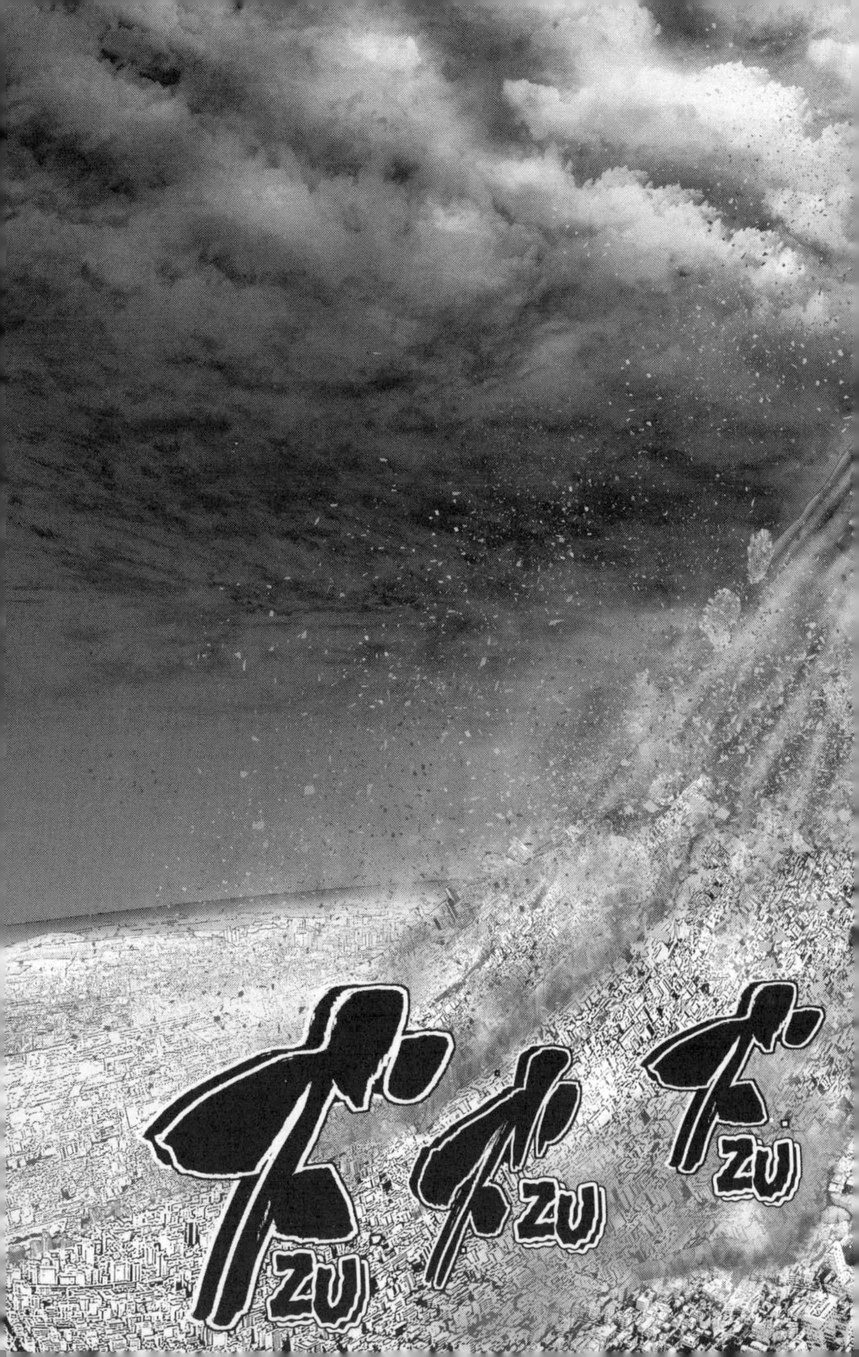
ZU
ZU
ZU

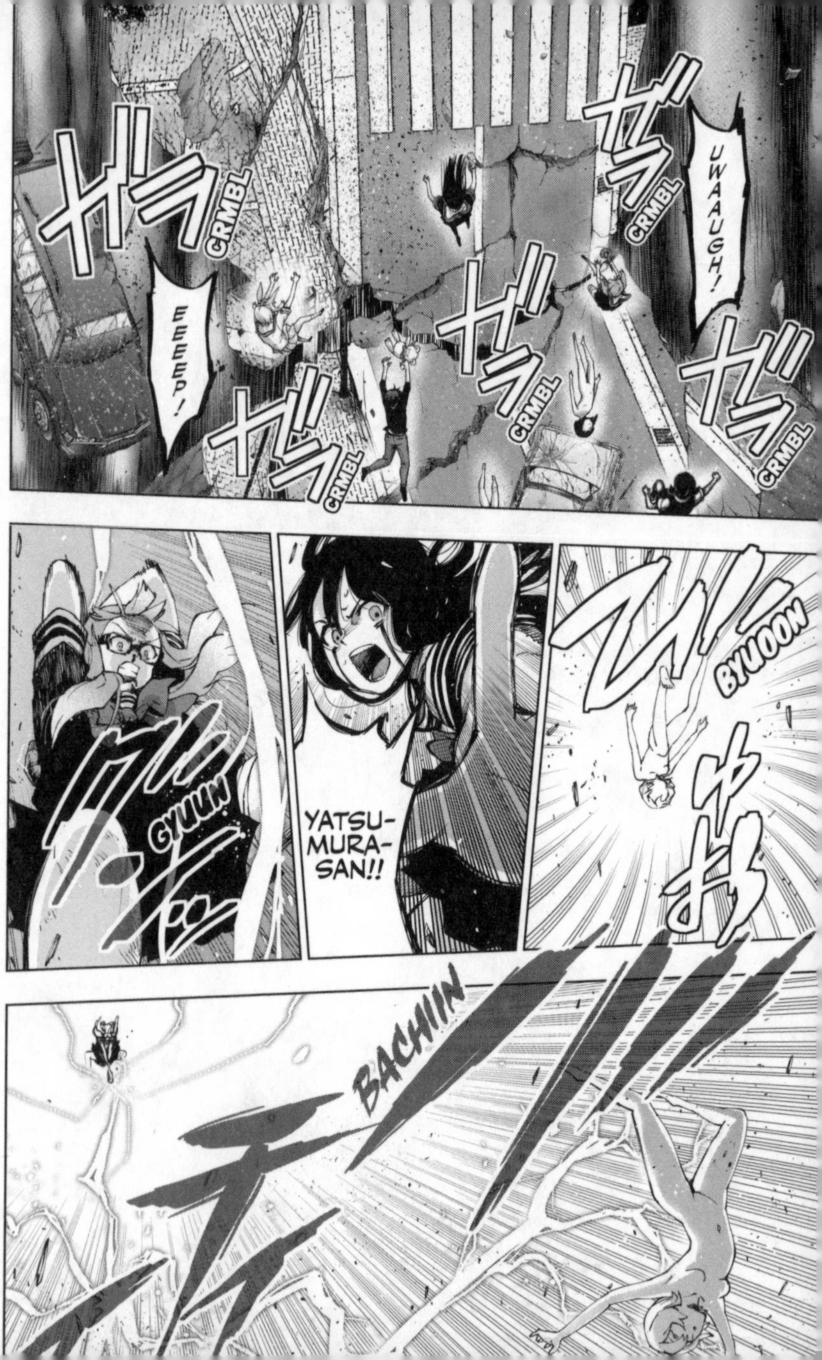
UWAAUGH!
GRMBL
GRMBL
GRMBL
GRMBL
EEEEP!
GRMBL
BYUOON
YATSU-MURA-SAN!!
GYUUN
BACHIIN

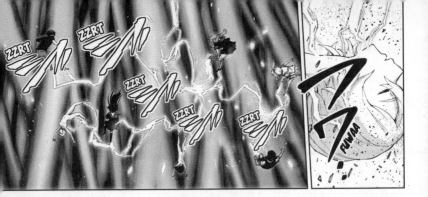

FUWAA
ZZRT
ZZRT
ZZRT
ZZRT
ZZRT
GRAB
THANK YOU, SHIORI-SAN!!
DOES THIS MEAN IT'S ALL OVER NOW?
IS THIS...
THE TEMPEST?

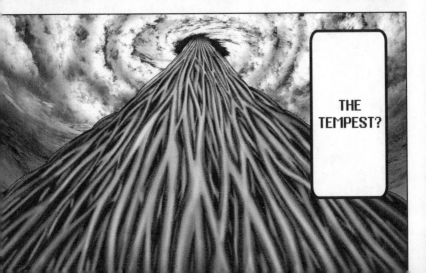

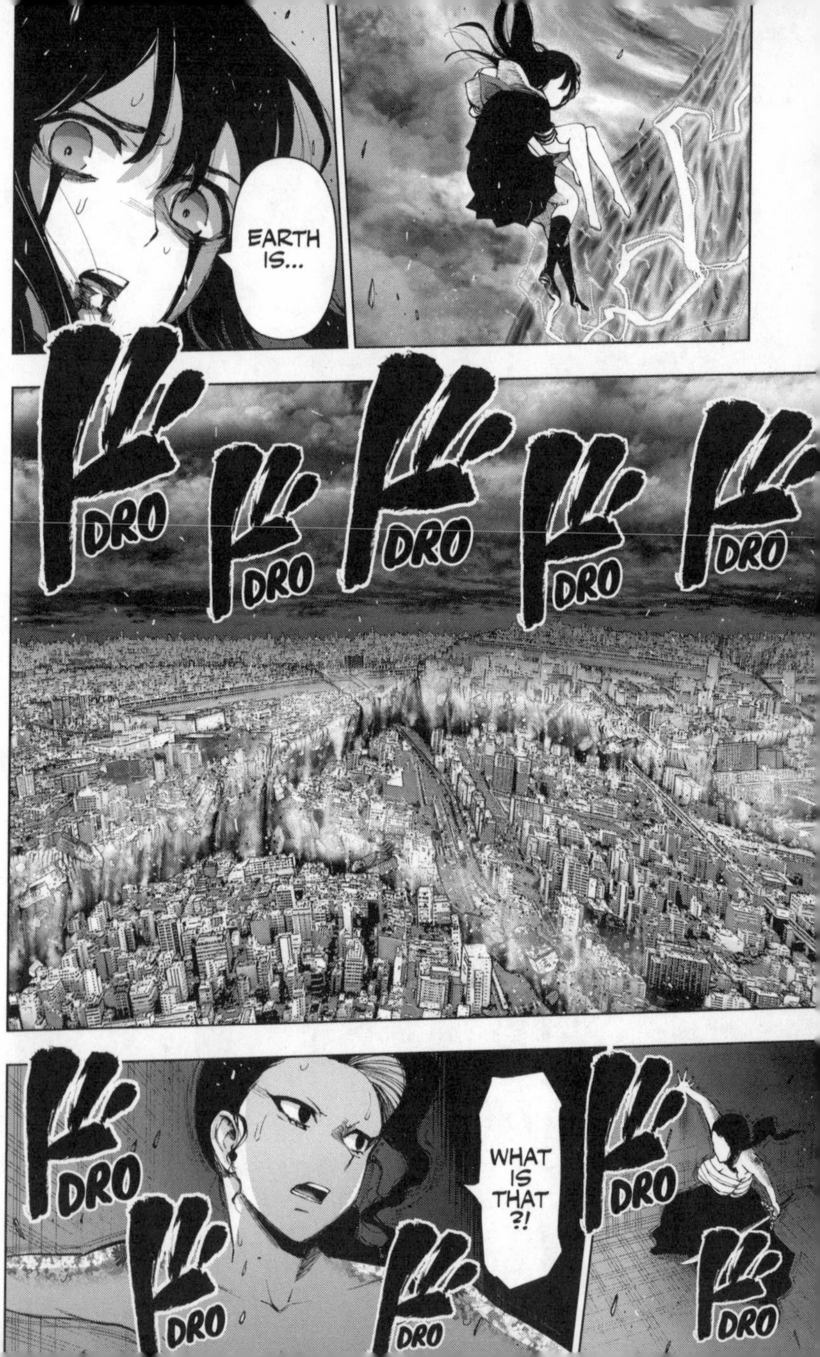
EARTH IS...
DRO
DRO
DRO
DRO
DRO
DRO
DRO
WHAT IS THAT?!
DRO
DRO
DRO

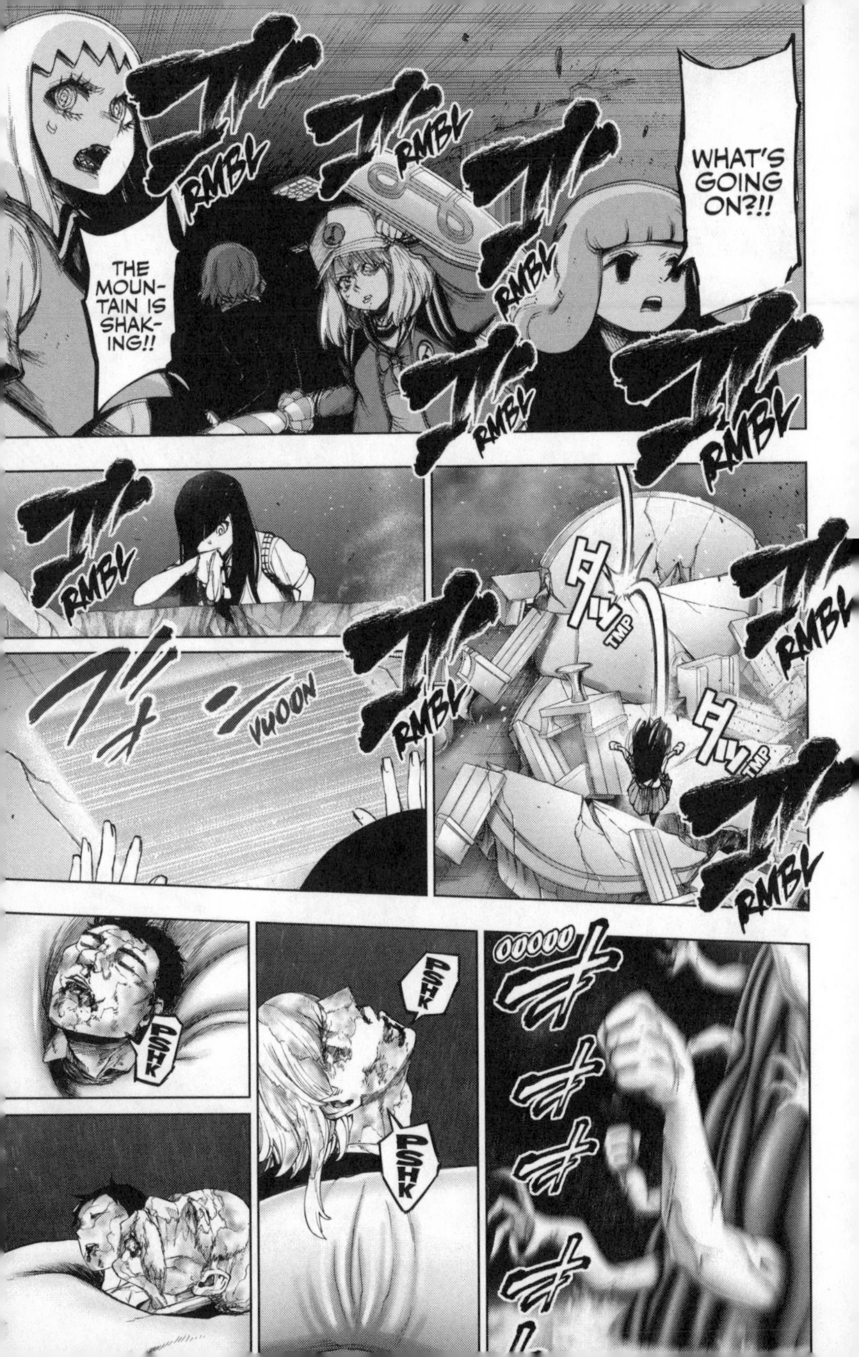
WHAT'S GOING ON?!!
RMBL
RMBL
RMBL
RMBL
RMBL
RMBL
THE MOUN-TAIN IS SHAK-ING!!
TMP
RMBL
TMP
RMBL
RMBL
RMBL
VUOON
OOOOO
PSHK
PSHK
PSHK

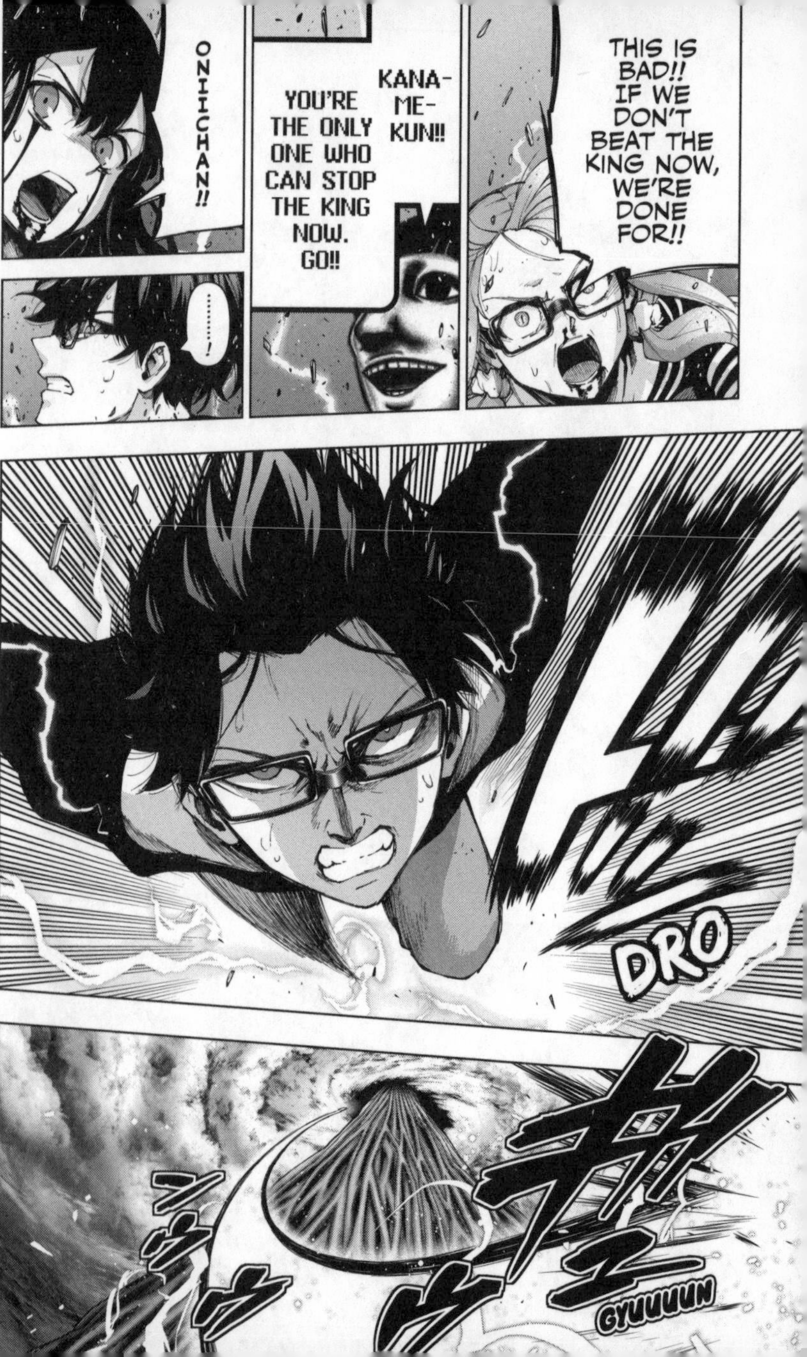
THIS IS BAD!! IF WE DON'T BEAT THE KING NOW, WE'RE DONE FOR!!
KANAME-KUN!!
YOU'RE THE ONLY ONE WHO CAN STOP THE KING NOW. GO!!
ONIICHAN!!
......!
DRO
GYUUUUN

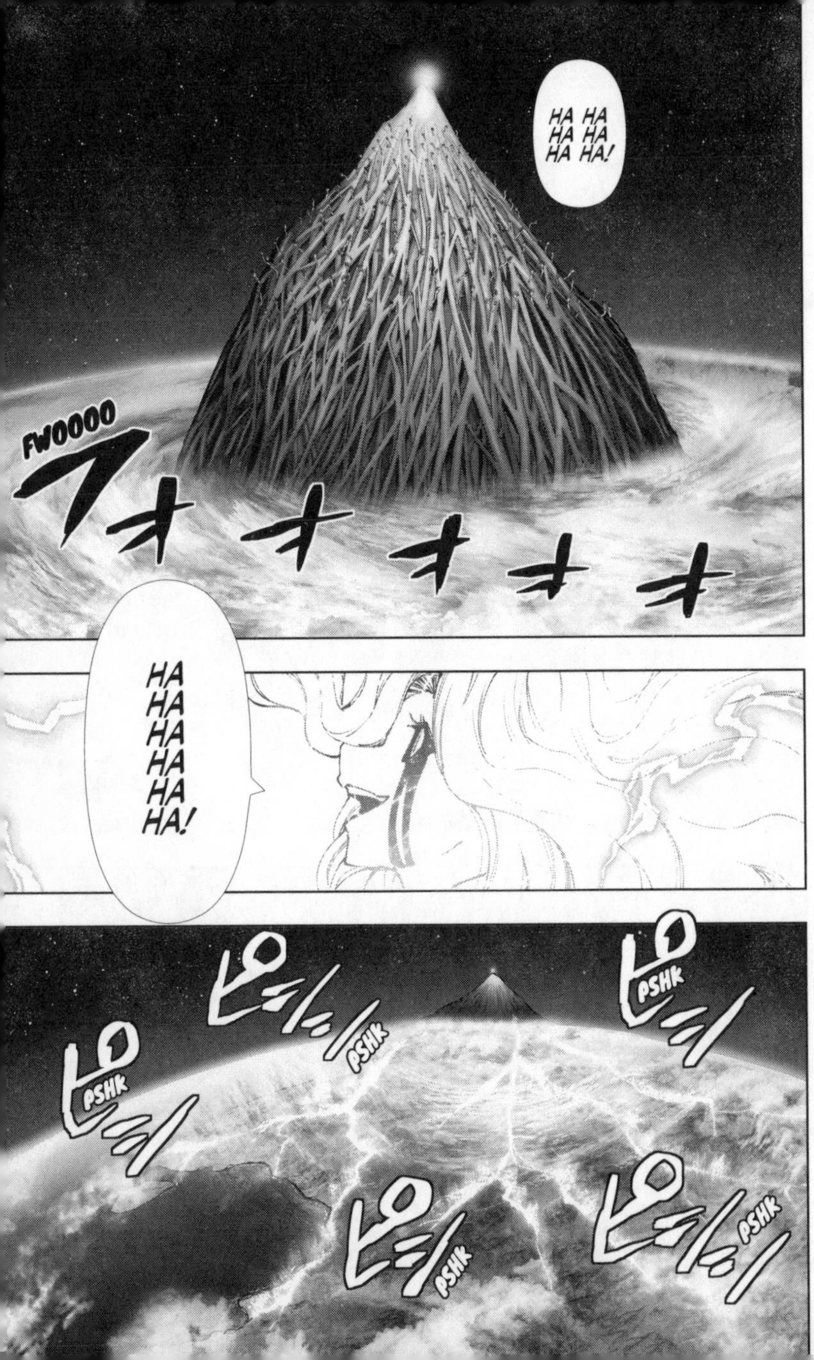
HA HA HA HA HA HA!
FWOOOO
HA HA HA HA HA HA!
PSHK
PSHK
PSHK
PSHK
PSHK

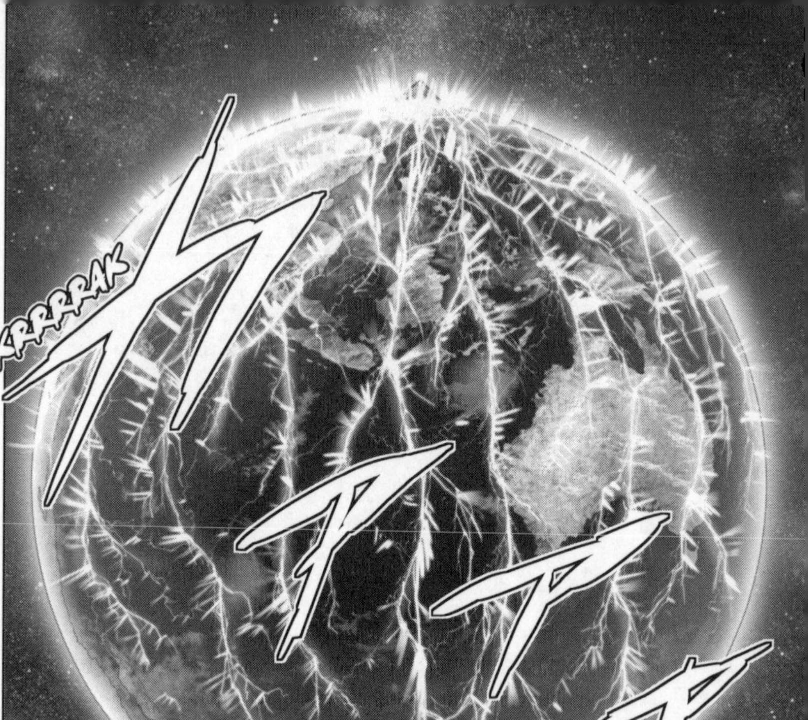
KRRRRAK
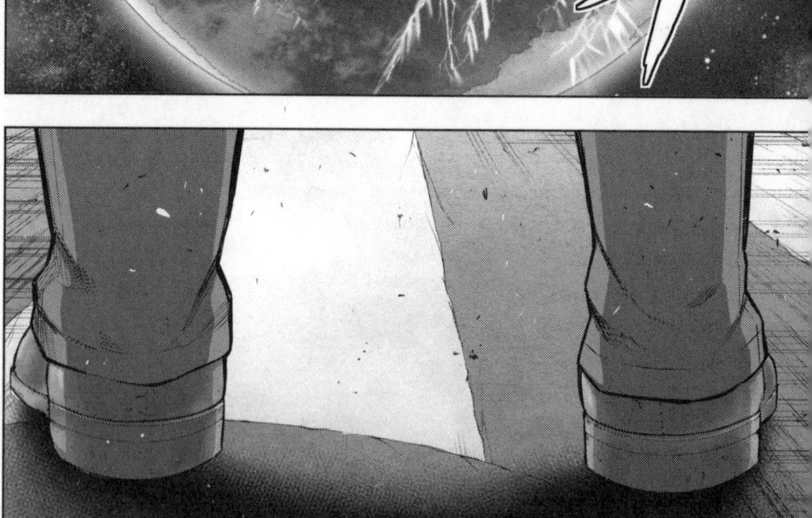

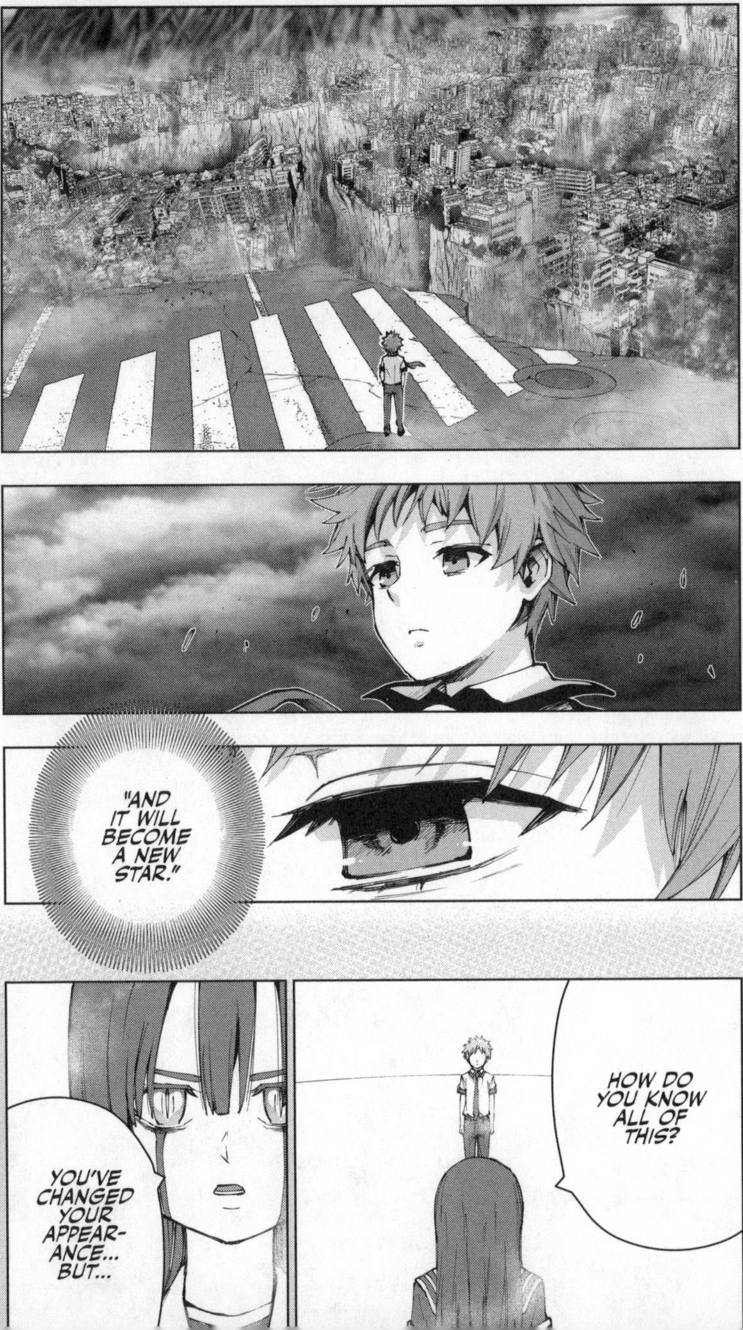
"AND IT WILL BECOME A NEW STAR."
HOW DO YOU KNOW ALL OF THIS?
YOU'VE CHANGED YOUR APPEAR-ANCE... BUT...

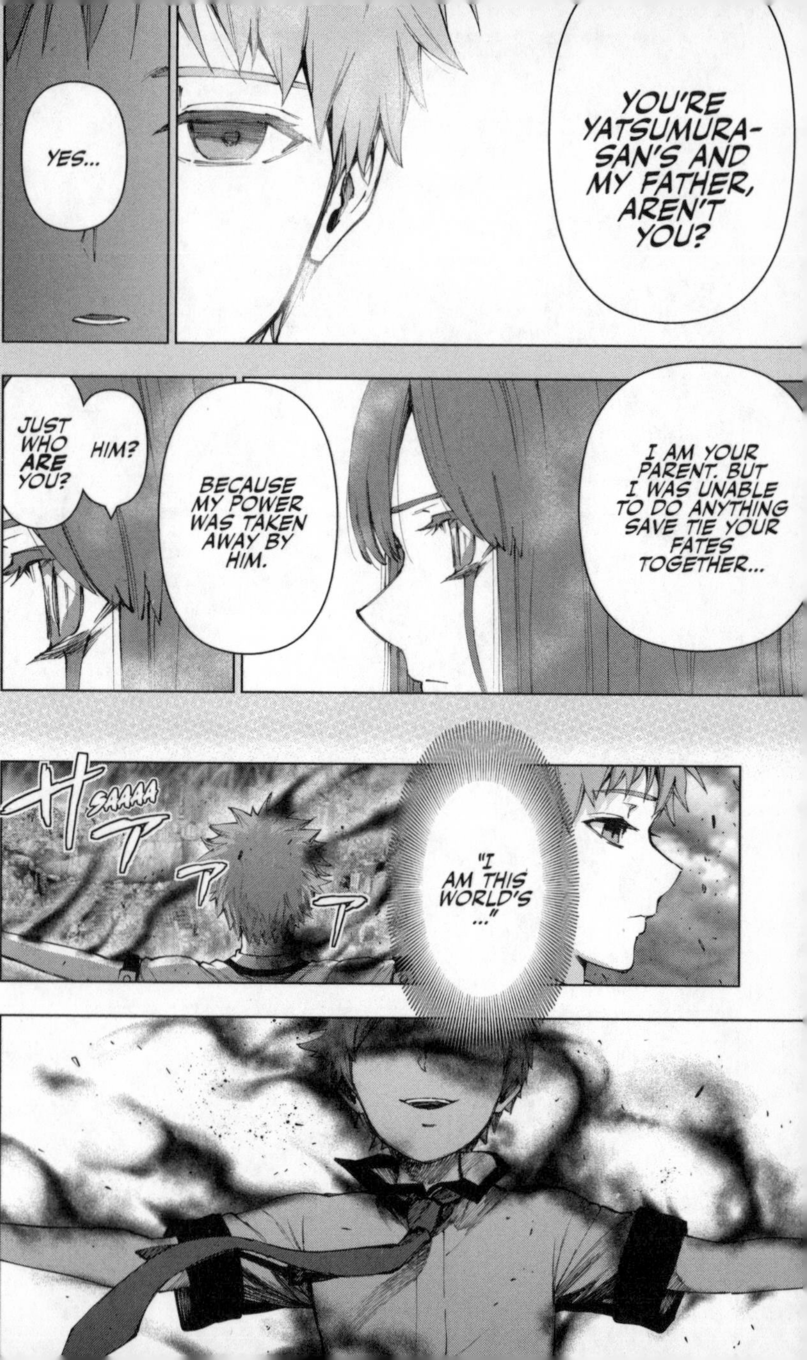
YOU'RE YATSUMURA-SAN'S AND MY FATHER, AREN'T YOU?
YES...
I AM YOUR PARENT. BUT I WAS UNABLE TO DO ANYTHING SAVE TIE YOUR FATES TOGETHER...
BECAUSE MY POWER WAS TAKEN AWAY BY HIM.
HIM?
JUST WHO ARE YOU?
"I AM THIS WORLD'S ..."
SAAAA

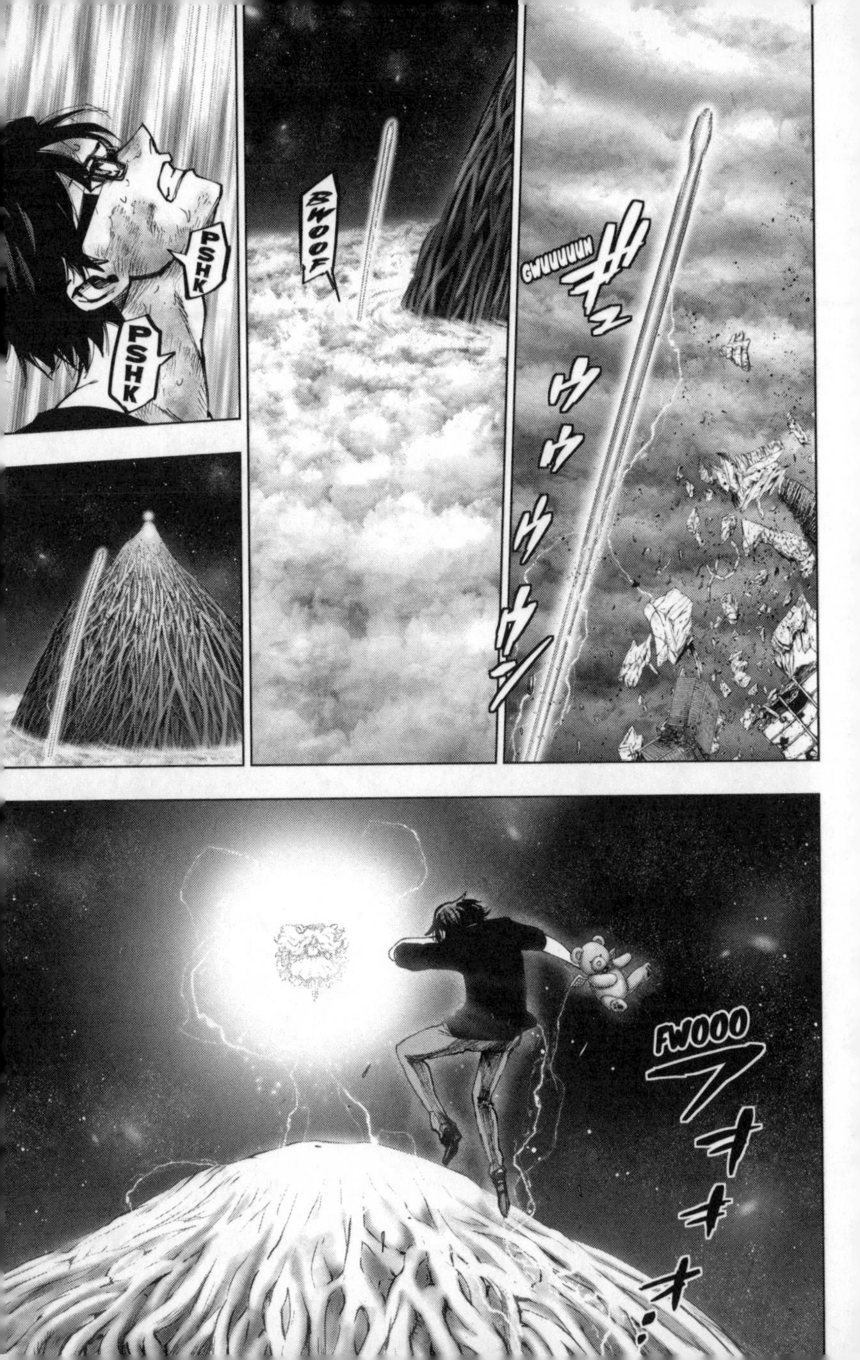
GWUUUUUN
BWOOF
PSHK
PSHK
FWOOO

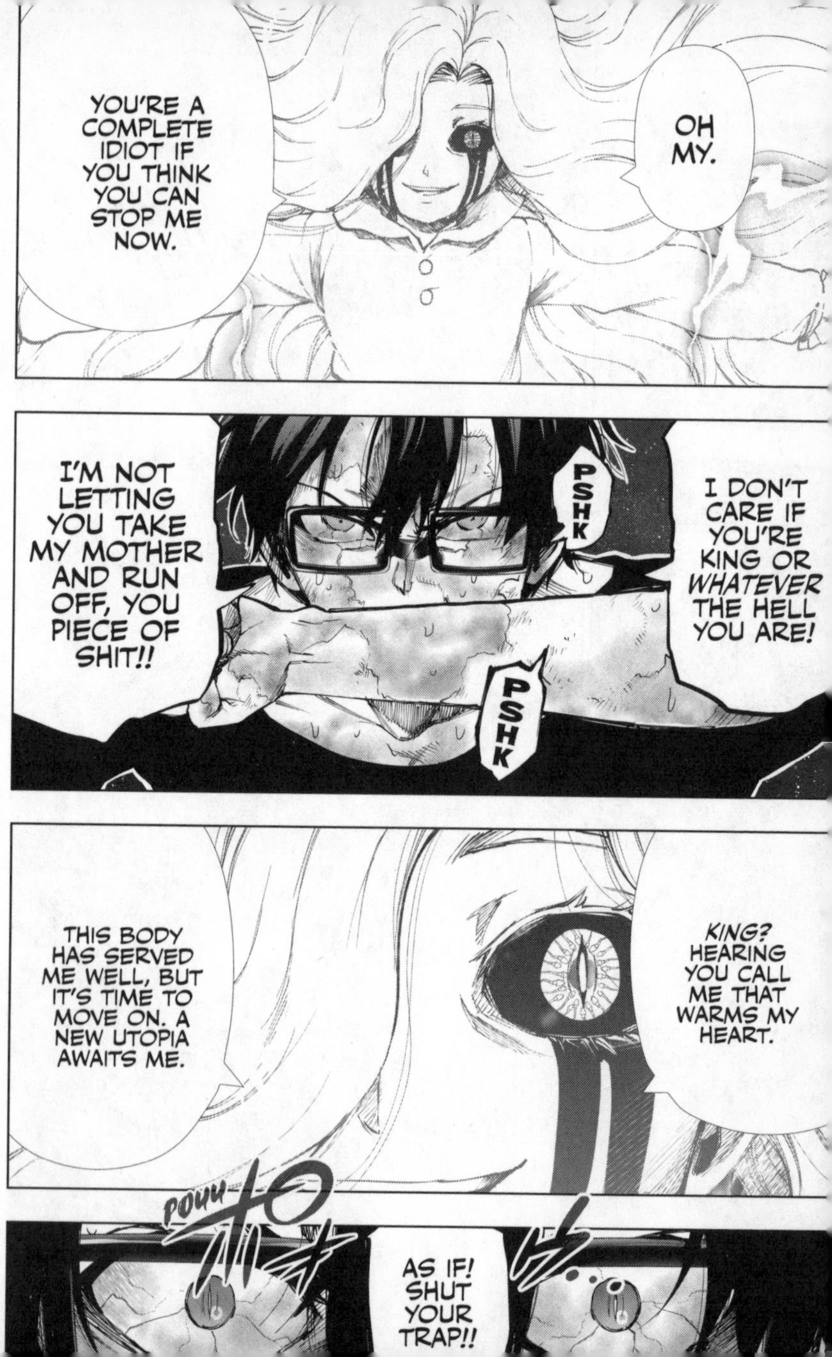
OH MY.
YOU'RE A COMPLETE IDIOT IF YOU THINK YOU CAN STOP ME NOW.
I DON'T CARE IF YOU'RE KING OR *WHATEVER* THE HELL YOU ARE!
PSHK
PSHK
I'M NOT LETTING YOU TAKE MY MOTHER AND RUN OFF, YOU PIECE OF SHIT!!
KING? HEARING YOU CALL ME THAT WARMS MY HEART.
THIS BODY HAS SERVED ME WELL, BUT IT'S TIME TO MOVE ON. A NEW UTOPIA AWAITS ME.
AS IF! SHUT YOUR TRAP!!
POUU

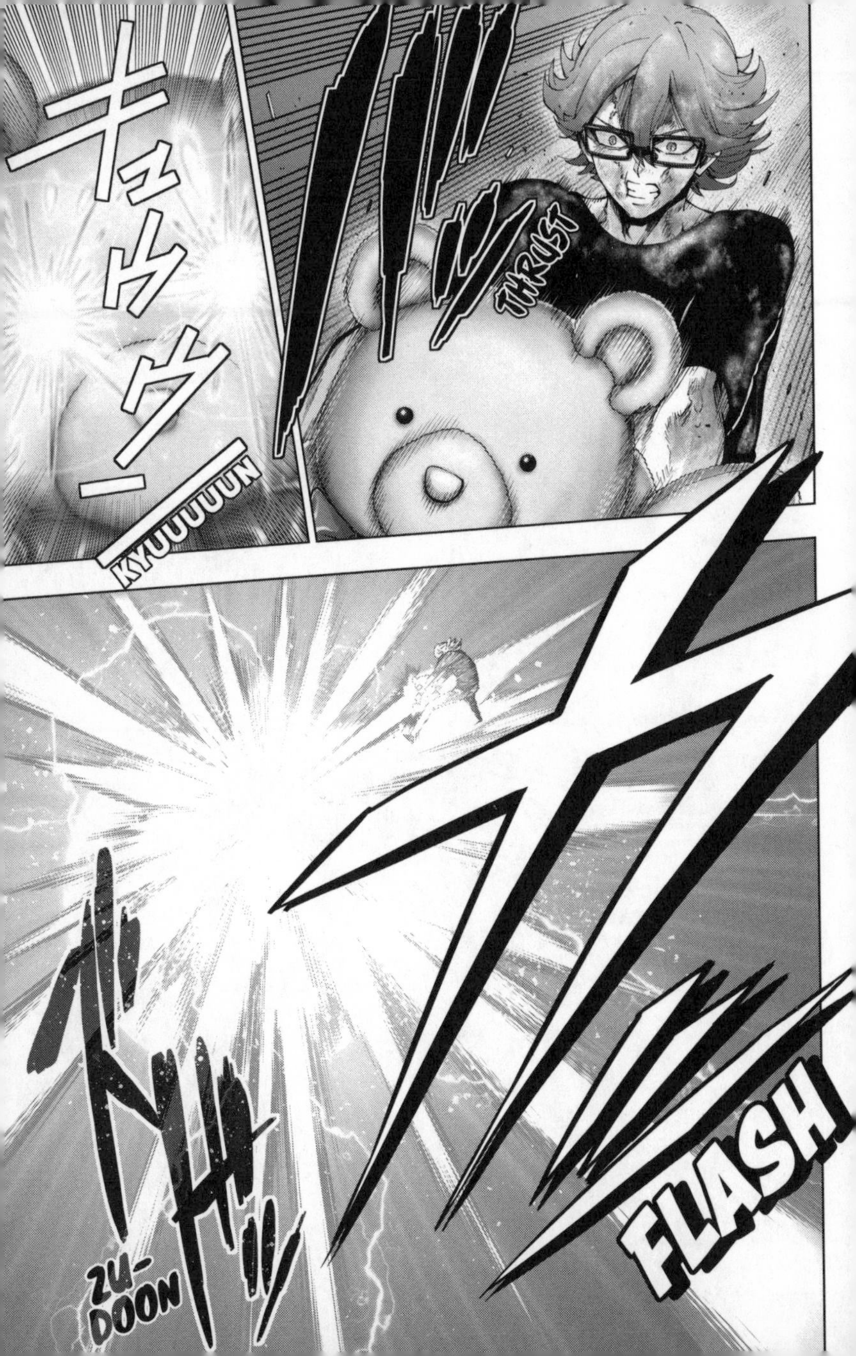
THRUST
KYUUUUUN
FLASH
ZU-DOON

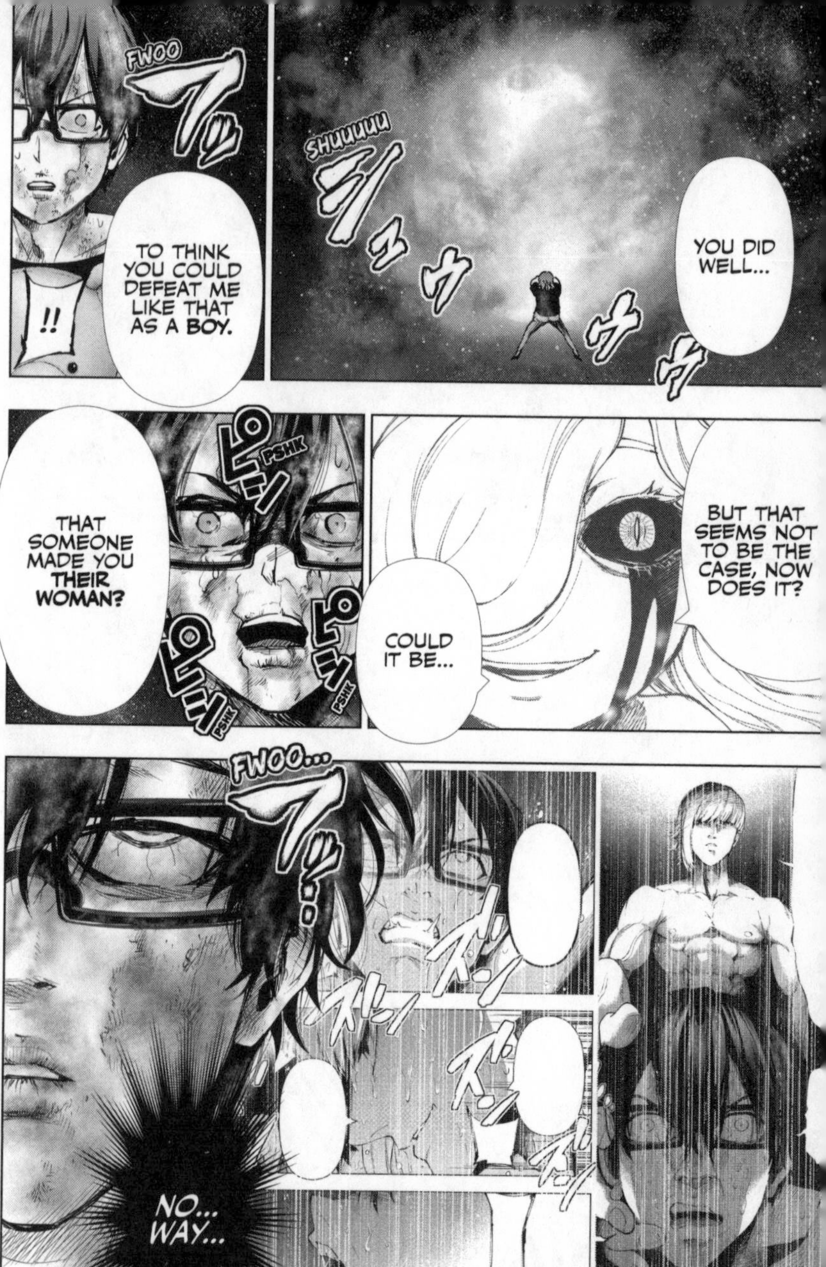
YOU DID WELL...
SHUUUUU
FWOO
TO THINK YOU COULD DEFEAT ME LIKE THAT AS A BOY.
!!
BUT THAT SEEMS NOT TO BE THE CASE, NOW DOES IT?
COULD IT BE...
PSHK
THAT SOMEONE MADE YOU THEIR WOMAN?
PSHK
PSHK
FWOO...
NO... WAY...

ENTER.133 CHECKMATE

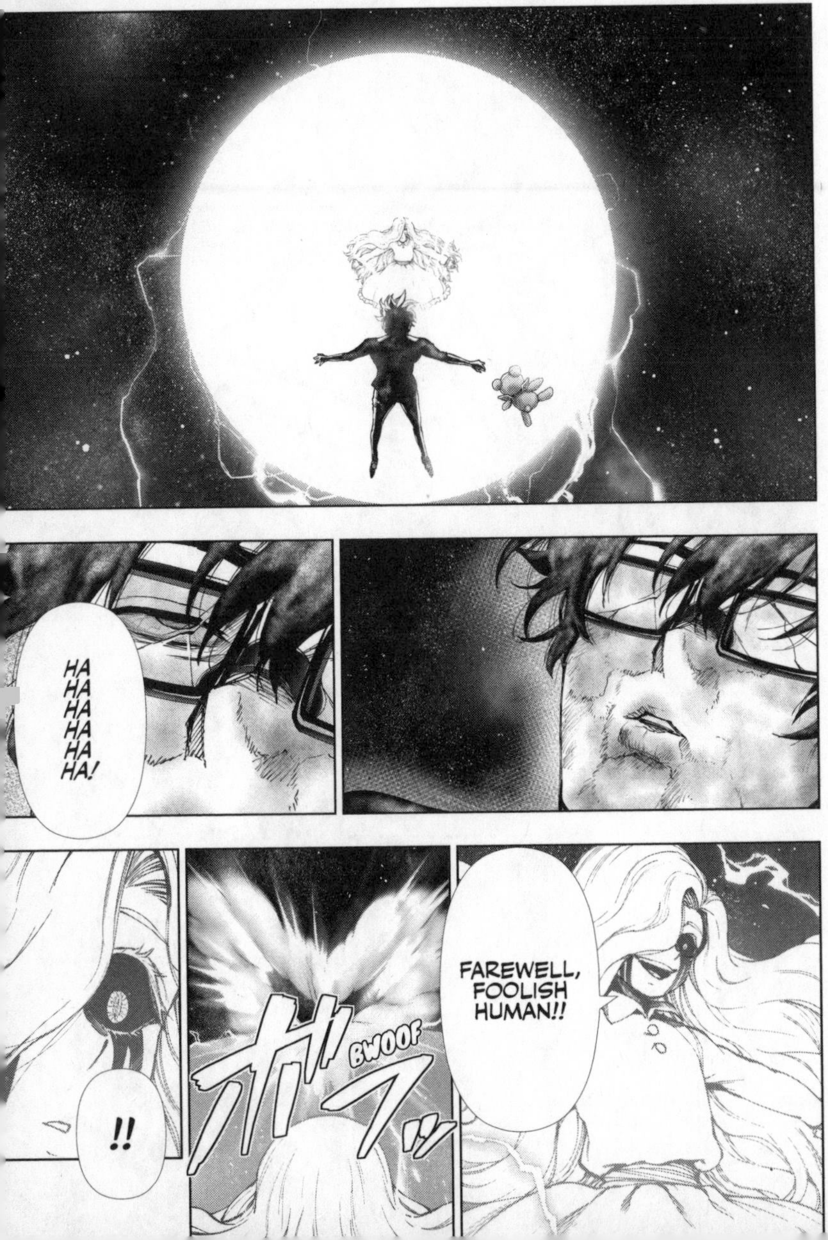
HA HA HA HA HA HA!
FAREWELL, FOOLISH HUMAN!!
BWOOF
!!

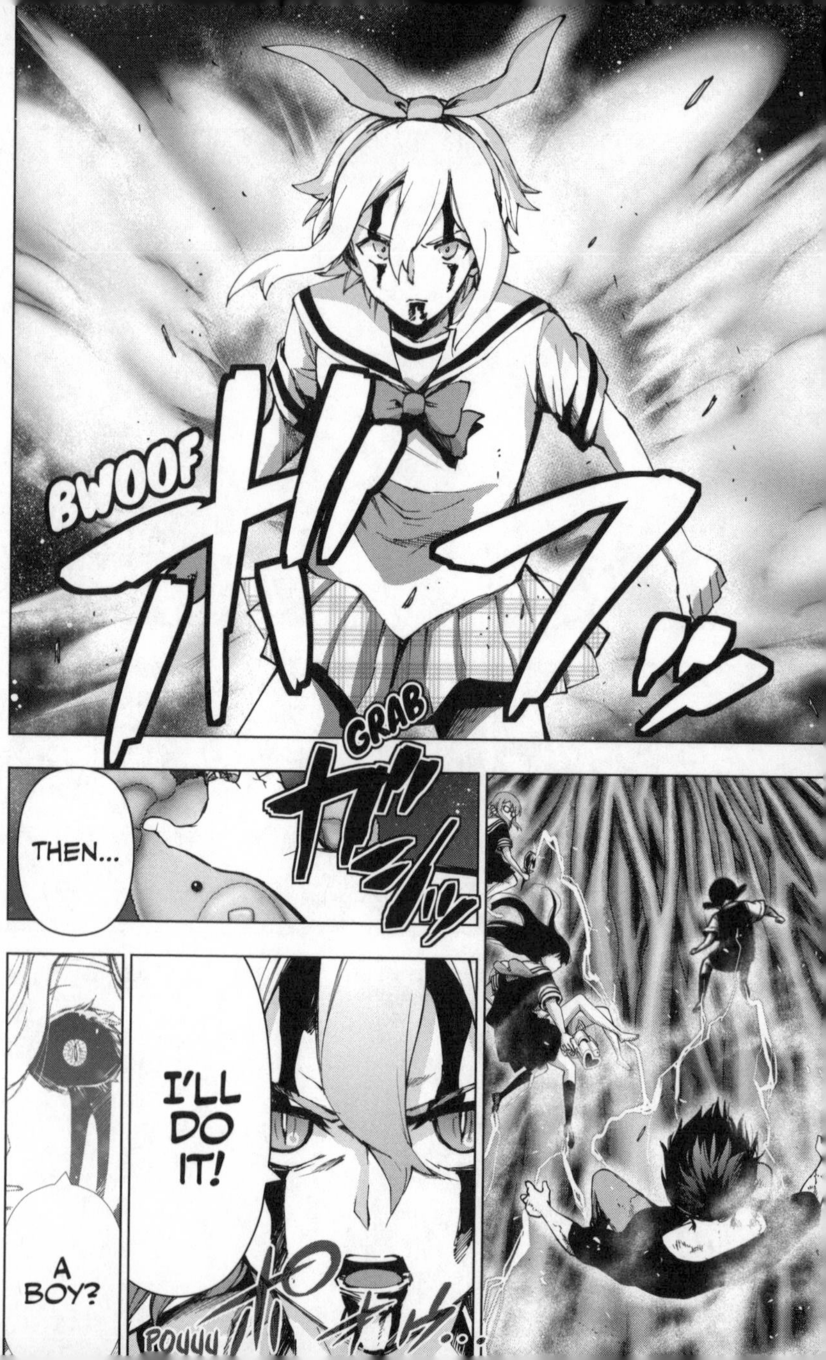
BWOOF
GRAB
THEN...
I'LL DO IT!
POUUU
A BOY?

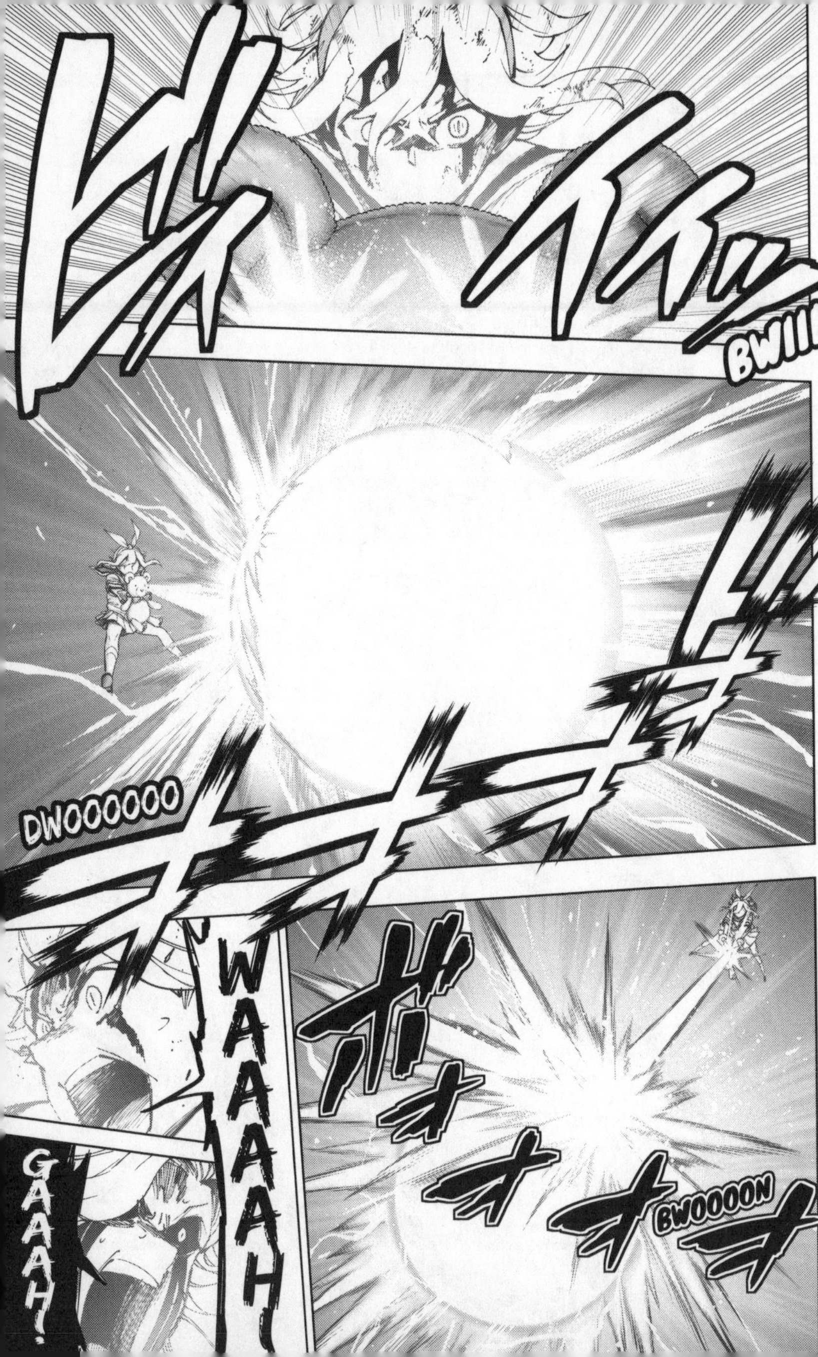
BWIII
DWOOOOOO
BWOOOON
WAAAAAH
GAAAH!

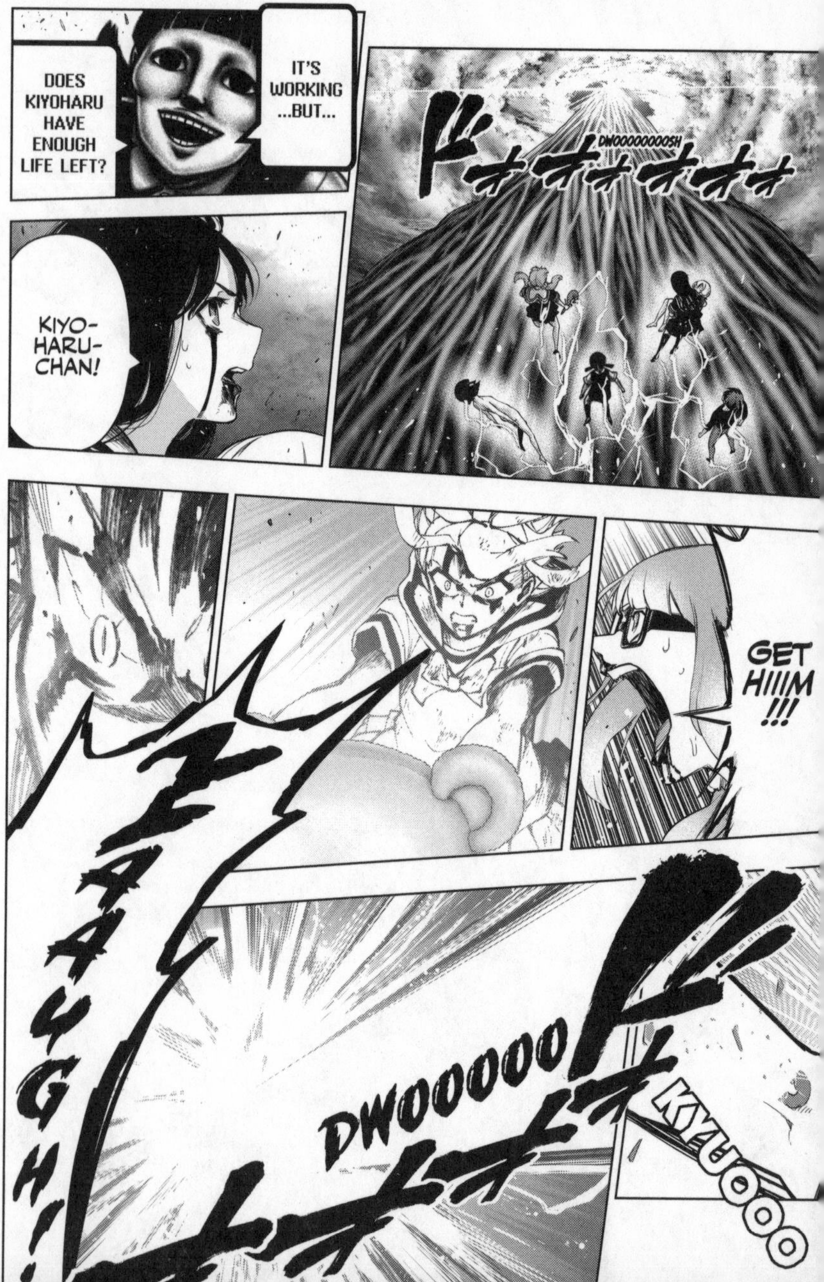
ドォォォォォォ
DWOOOOOOOOOOSH
IT'S WORKING ...BUT...
DOES KIYOHARU HAVE ENOUGH LIFE LEFT?
KIYO-HARU-CHAN!
GET HIIIM !!!
KYUOOOO
DWOOOOOOM
AAAUGH!

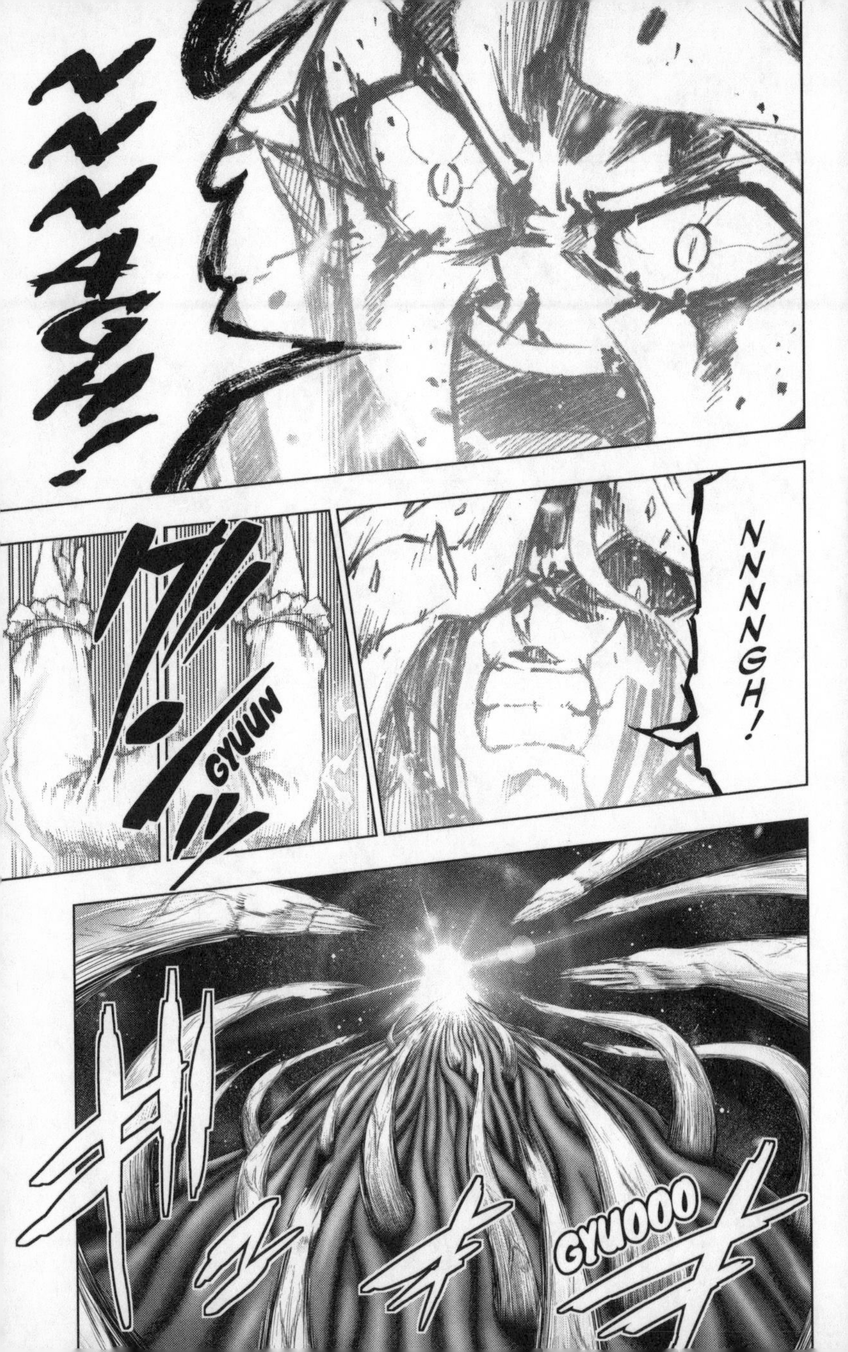
NNNAGH!!
NNNNGH!
GYUUN
GYUOOO

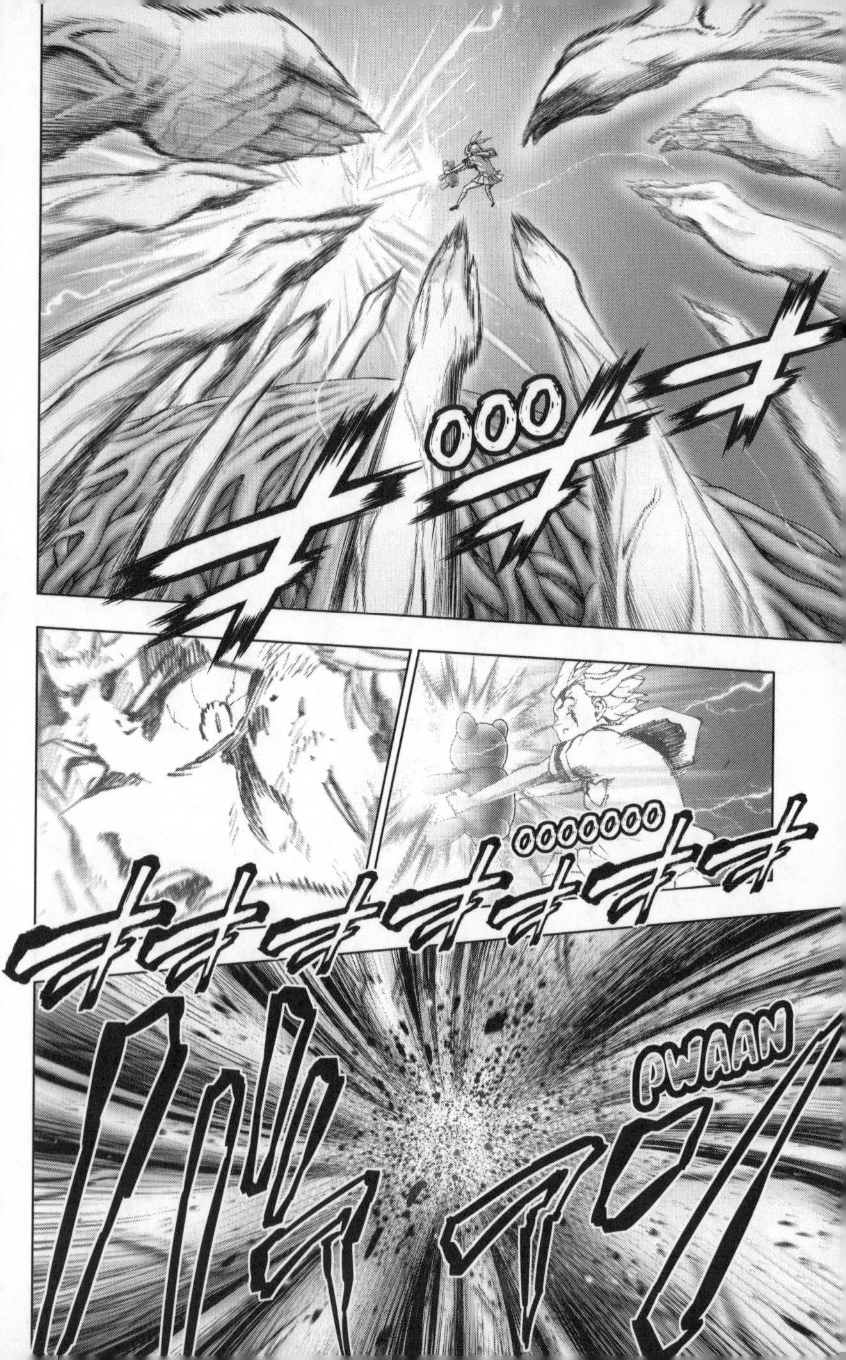
OOO
OOOOOOO
PWAAN

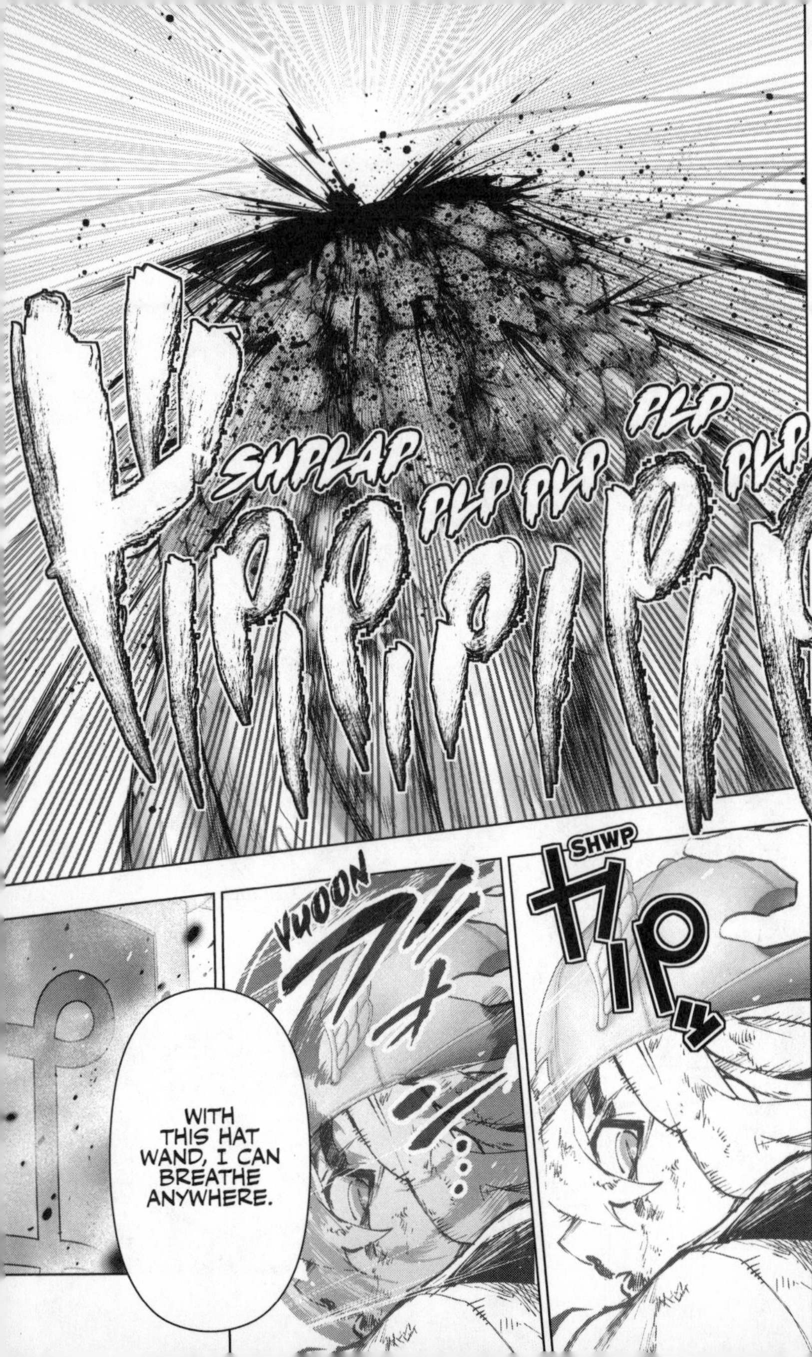
PLP
PLP
PLP
PLP
SHPLAP
SHWP
VUOON
WITH THIS HAT WAND, I CAN BREATHE ANYWHERE.

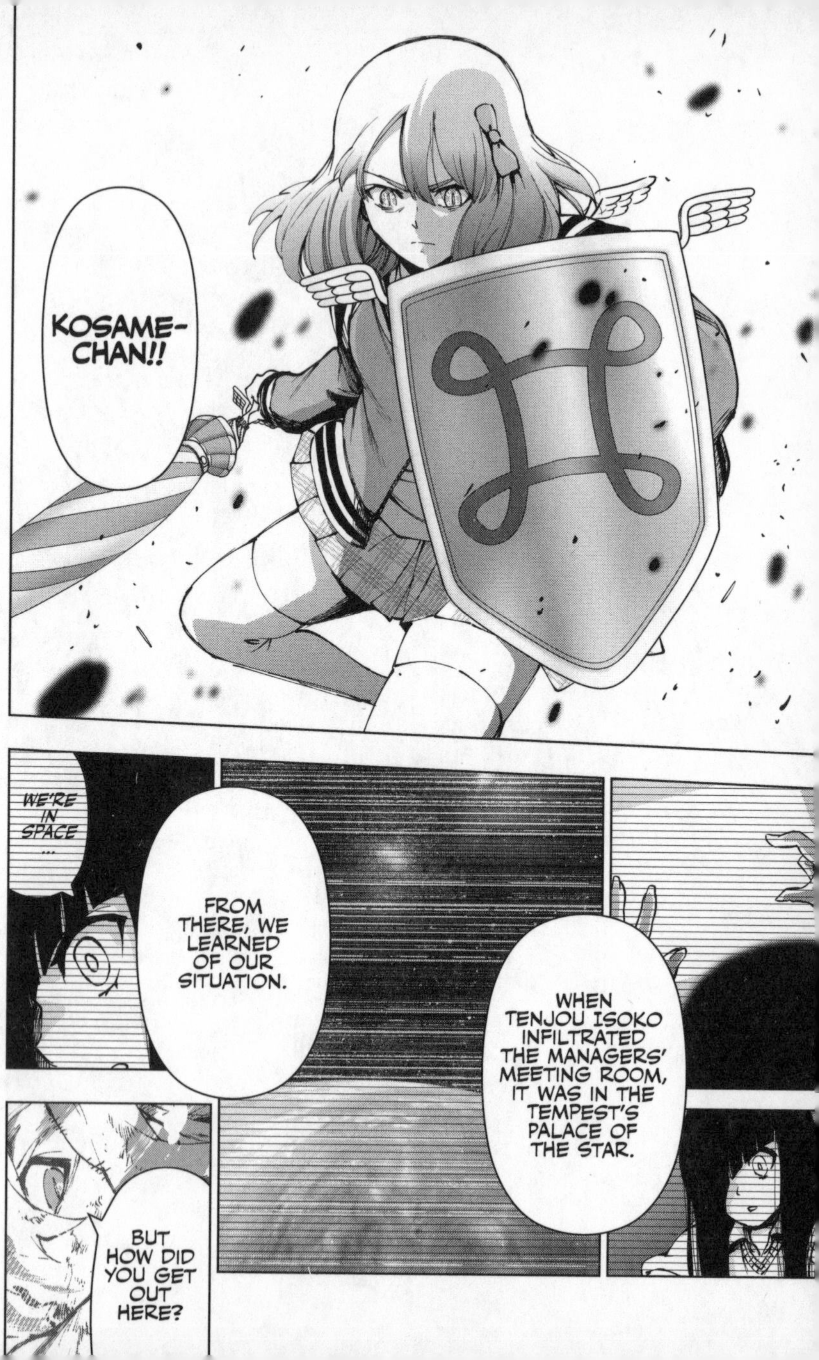
KOSAME-CHAN!!
WHEN TENJOU ISOKO INFILTRATED THE MANAGERS' MEETING ROOM, IT WAS IN THE TEMPEST'S PALACE OF THE STAR.
FROM THERE, WE LEARNED OF OUR SITUATION.
WE'RE IN SPACE...
BUT HOW DID YOU GET OUT HERE?

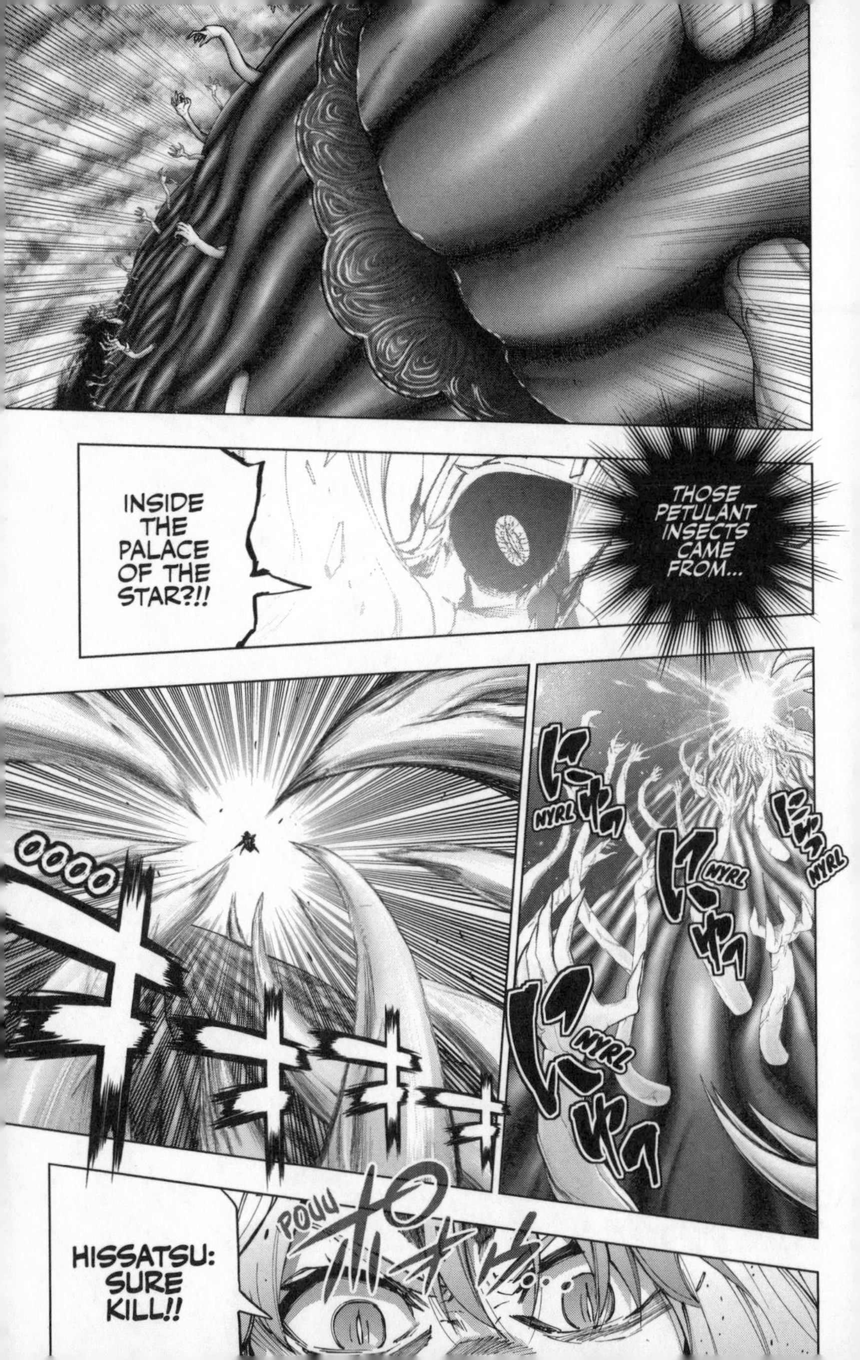
THOSE PETULANT INSECTS CAME FROM...
INSIDE THE PALACE OF THE STAR?!!
NYRL
NYRL
NYRL
NYRL
OOOO
POUU
HISSATSU: SURE KILL!!

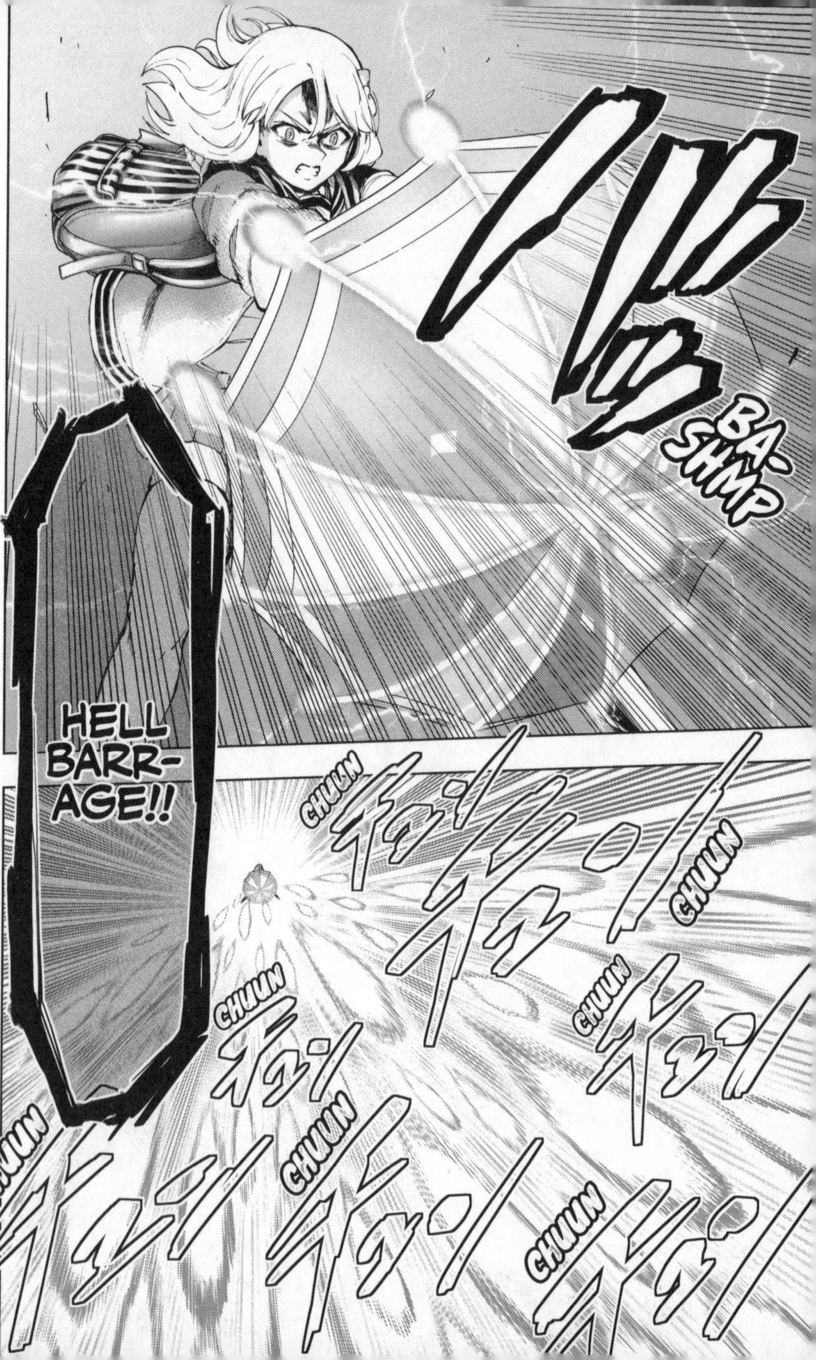
BA-
SHMP
HELL
BARR-
AGE!!
CHUUN
CHUUN
CHUUN
CHUUN
CHUUN
CHUUN
CHUUN

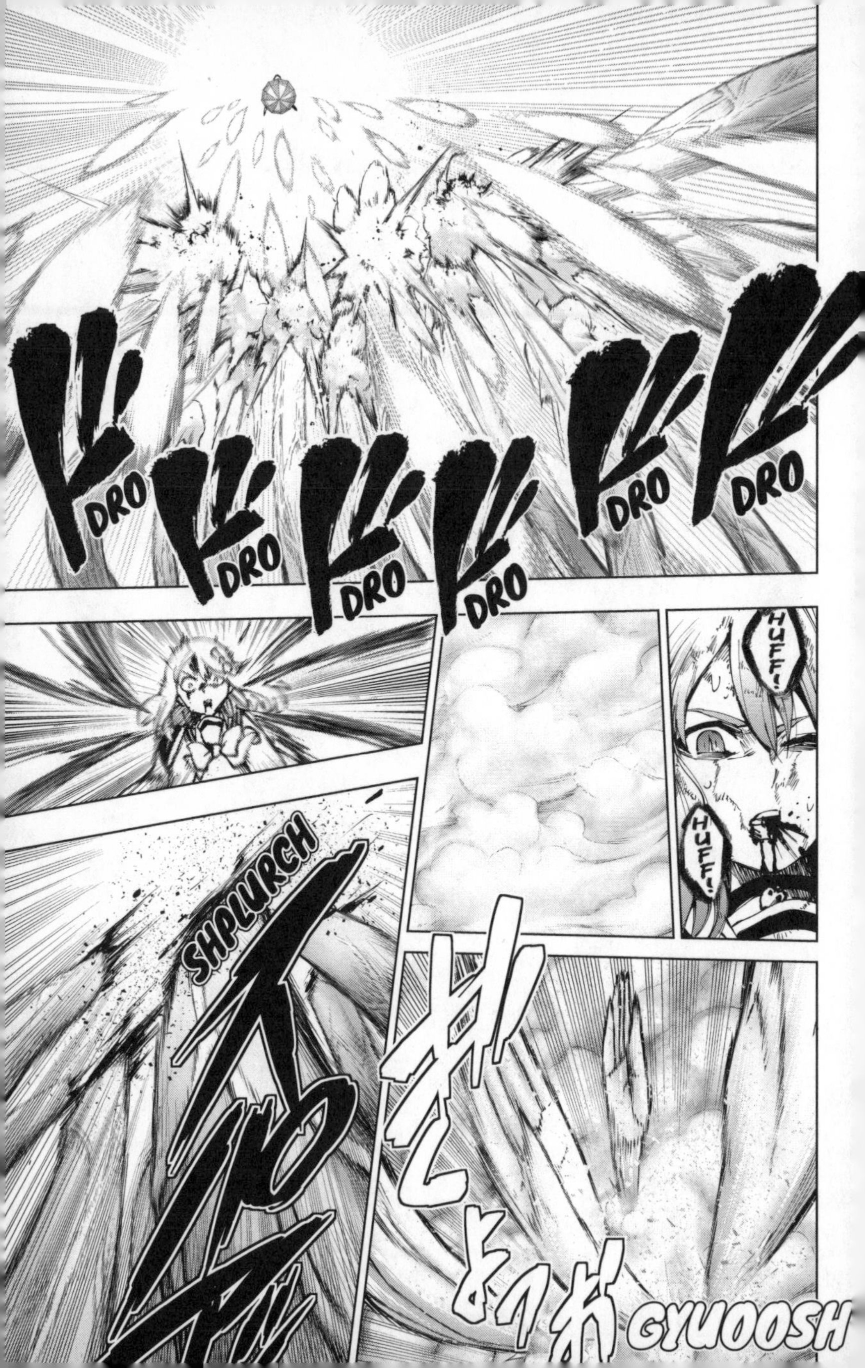
DRO
DRO
DRO
DRO
DRO
DRO
HUFF!
HUFF!
GYUOOSH
SHPLURCH

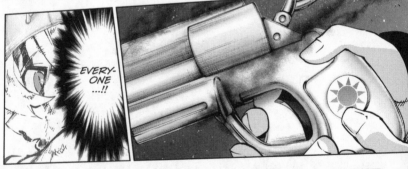

EVERY-
ONE
....!!

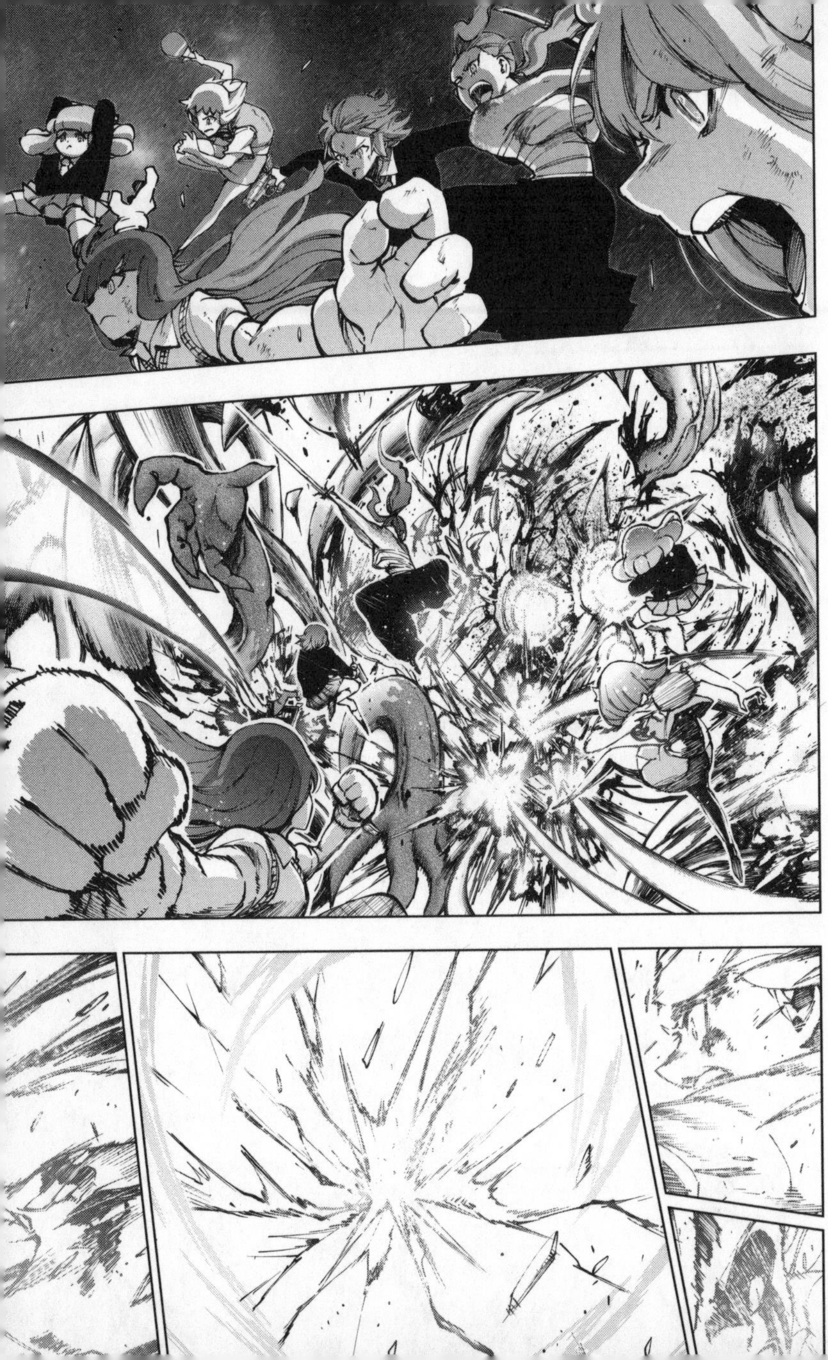

FAINT

!!

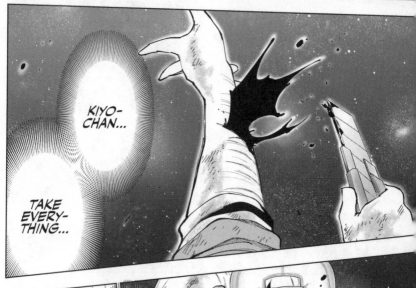

KIYO-
CHAN...

TAKE
EVERY-
THING...

THAT
I'VE
GOT!

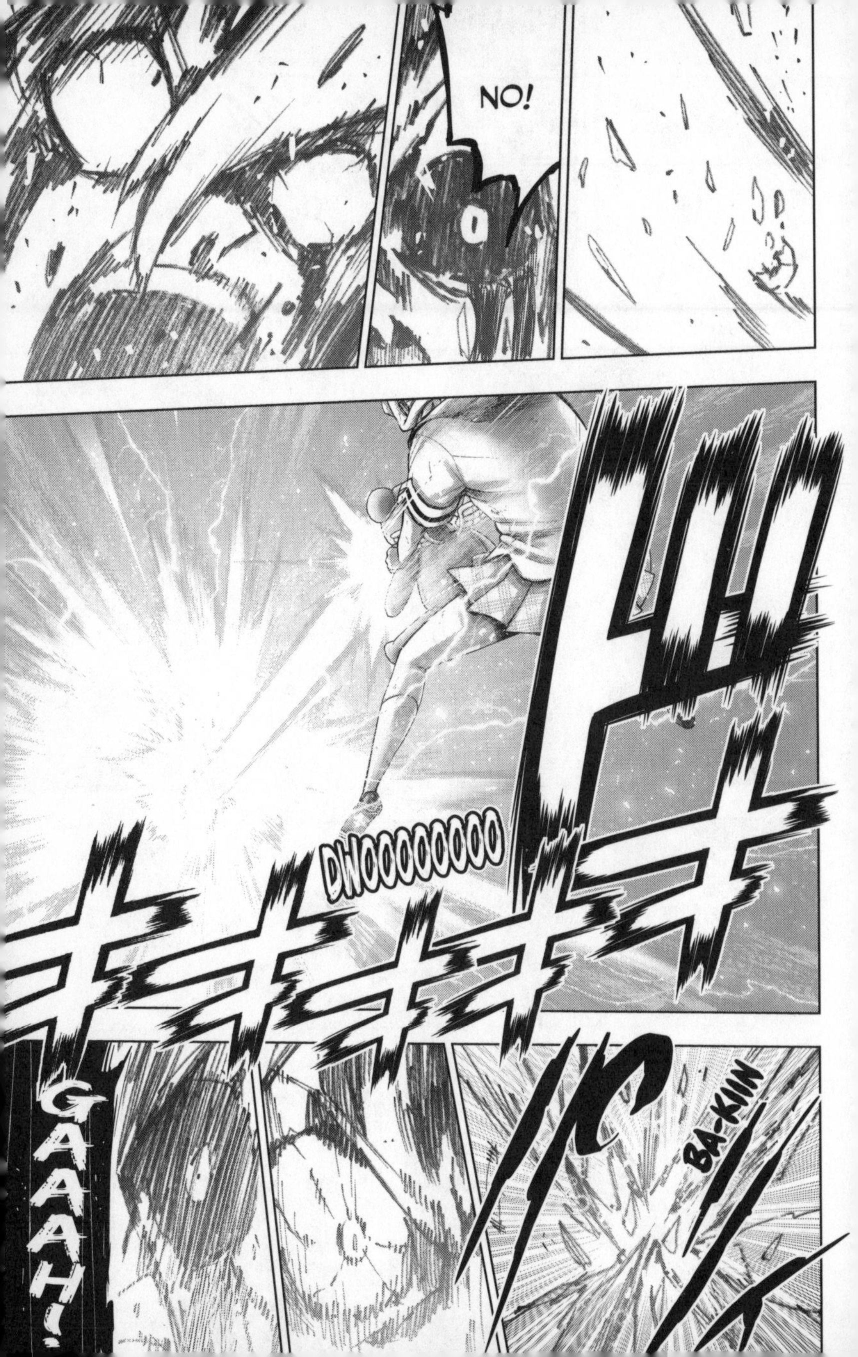
NO!
DWOOOOOOOO
BA-KIIN
GAAAH!

FAINT

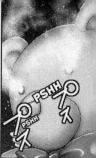

PSHH

PSHH

HAH
...

HA HA HA HA HA! YOU PATHETIC BUGS MAY HAVE GROWN IN NUMBER ...

BUT YOU'RE NO MATCH FOR ME!!

HA HA HA HA HA!

......!!

YOU WERE SO CLOSE TO VICTORY! TOO BAD!!

KAYO...

POW

TP

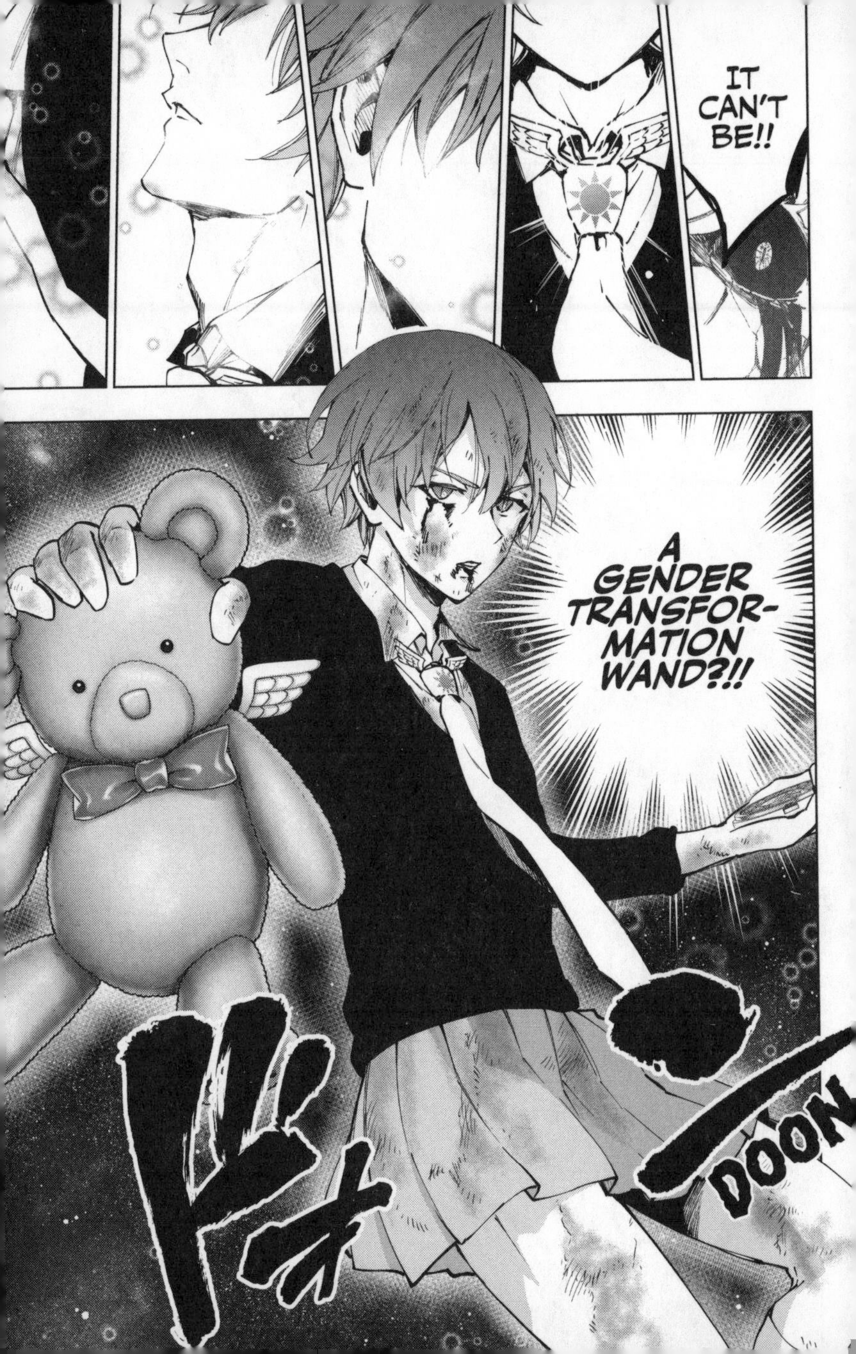
IT CAN'T BE!!
A GENDER TRANSFORMATION WAND?!!
DOON

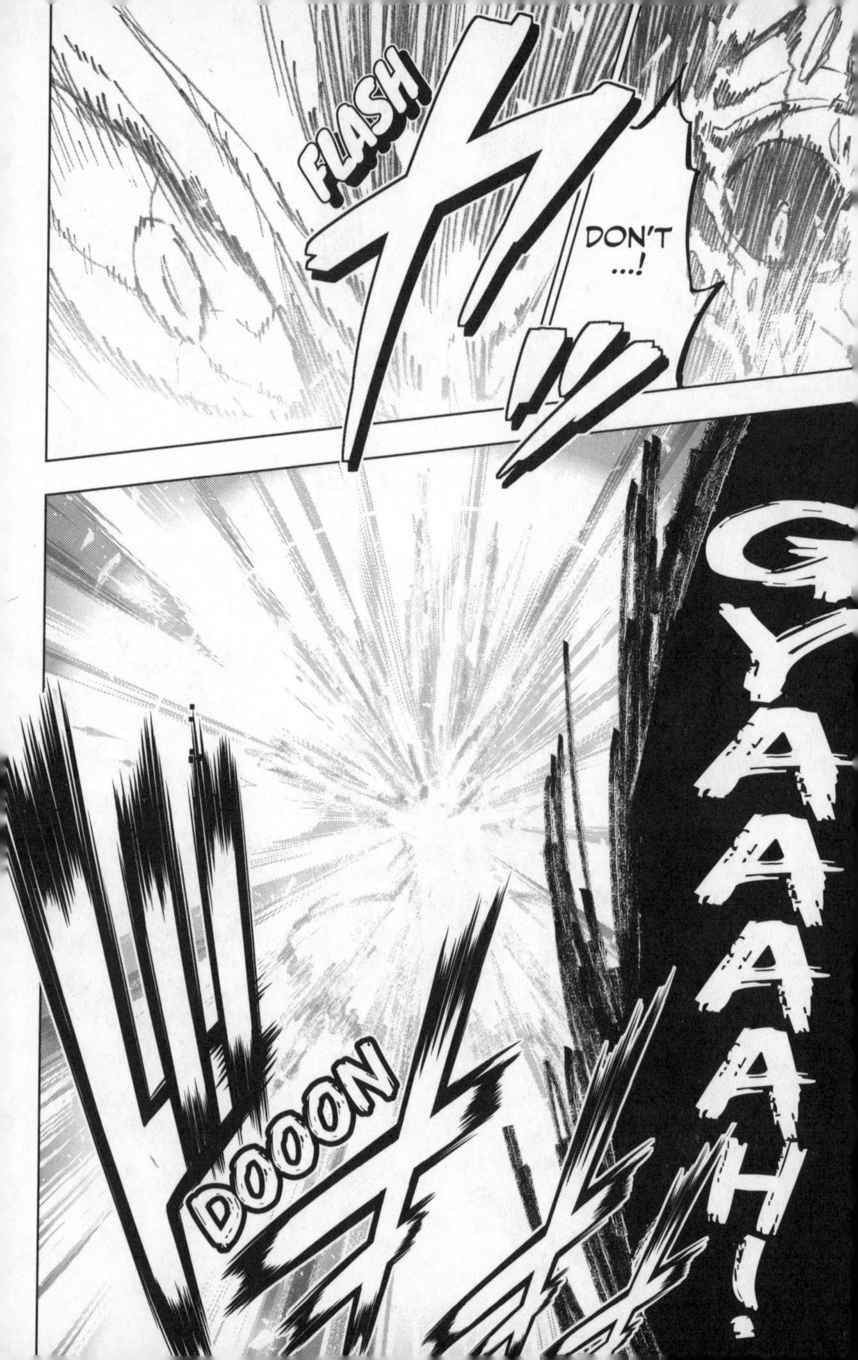
FLASH
DON'T ...!
GYAAAAAH!
DOOON

ENTER.134 THE WORLD EVERYONE I LOVE IS IN

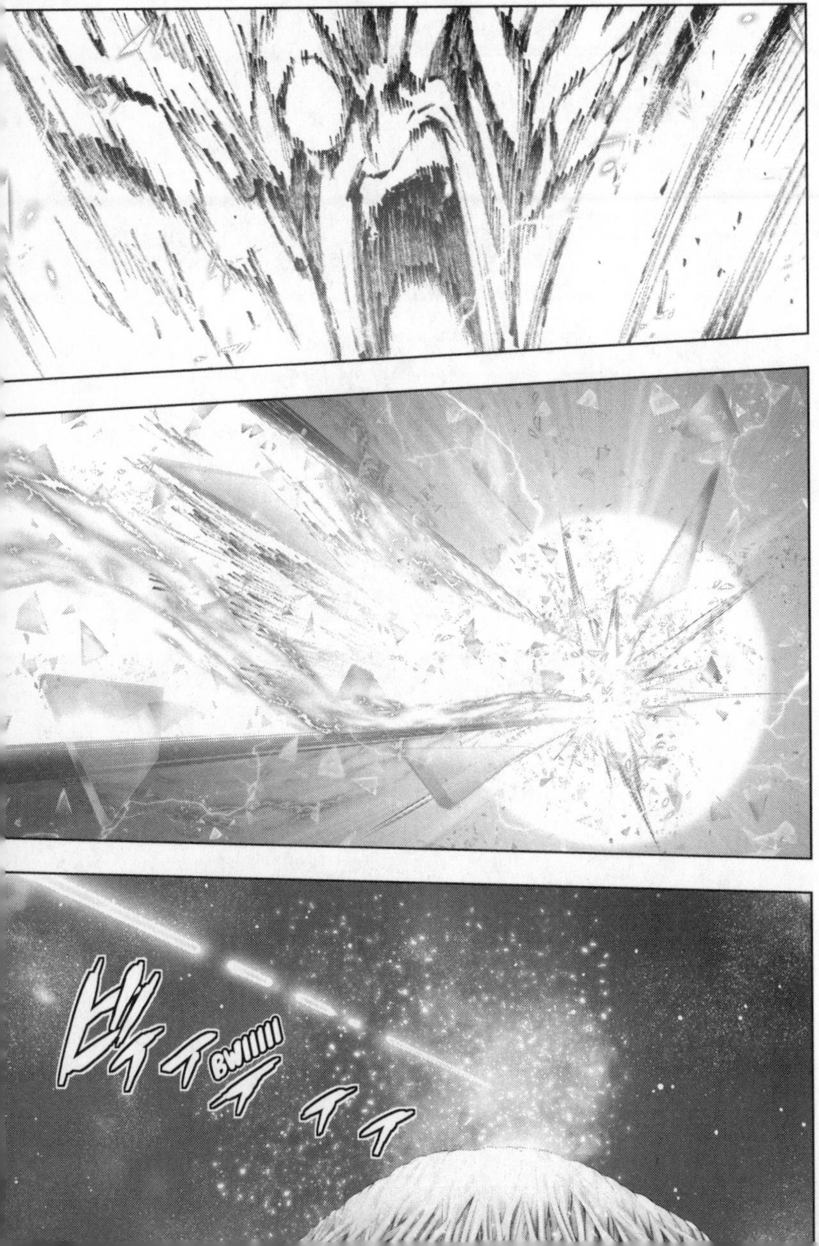
BWIIIII

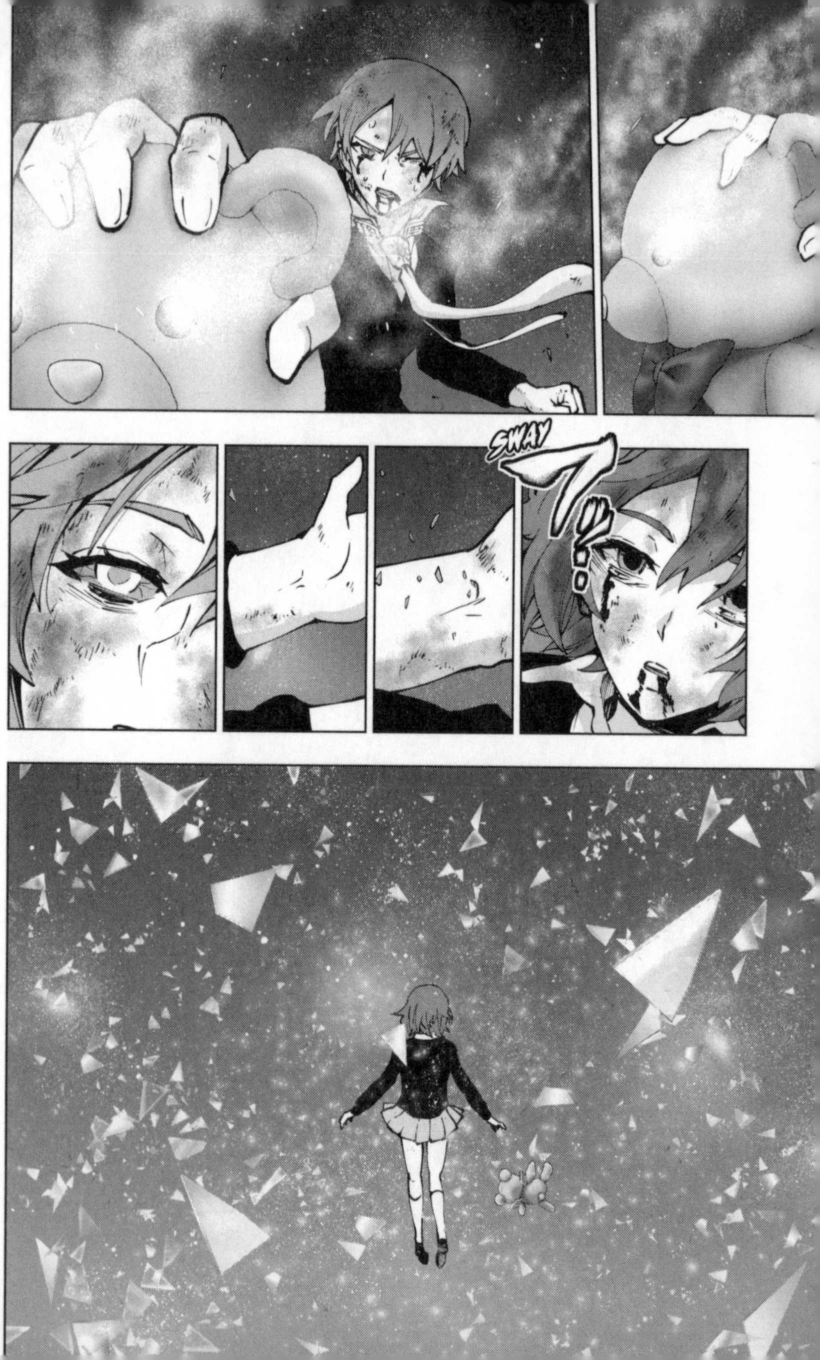
SWAY

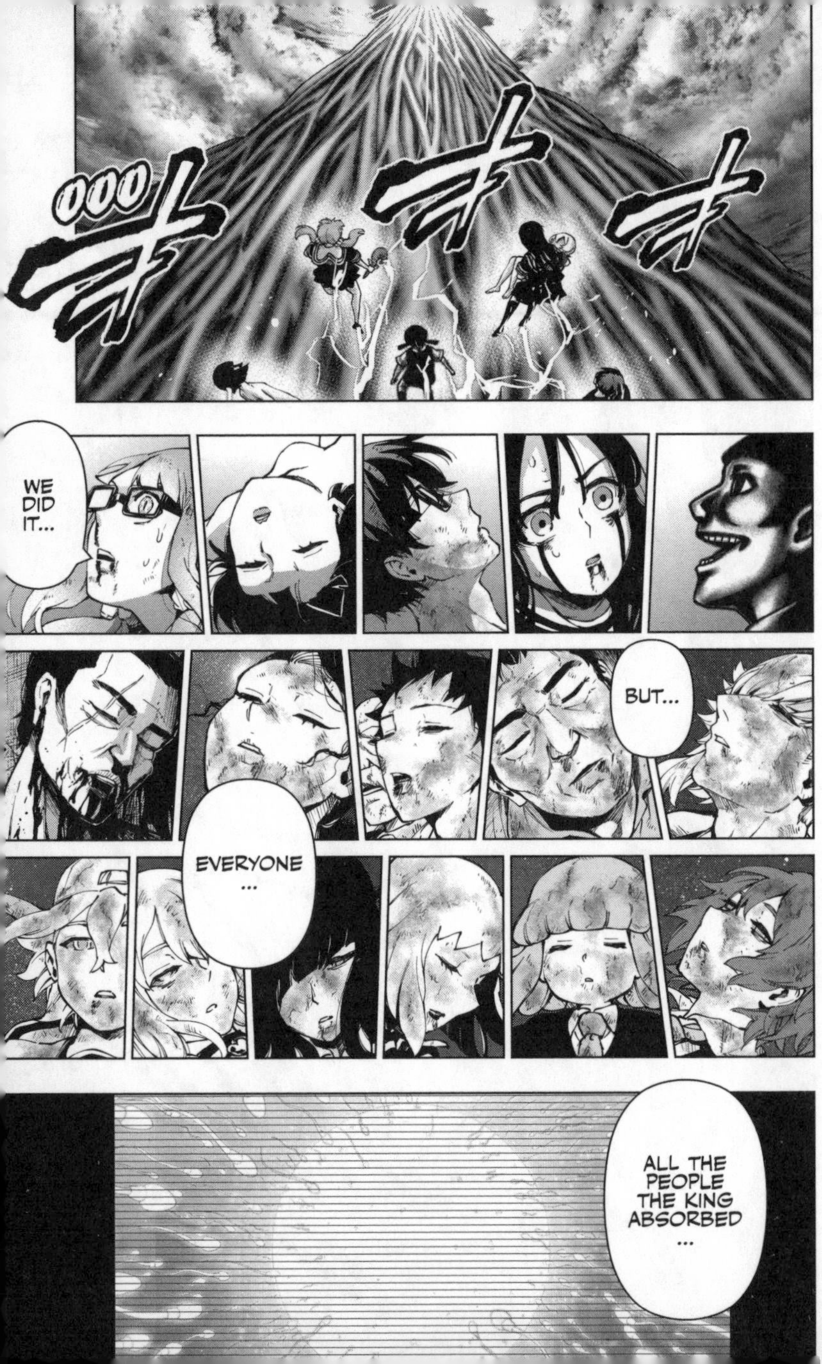
OOO
WE DID IT...
BUT...
EVERYONE ...
ALL THE PEOPLE THE KING ABSORBED ...

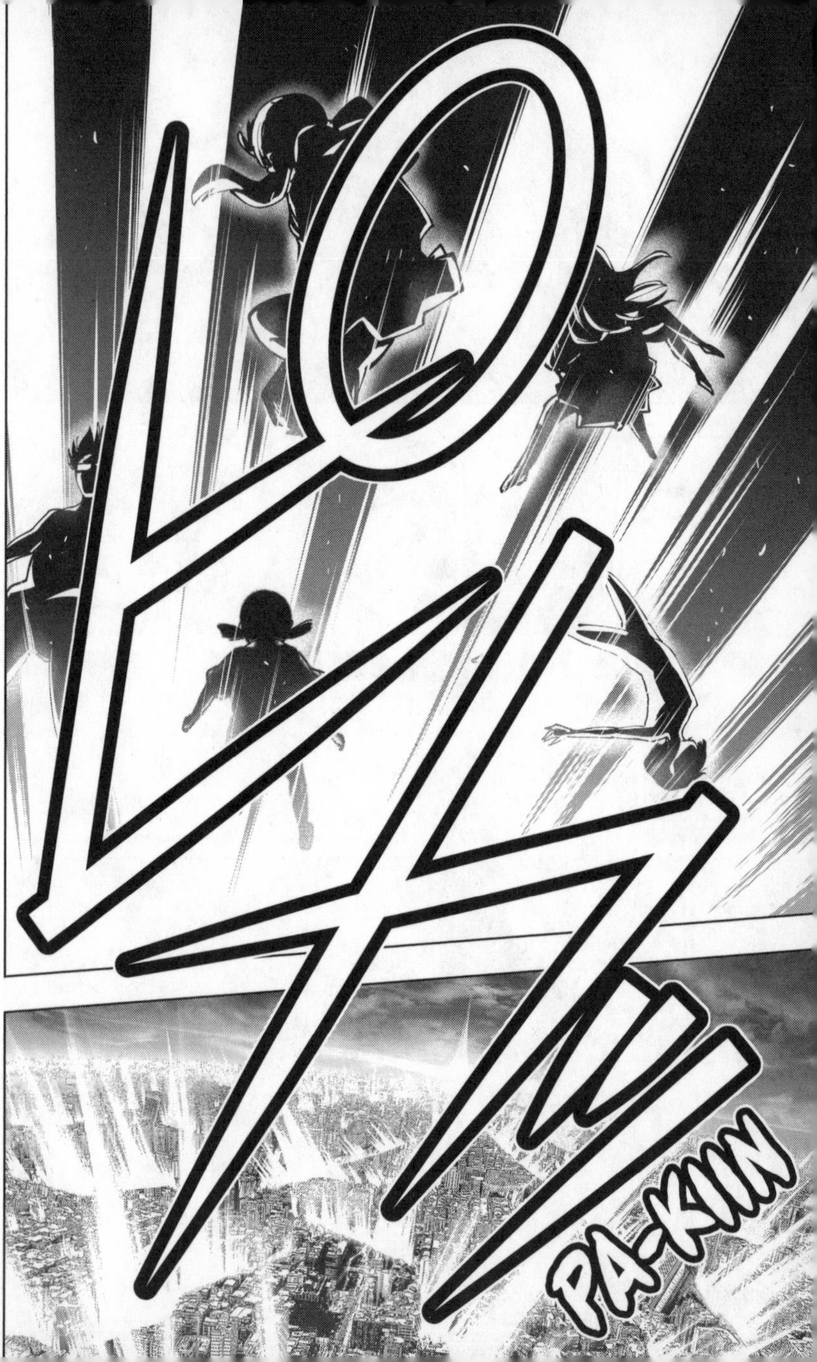
PA-KIIN

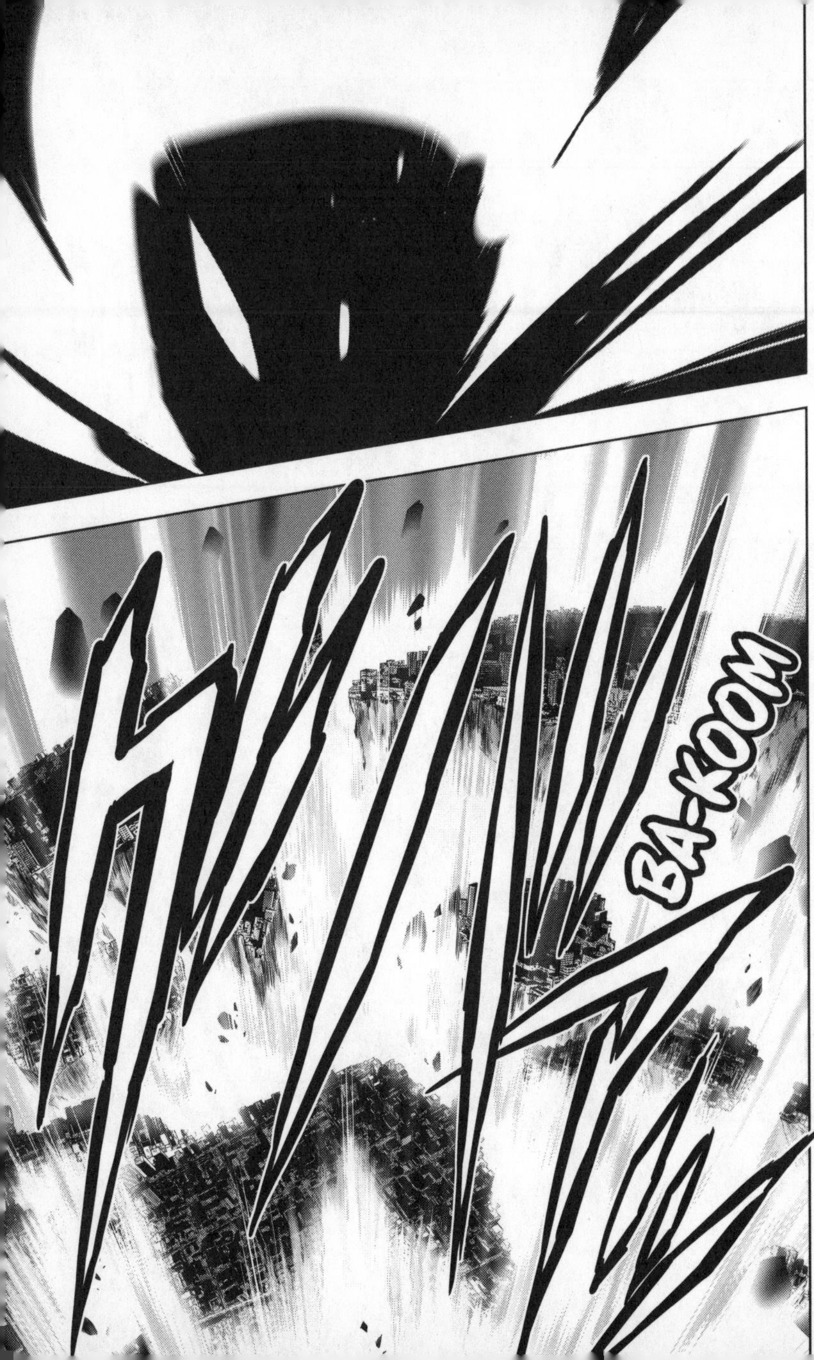
BA-KOOM

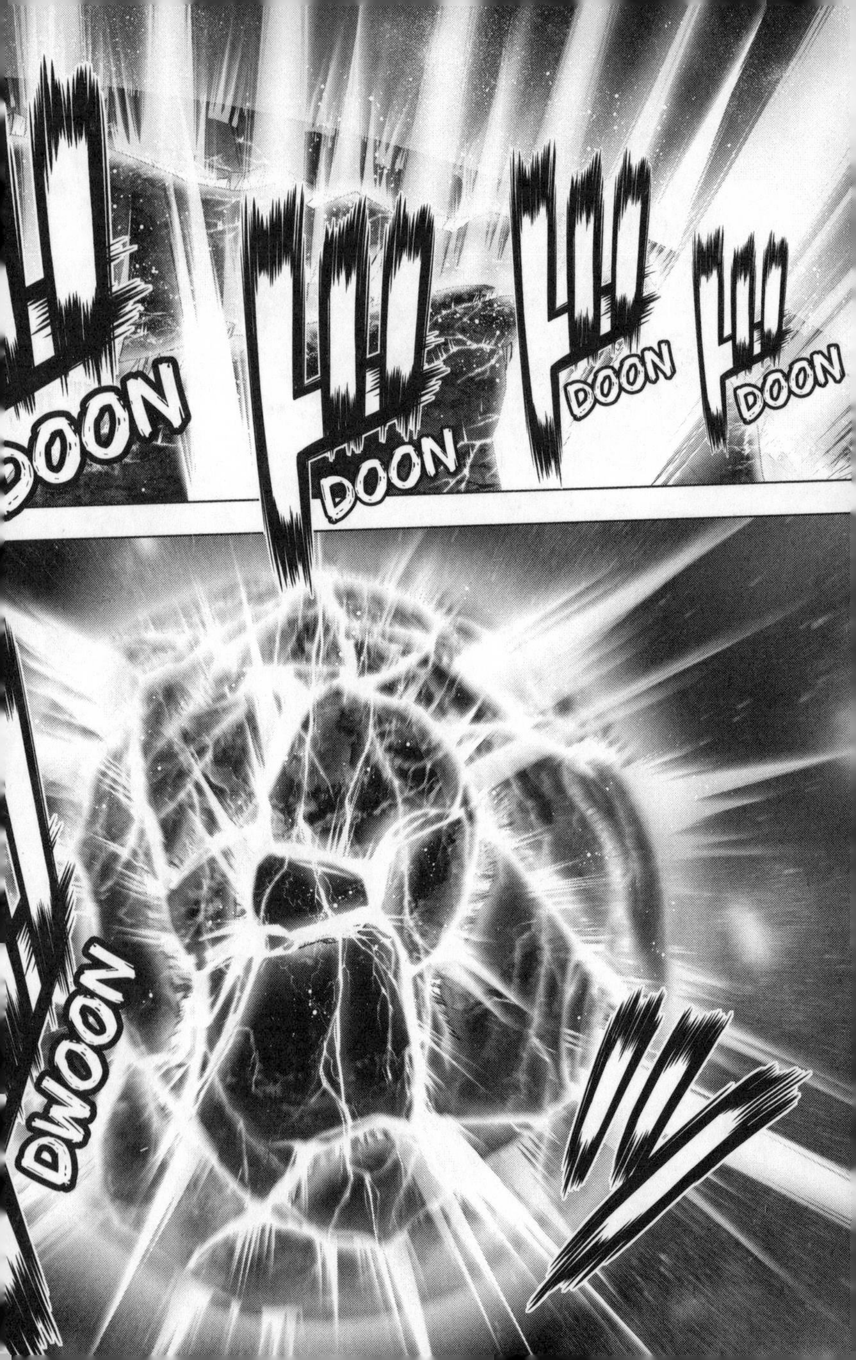
DOON
DOON
DOON
DOON
DWOON

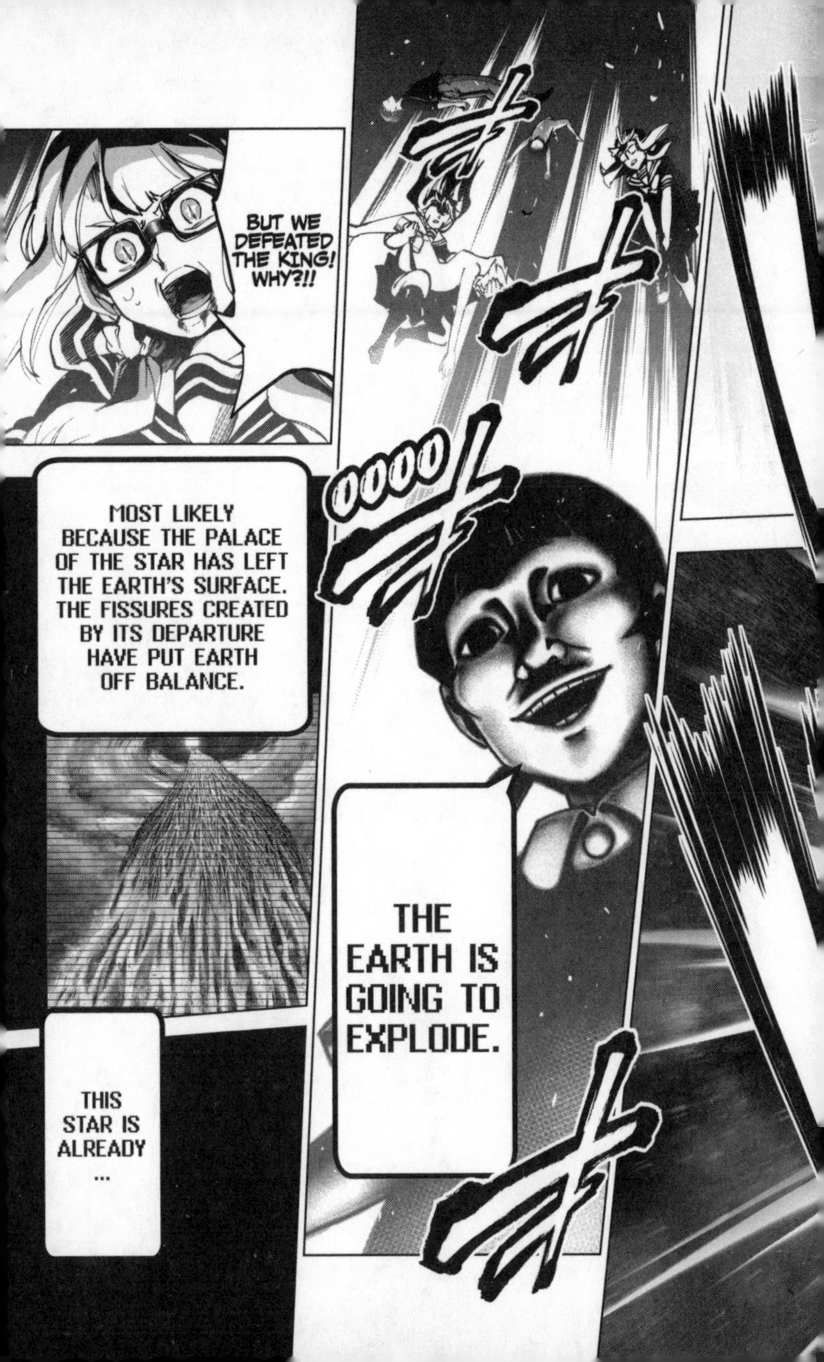
THE EARTH IS GOING TO EXPLODE.
BUT WE DEFEATED THE KING! WHY?!!
MOST LIKELY BECAUSE THE PALACE OF THE STAR HAS LEFT THE EARTH'S SURFACE. THE FISSURES CREATED BY ITS DEPARTURE HAVE PUT EARTH OFF BALANCE.
THIS STAR IS ALREADY ...

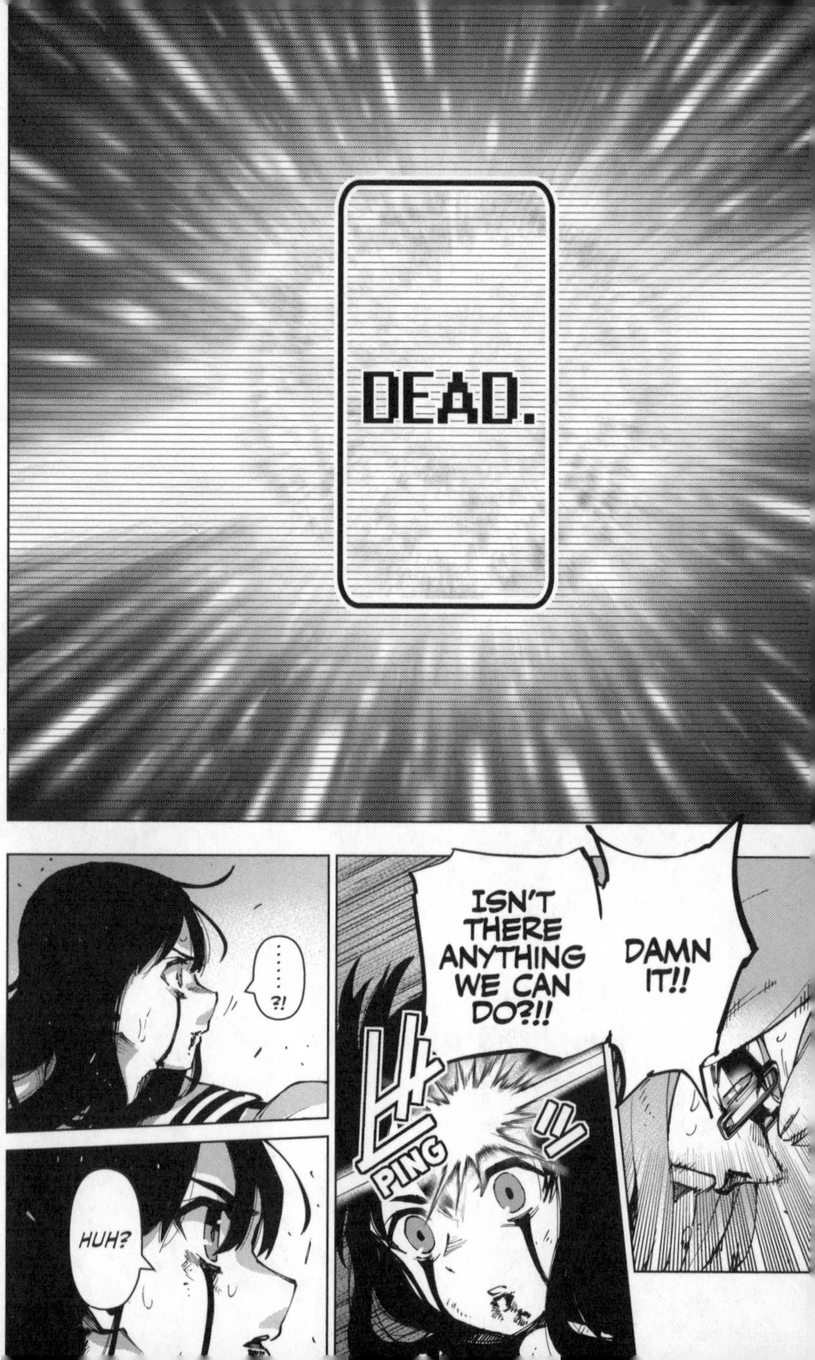
DEAD.
DAMN IT!!
ISN'T THERE ANYTHING WE CAN DO?!!
PING
......?!
HUH?

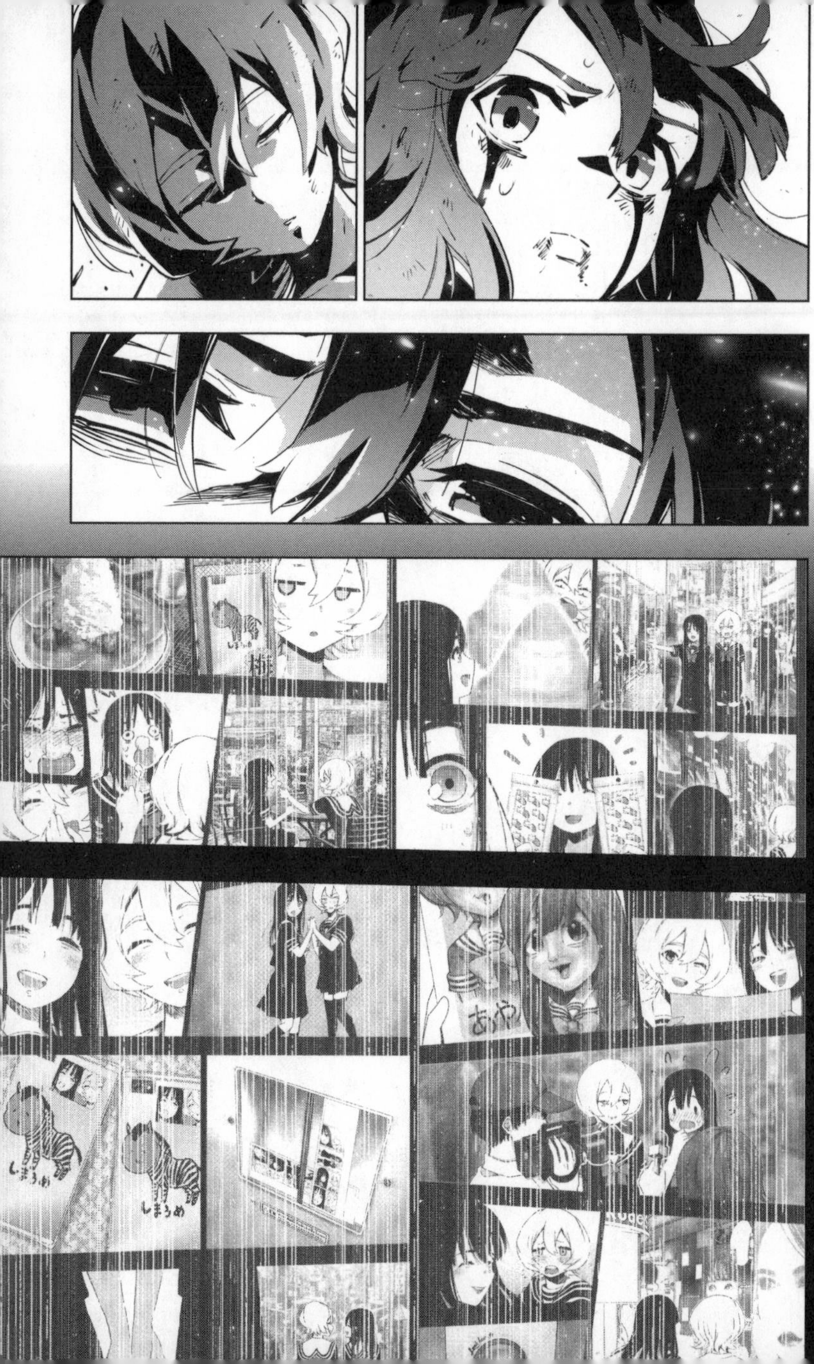
しまうめ
あや
しまうめ
しまうめ

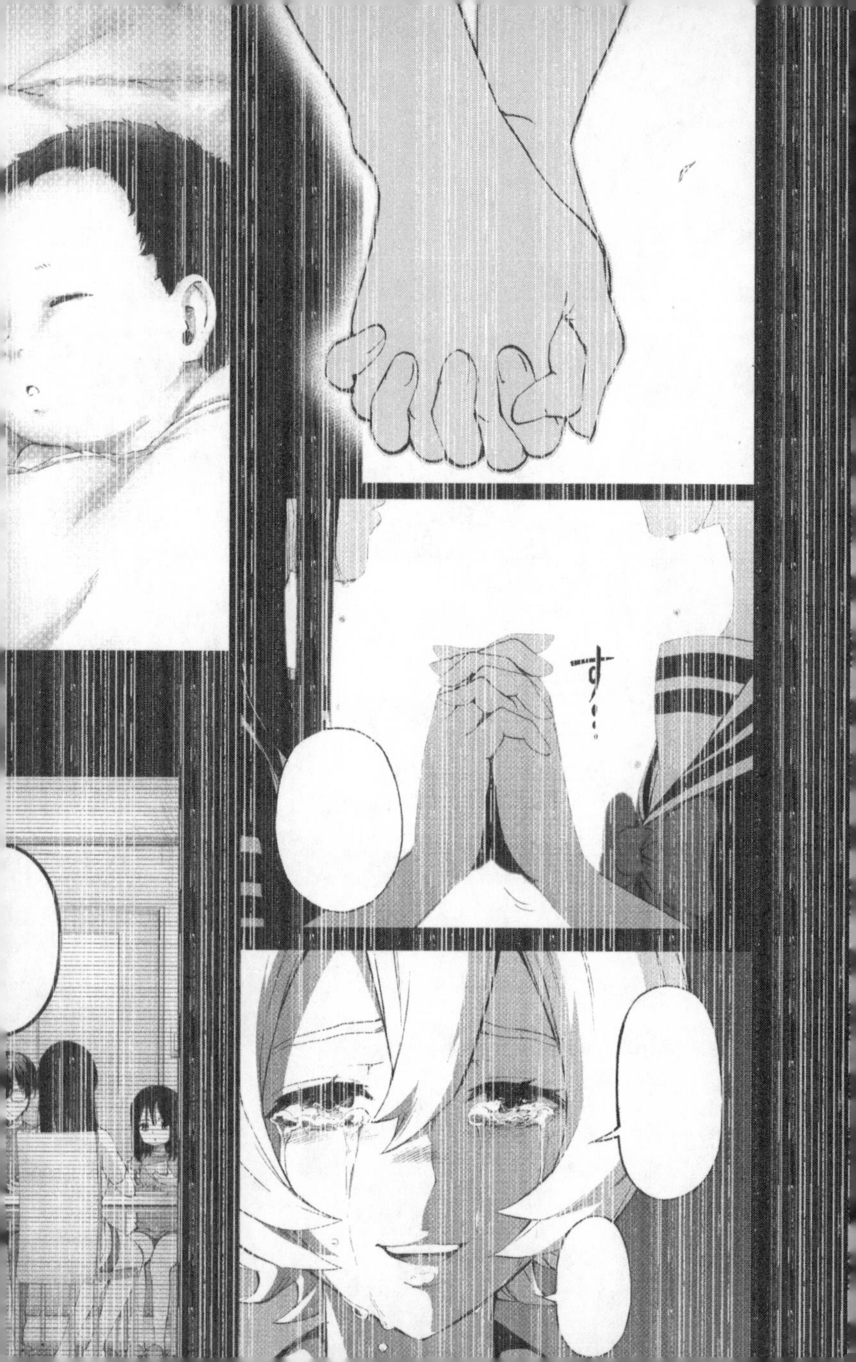
す…

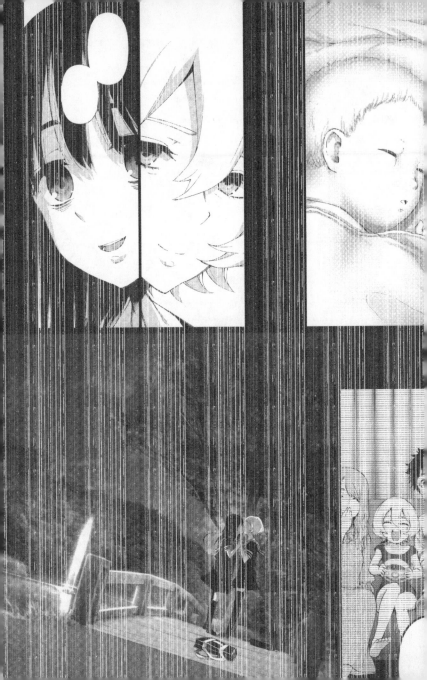

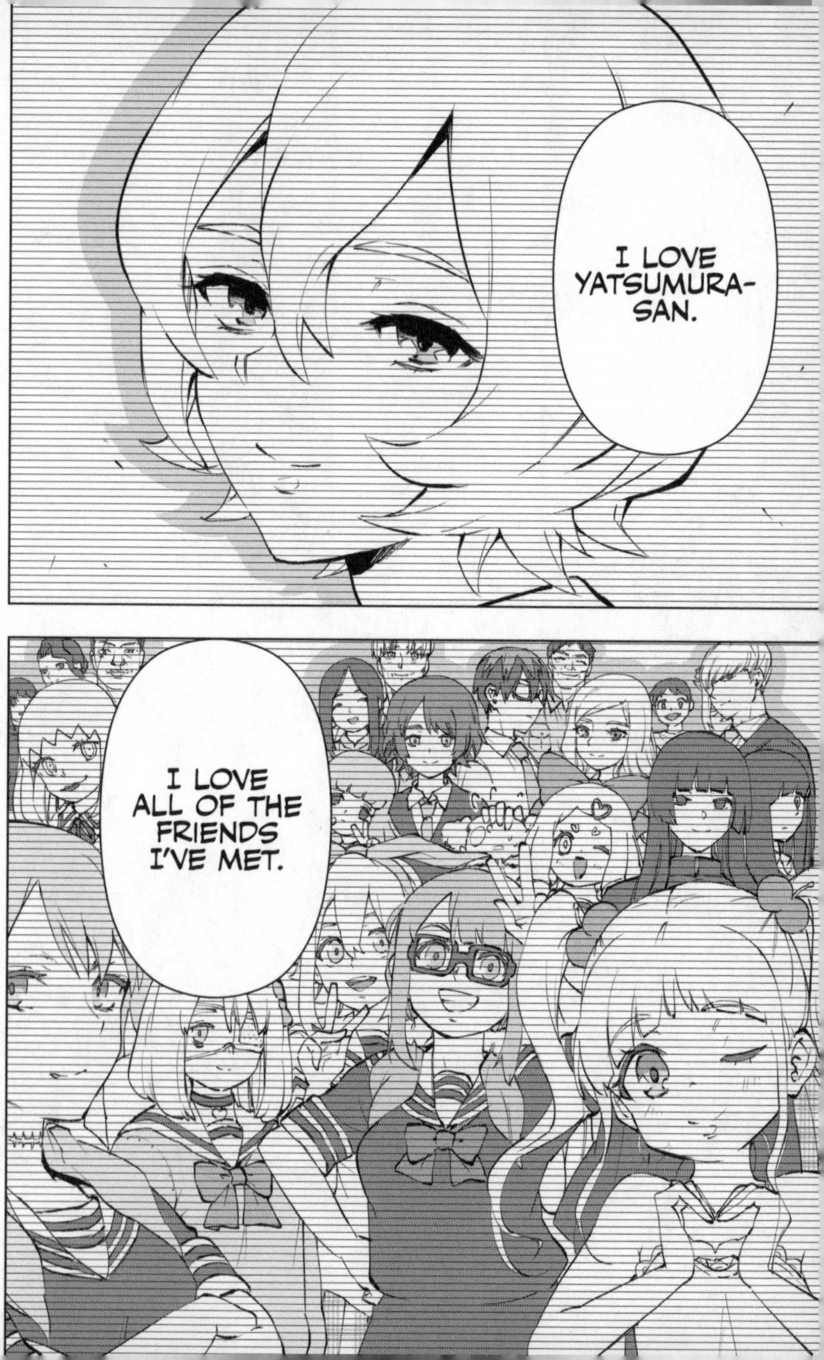
I LOVE YATSUMURA-SAN.
I LOVE ALL OF THE FRIENDS I'VE MET.

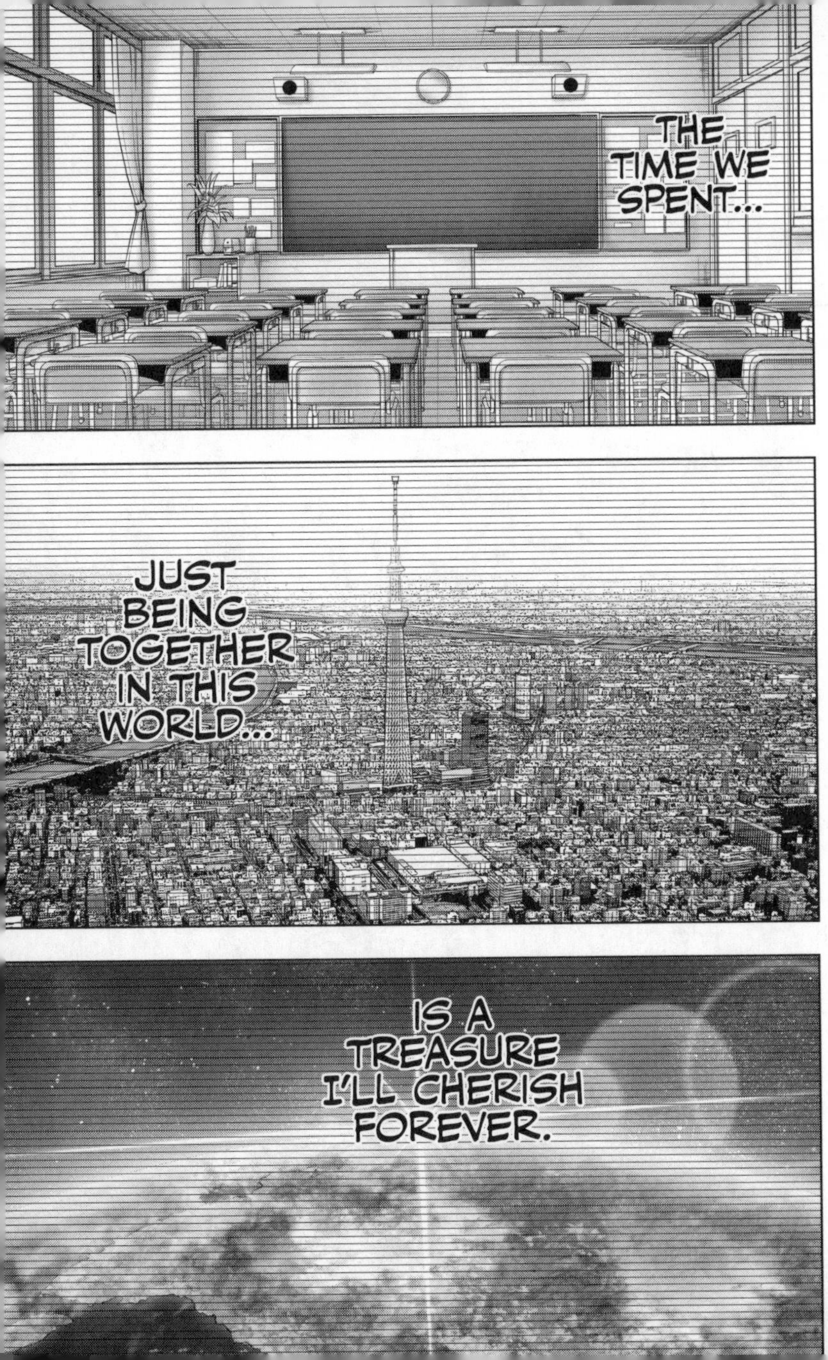
THE TIME WE SPENT...
JUST BEING TOGETHER IN THIS WORLD...
IS A TREASURE I'LL CHERISH FOREVER.

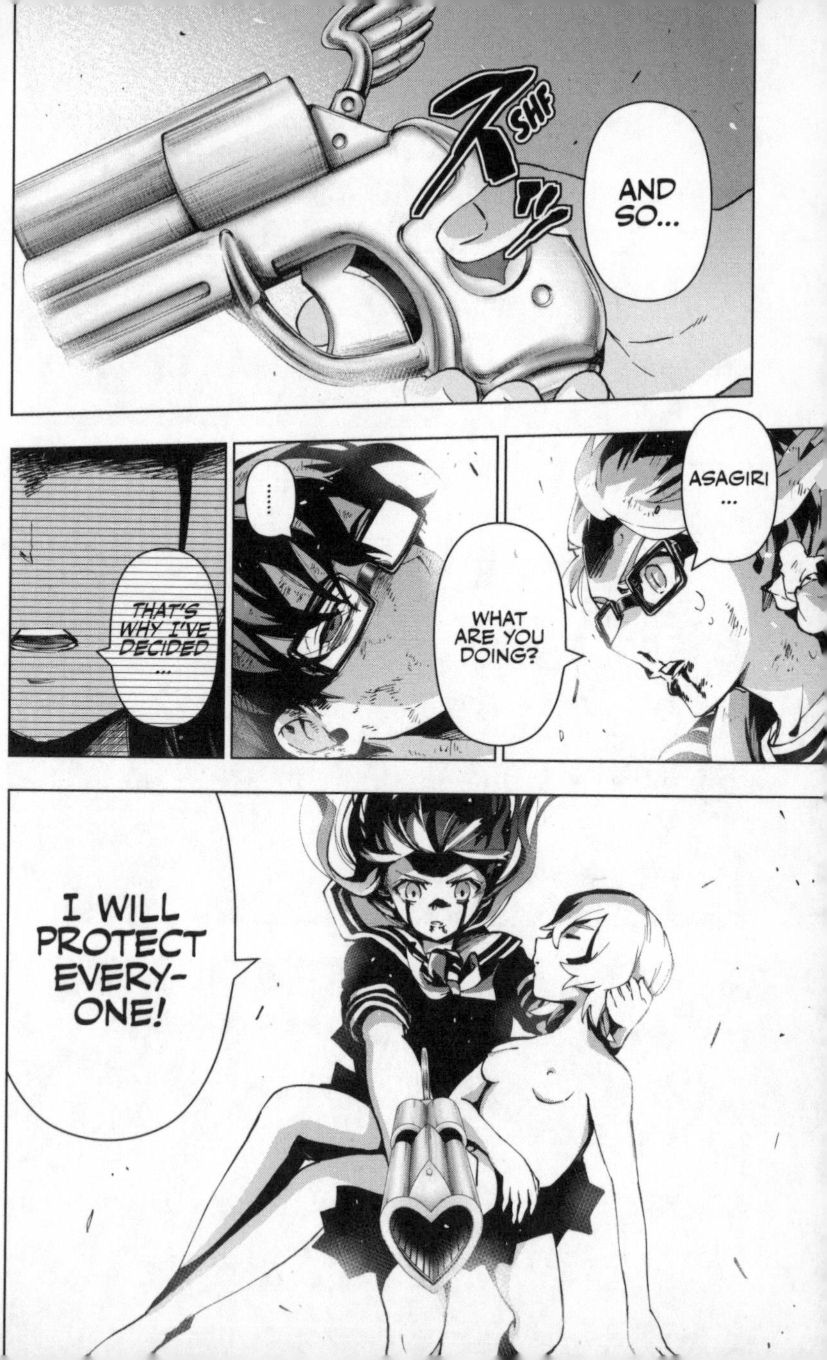
AND SO...
SHF
ASAGIRI...
WHAT ARE YOU DOING?
......
THAT'S WHY I'VE DECIDED...
I WILL PROTECT EVERY-ONE!

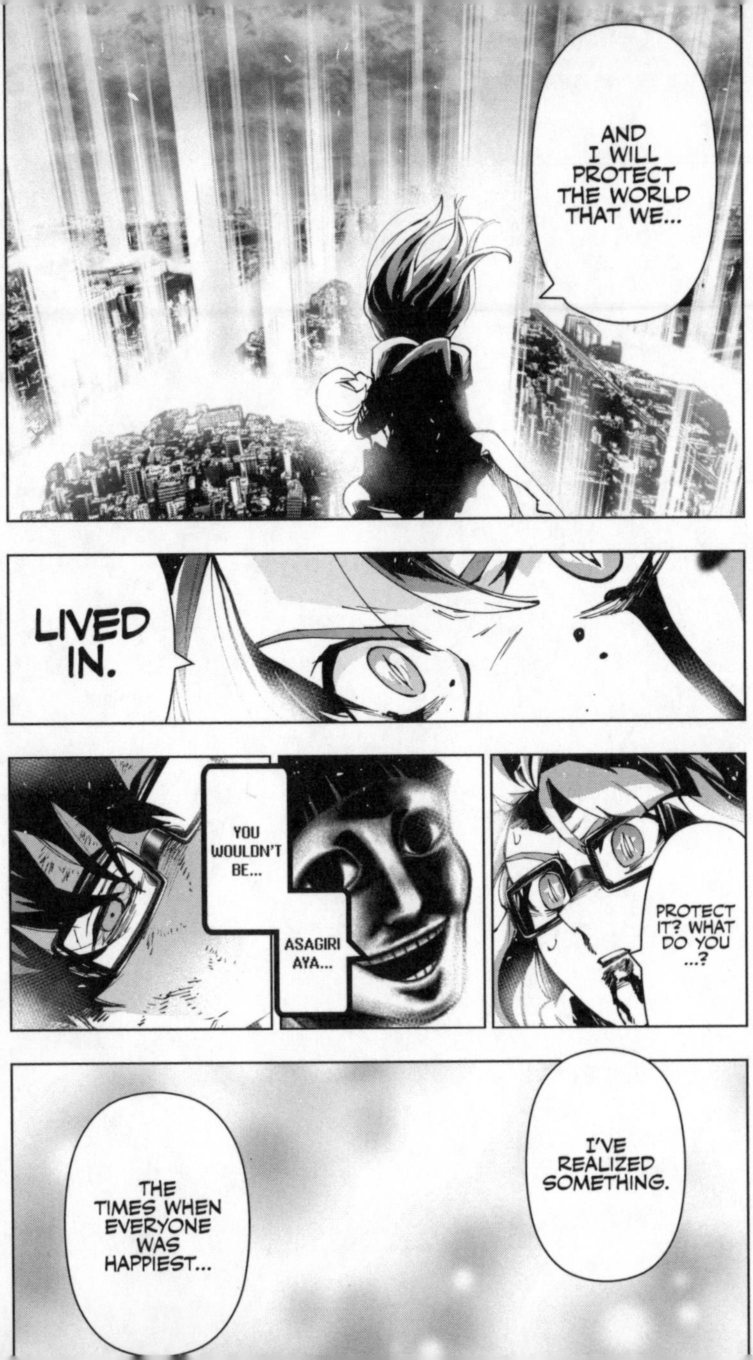
AND I WILL PROTECT THE WORLD THAT WE...
LIVED IN.
PROTECT IT? WHAT DO YOU ...?
YOU WOULDN'T BE...
ASAGIRI AYA...
I'VE REALIZED SOMETHING.
THE TIMES WHEN EVERYONE WAS HAPPIEST...

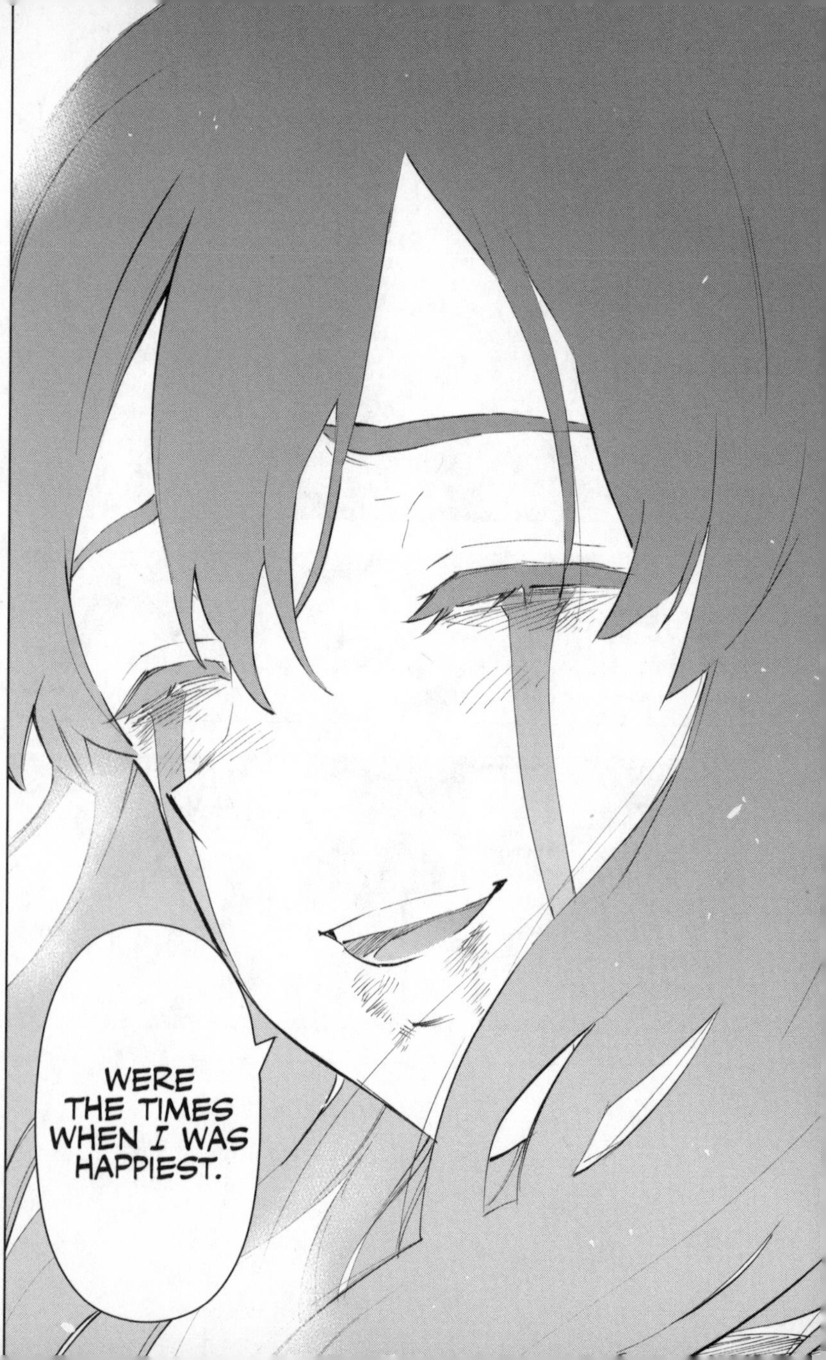
WERE THE TIMES WHEN I WAS HAPPIEST.

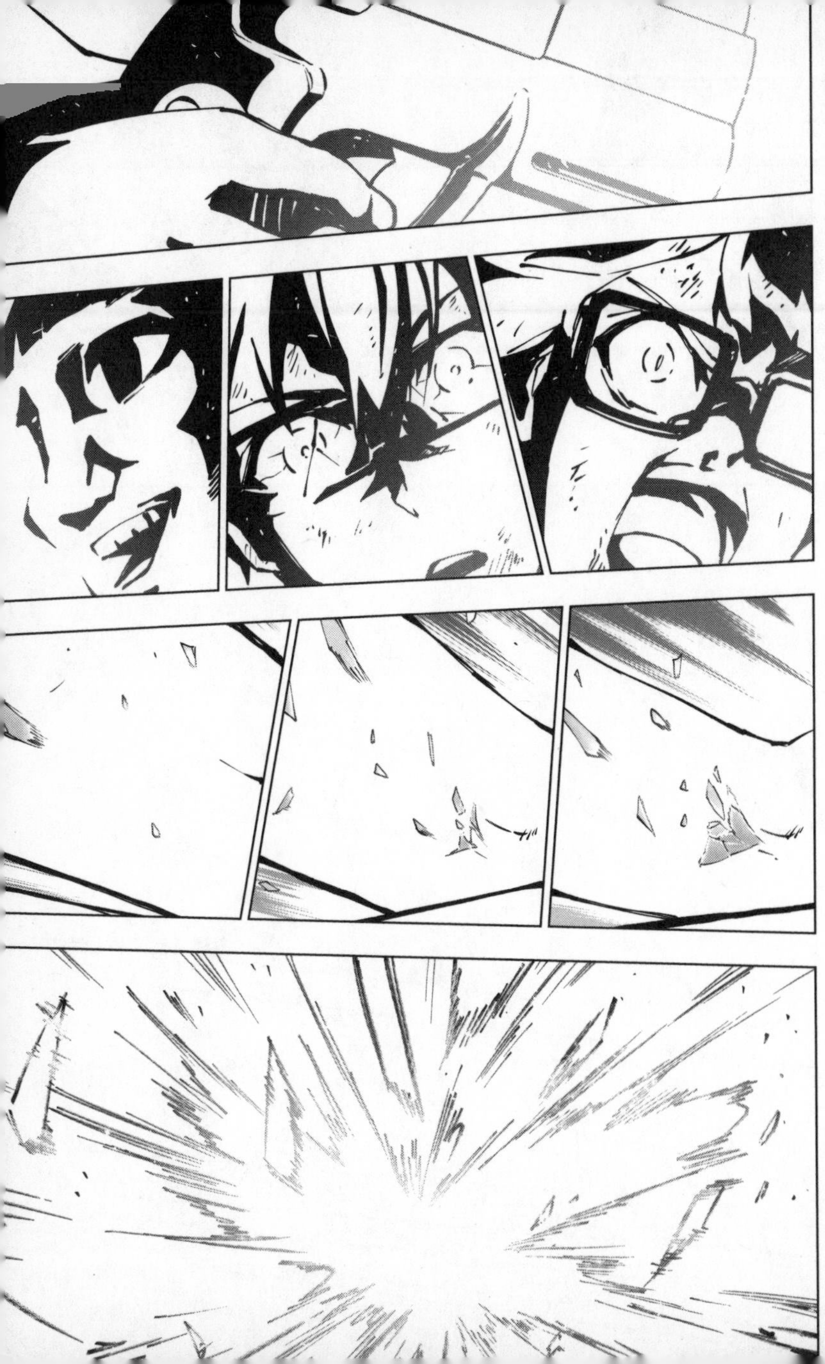

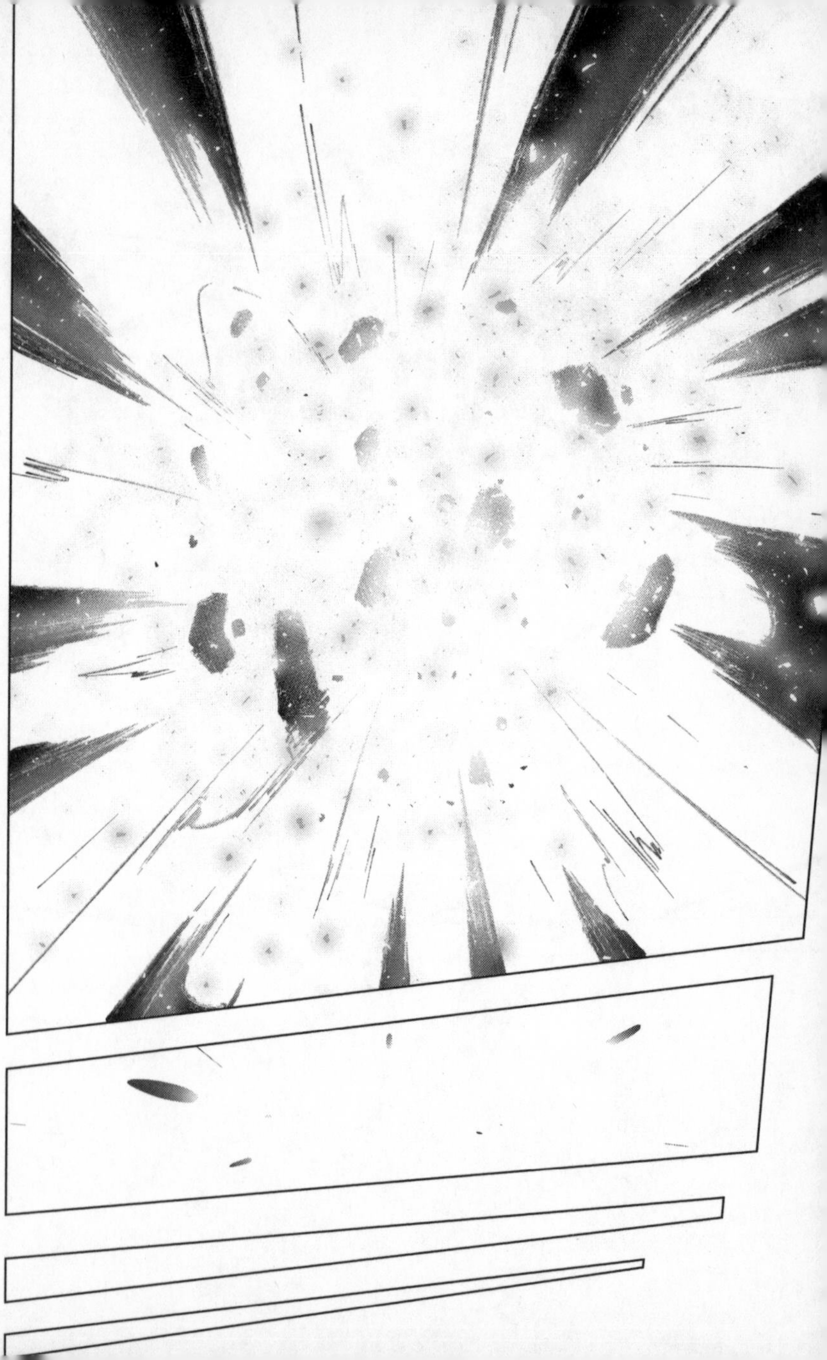

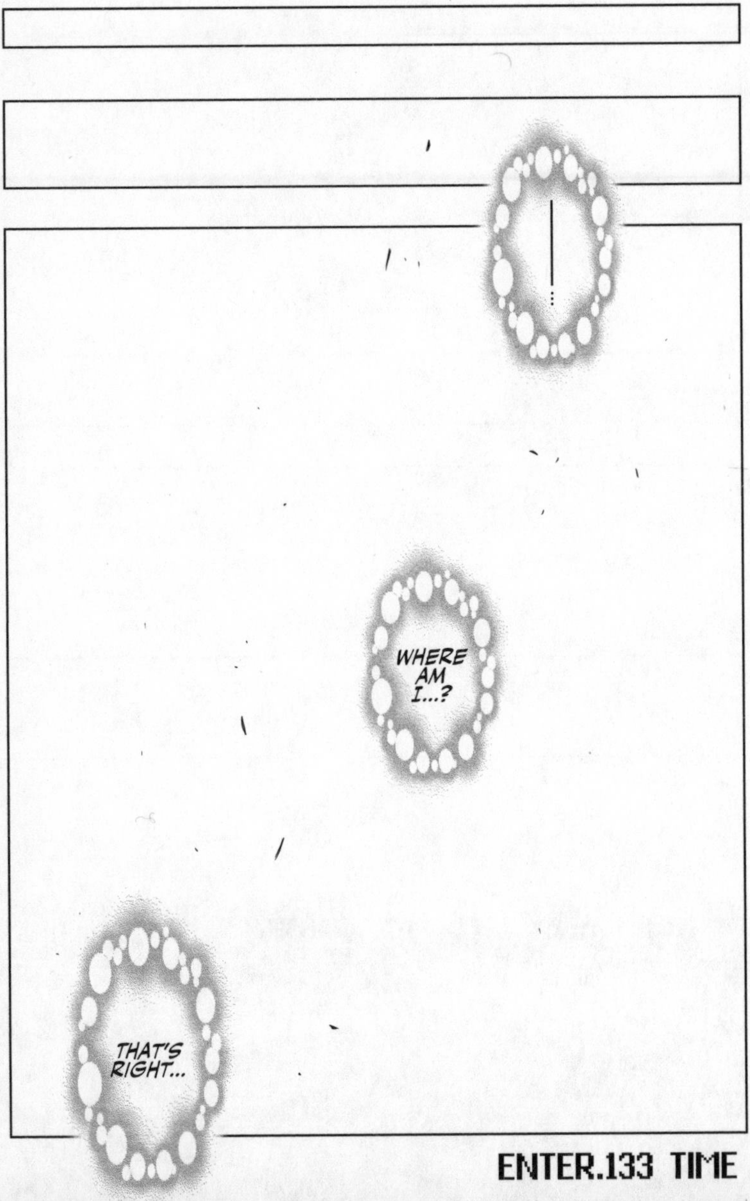
—...
WHERE AM I...?
THAT'S RIGHT...

ENTER.133 TIME

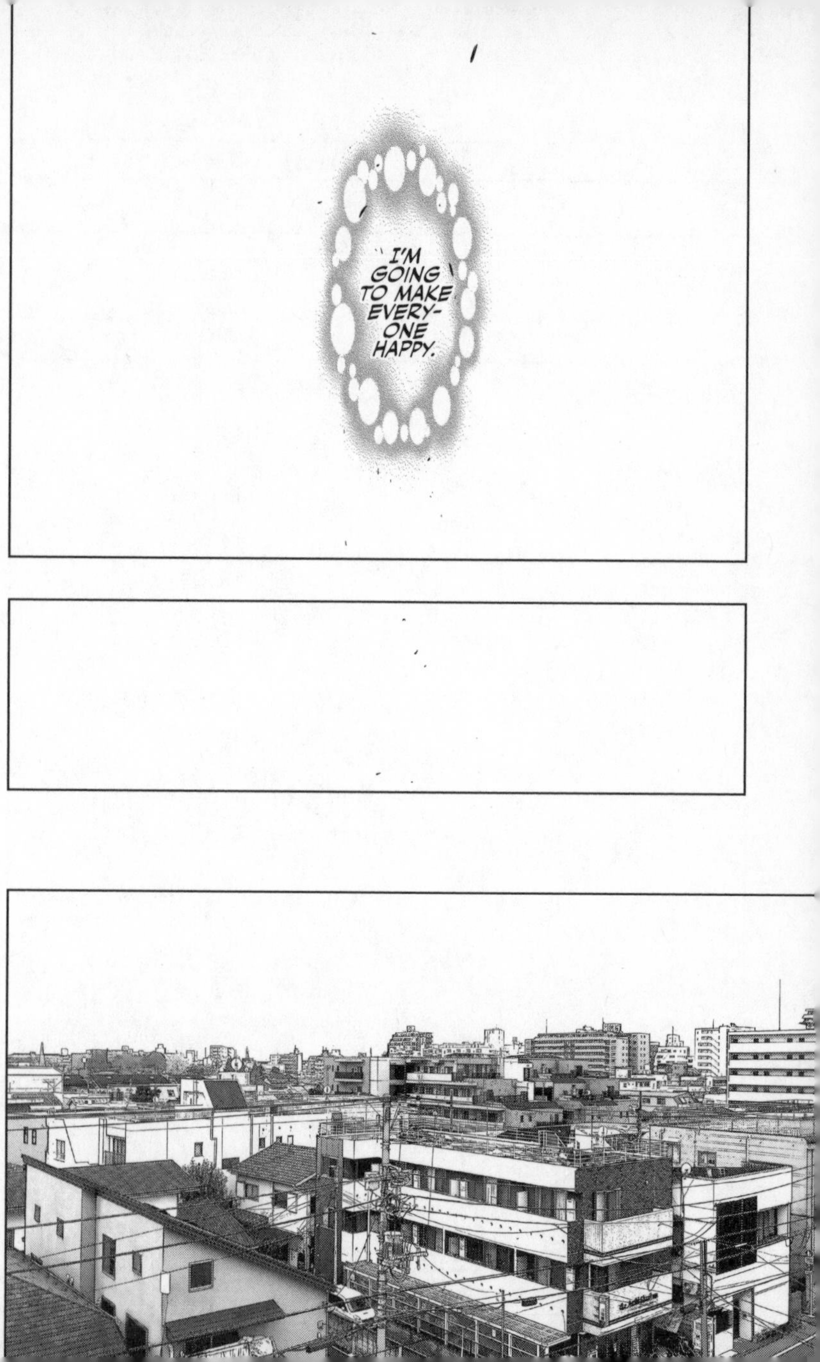
I'M GOING TO MAKE EVERY-ONE HAPPY.

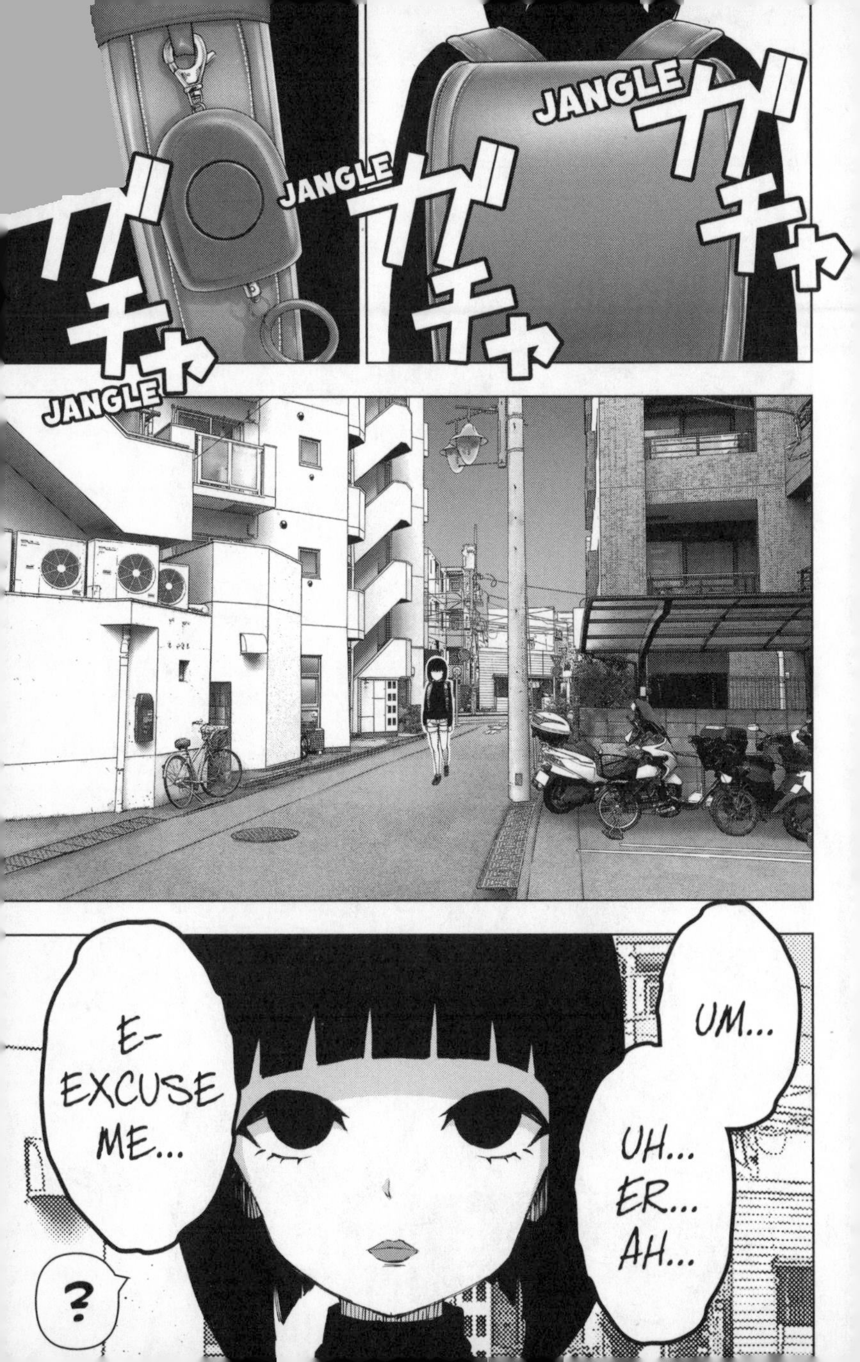
JANGLE
ガチャ
JANGLE
ガチャ
ガチャ
JANGLE
UM...
UH... ER... AH...
E-EXCUSE ME...
?

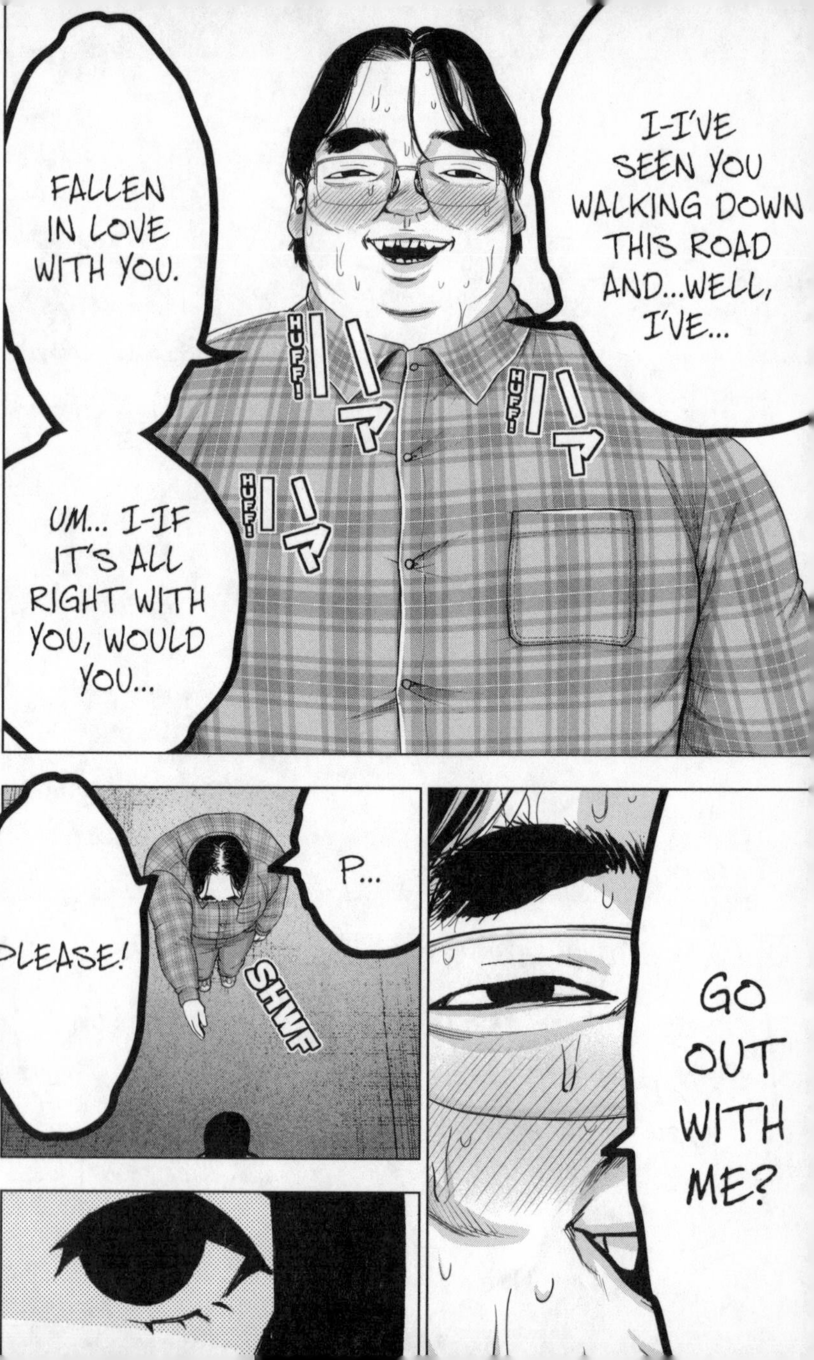
I-I'VE SEEN YOU WALKING DOWN THIS ROAD AND...WELL, I'VE...
FALLEN IN LOVE WITH YOU.
HUFF! ハア
HUFF! ハア
HUFF! ハア
UM... I-IF IT'S ALL RIGHT WITH YOU, WOULD YOU...
GO OUT WITH ME?
P...
PLEASE!
SHWF

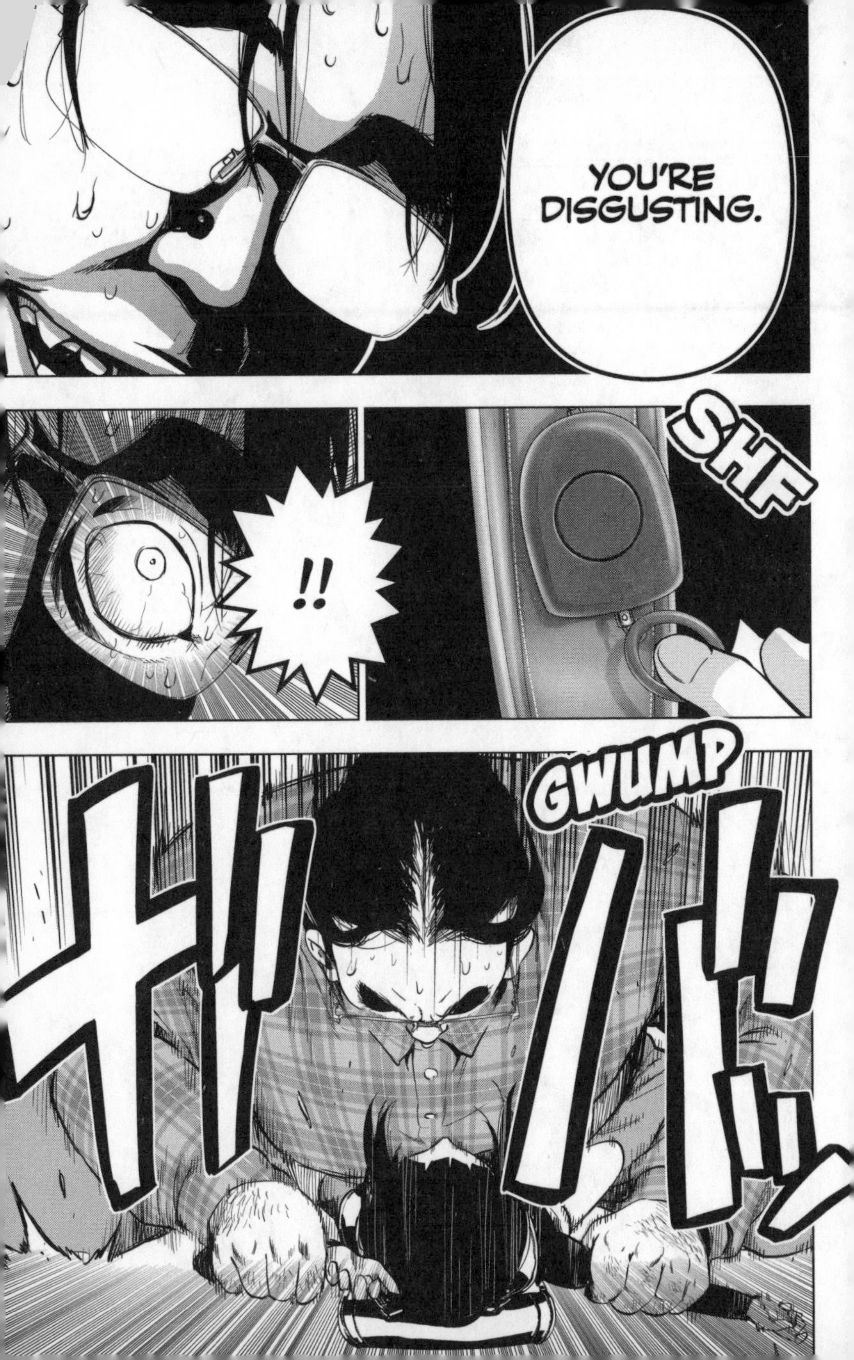
YOU'RE DISGUSTING.
SHF
!!
GWUMP

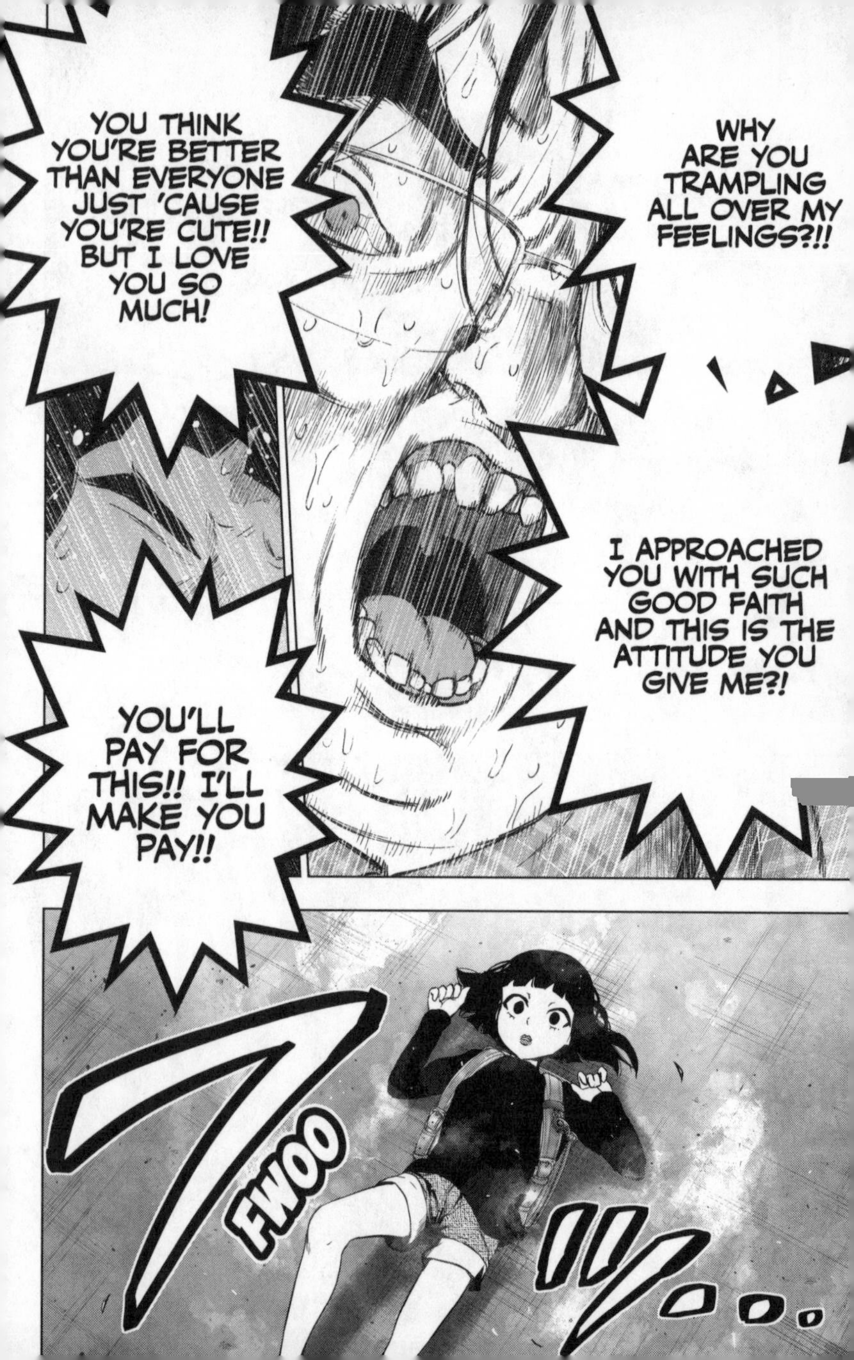
WHY ARE YOU TRAMPLING ALL OVER MY FEELINGS?!!
YOU THINK YOU'RE BETTER THAN EVERYONE JUST 'CAUSE YOU'RE CUTE!! BUT I LOVE YOU SO MUCH!
I APPROACHED YOU WITH SUCH GOOD FAITH AND THIS IS THE ATTITUDE YOU GIVE ME?!
YOU'LL PAY FOR THIS!! I'LL MAKE YOU PAY!!
FWOO

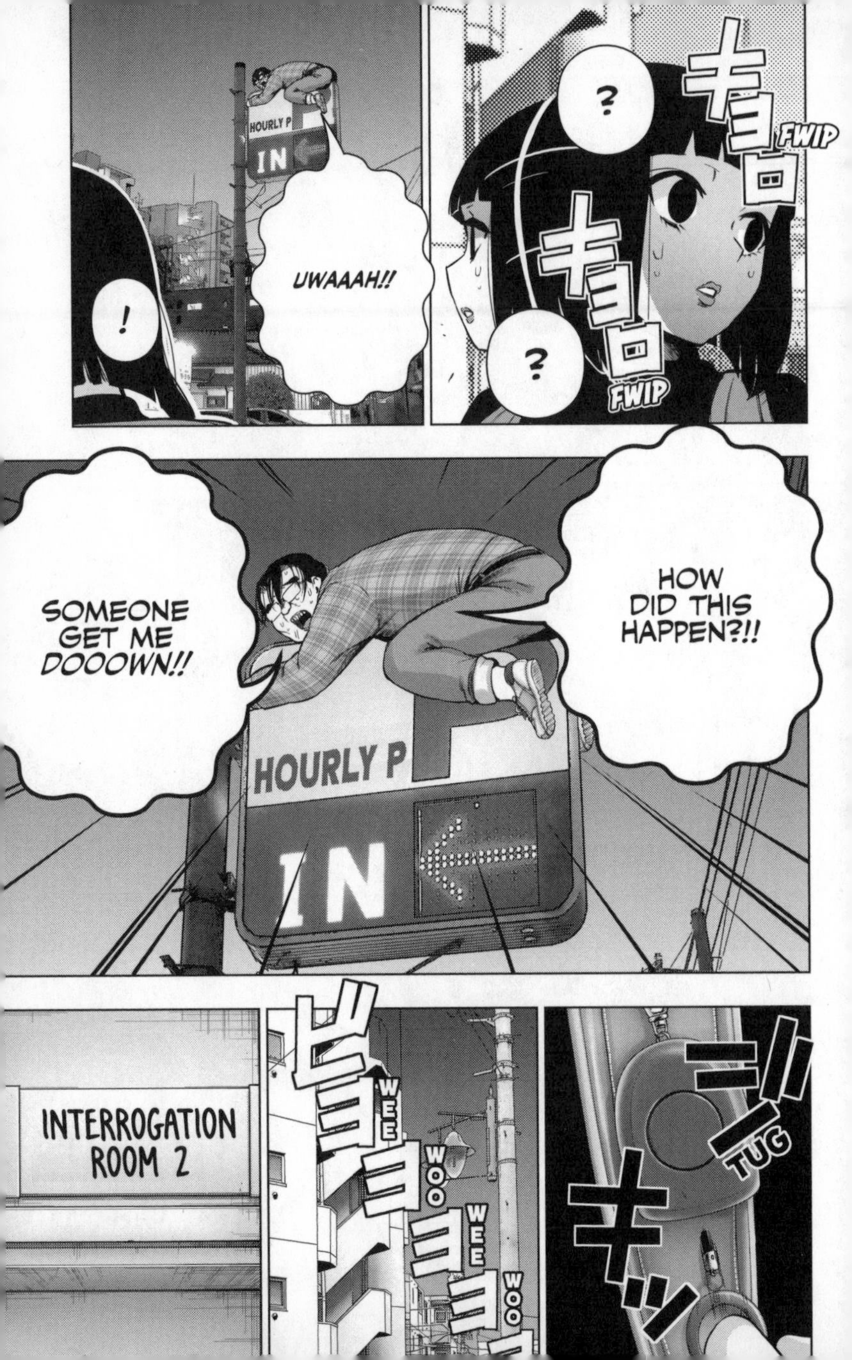

キョロ
FWIP
?
キョロ
?
FWIP
HOURLY P
IN
UWAAAH!!
!
HOW DID THIS HAPPEN?!!
SOMEONE GET ME DOOOWN!!
HOURLY P
IN
TUG
WEE
WOO
WEE
WOO
INTERROGATION ROOM 2

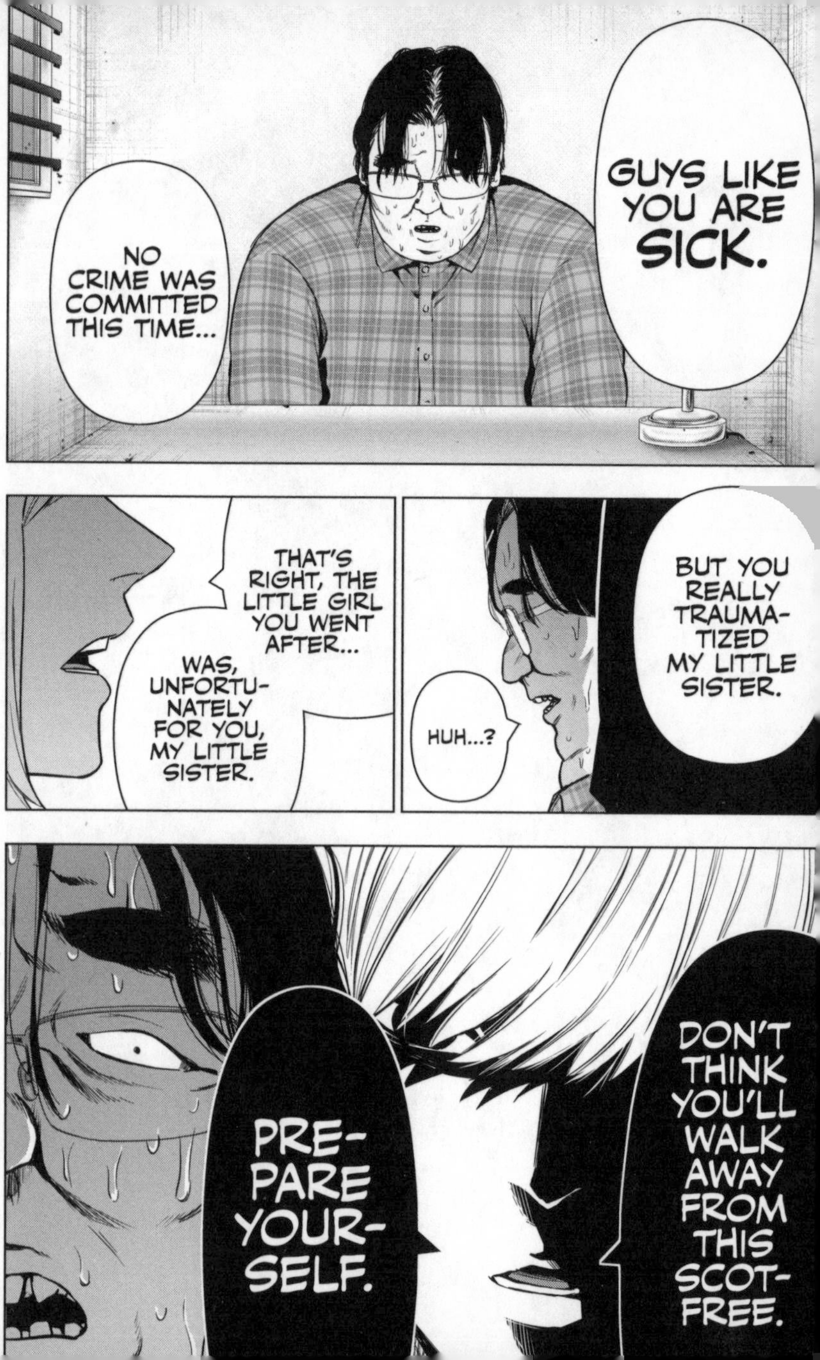
GUYS LIKE YOU ARE SICK.
NO CRIME WAS COMMITTED THIS TIME...
BUT YOU REALLY TRAUMATIZED MY LITTLE SISTER.
HUH...?
THAT'S RIGHT, THE LITTLE GIRL YOU WENT AFTER...
WAS, UNFORTUNATELY FOR YOU, MY LITTLE SISTER.
DON'T THINK YOU'LL WALK AWAY FROM THIS SCOT-FREE.
PREPARE YOURSELF.

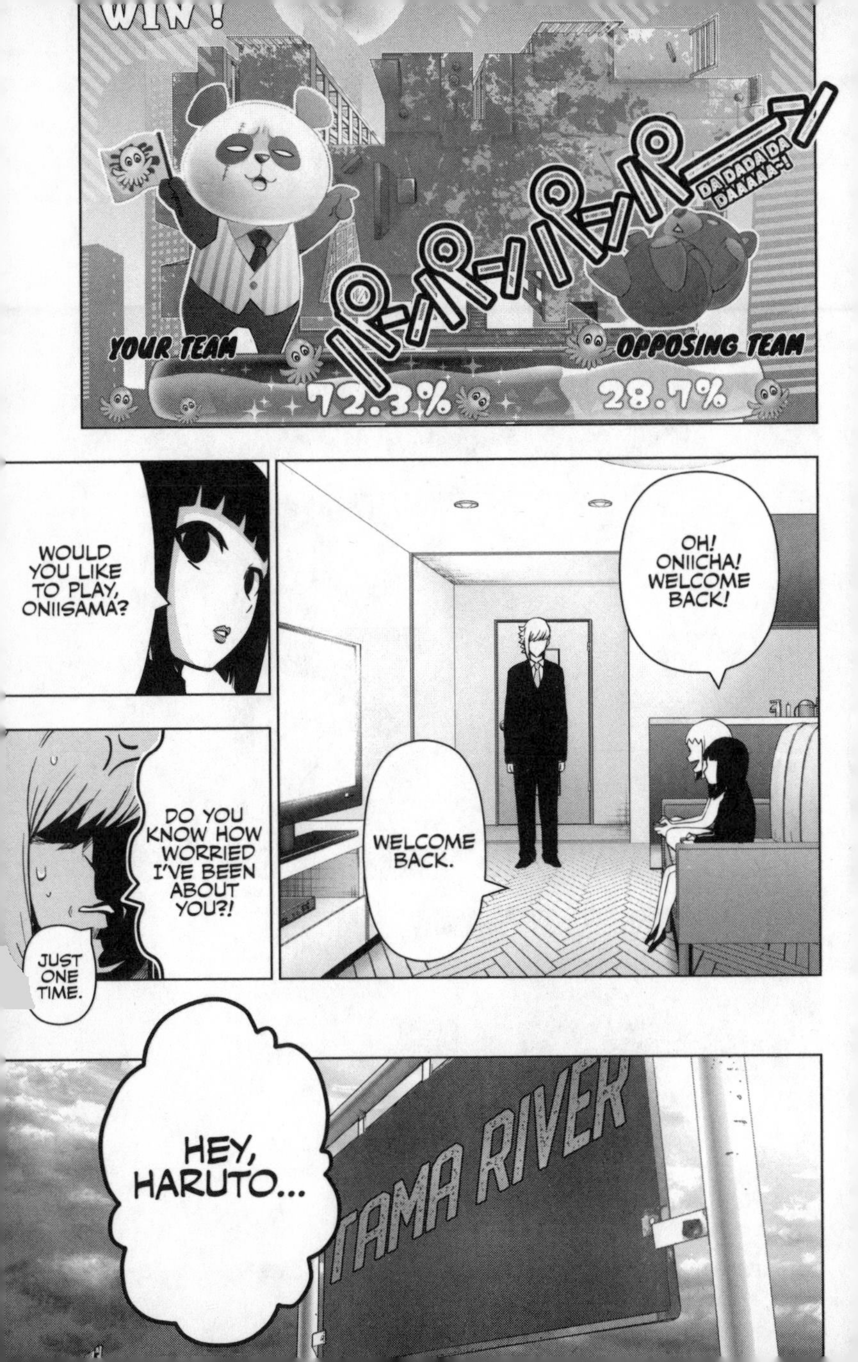
WIN!
DA DADA DA DAAAAA~!
YOUR TEAM
OPPOSING TEAM
72.3%
28.7%
OH! ONIICHA! WELCOME BACK!
WELCOME BACK.
WOULD YOU LIKE TO PLAY, ONIISAMA?
DO YOU KNOW HOW WORRIED I'VE BEEN ABOUT YOU?!
JUST ONE TIME.
TAMA RIVER
HEY, HARUTO...

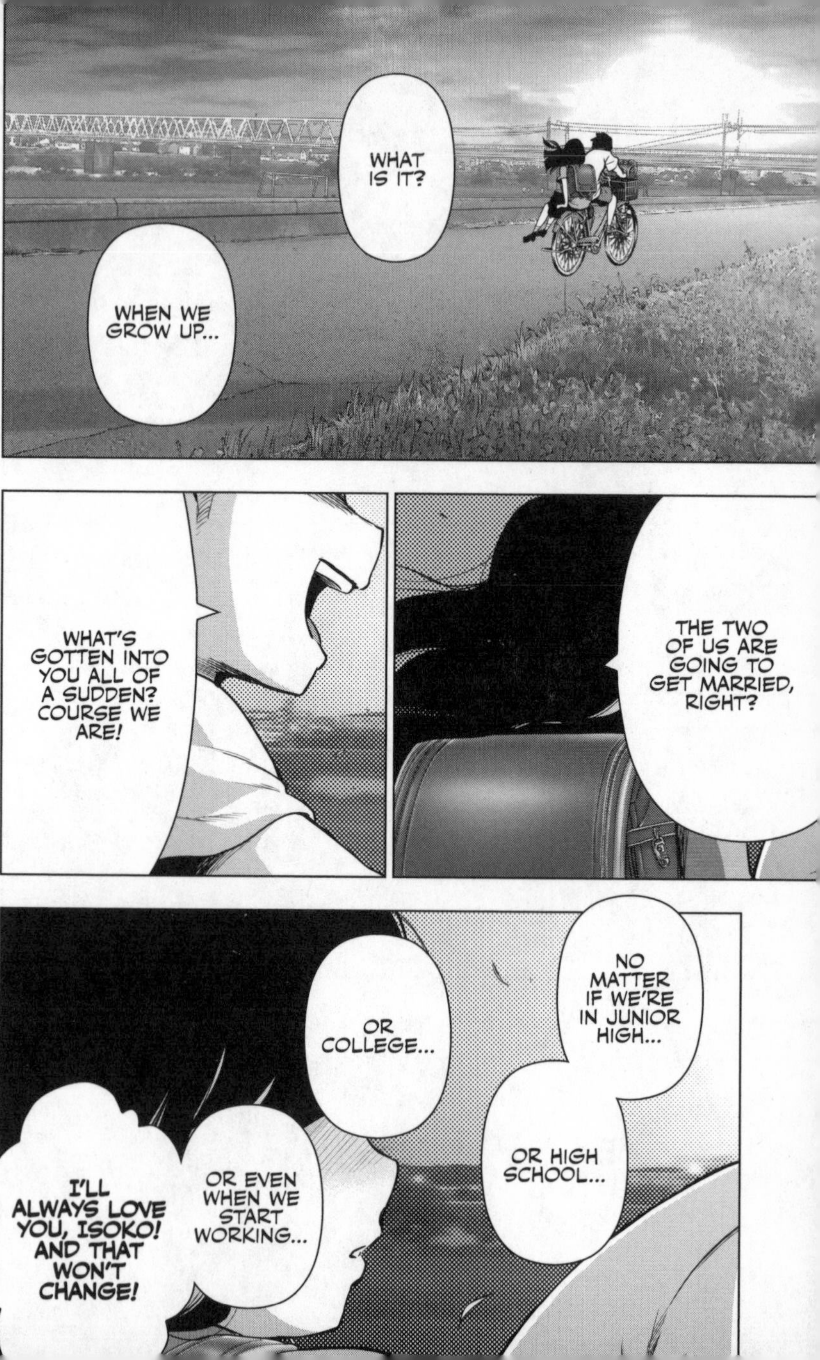
WHAT IS IT?
WHEN WE GROW UP...
THE TWO OF US ARE GOING TO GET MARRIED, RIGHT?
WHAT'S GOTTEN INTO YOU ALL OF A SUDDEN? COURSE WE ARE!
NO MATTER IF WE'RE IN JUNIOR HIGH...
OR HIGH SCHOOL...
OR COLLEGE...
OR EVEN WHEN WE START WORKING...
I'LL ALWAYS LOVE YOU, ISOKO! AND THAT WON'T CHANGE!

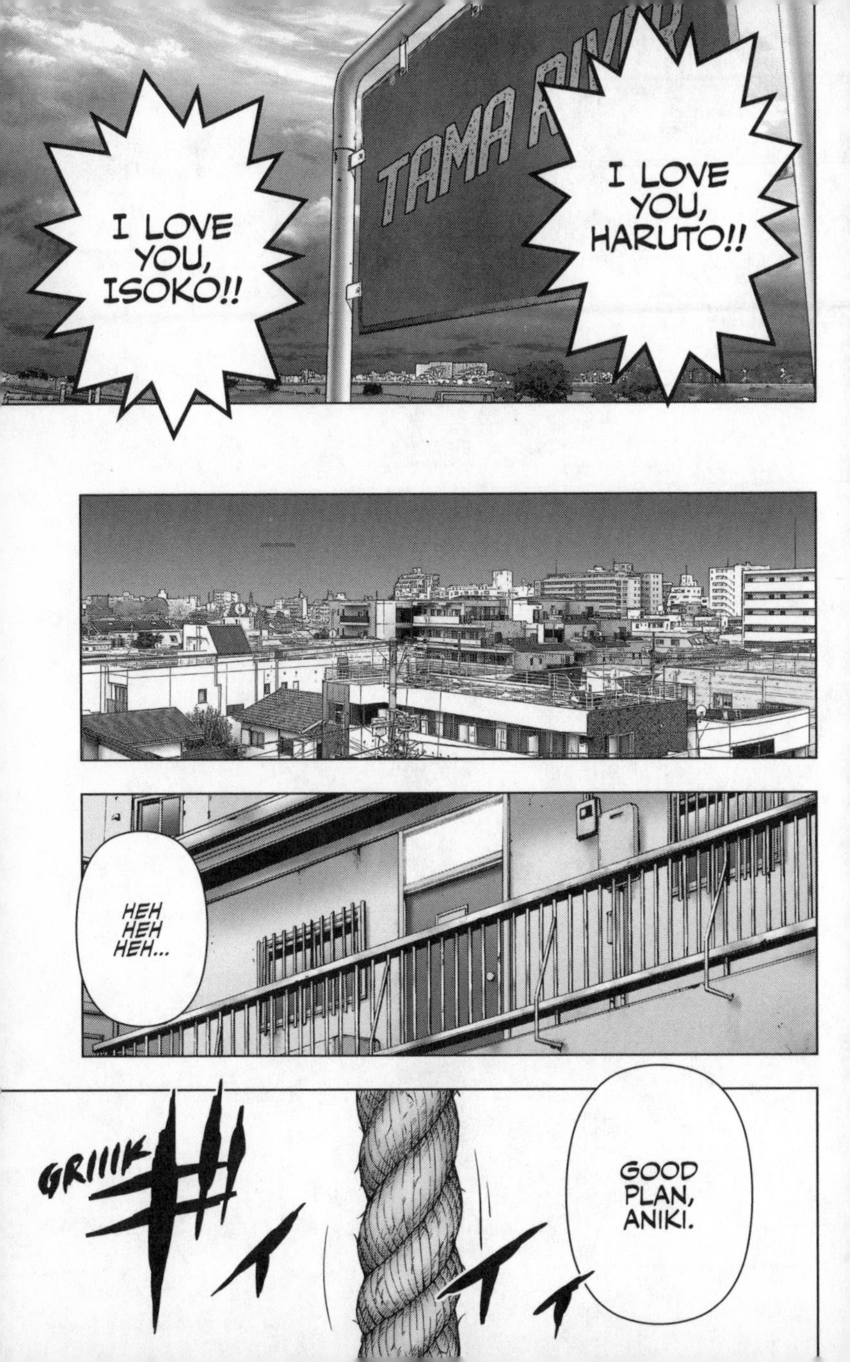
I LOVE YOU, HARUTO!!
I LOVE YOU, ISOKO!!
TAMA
HEH HEH HEH...
GOOD PLAN, ANIKI.
GRIIIK

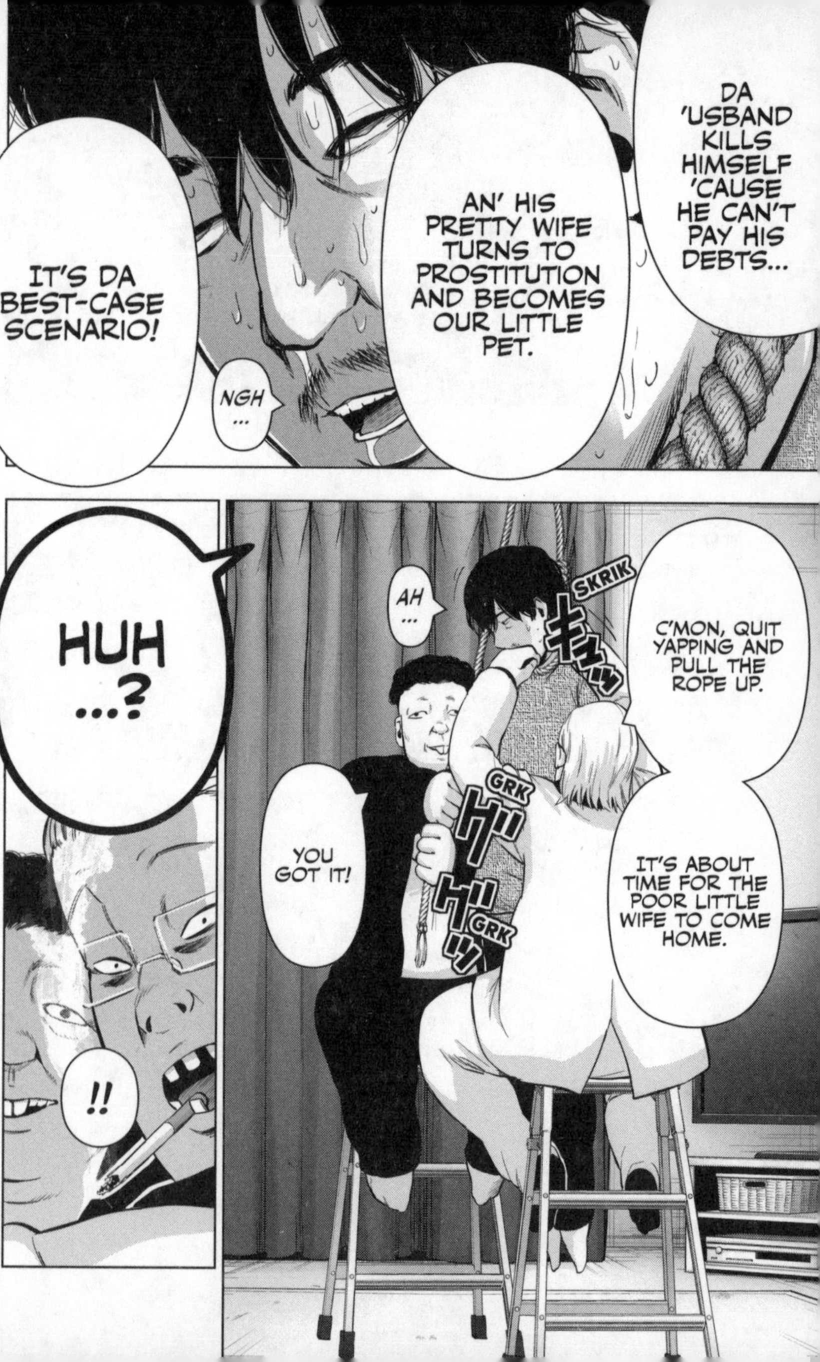
DA 'USBAND KILLS HIMSELF 'CAUSE HE CAN'T PAY HIS DEBTS...
AN' HIS PRETTY WIFE TURNS TO PROSTITUTION AND BECOMES OUR LITTLE PET.
NGH ...
IT'S DA BEST-CASE SCENARIO!
SKRIK
C'MON, QUIT YAPPING AND PULL THE ROPE UP.
AH ...
IT'S ABOUT TIME FOR THE POOR LITTLE WIFE TO COME HOME.
YOU GOT IT!
GRK
GRK
HUH ...?
!!

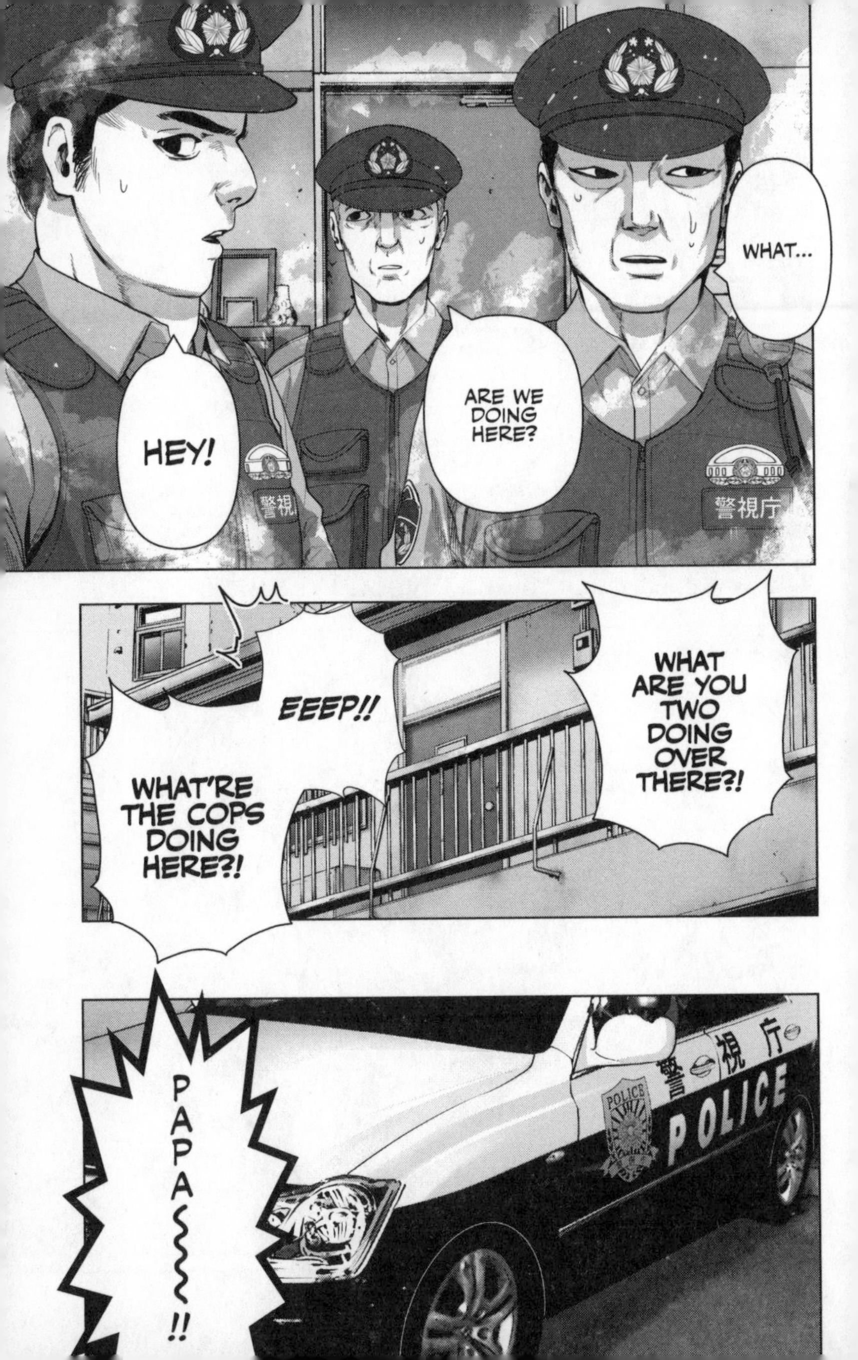
WHAT...
ARE WE DOING HERE?
警視庁
HEY!
警視
WHAT ARE YOU TWO DOING OVER THERE?!
EEEP!!
WHAT'RE THE COPS DOING HERE?!
警視庁
POLICE
PAPA~~!!

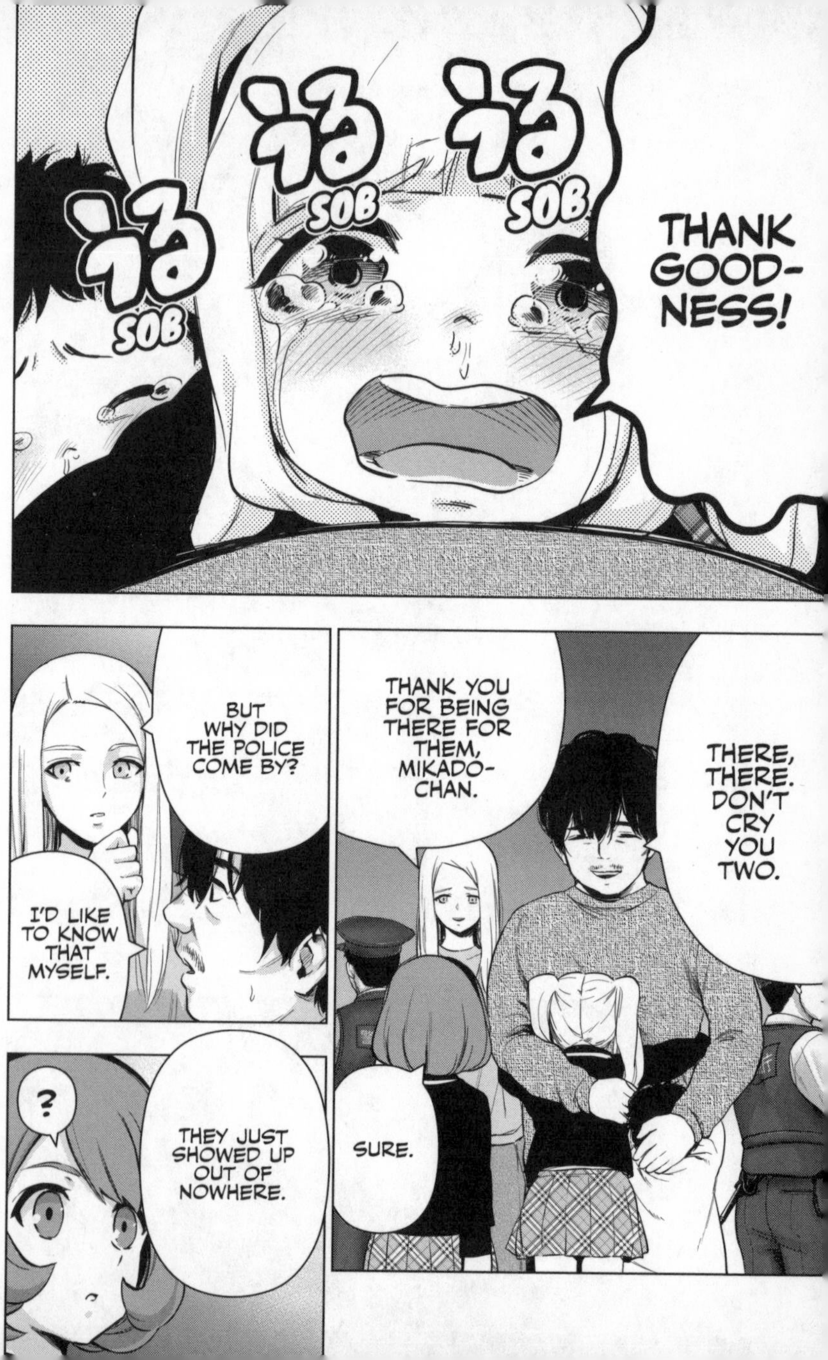
THANK GOODNESS!
SOB
SOB
SOB
THERE, THERE. DON'T CRY YOU TWO.
THANK YOU FOR BEING THERE FOR THEM, MIKADO-CHAN.
SURE.
BUT WHY DID THE POLICE COME BY?
I'D LIKE TO KNOW THAT MYSELF.
?
THEY JUST SHOWED UP OUT OF NOWHERE.

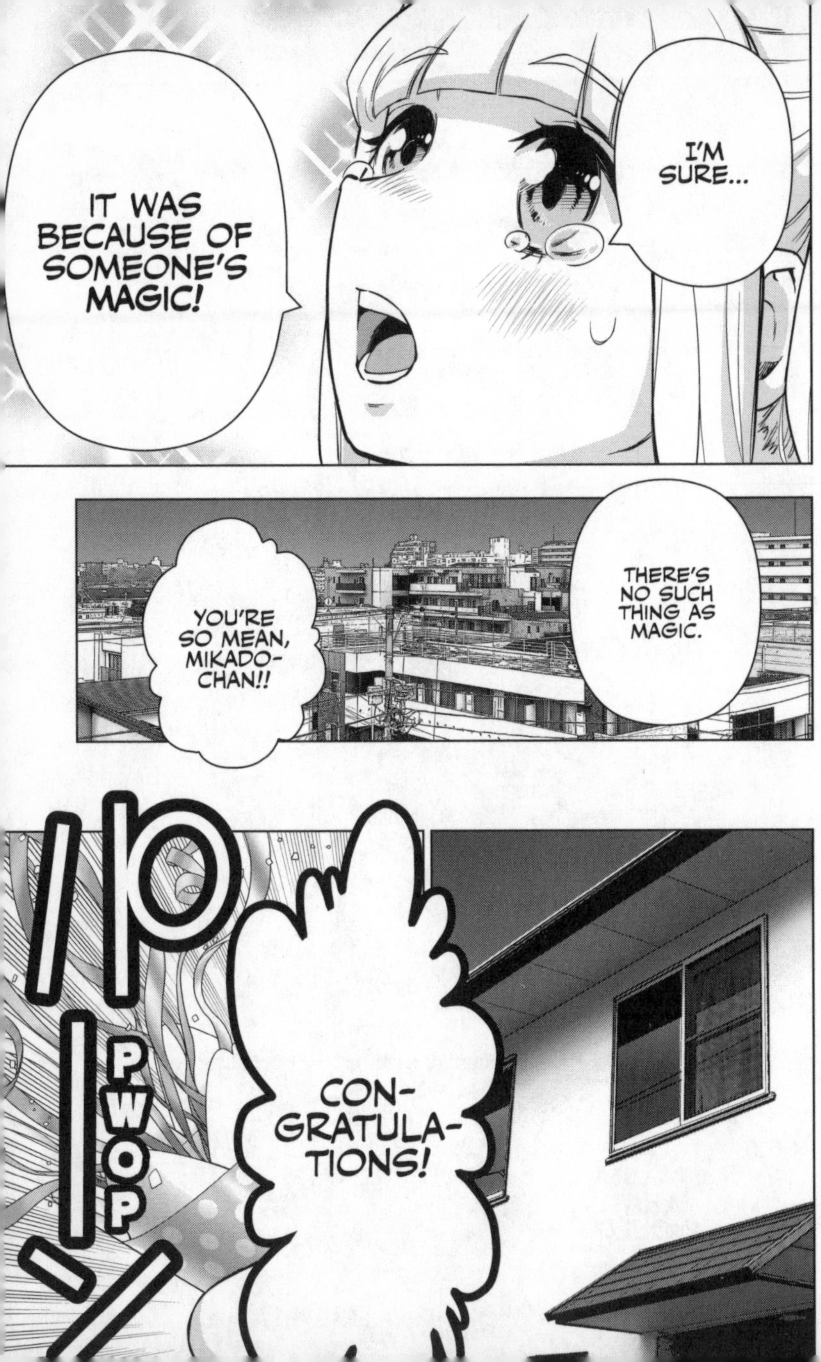
I'M SURE...
IT WAS BECAUSE OF SOMEONE'S MAGIC!
THERE'S NO SUCH THING AS MAGIC.
YOU'RE SO MEAN, MIKADO-CHAN!!
CON-GRATULA-TIONS!
PWOP

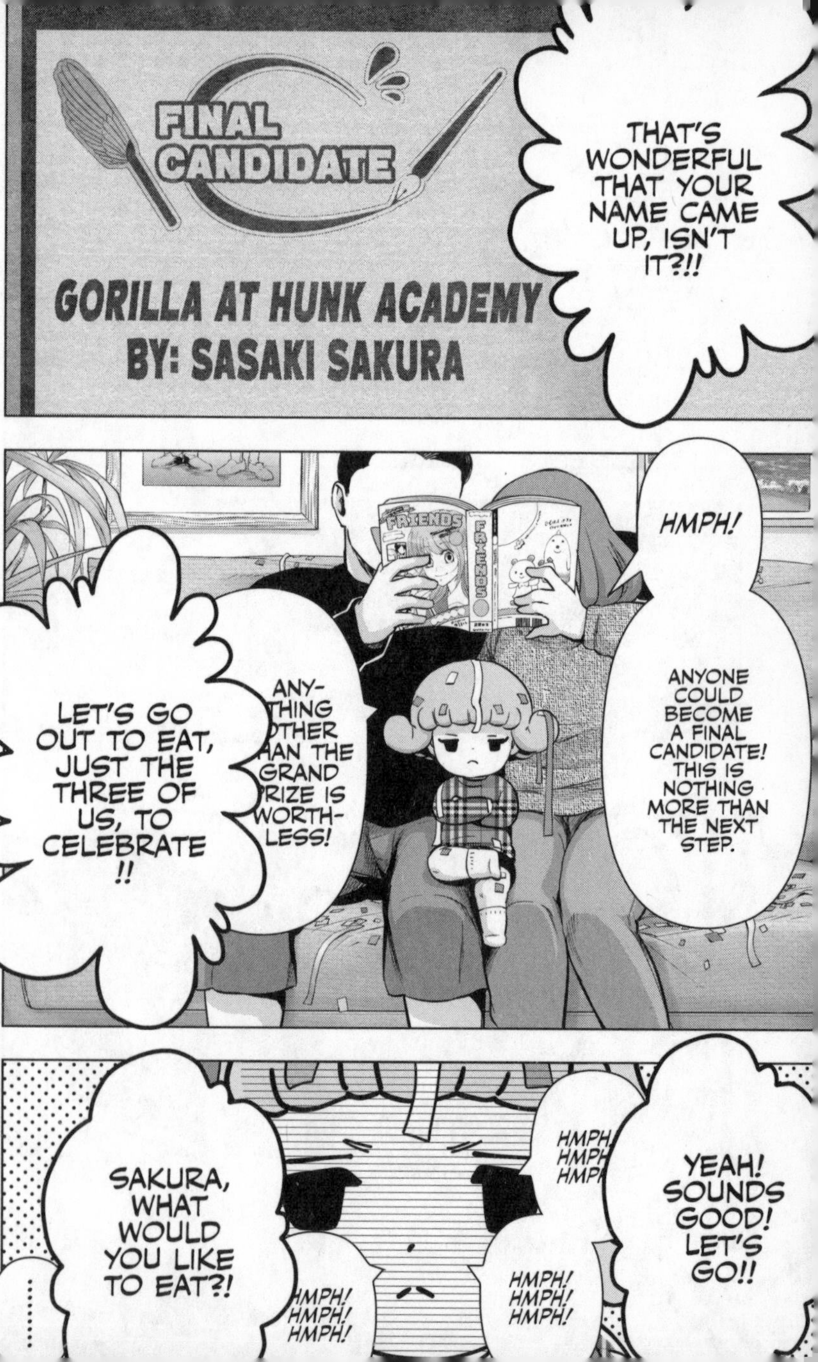
THAT'S WONDERFUL THAT YOUR NAME CAME UP, ISN'T IT?!!
FINAL CANDIDATE
GORILLA AT HUNK ACADEMY
BY: SASAKI SAKURA
HMPH!
ANYONE COULD BECOME A FINAL CANDIDATE! THIS IS NOTHING MORE THAN THE NEXT STEP.
ANYTHING OTHER THAN THE GRAND PRIZE IS WORTHLESS!
LET'S GO OUT TO EAT, JUST THE THREE OF US, TO CELEBRATE!!
YEAH! SOUNDS GOOD! LET'S GO!!
HMPH! HMPH! HMPH!
HMPH! HMPH! HMPH!
SAKURA, WHAT WOULD YOU LIKE TO EAT?!
HMPH! HMPH! HMPH!
......

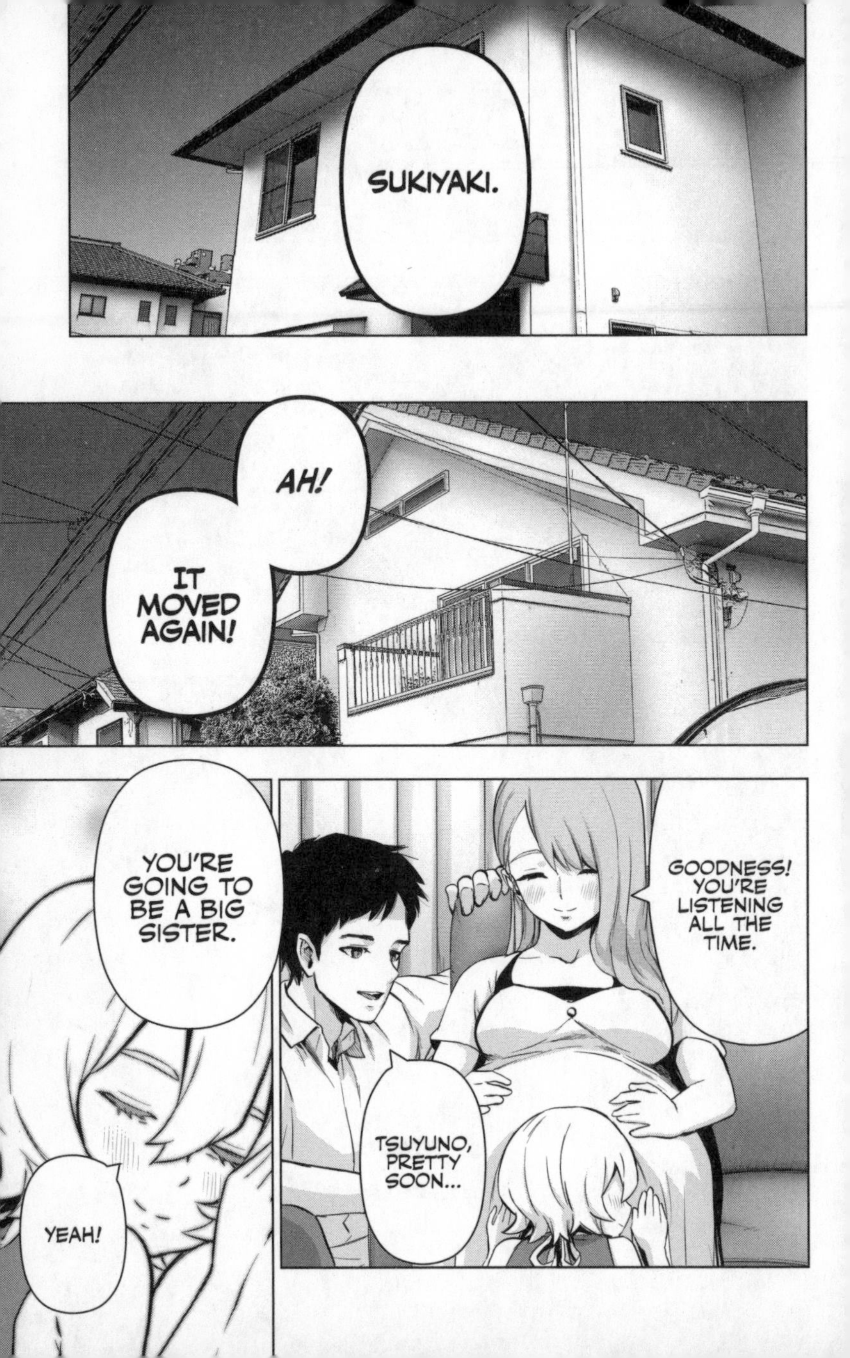
SUKIYAKI.
AH!
IT MOVED AGAIN!
GOODNESS! YOU'RE LISTENING ALL THE TIME.
TSUYUNO, PRETTY SOON...
YOU'RE GOING TO BE A BIG SISTER.
YEAH!

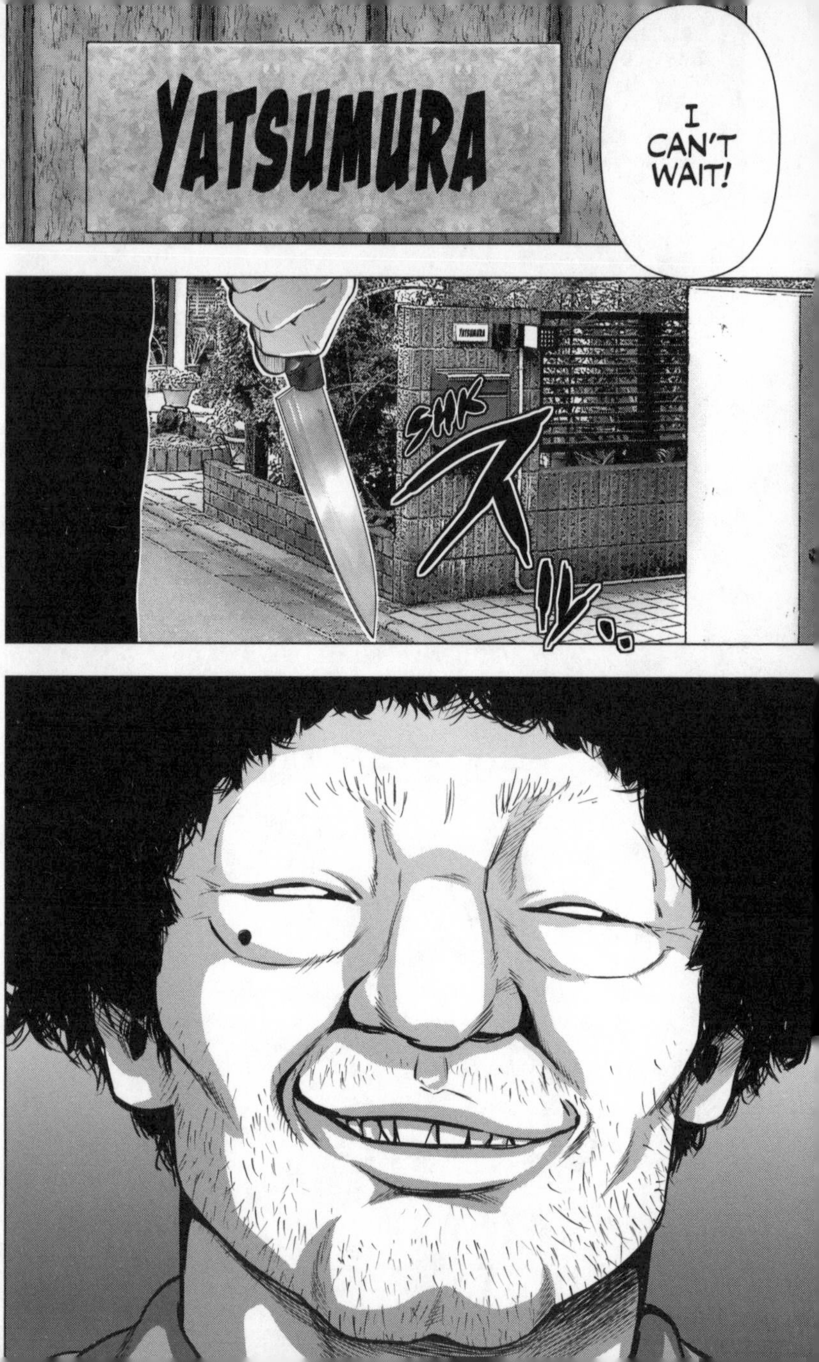
I CAN'T WAIT!
YATSUMURA
YATSUMURA
SHK
スッ

ENTER.136 TO SAY

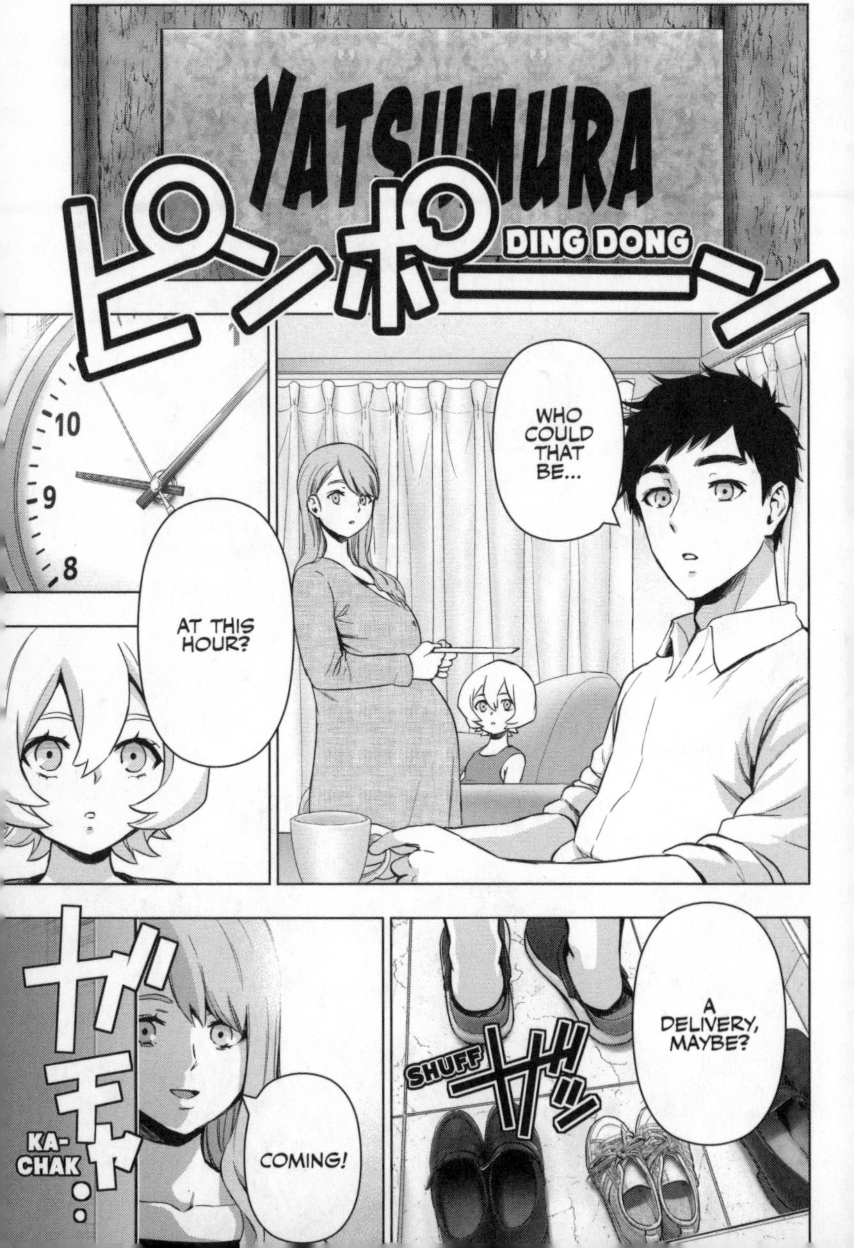
YATSUMURA
DING DONG
WHO COULD THAT BE...
AT THIS HOUR?
A DELIVERY, MAYBE?
SHUFF
KA-CHAK
COMING!

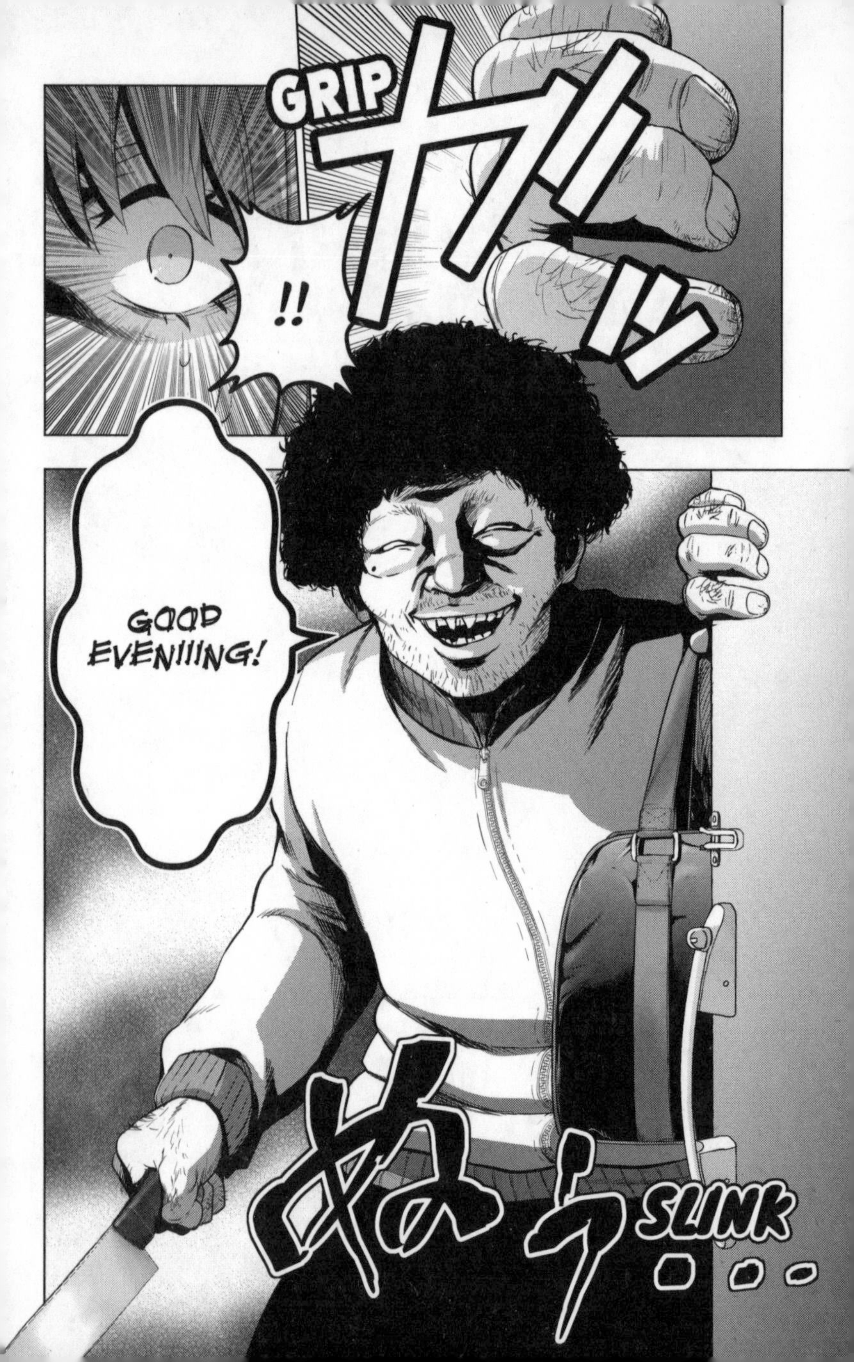
GRIP
!!
GOOD EVENIIING!
SLINK...

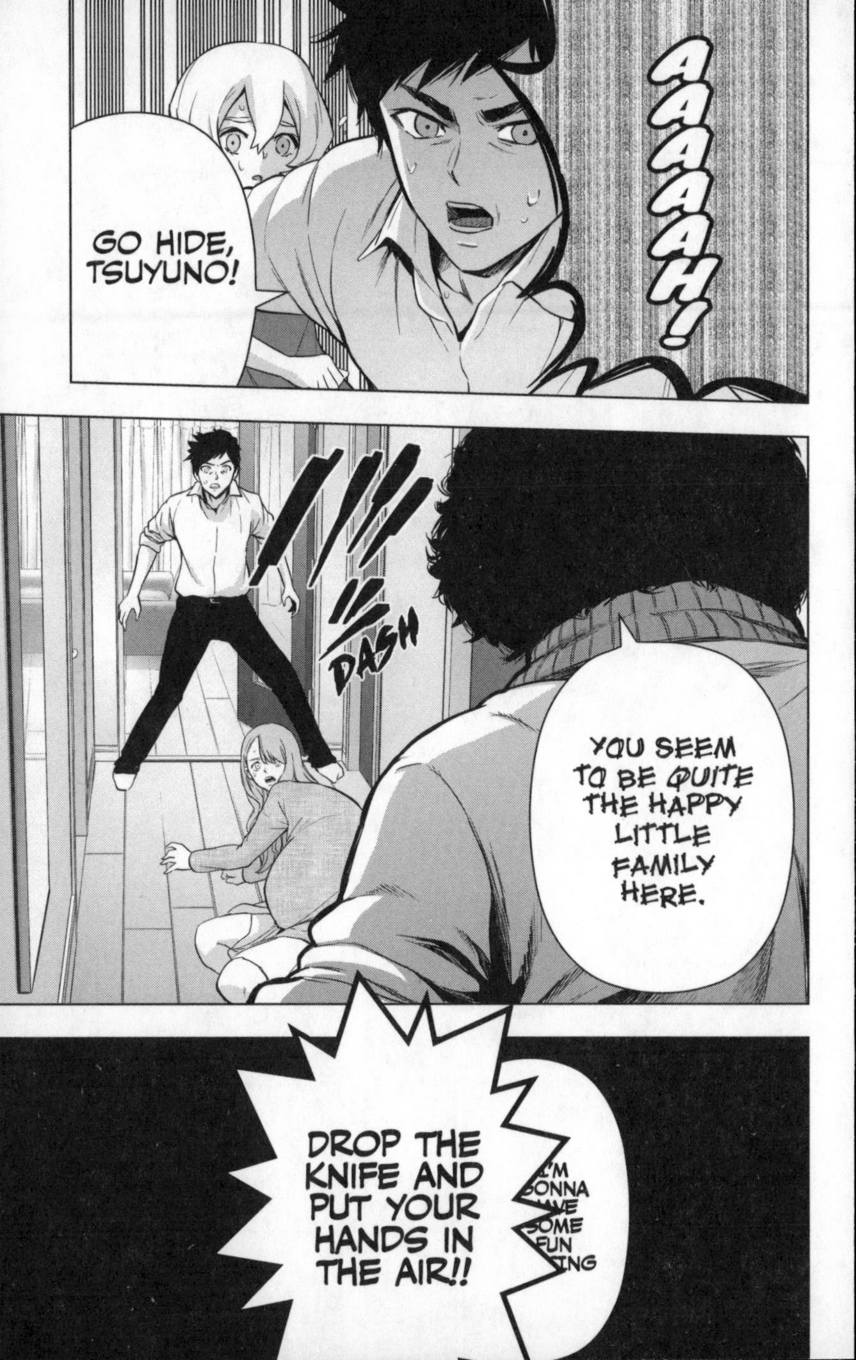
AAAAAAH!
GO HIDE, TSUYUNO!
YOU SEEM TO BE QUITE THE HAPPY LITTLE FAMILY HERE.
DASH
DROP THE KNIFE AND PUT YOUR HANDS IN THE AIR!!

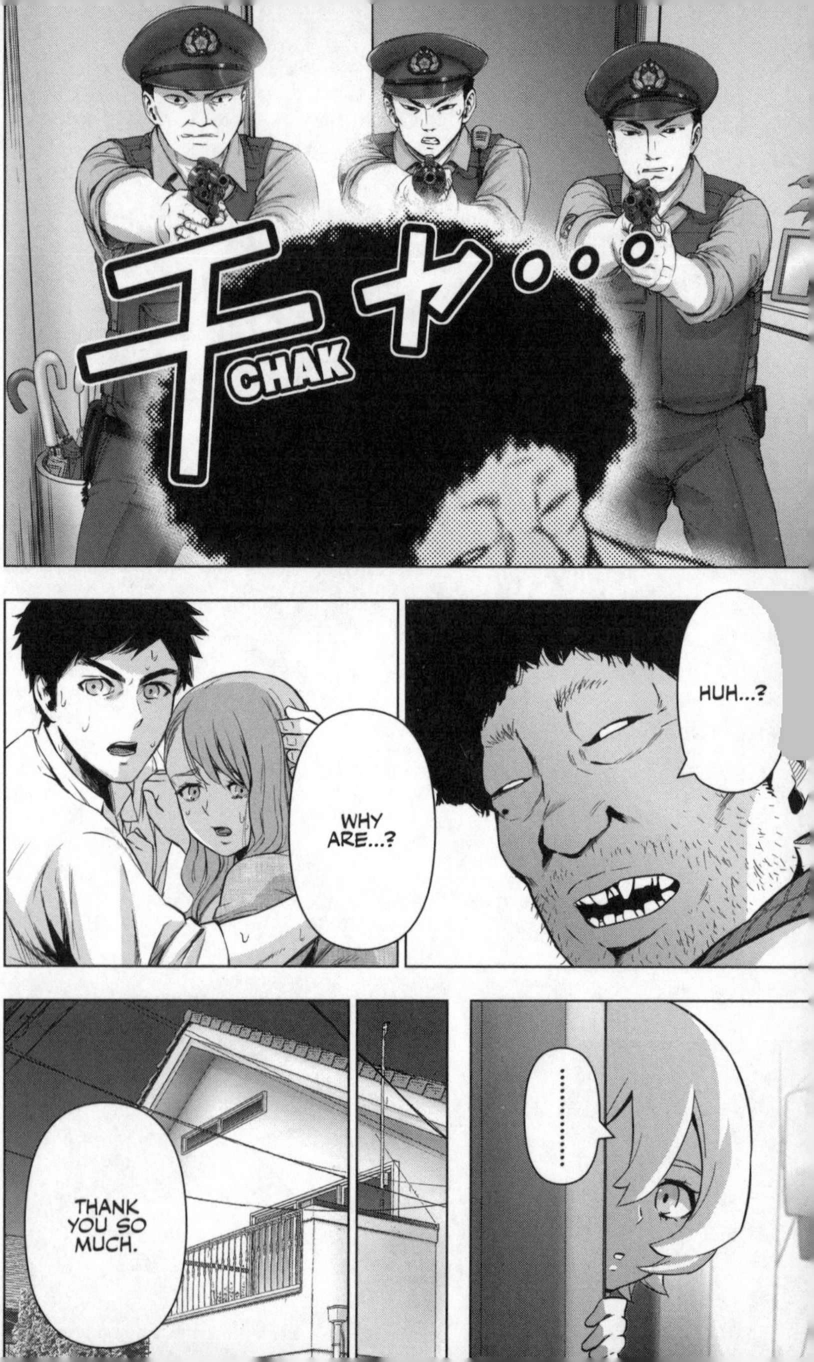
チャ…
CHAK
HUH...?
WHY ARE...?
......
THANK YOU SO MUCH.

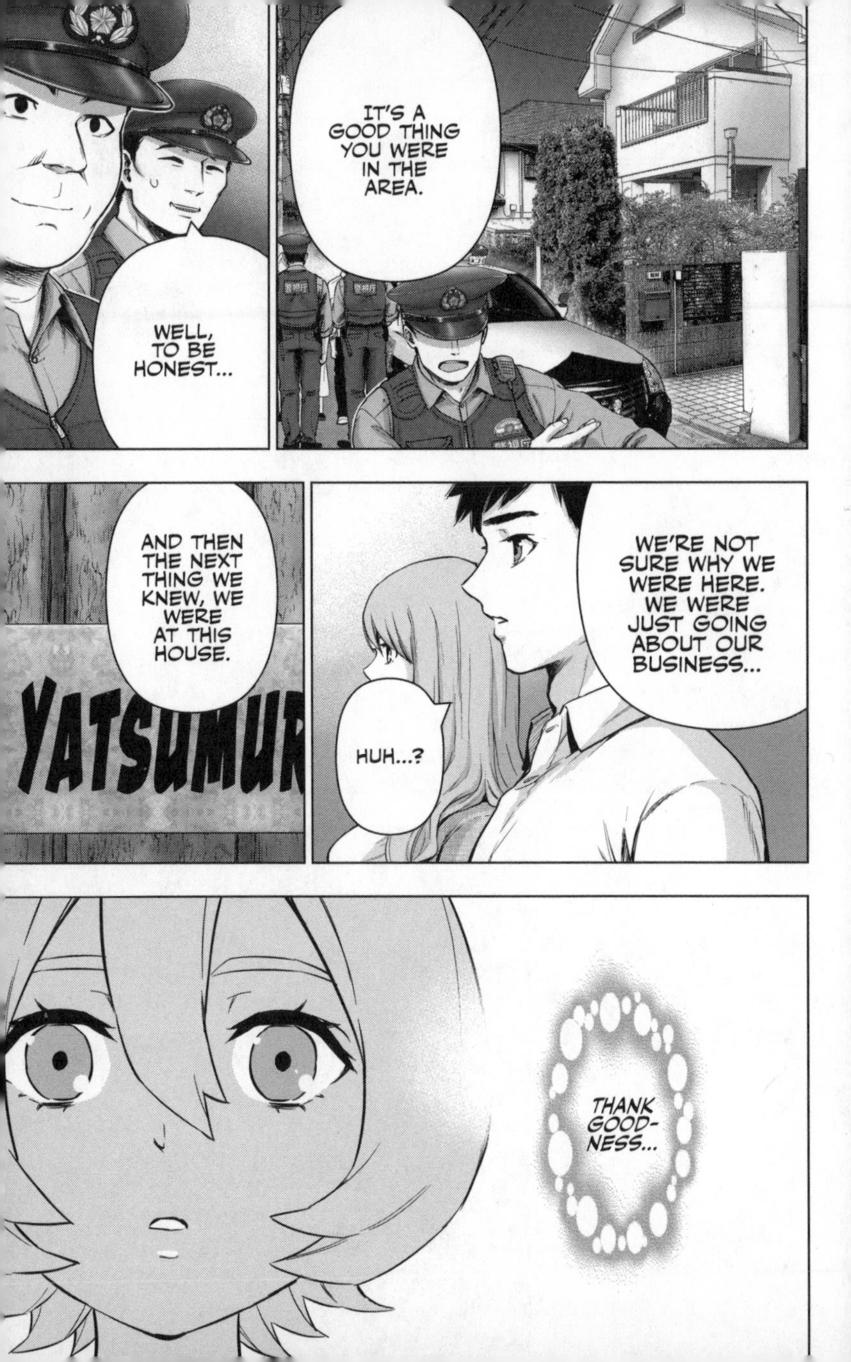
IT'S A GOOD THING YOU WERE IN THE AREA.
WELL, TO BE HONEST...
WE'RE NOT SURE WHY WE WERE HERE. WE WERE JUST GOING ABOUT OUR BUSINESS...
HUH...?
AND THEN THE NEXT THING WE KNEW, WE WERE AT THIS HOUSE.
YATSUMUR
THANK GOOD-NESS...

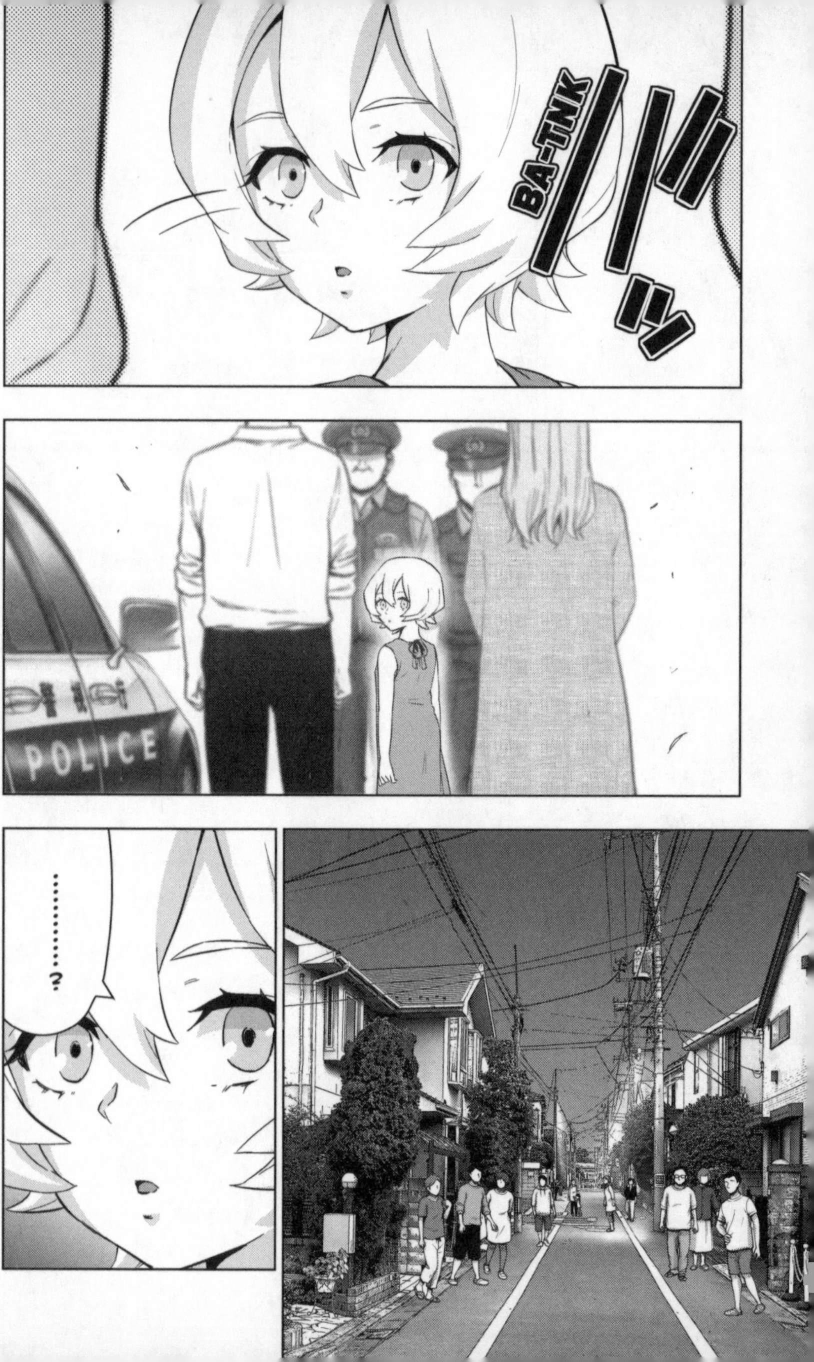
BA-TNK
POLICE
......?

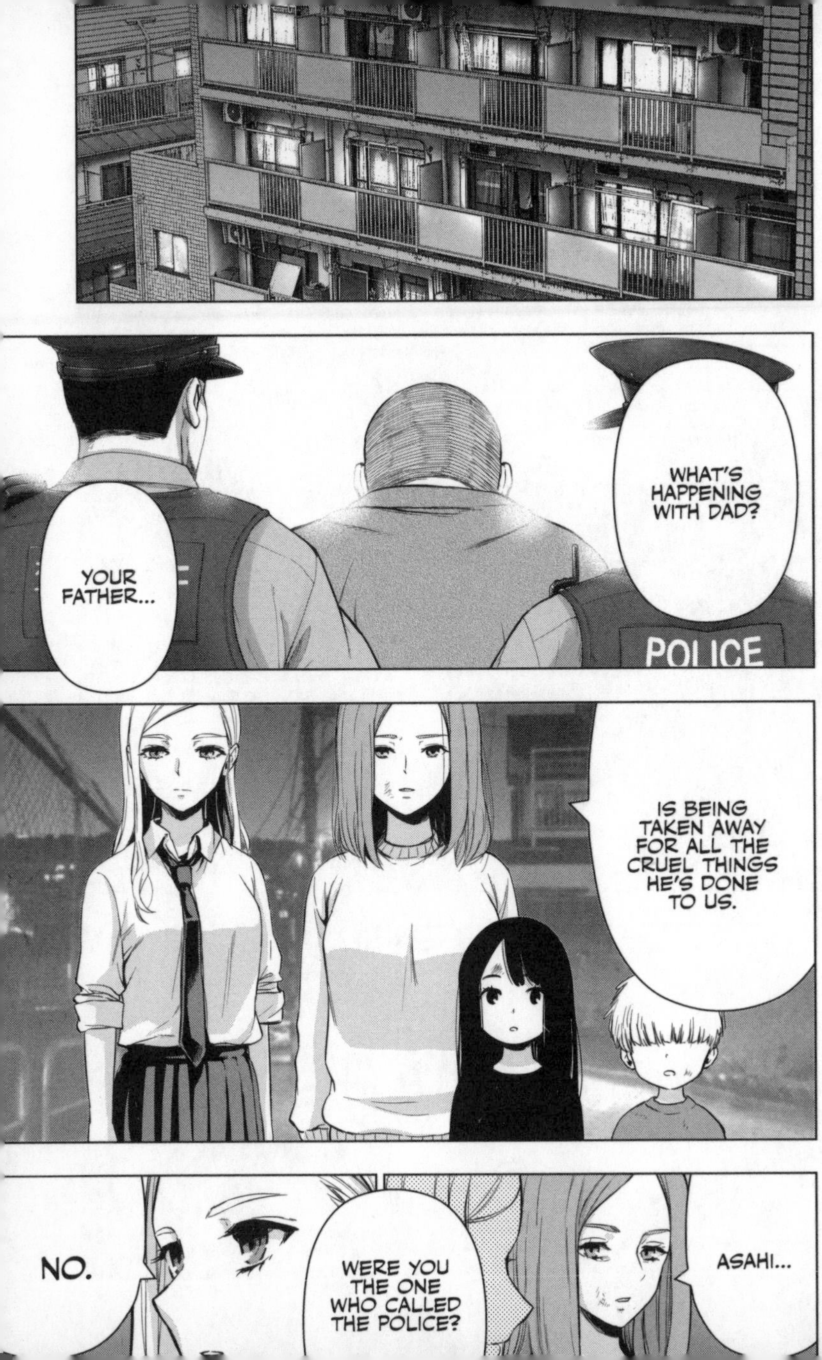
WHAT'S HAPPENING WITH DAD?
YOUR FATHER...
POLICE
IS BEING TAKEN AWAY FOR ALL THE CRUEL THINGS HE'S DONE TO US.
ASAHI...
WERE YOU THE ONE WHO CALLED THE POLICE?
NO.

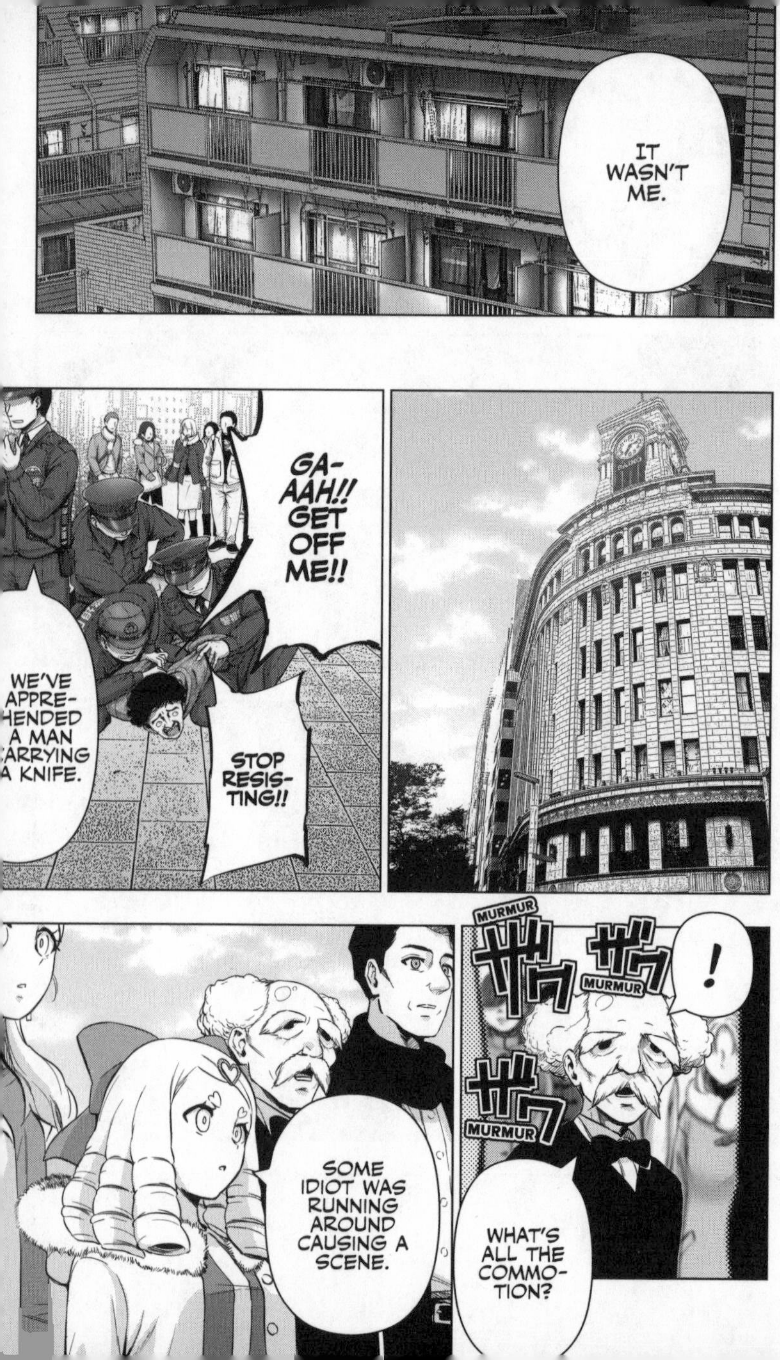
IT WASN'T ME.
GA-AAH!! GET OFF ME!!
STOP RESIS-TING!!
WE'VE APPRE-HENDED A MAN CARRYING A KNIFE.
ザワ MURMUR
ザワ MURMUR
!
ザワ MURMUR
WHAT'S ALL THE COMMO-TION?
SOME IDIOT WAS RUNNING AROUND CAUSING A SCENE.

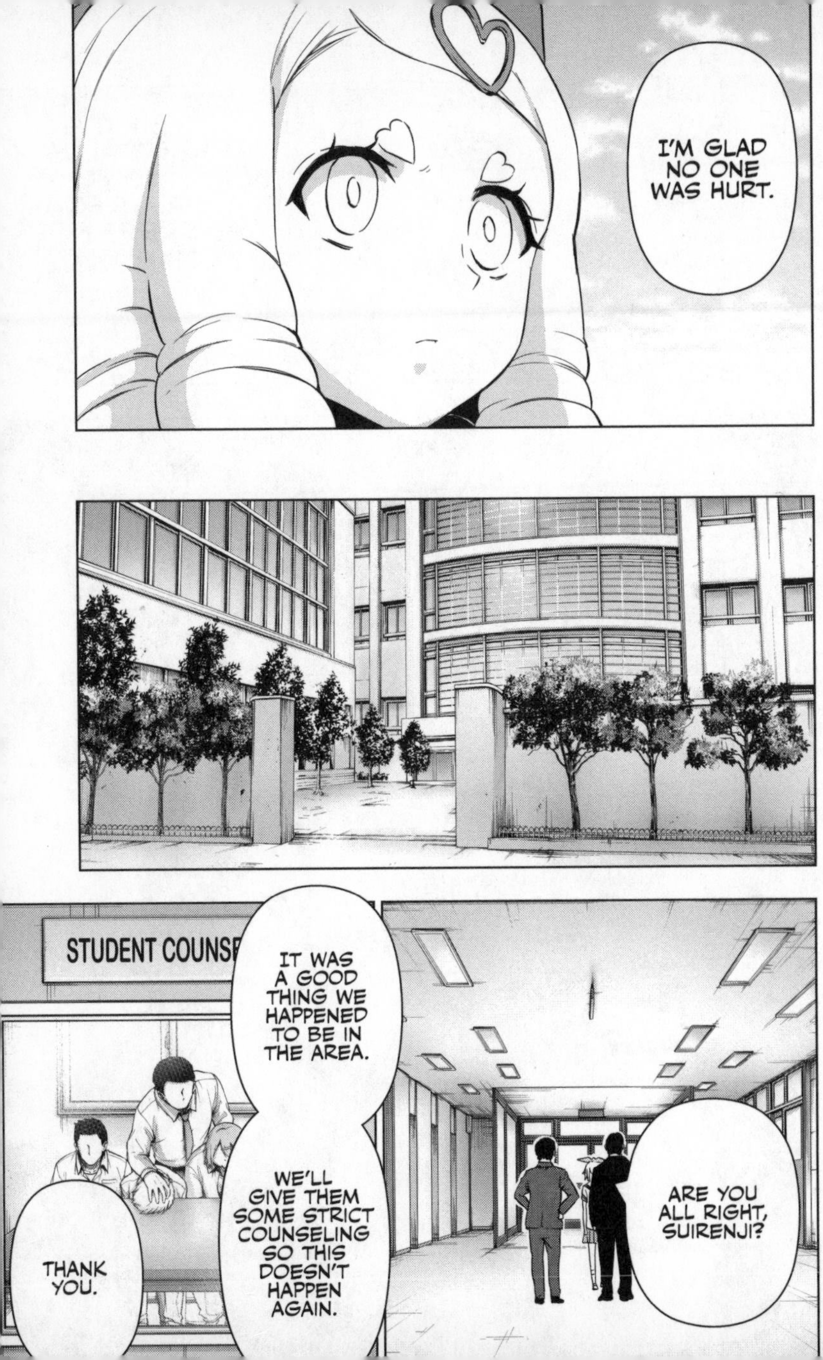
I'M GLAD NO ONE WAS HURT.
ARE YOU ALL RIGHT, SUIRENJI?
IT WAS A GOOD THING WE HAPPENED TO BE IN THE AREA.
WE'LL GIVE THEM SOME STRICT COUNSELING SO THIS DOESN'T HAPPEN AGAIN.
STUDENT COUNSE
THANK YOU.

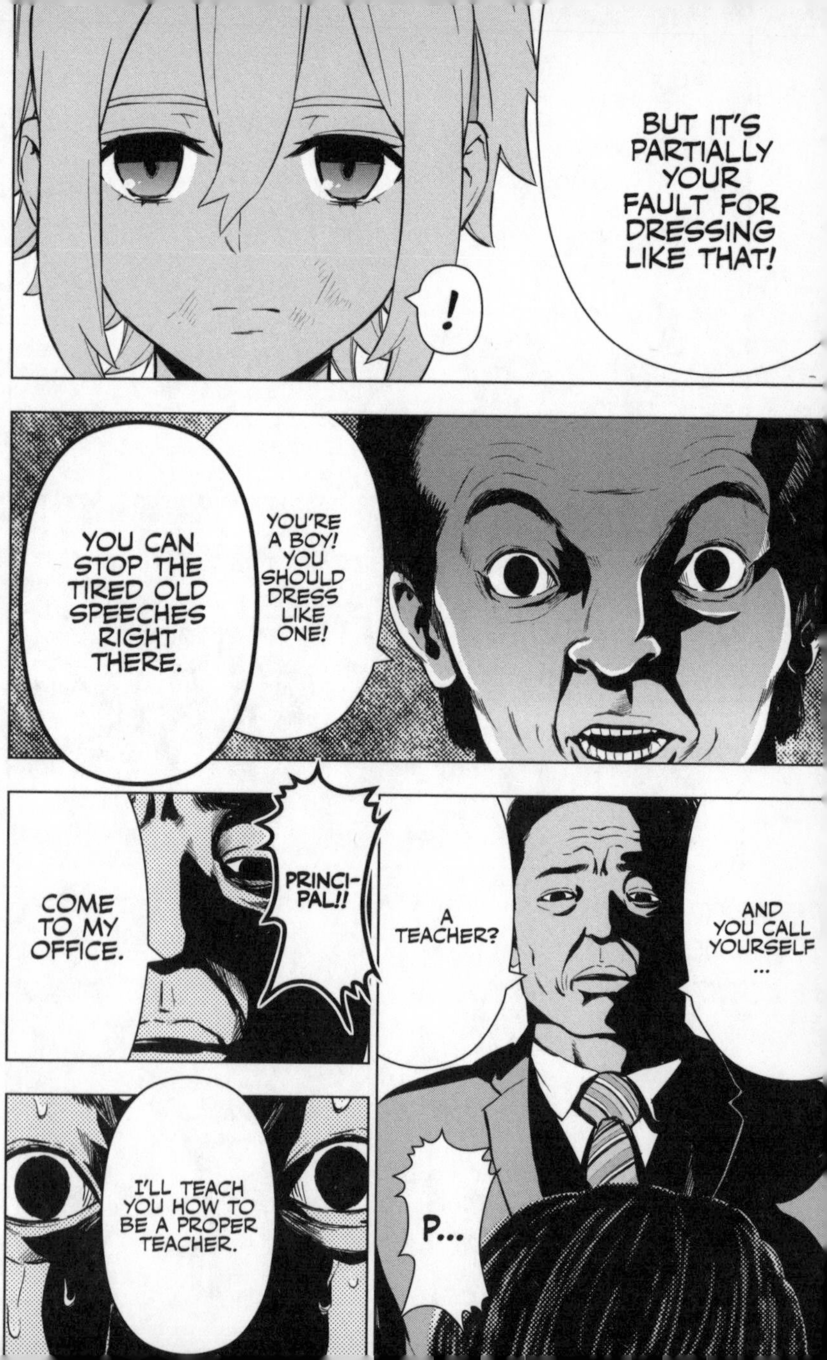
BUT IT'S PARTIALLY YOUR FAULT FOR DRESSING LIKE THAT!
!
YOU'RE A BOY! YOU SHOULD DRESS LIKE ONE!
YOU CAN STOP THE TIRED OLD SPEECHES RIGHT THERE.
AND YOU CALL YOURSELF ...
A TEACHER?
P...
PRINCI-PAL!!
COME TO MY OFFICE.
I'LL TEACH YOU HOW TO BE A PROPER TEACHER.

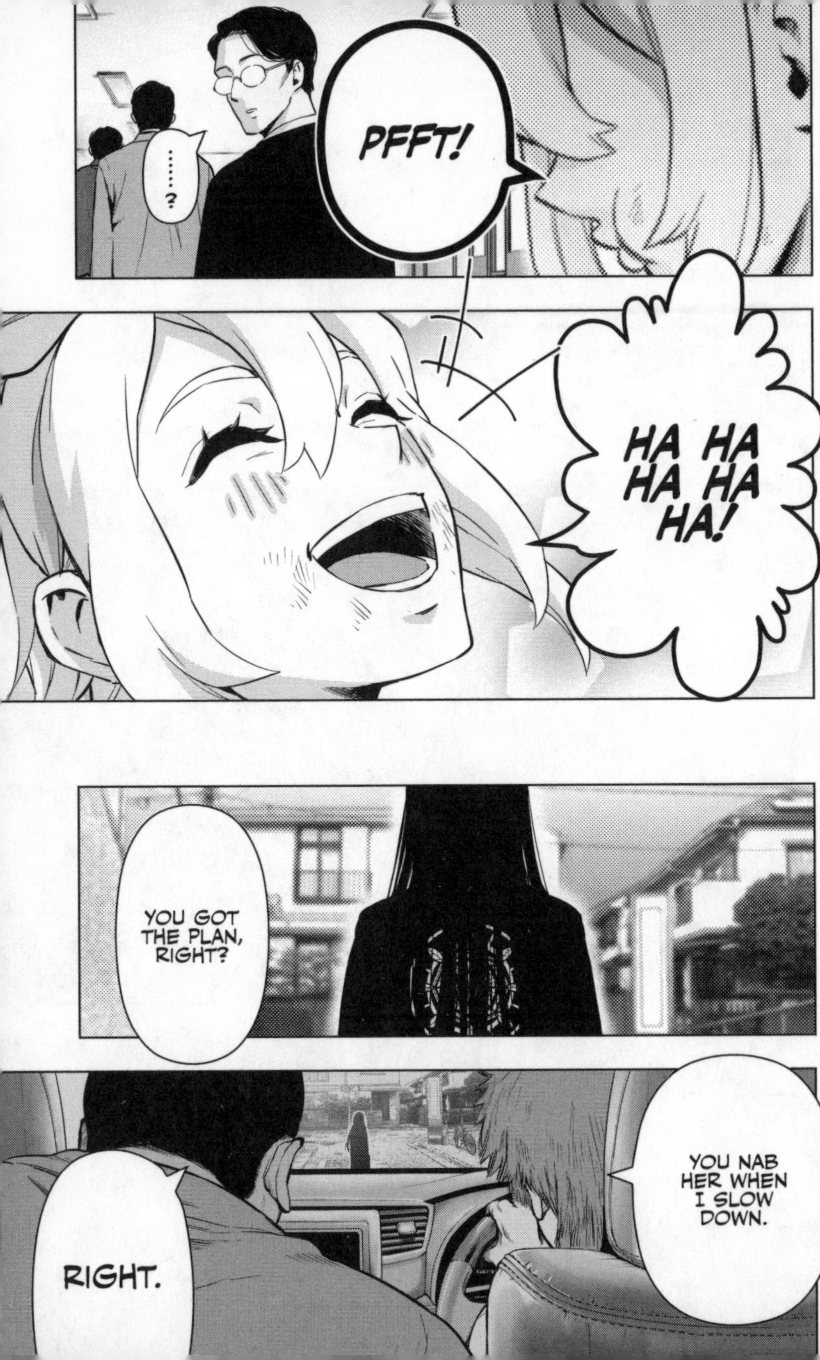
PFFT!
......?
HA HA HA HA HA!
YOU GOT THE PLAN, RIGHT?
YOU NAB HER WHEN I SLOW DOWN.
RIGHT.

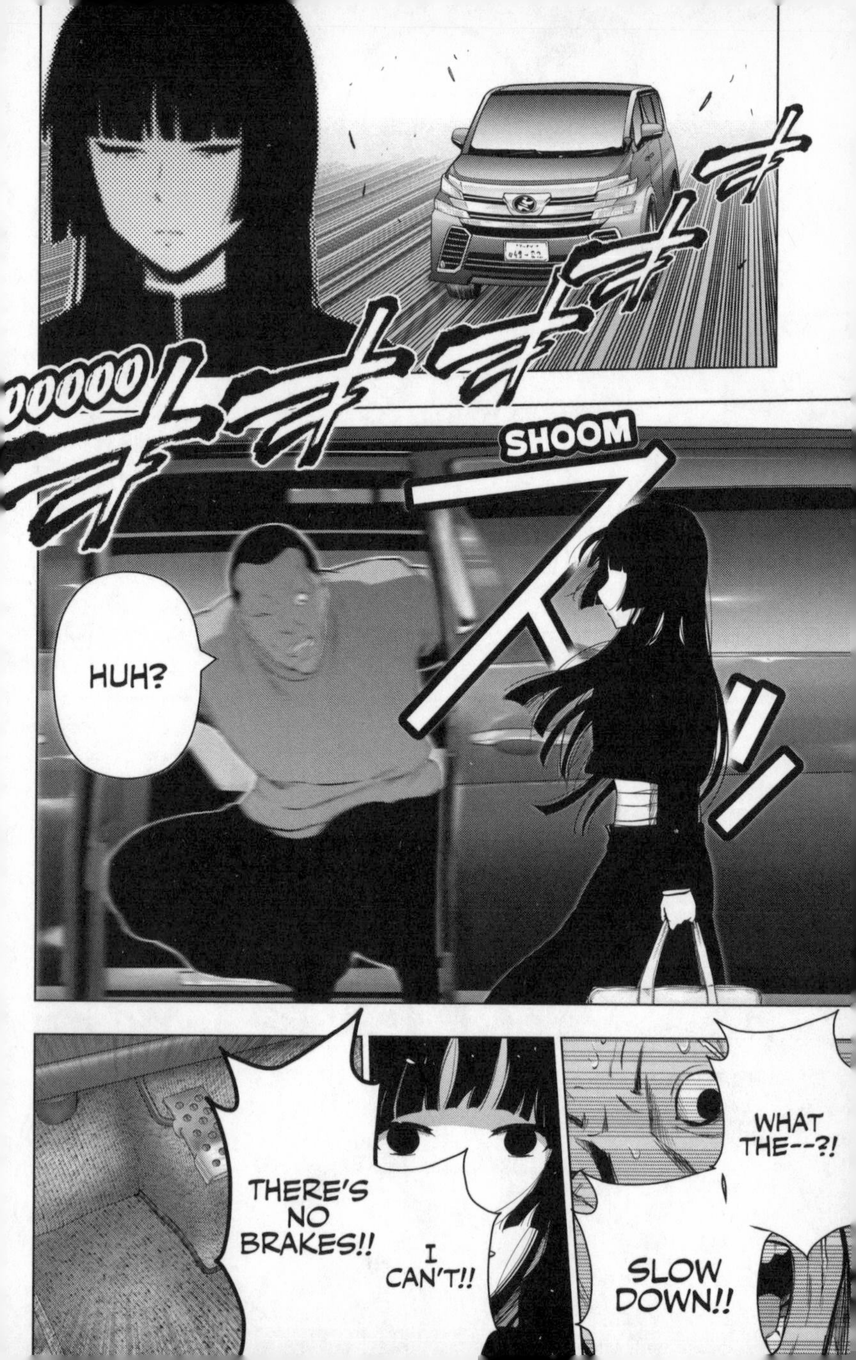
OOOOO
SHOOM
HUH?
WHAT THE--?!
SLOW DOWN!!
I CAN'T!!
THERE'S NO BRAKES!!

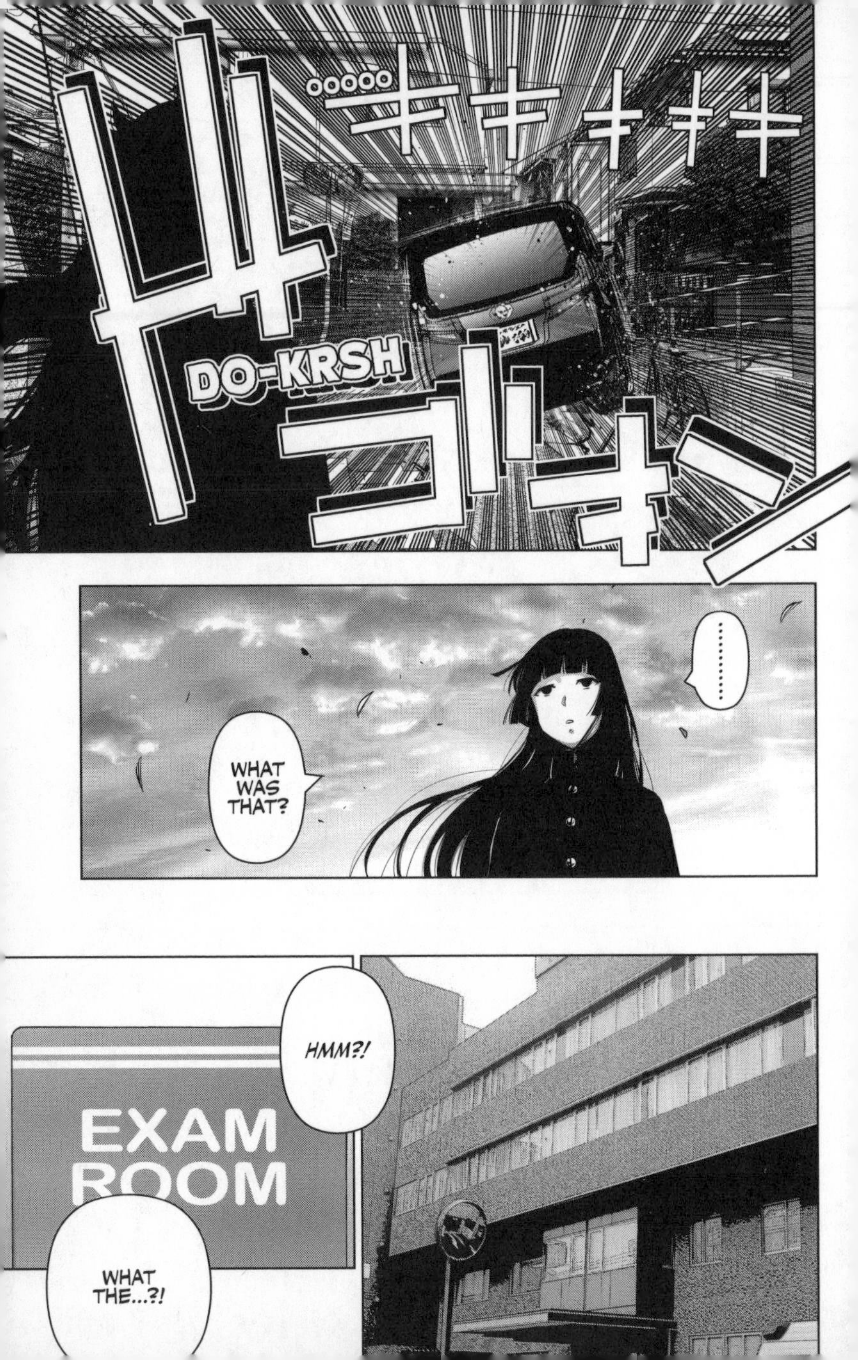
DO-KRSH
……
WHAT WAS THAT?
HMM?!
EXAM ROOM
WHAT THE...?!

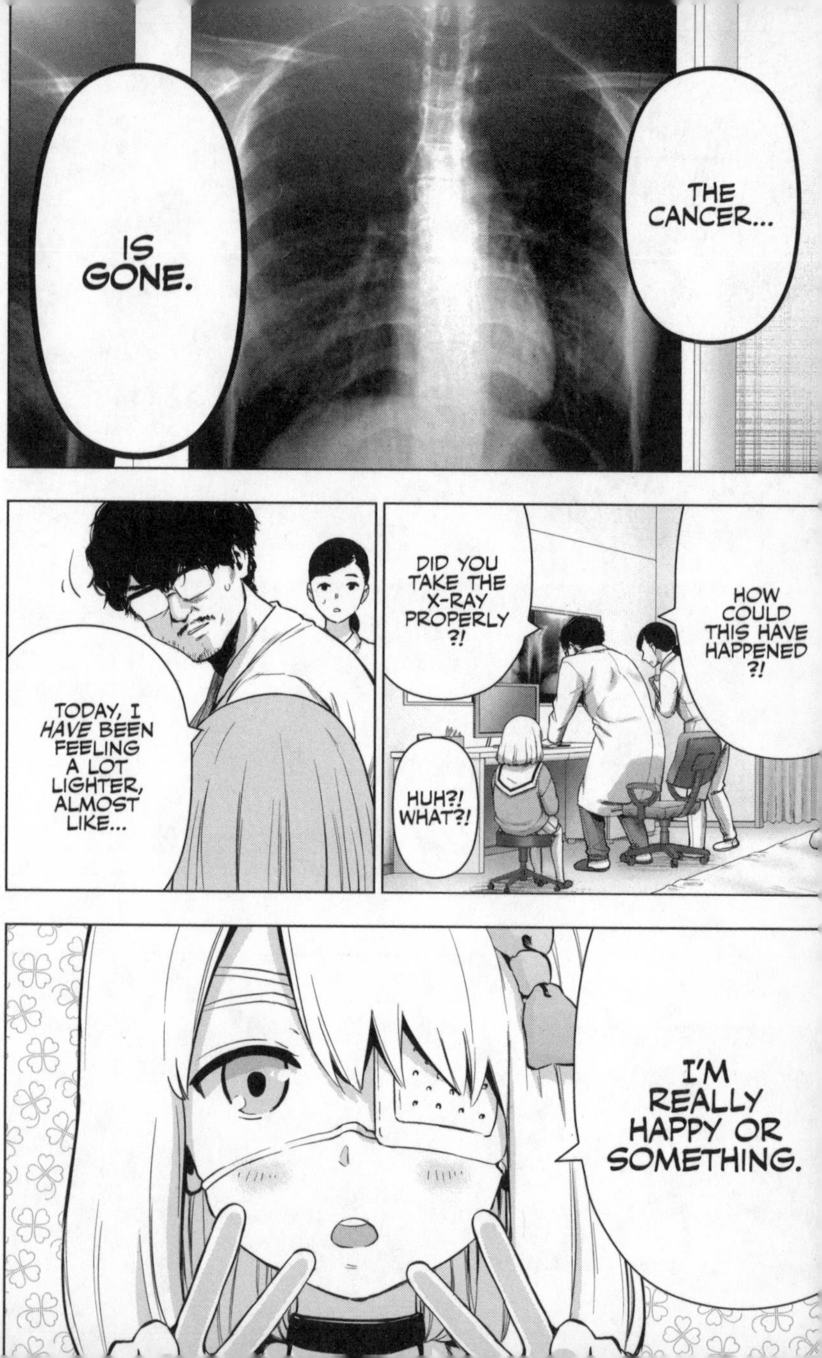
THE CANCER...
IS GONE.
HOW COULD THIS HAVE HAPPENED?!
DID YOU TAKE THE X-RAY PROPERLY?!
HUH?! WHAT?!
TODAY, I *HAVE* BEEN FEELING A LOT LIGHTER, ALMOST LIKE...
I'M REALLY HAPPY OR SOMETHING.

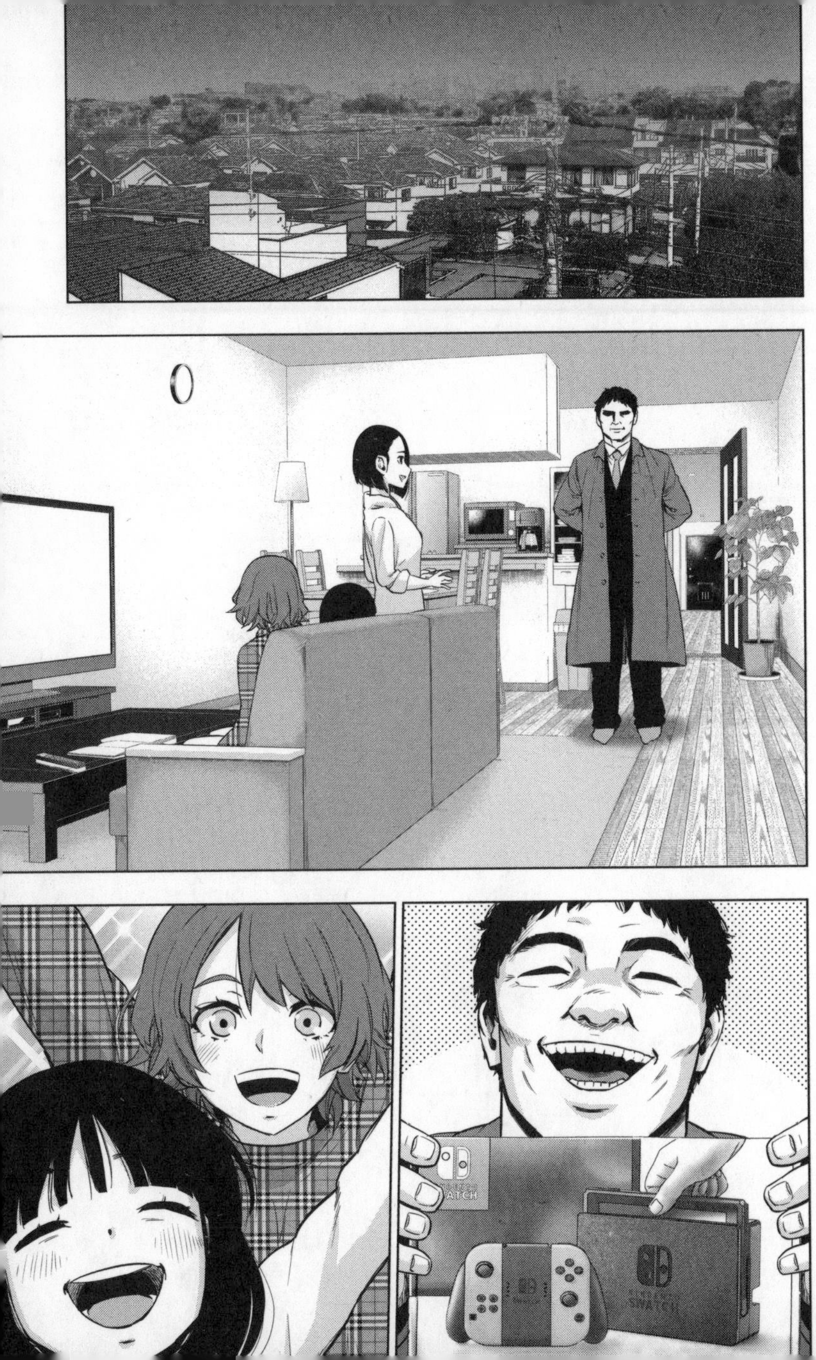

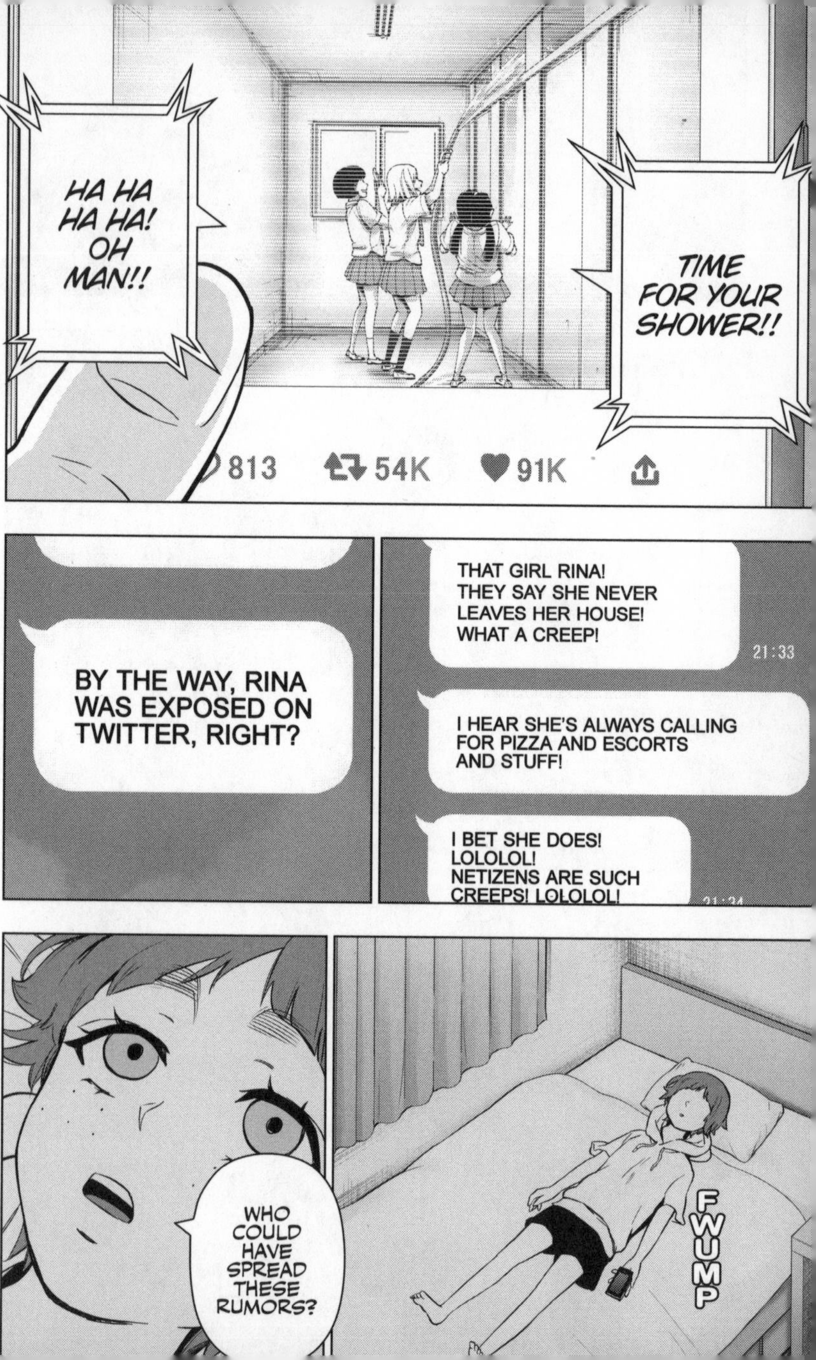
TIME FOR YOUR SHOWER!!
HA HA HA HA! OH MAN!!
813
54K
91K
THAT GIRL RINA! THEY SAY SHE NEVER LEAVES HER HOUSE! WHAT A CREEP!
21:33
I HEAR SHE'S ALWAYS CALLING FOR PIZZA AND ESCORTS AND STUFF!
I BET SHE DOES! LOLOLOL! NETIZENS ARE SUCH CREEPS! LOLOLOL!
BY THE WAY, RINA WAS EXPOSED ON TWITTER, RIGHT?
FWUMP
WHO COULD HAVE SPREAD THESE RUMORS?

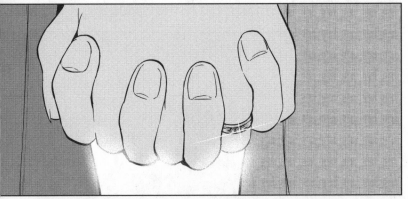

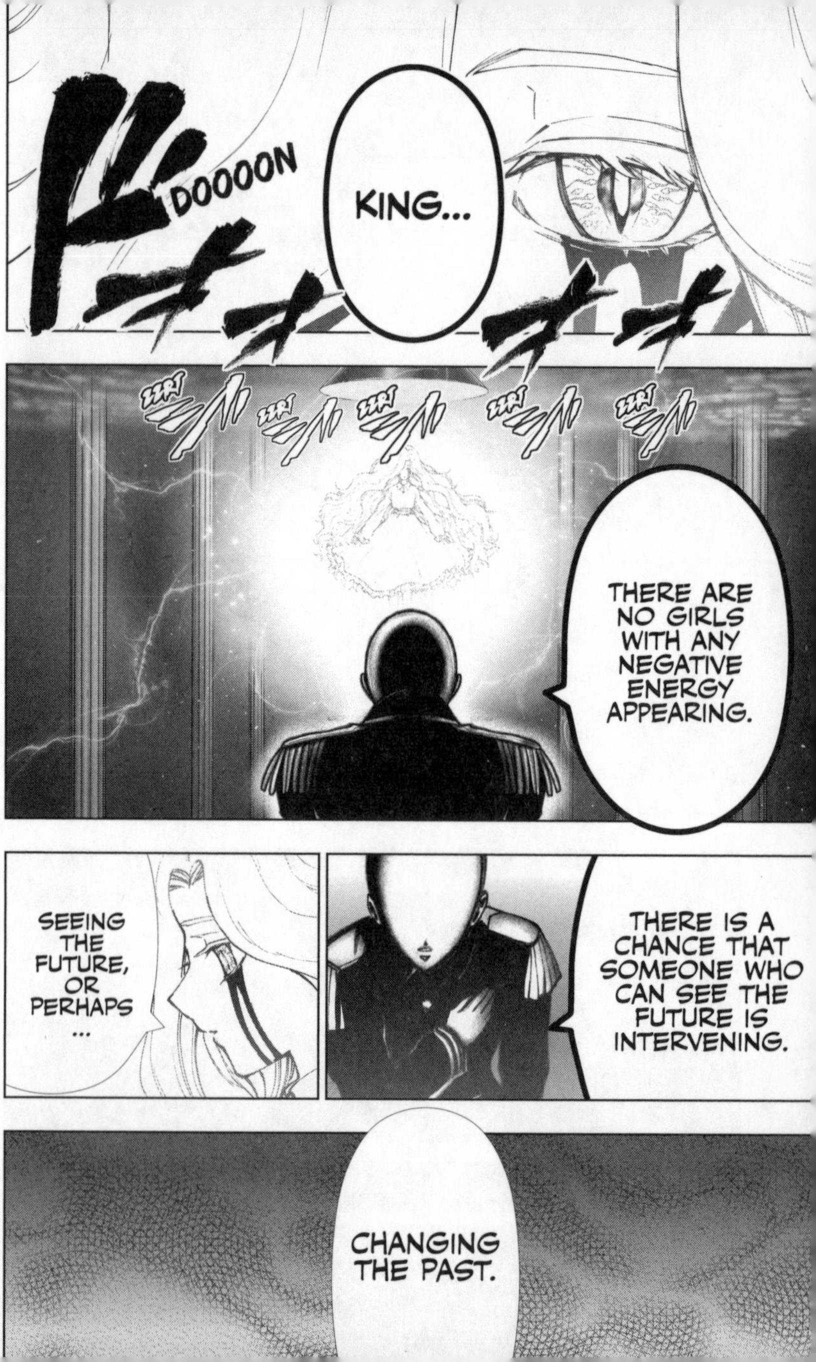

KING...
DOOOON
ZZRT
ZZRT
ZZRT
ZZRT
ZZRT
THERE ARE NO GIRLS WITH ANY NEGATIVE ENERGY APPEARING.
THERE IS A CHANCE THAT SOMEONE WHO CAN SEE THE FUTURE IS INTERVENING.
SEEING THE FUTURE, OR PERHAPS ...
CHANGING THE PAST.

ENTER.137 "GOODBYE"

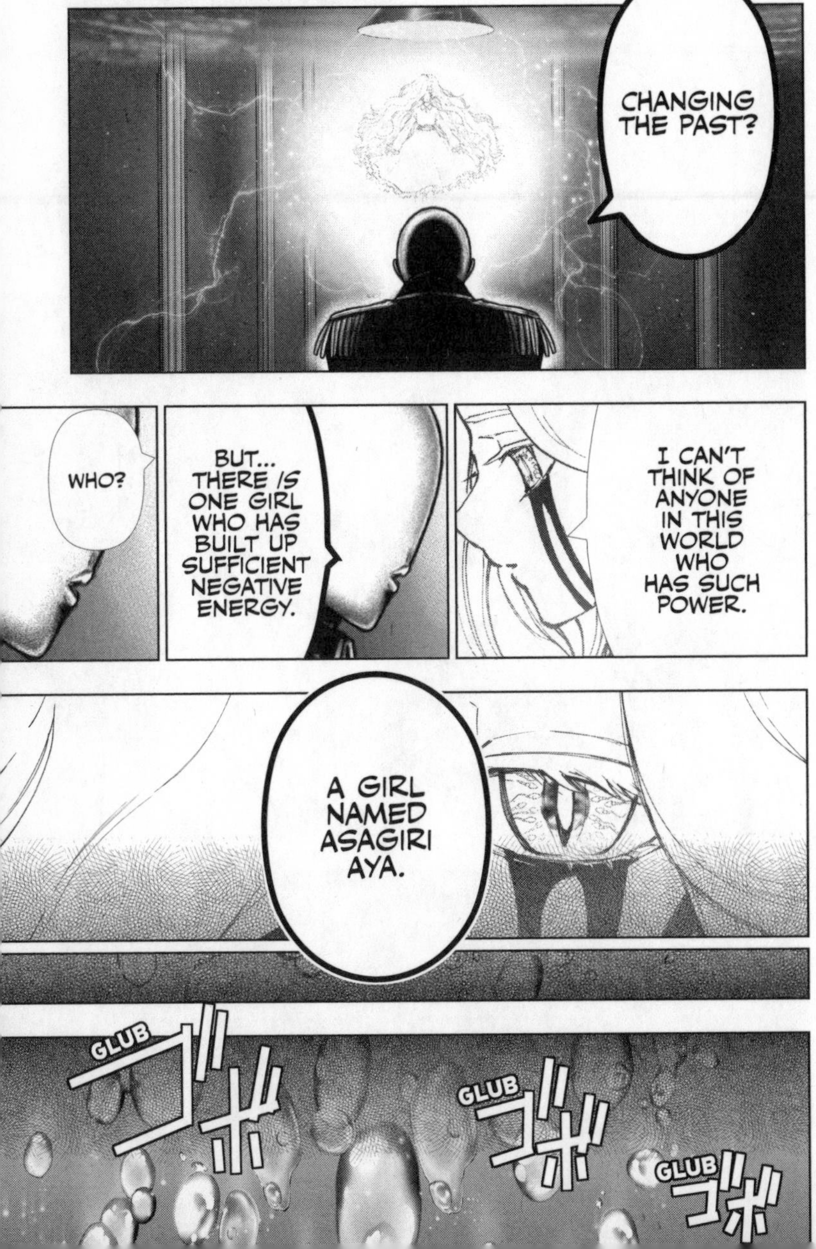
CHANGING THE PAST?
I CAN'T THINK OF ANYONE IN THIS WORLD WHO HAS SUCH POWER.
BUT... THERE *IS* ONE GIRL WHO HAS BUILT UP SUFFICIENT NEGATIVE ENERGY.
WHO?
A GIRL NAMED ASAGIRI AYA.
GLUB ゴボ
GLUB ゴボ
GLUB ゴボ

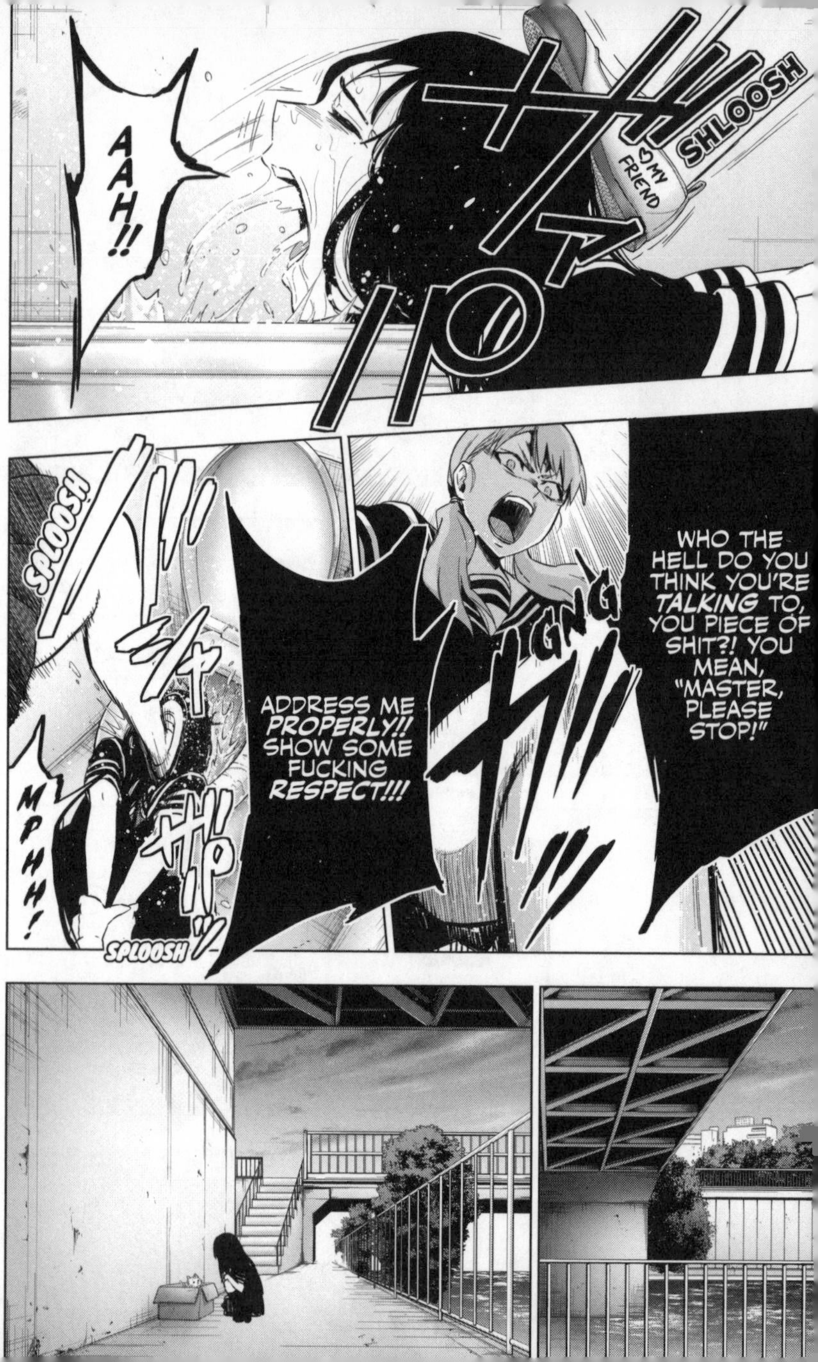
AAH!!
SHLOOSH
♡MY FRIEND
WHO THE HELL DO YOU THINK YOU'RE *TALKING* TO, YOU PIECE OF SHIT?! YOU MEAN, "MASTER, PLEASE STOP!"
IGNG
ADDRESS ME *PROPERLY*!! SHOW SOME FUCKING *RESPECT*!!!
SPLOOSH
MPHH!
SPLOOSH

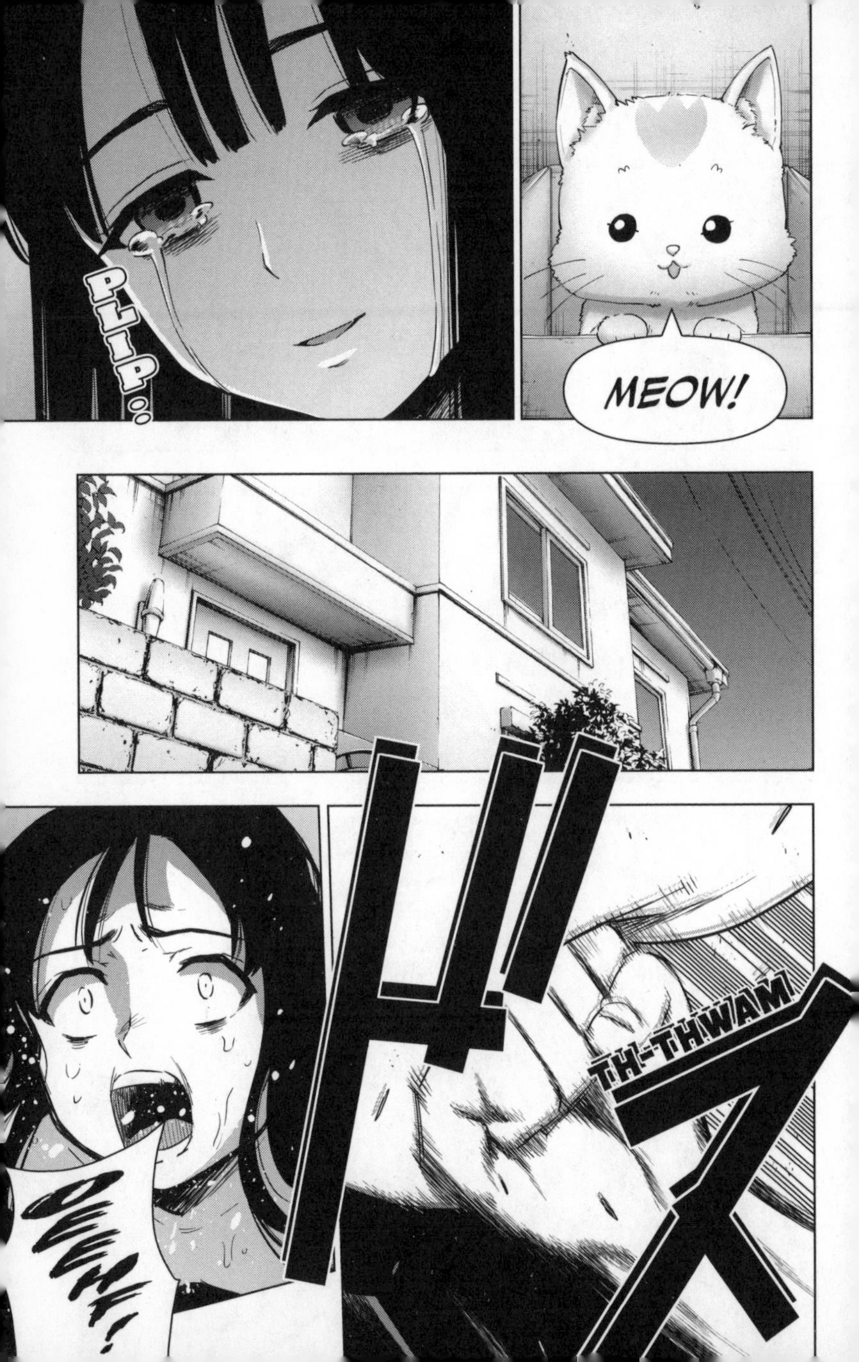
MEOW!
PLIP
TH-THWAM

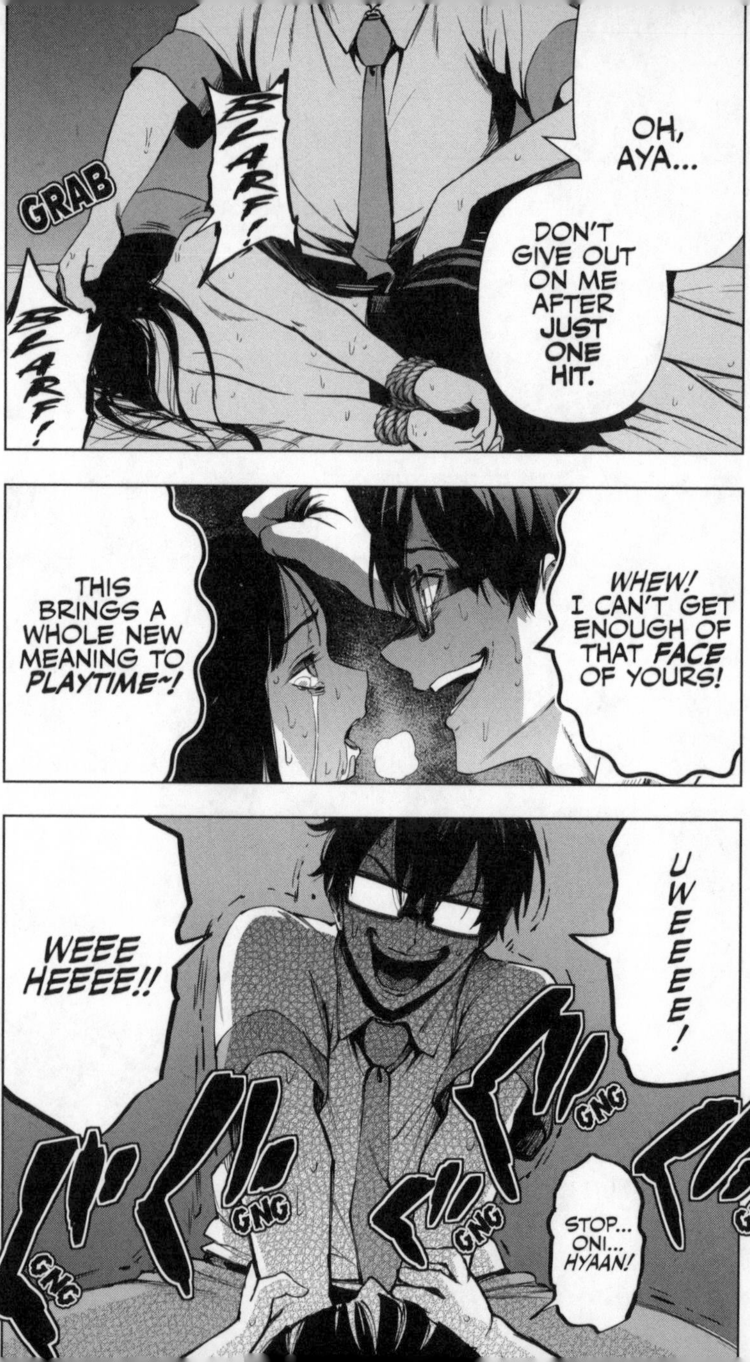
OH, AYA...
DON'T GIVE OUT ON ME AFTER JUST ONE HIT.
BLARF!
BLARF!
GRAB
WHEW! I CAN'T GET ENOUGH OF THAT FACE OF YOURS!
THIS BRINGS A WHOLE NEW MEANING TO PLAYTIME~!
UWEEEEE!
WEEE HEEEEE!!
GNG
STOP... ONI... HYAAN!
GNG
GNG
GNG
GNG
GNG

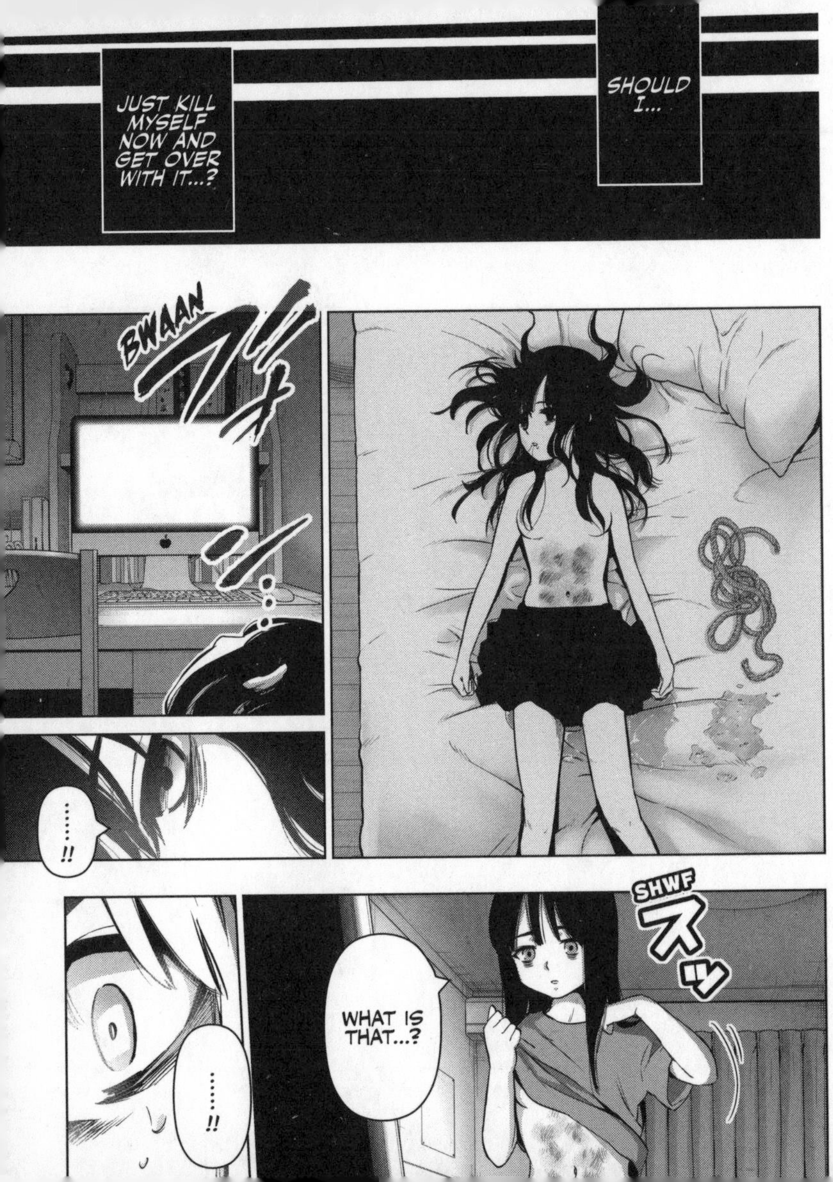
SHOULD I...
JUST KILL MYSELF NOW AND GET OVER WITH IT...?
BWAAN
......!!
SHWF
スッ
WHAT IS THAT...?
......!!

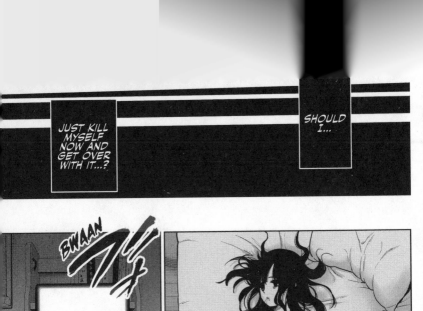

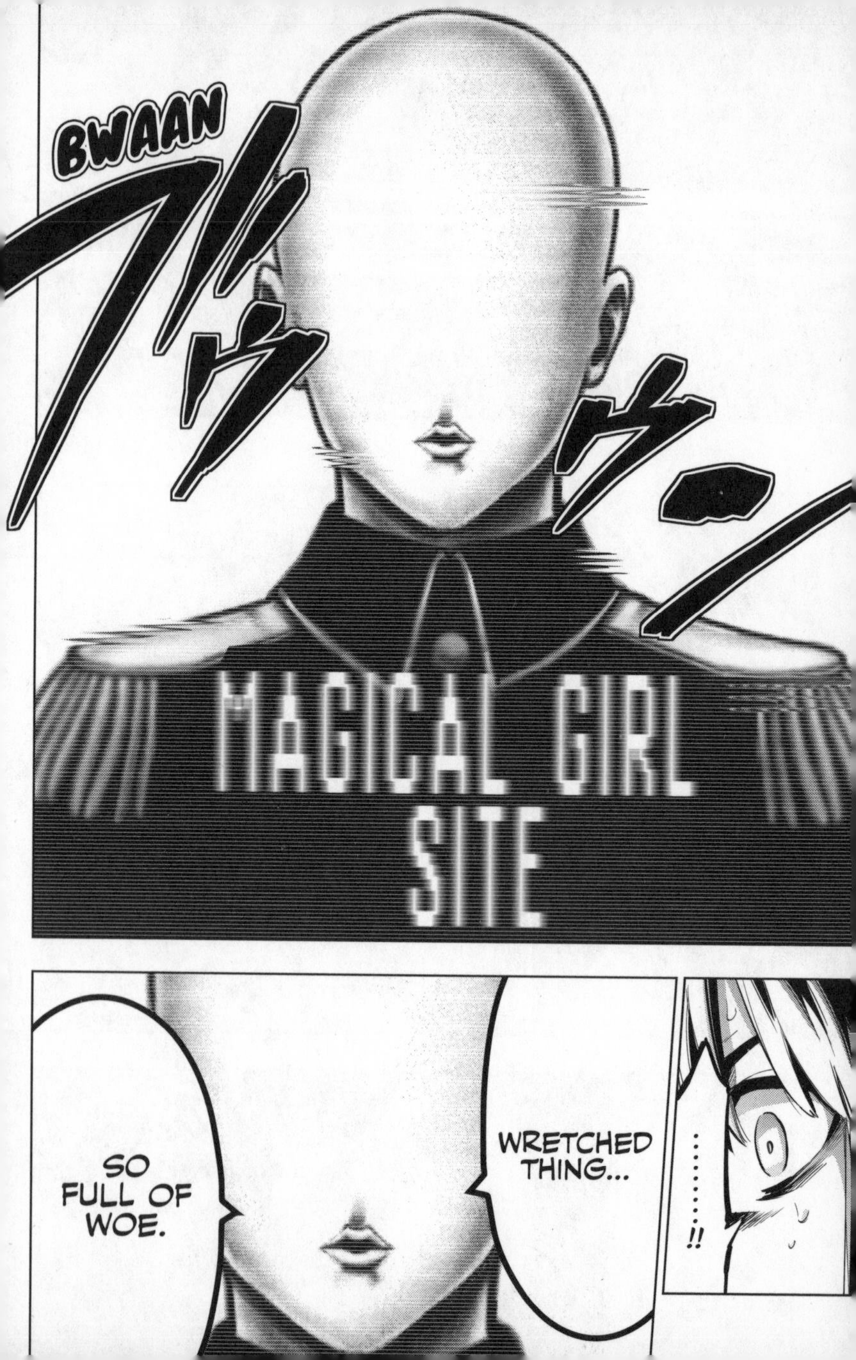
BWAAN
MAGICAL GIRL SITE
.........!!
WRETCHED THING...
SO FULL OF WOE.

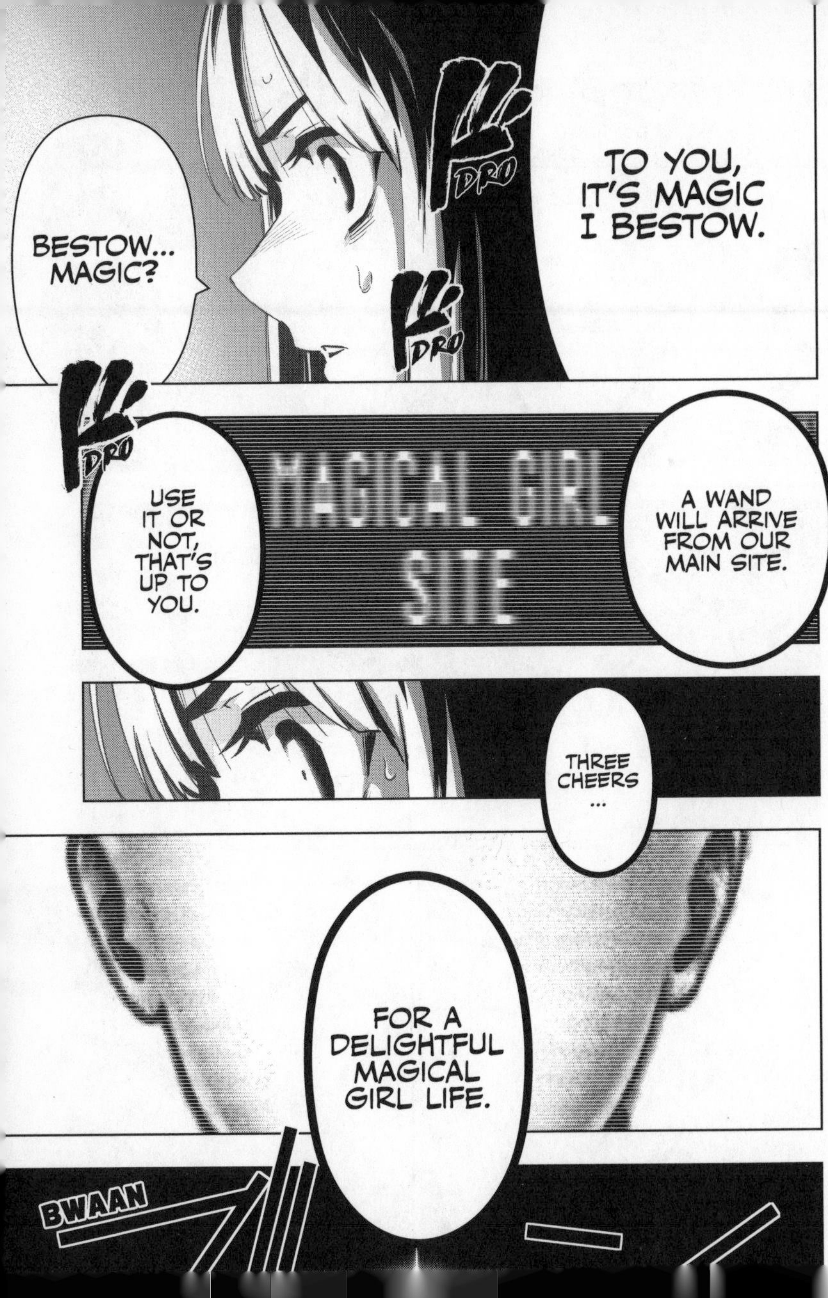
TO YOU, IT'S MAGIC I BESTOW.
DRO
DRO
BESTOW... MAGIC?
A WAND WILL ARRIVE FROM OUR MAIN SITE.
MAGICAL GIRL SITE
DRO
USE IT OR NOT, THAT'S UP TO YOU.
THREE CHEERS ...
FOR A DELIGHTFUL MAGICAL GIRL LIFE.
BWAAN

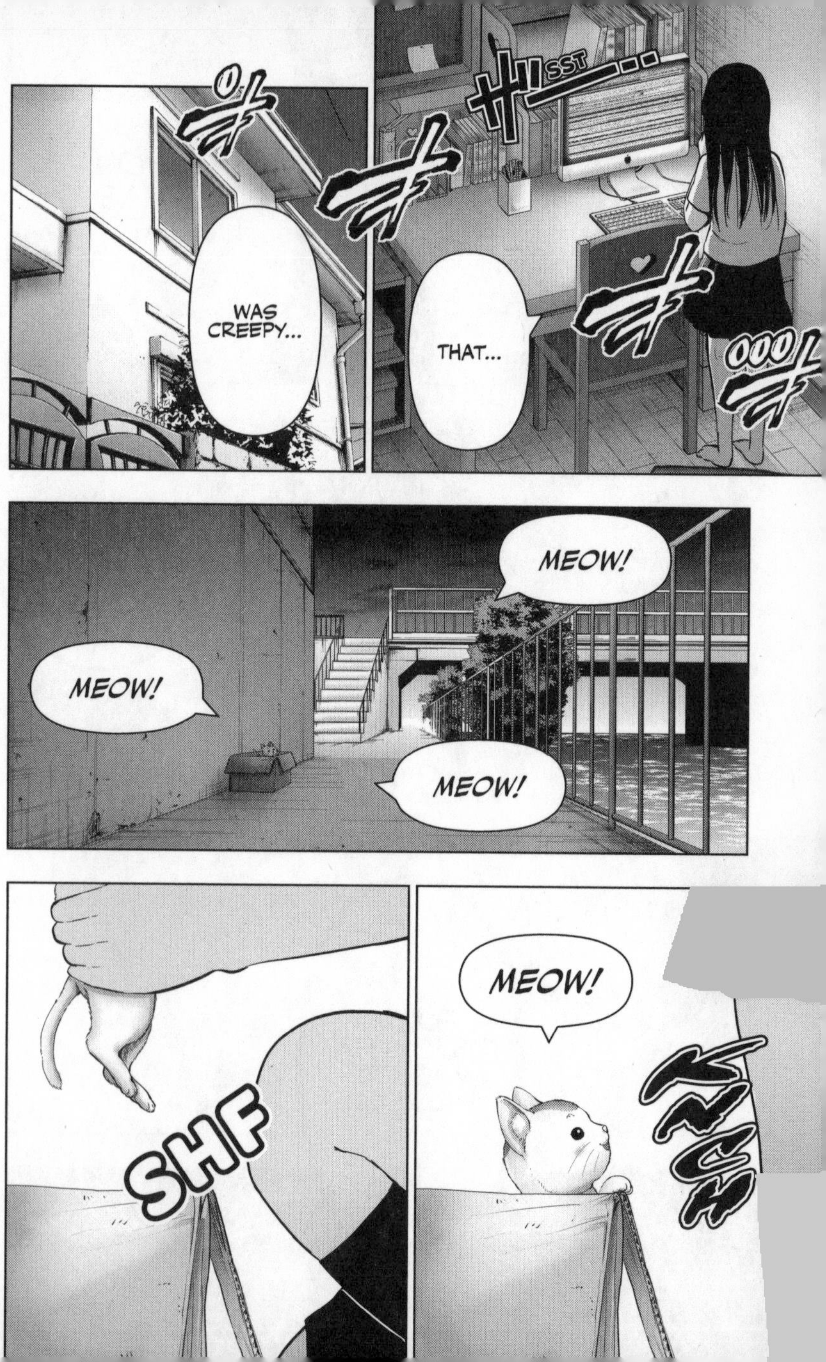
SST
THAT...
OOO
WAS CREEPY...
MEOW!
MEOW!
MEOW!
MEOW!
KNCH
SHF

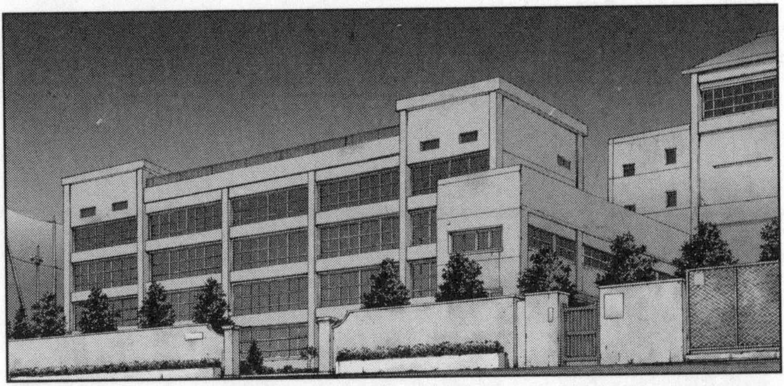

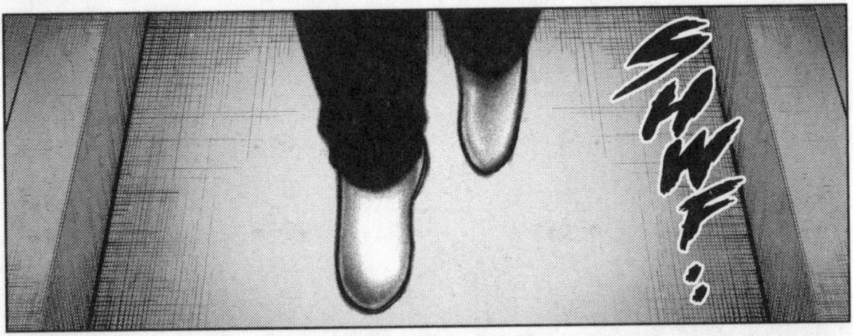
SHWF..

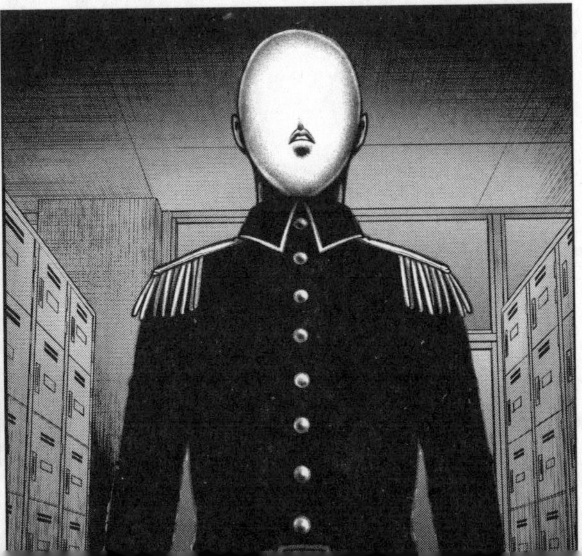

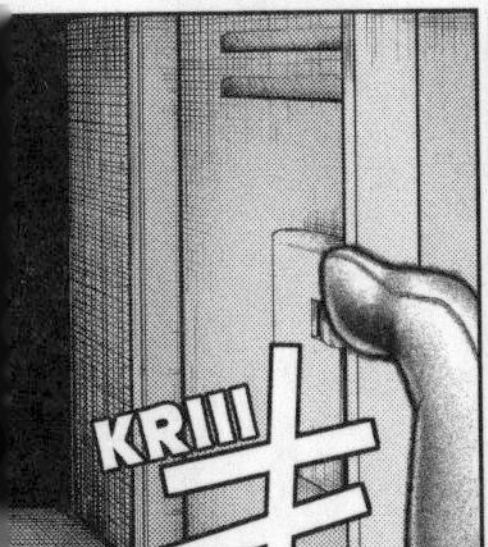
KRIII
キイイイ

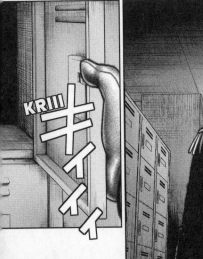

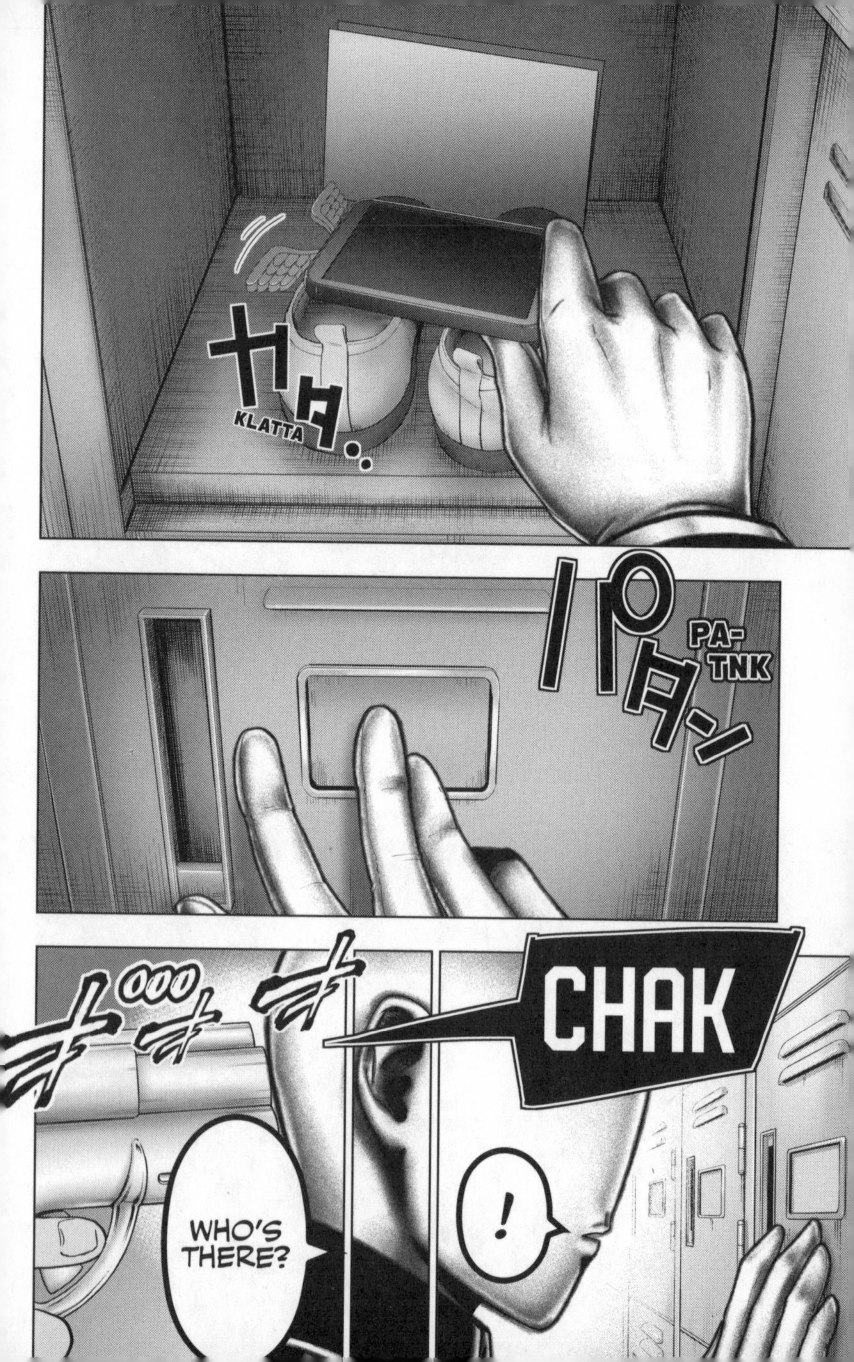
KLATTA
PA-TNK
CHAK
!
WHO'S THERE?

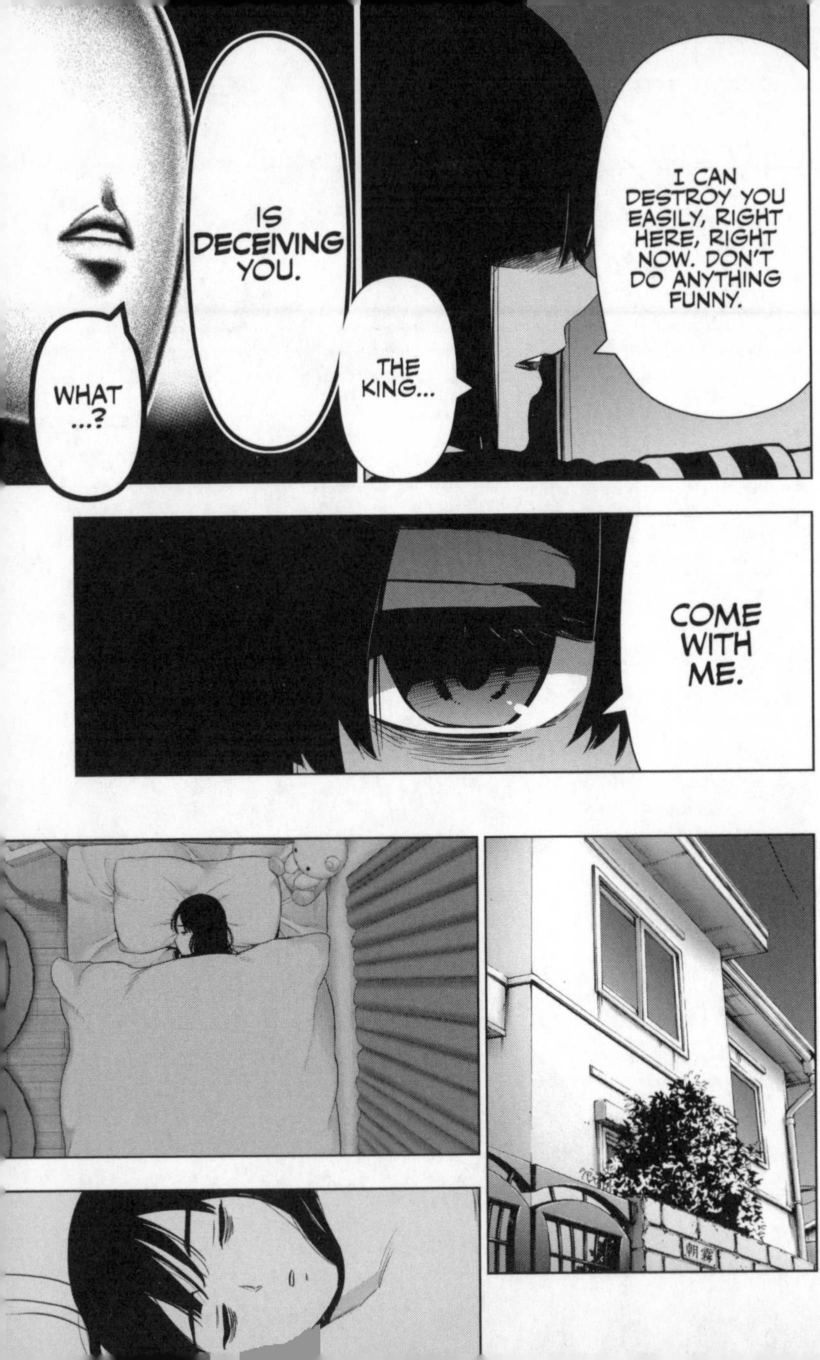
I CAN DESTROY YOU EASILY, RIGHT HERE, RIGHT NOW. DON'T DO ANYTHING FUNNY.
THE KING...
IS DECEIVING YOU.
WHAT ...?
COME WITH ME.
朝霧

FWF

SHF...

HM...?

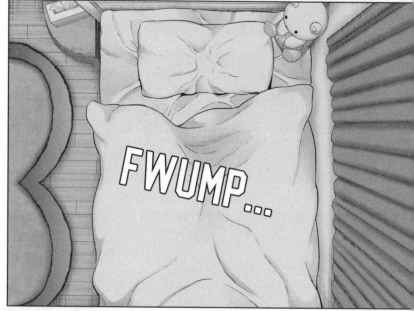

FWUMP...

BWOOF

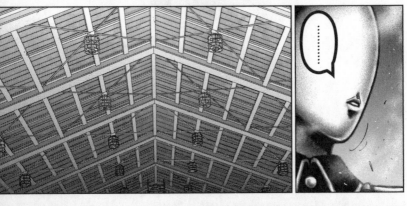

ASAGIRI AYA.

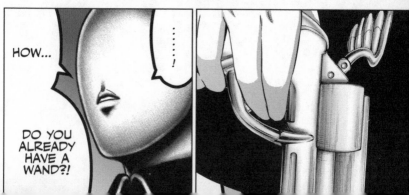

HOW...

......!

DO YOU ALREADY HAVE A WAND?!

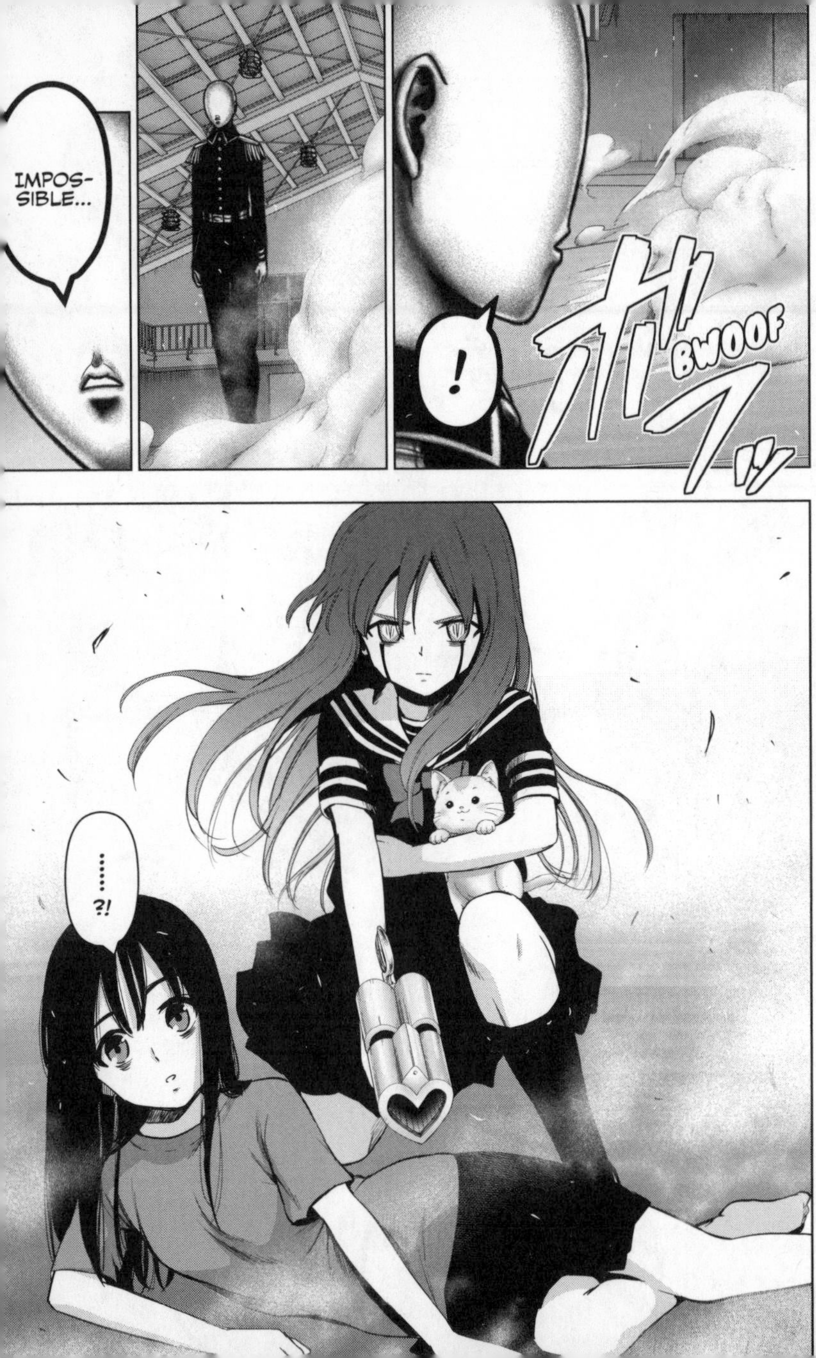
!
BWOOF
IMPOS-SIBLE...
......?!

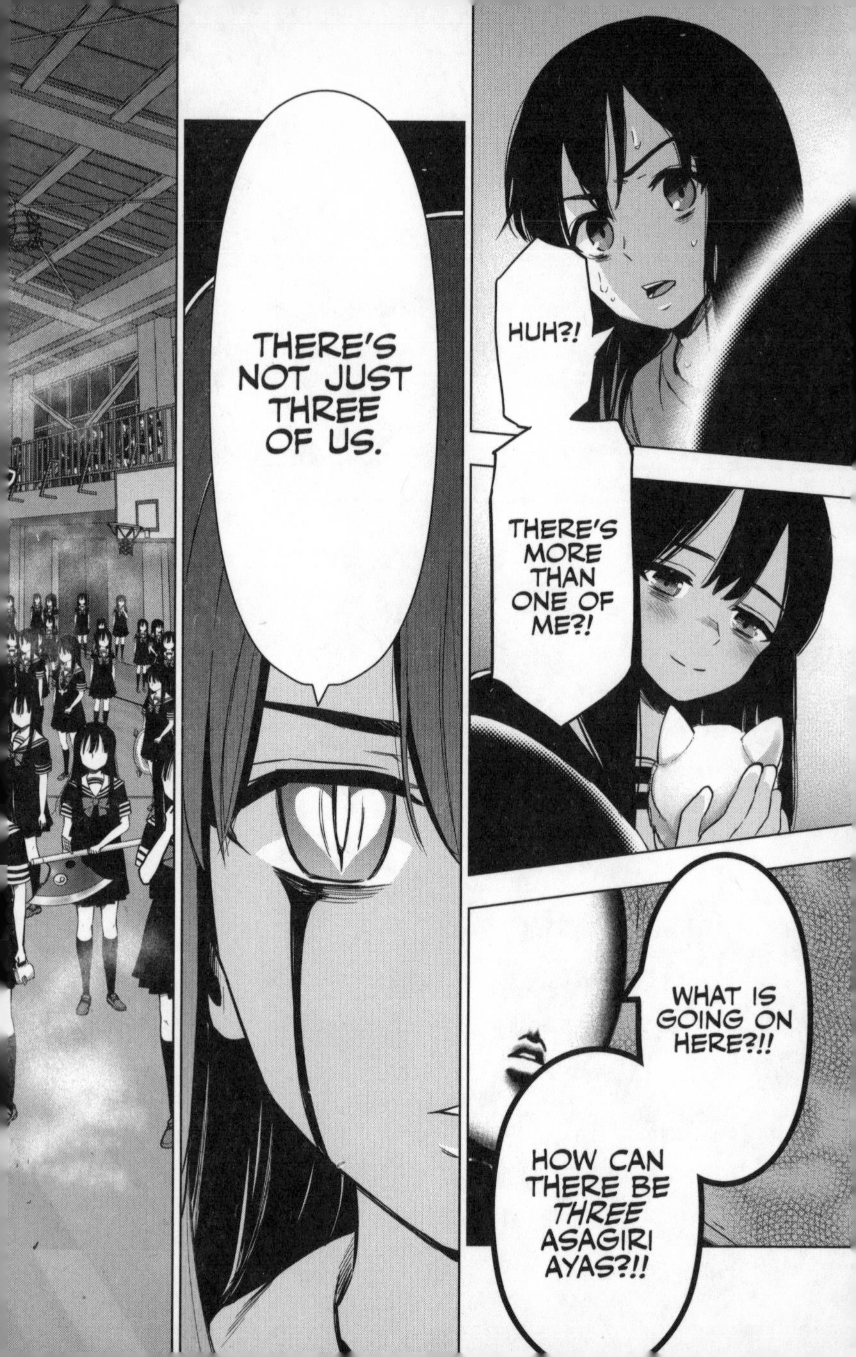
HUH?!
THERE'S MORE THAN ONE OF ME?!
WHAT IS GOING ON HERE?!!
HOW CAN THERE BE *THREE* ASAGIRI AYAS?!!
THERE'S NOT JUST THREE OF US.

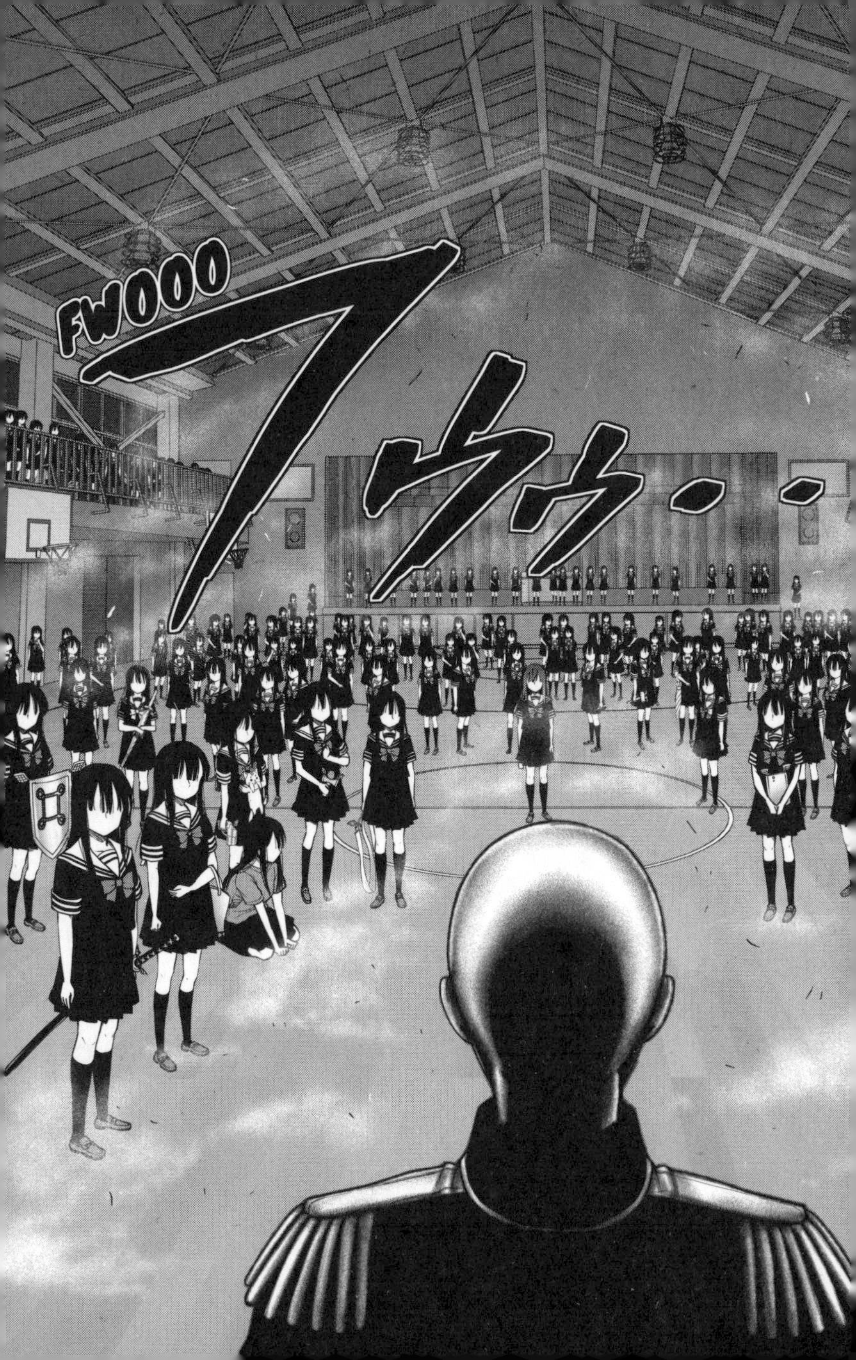
FWOOO
フウウ・・

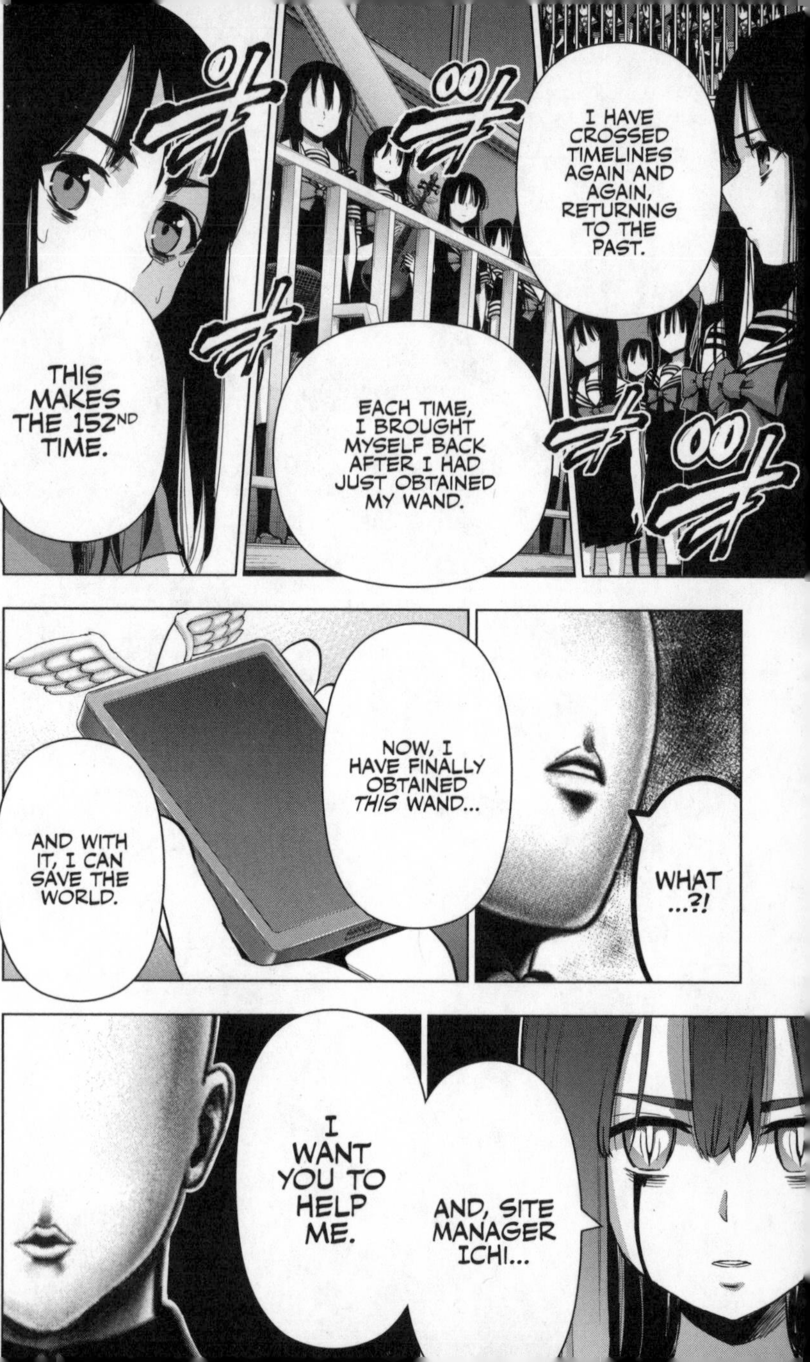
I HAVE CROSSED TIMELINES AGAIN AND AGAIN, RETURNING TO THE PAST.
EACH TIME, I BROUGHT MYSELF BACK AFTER I HAD JUST OBTAINED MY WAND.
THIS MAKES THE 152ND TIME.
WHAT ...?!
NOW, I HAVE FINALLY OBTAINED *THIS* WAND...
AND WITH IT, I CAN SAVE THE WORLD.
AND, SITE MANAGER ICHI...
I WANT YOU TO HELP ME.

ENTER.138 HAPPINESS

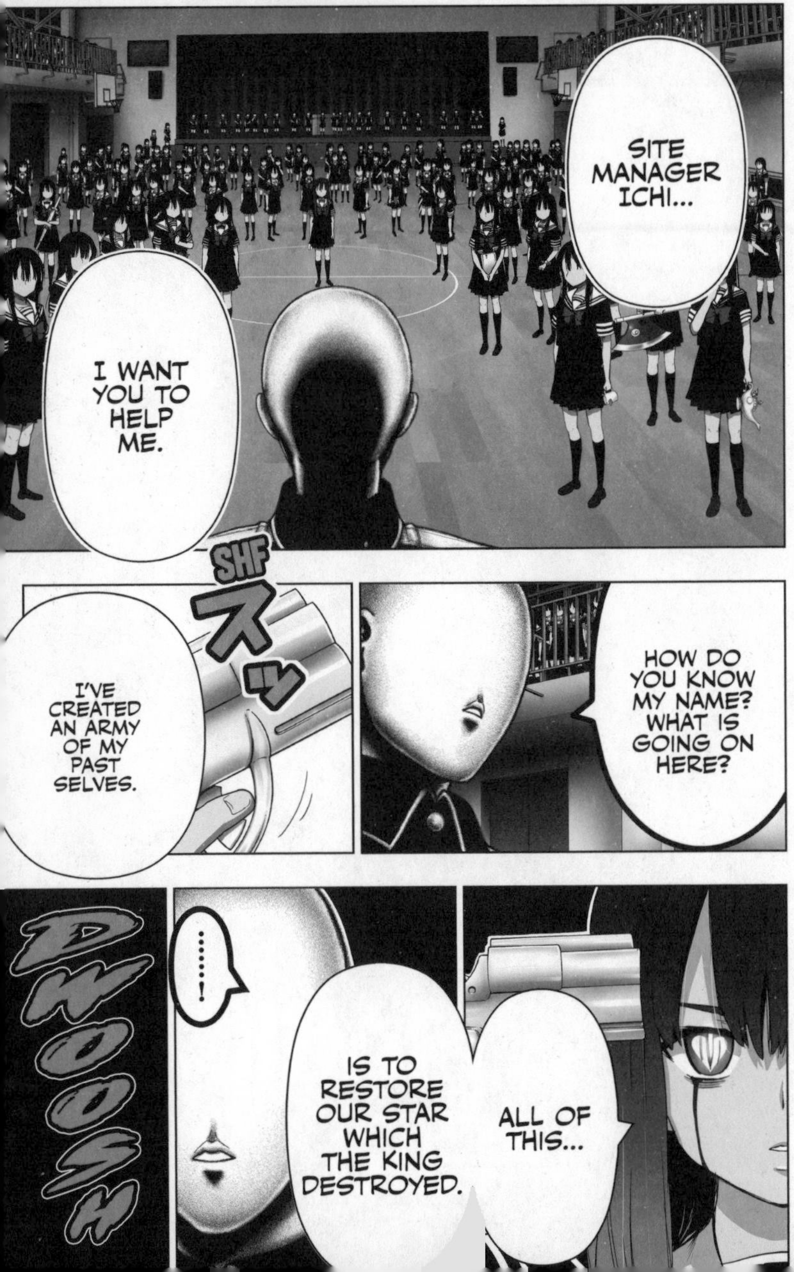
SITE MANAGER ICHI...
I WANT YOU TO HELP ME.
HOW DO YOU KNOW MY NAME? WHAT IS GOING ON HERE?
SHF
I'VE CREATED AN ARMY OF MY PAST SELVES.
ALL OF THIS...
IS TO RESTORE OUR STAR WHICH THE KING DESTROYED.
......!
DWOOSH

MAGICAL
GIRL SITE

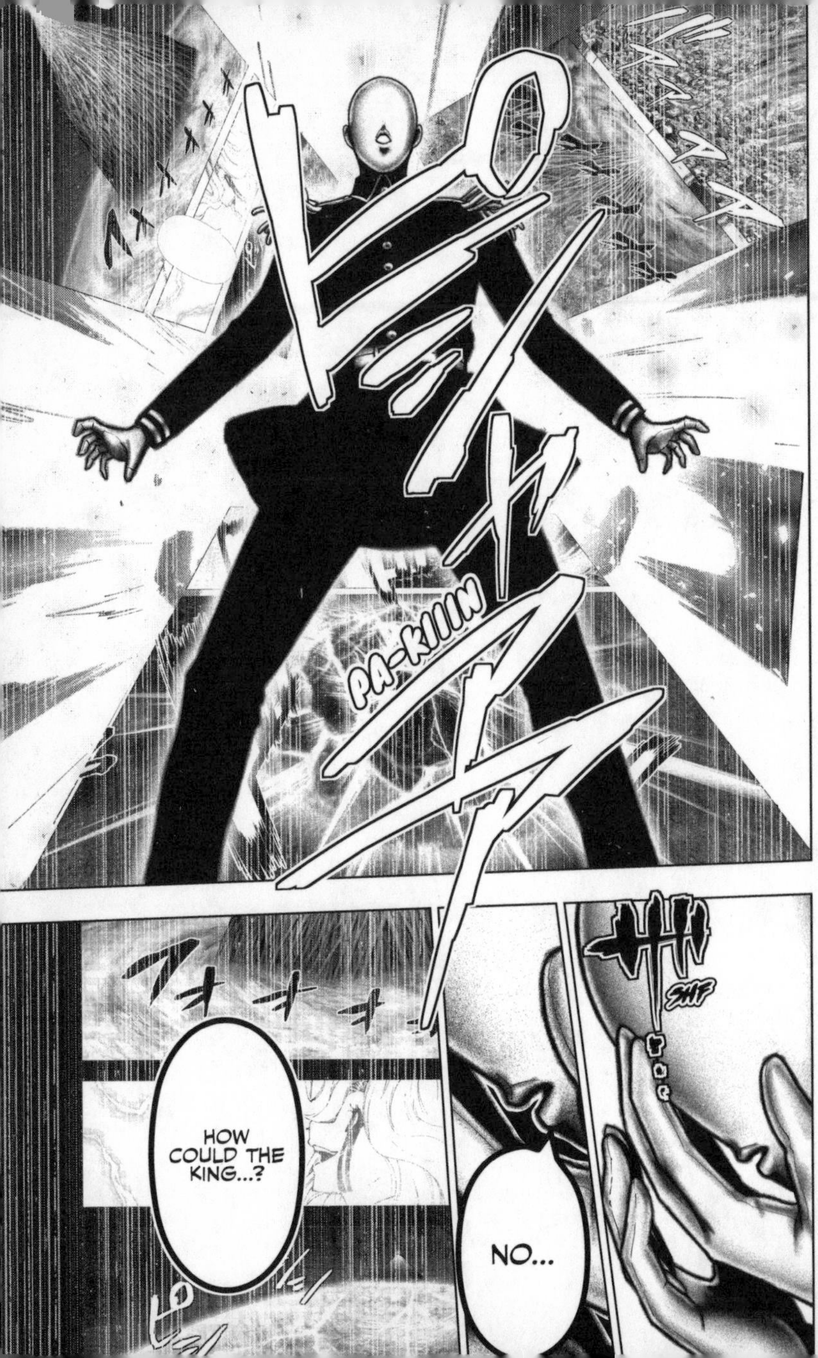
PA-KIIIN
SHF
NO...
HOW COULD THE KING...?

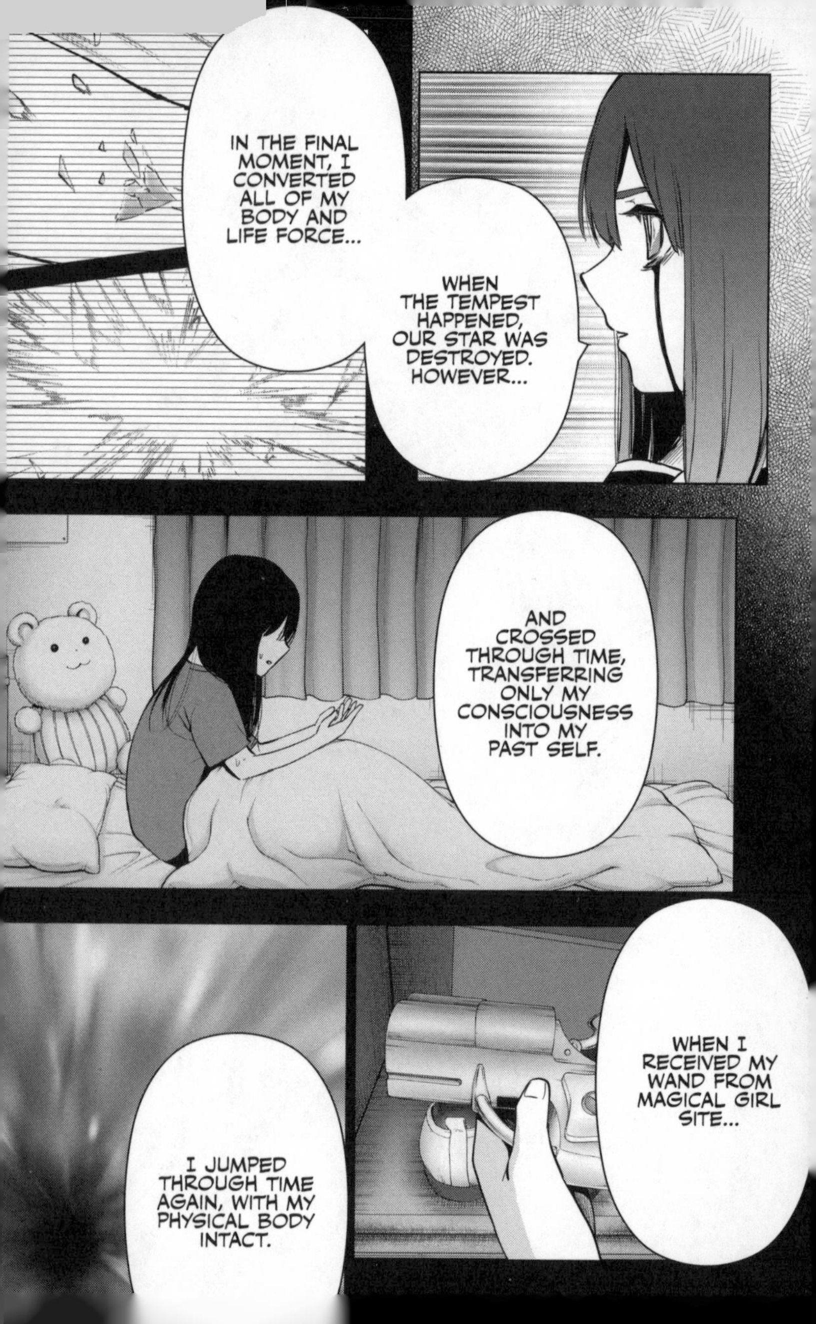
WHEN THE TEMPEST HAPPENED, OUR STAR WAS DESTROYED. HOWEVER...
IN THE FINAL MOMENT, I CONVERTED ALL OF MY BODY AND LIFE FORCE...
AND CROSSED THROUGH TIME, TRANSFERRING ONLY MY CONSCIOUSNESS INTO MY PAST SELF.
WHEN I RECEIVED MY WAND FROM MAGICAL GIRL SITE...
I JUMPED THROUGH TIME AGAIN, WITH MY PHYSICAL BODY INTACT.

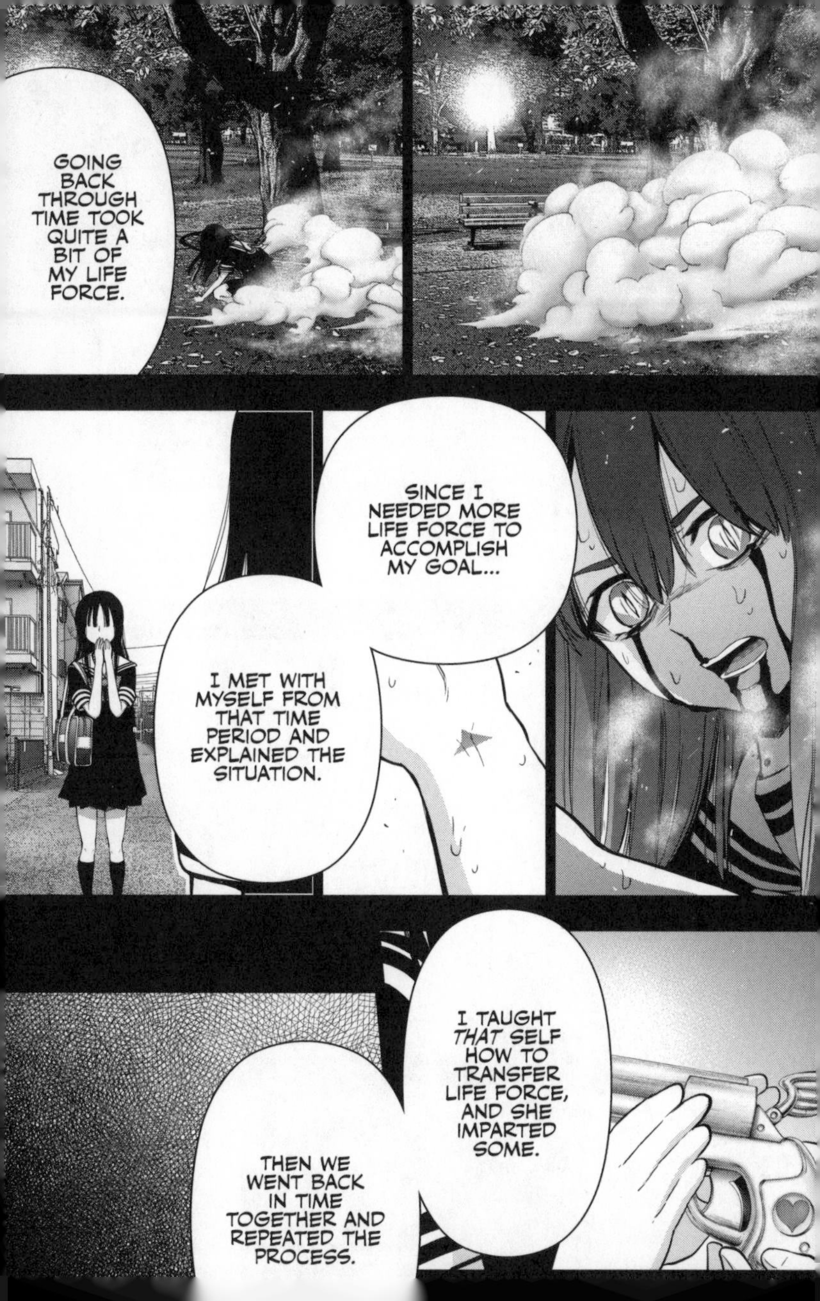
GOING BACK THROUGH TIME TOOK QUITE A BIT OF MY LIFE FORCE.
SINCE I NEEDED MORE LIFE FORCE TO ACCOMPLISH MY GOAL...
I MET WITH MYSELF FROM THAT TIME PERIOD AND EXPLAINED THE SITUATION.
I TAUGHT *THAT* SELF HOW TO TRANSFER LIFE FORCE, AND SHE IMPARTED SOME.
THEN WE WENT BACK IN TIME TOGETHER AND REPEATED THE PROCESS.

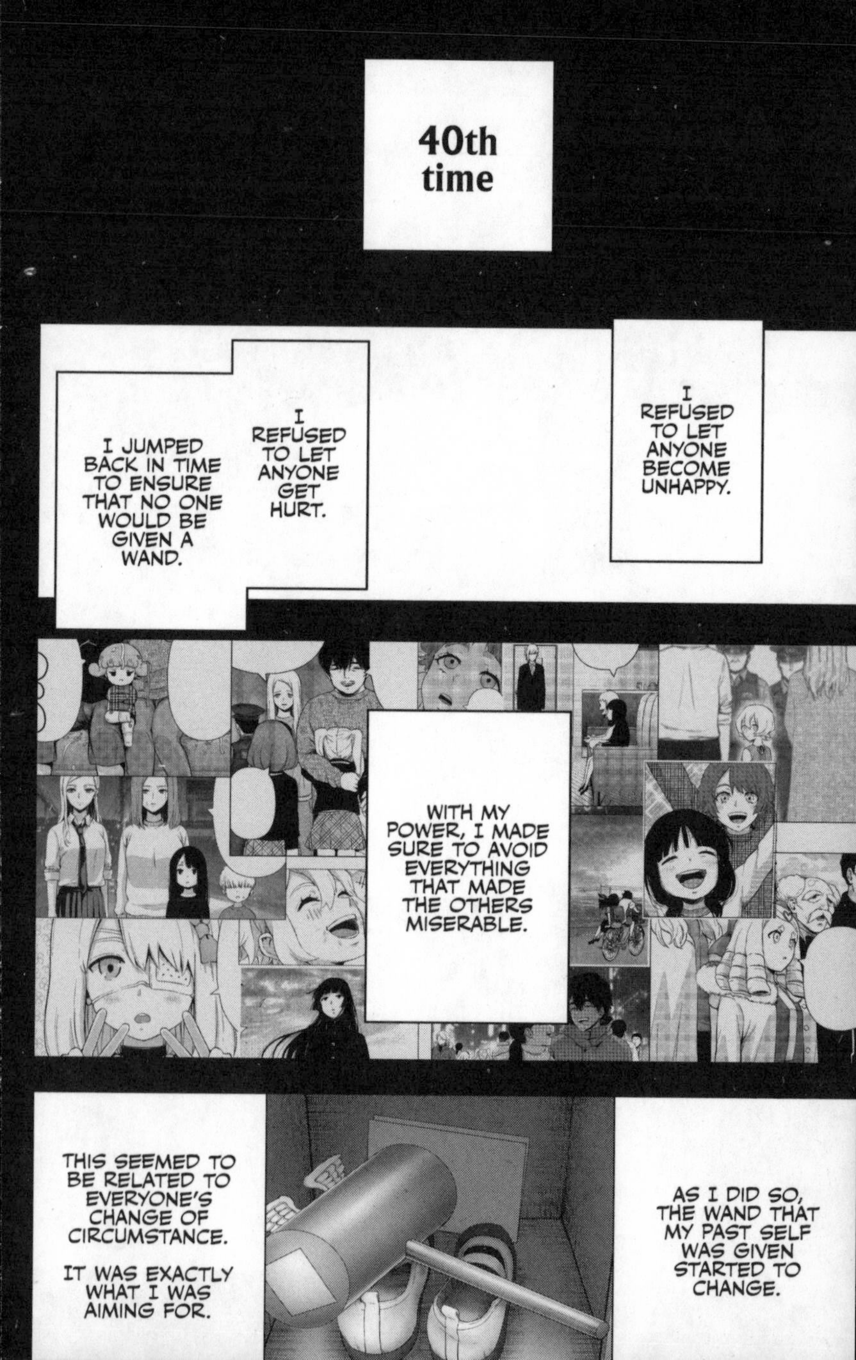
40th time
I REFUSED TO LET ANYONE BECOME UNHAPPY.
I REFUSED TO LET ANYONE GET HURT.
I JUMPED BACK IN TIME TO ENSURE THAT NO ONE WOULD BE GIVEN A WAND.
WITH MY POWER, I MADE SURE TO AVOID EVERYTHING THAT MADE THE OTHERS MISERABLE.
AS I DID SO, THE WAND THAT MY PAST SELF WAS GIVEN STARTED TO CHANGE.
THIS SEEMED TO BE RELATED TO EVERYONE'S CHANGE OF CIRCUMSTANCE.
IT WAS EXACTLY WHAT I WAS AIMING FOR.

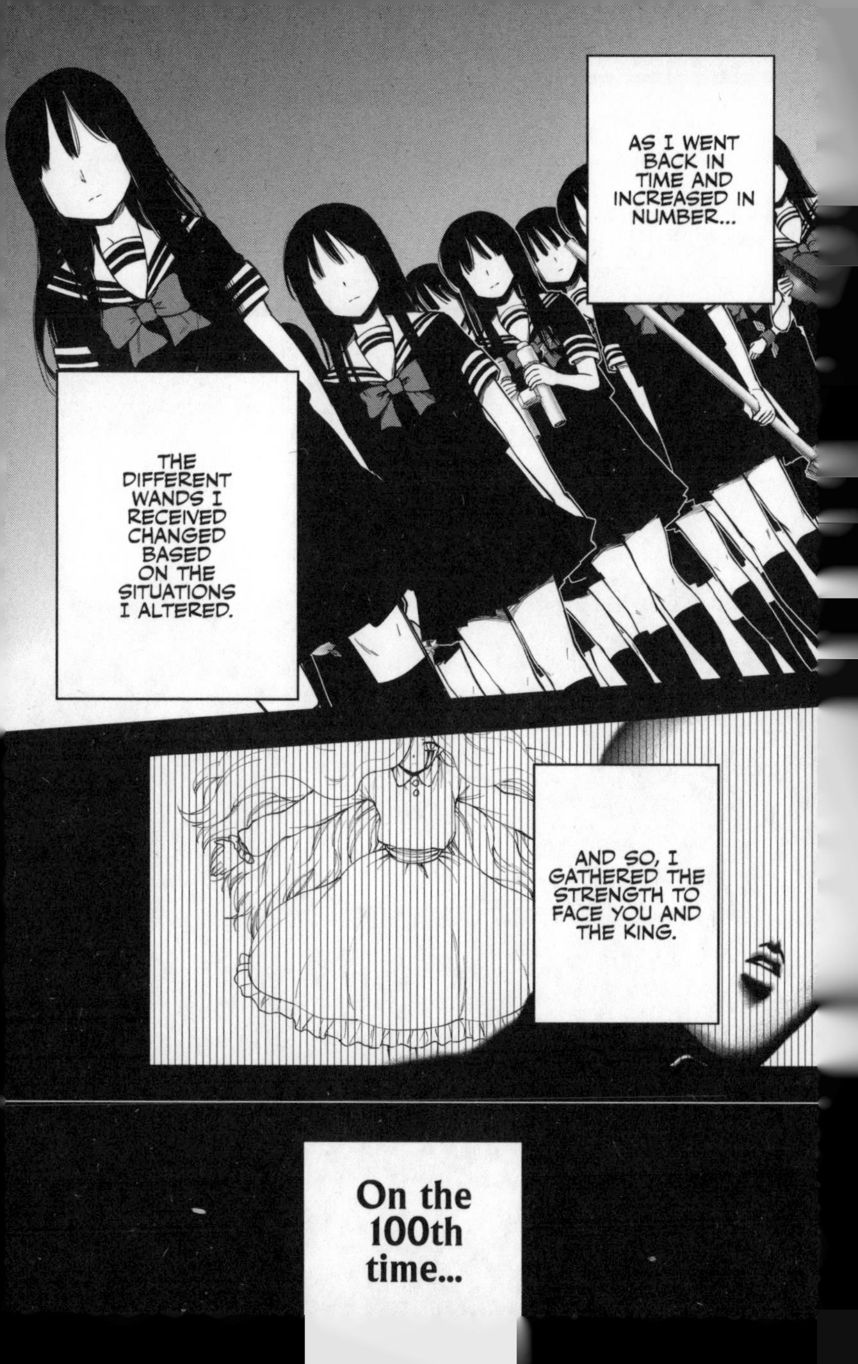
AS I WENT BACK IN TIME AND INCREASED IN NUMBER...
THE DIFFERENT WANDS I RECEIVED CHANGED BASED ON THE SITUATIONS I ALTERED.
AND SO, I GATHERED THE STRENGTH TO FACE YOU AND THE KING.
On the 100th time...

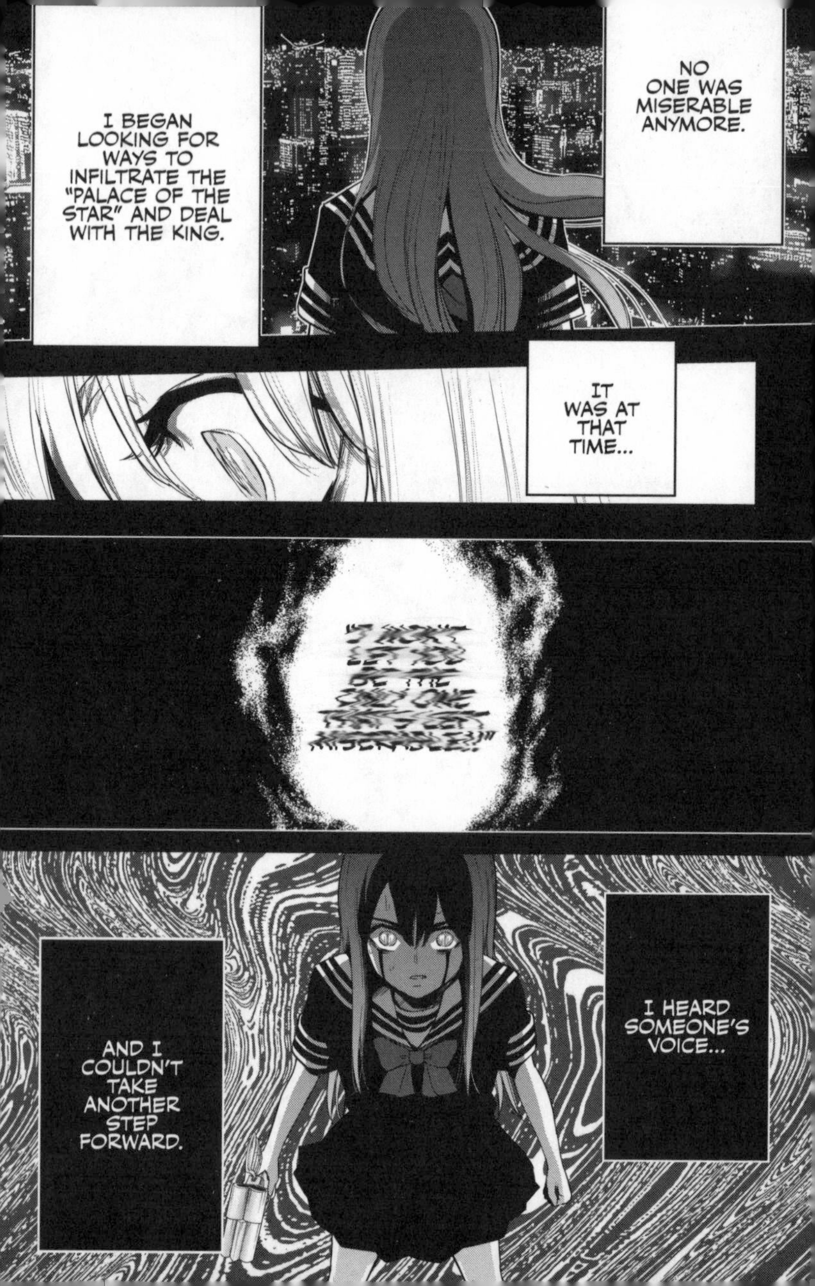
NO ONE WAS MISERABLE ANYMORE.
I BEGAN LOOKING FOR WAYS TO INFILTRATE THE "PALACE OF THE STAR" AND DEAL WITH THE KING.
IT WAS AT THAT TIME...
I HEARD SOMEONE'S VOICE...
AND I COULDN'T TAKE ANOTHER STEP FORWARD.

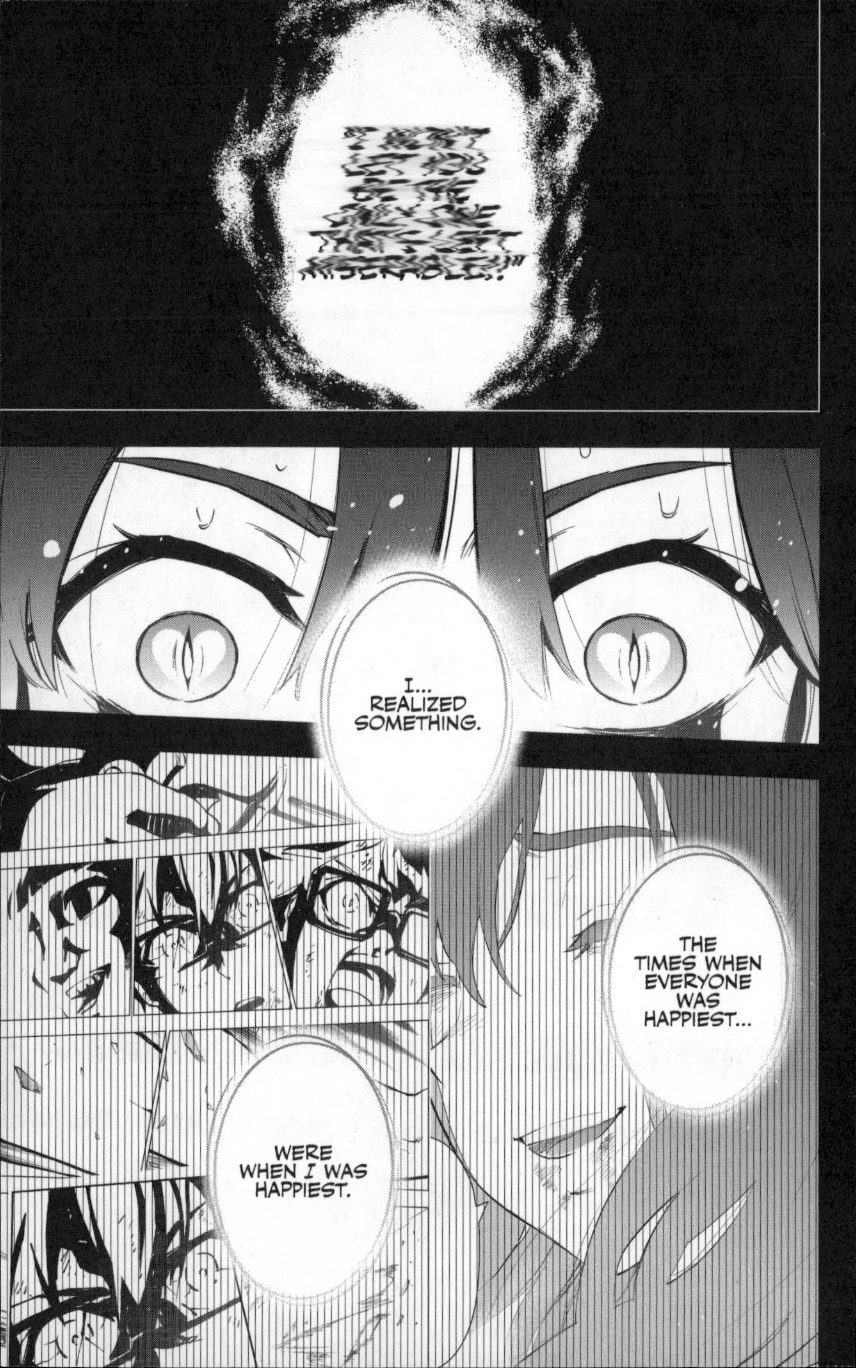
I... REALIZED SOMETHING.
THE TIMES WHEN EVERYONE WAS HAPPIEST...
WERE WHEN I WAS HAPPIEST.

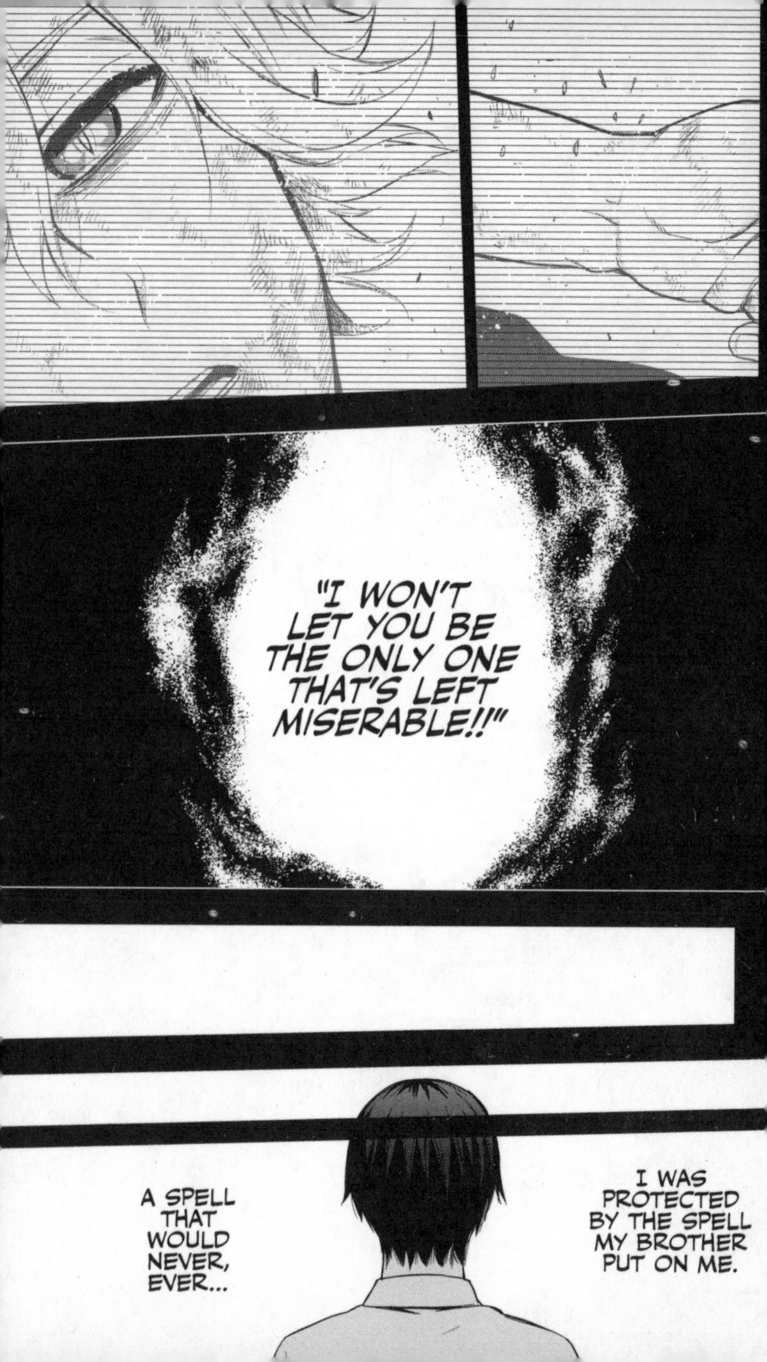
"I WON'T LET YOU BE THE ONLY ONE THAT'S LEFT MISERABLE!!"
I WAS PROTECTED BY THE SPELL MY BROTHER PUT ON ME.
A SPELL THAT WOULD NEVER, EVER...

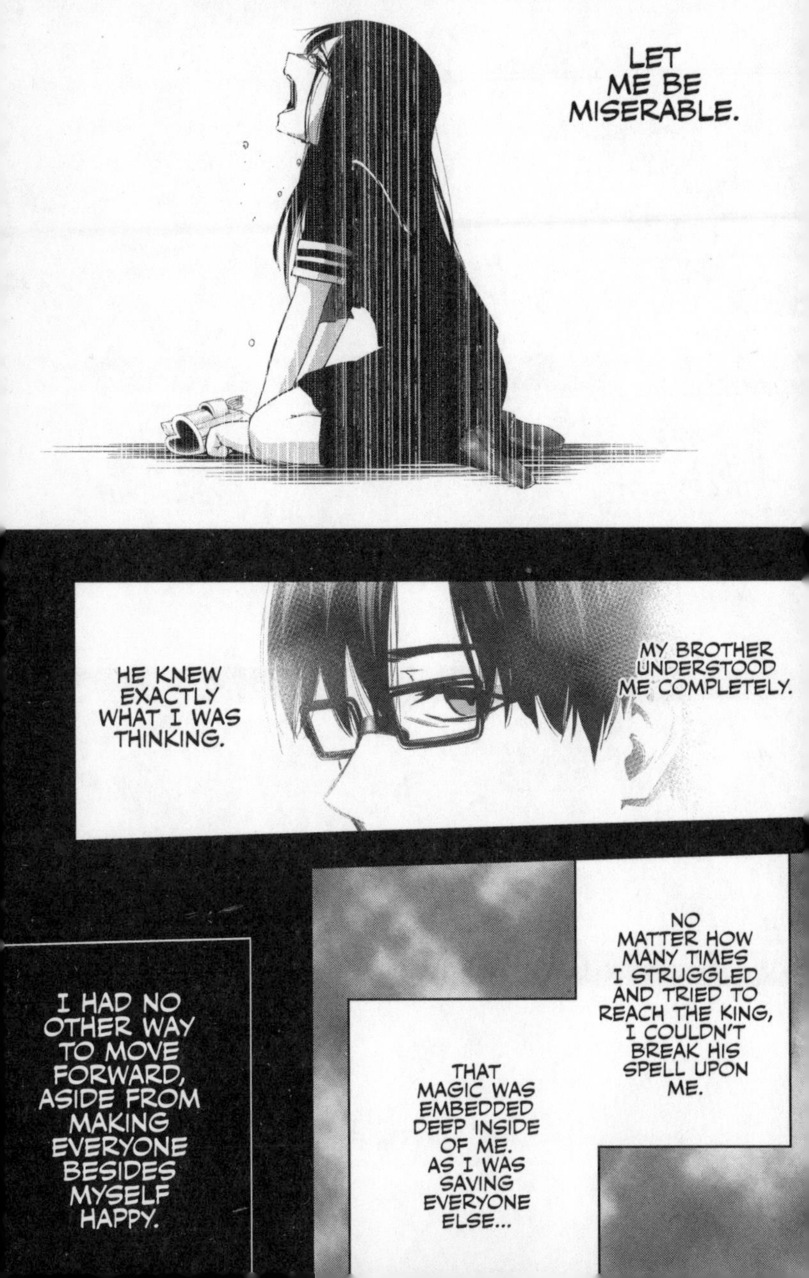
LET ME BE MISERABLE.
MY BROTHER UNDERSTOOD ME COMPLETELY.
HE KNEW EXACTLY WHAT I WAS THINKING.
NO MATTER HOW MANY TIMES I STRUGGLED AND TRIED TO REACH THE KING, I COULDN'T BREAK HIS SPELL UPON ME.
THAT MAGIC WAS EMBEDDED DEEP INSIDE OF ME. AS I WAS SAVING EVERYONE ELSE...
I HAD NO OTHER WAY TO MOVE FORWARD, ASIDE FROM MAKING EVERYONE BESIDES MYSELF HAPPY.

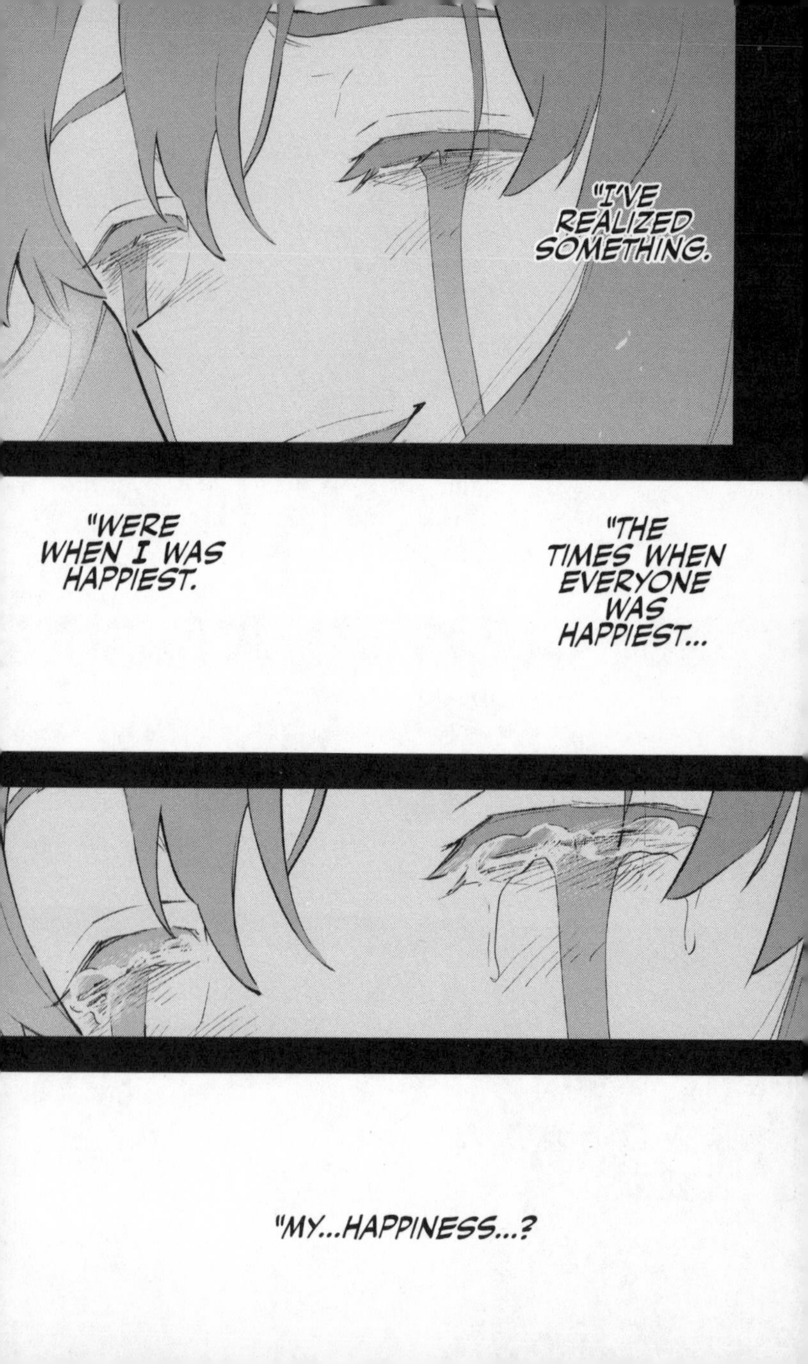
"I'VE REALIZED SOMETHING.
"THE TIMES WHEN EVERYONE WAS HAPPIEST...
"WERE WHEN I WAS HAPPIEST.
"MY...HAPPINESS...?

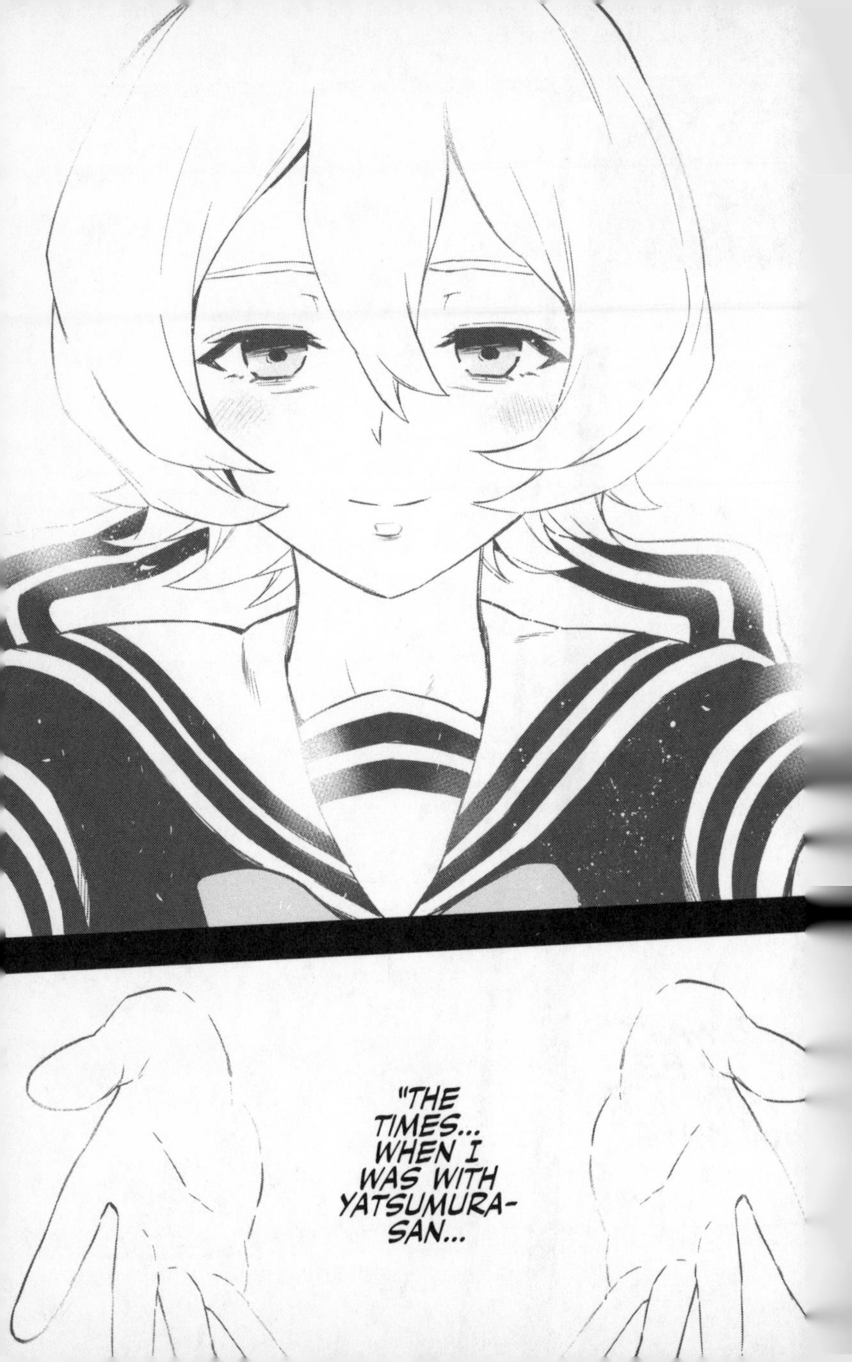
"THE TIMES... WHEN I WAS WITH YATSUMURA-SAN...

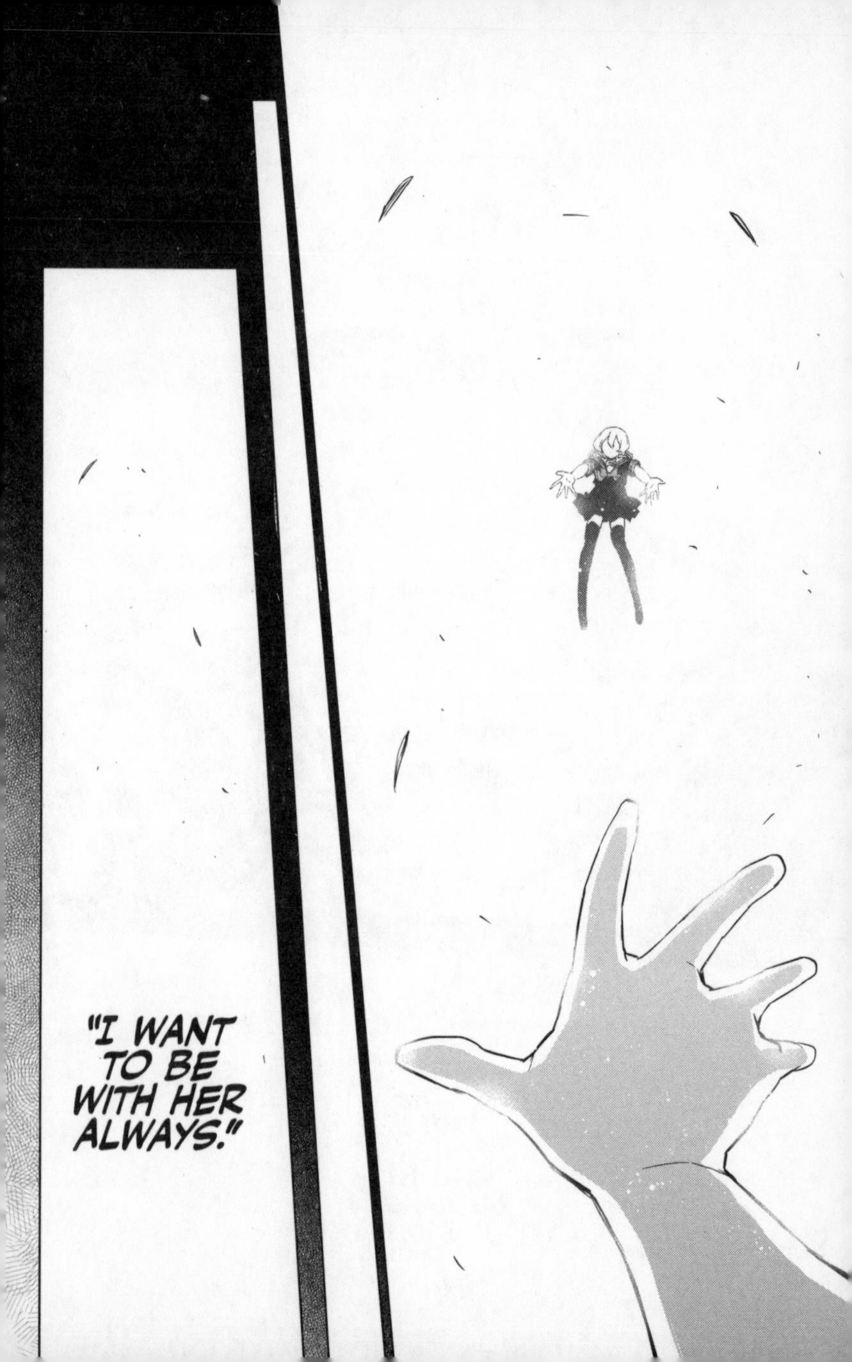
"I WANT TO BE WITH HER ALWAYS."

THERE WAS ONLY ONE WAY...
TO RESOLVE EVERYTHING.
I WAITED FOR YOU.
......!
WE NEED TO RETURN TO THE POINT WHEN THE EARTH EXPLODED.
WHILE TIME IS STOPPED WITH THIS WAND...
YOU NEED TO REMAKE THE WORLD.

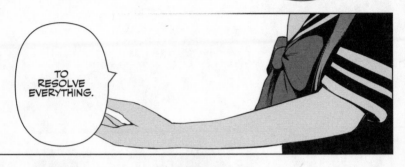

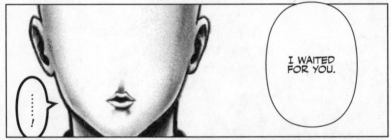

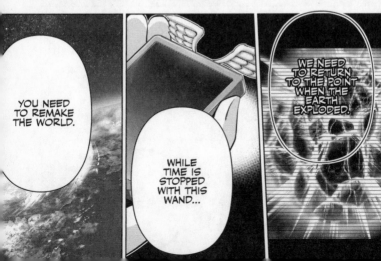

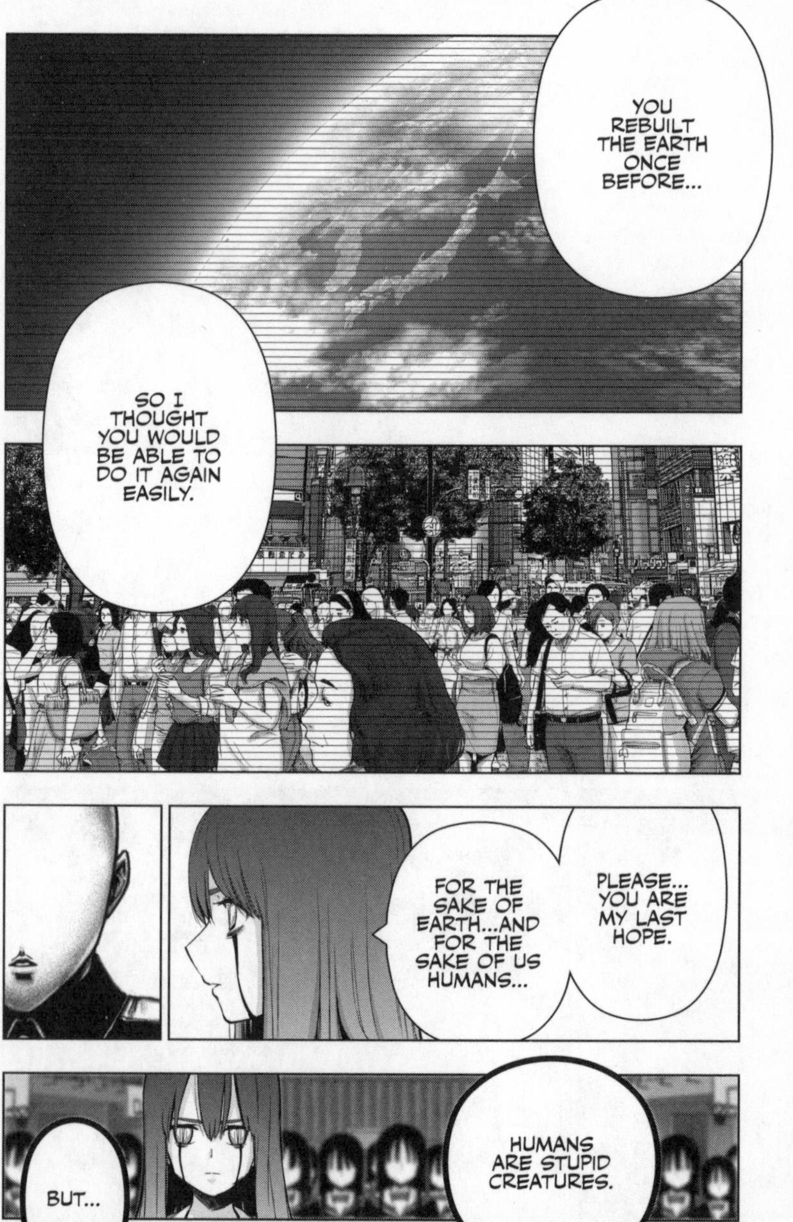
YOU REBUILT THE EARTH ONCE BEFORE...
SO I THOUGHT YOU WOULD BE ABLE TO DO IT AGAIN EASILY.
PLEASE... YOU ARE MY LAST HOPE.
FOR THE SAKE OF EARTH...AND FOR THE SAKE OF US HUMANS...
HUMANS ARE STUPID CREATURES.
BUT...

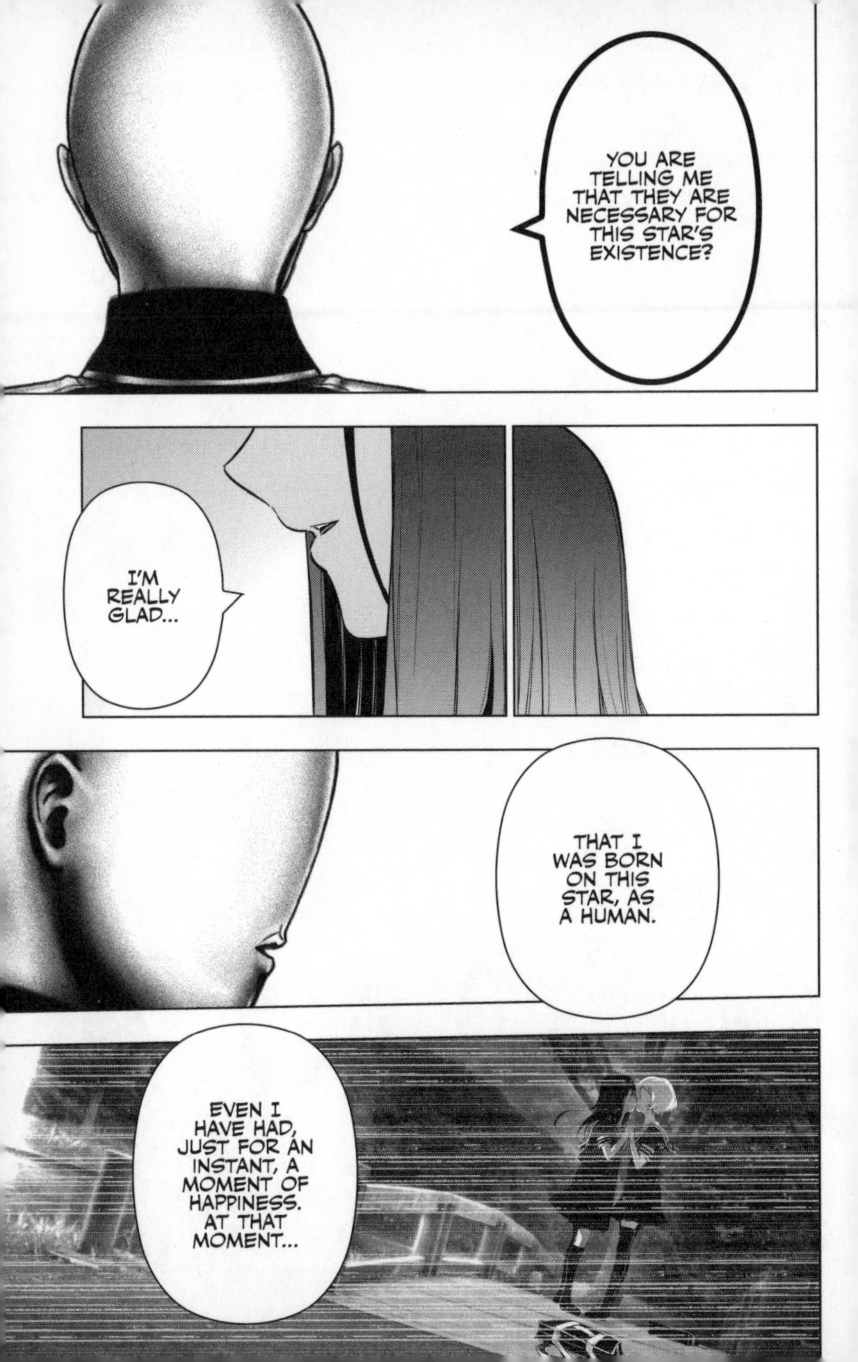
YOU ARE TELLING ME THAT THEY ARE NECESSARY FOR THIS STAR'S EXISTENCE?
I'M REALLY GLAD...
THAT I WAS BORN ON THIS STAR, AS A HUMAN.
EVEN I HAVE HAD, JUST FOR AN INSTANT, A MOMENT OF HAPPINESS. AT THAT MOMENT...

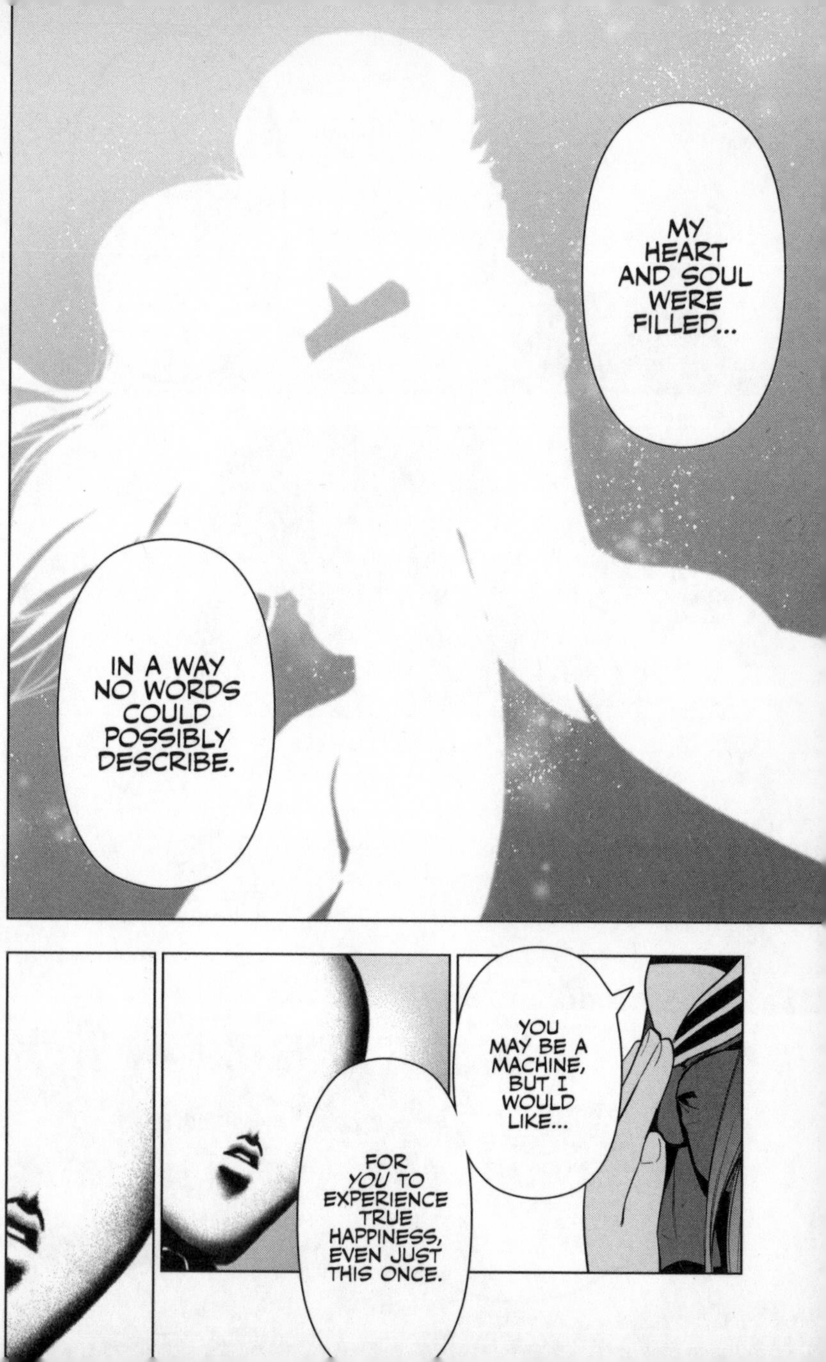
MY HEART AND SOUL WERE FILLED...
IN A WAY NO WORDS COULD POSSIBLY DESCRIBE.
YOU MAY BE A MACHINE, BUT I WOULD LIKE...
FOR *YOU* TO EXPERIENCE TRUE HAPPINESS, EVEN JUST THIS ONCE.

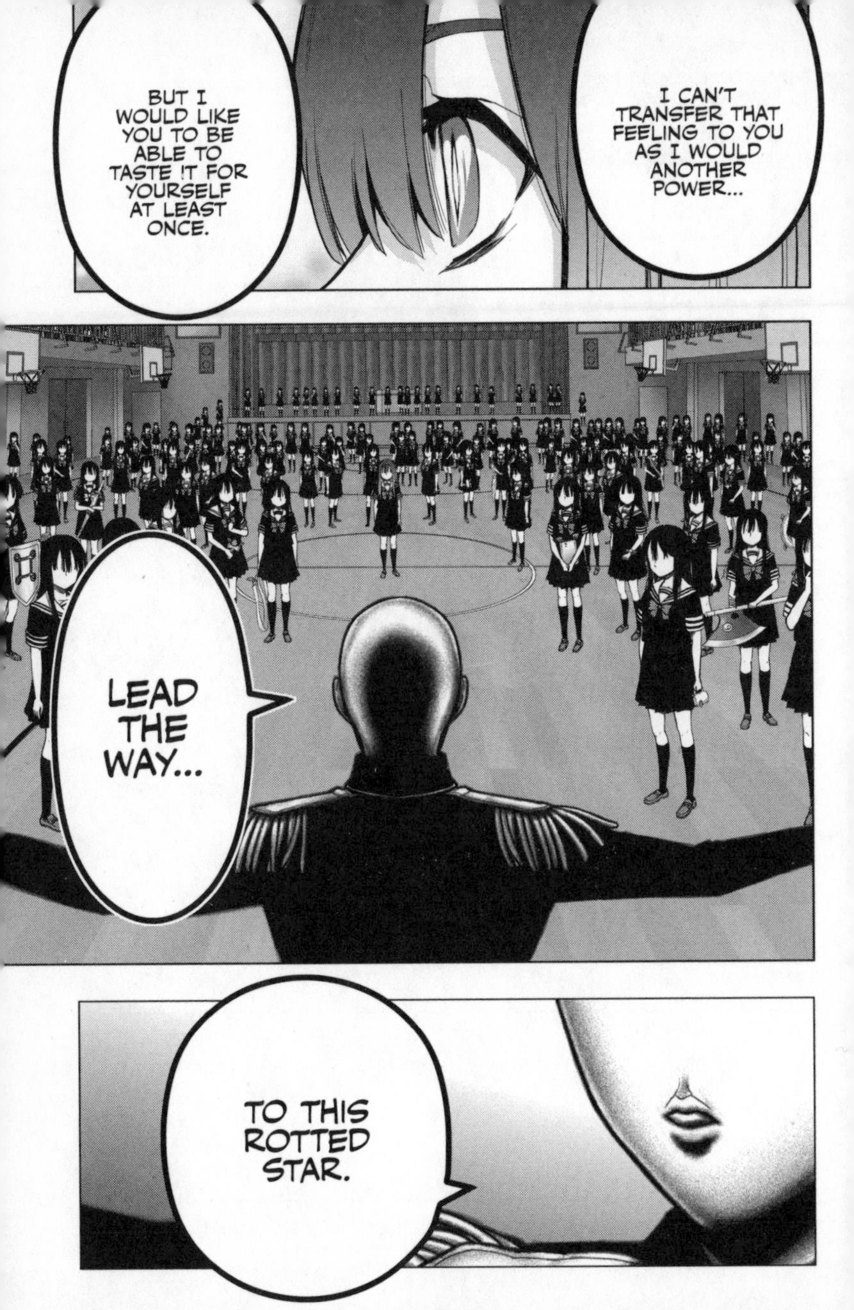
I CAN'T TRANSFER THAT FEELING TO YOU AS I WOULD ANOTHER POWER...
BUT I WOULD LIKE YOU TO BE ABLE TO TASTE IT FOR YOURSELF AT LEAST ONCE.
LEAD THE WAY...
TO THIS ROTTED STAR.

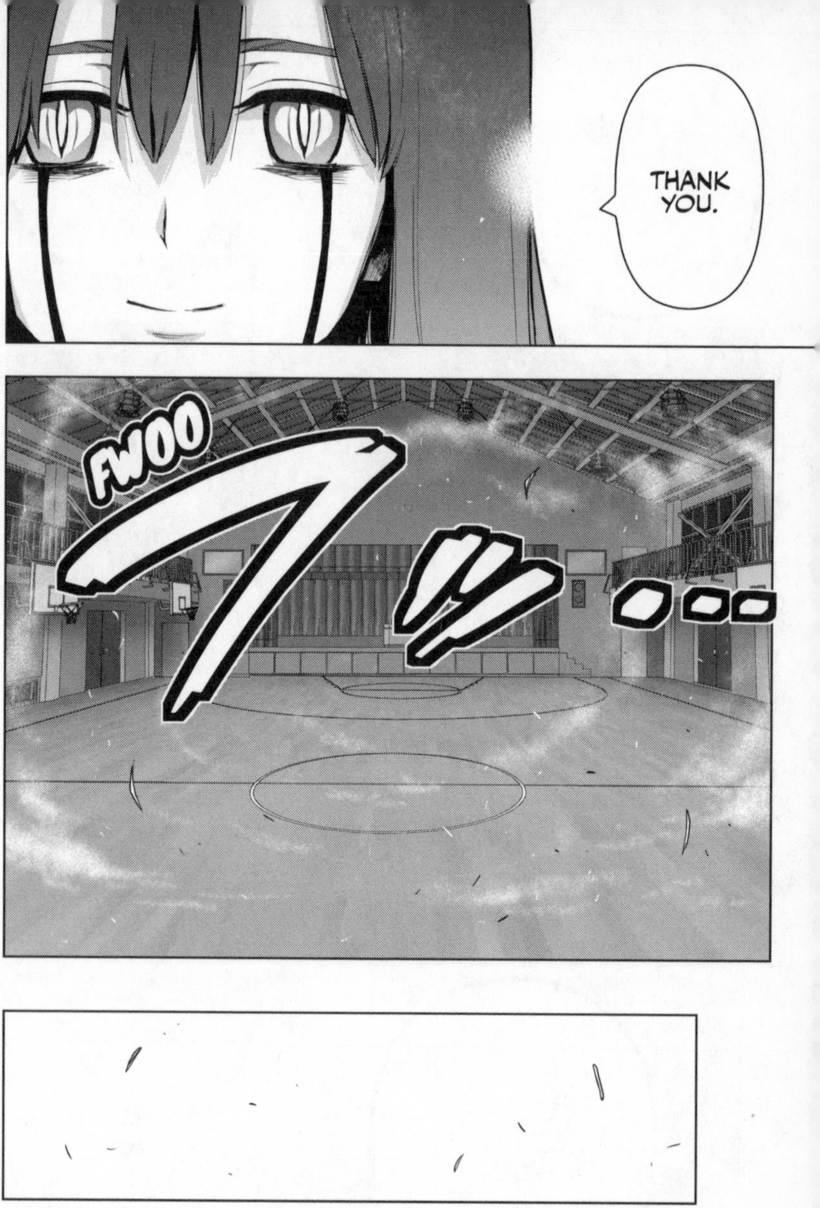
THANK YOU.
FWOO

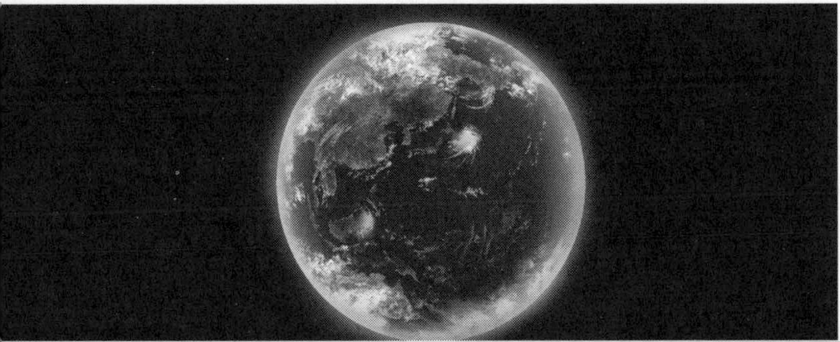

MAGICAL GIRL SITE

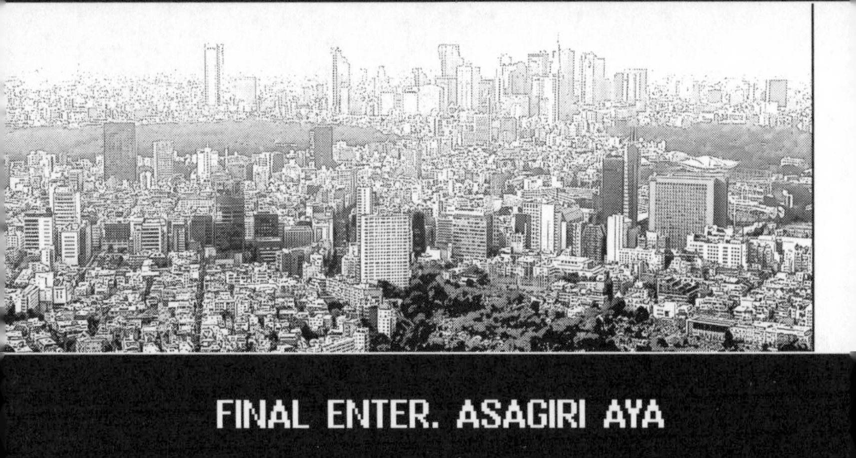

FINAL ENTER. ASAGIRI AYA

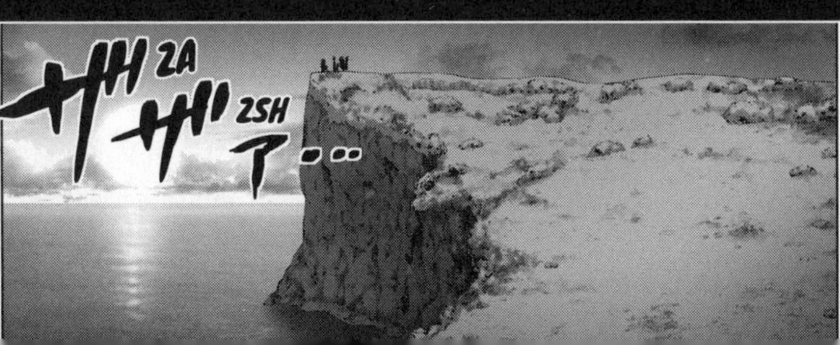
ZA
ZSH

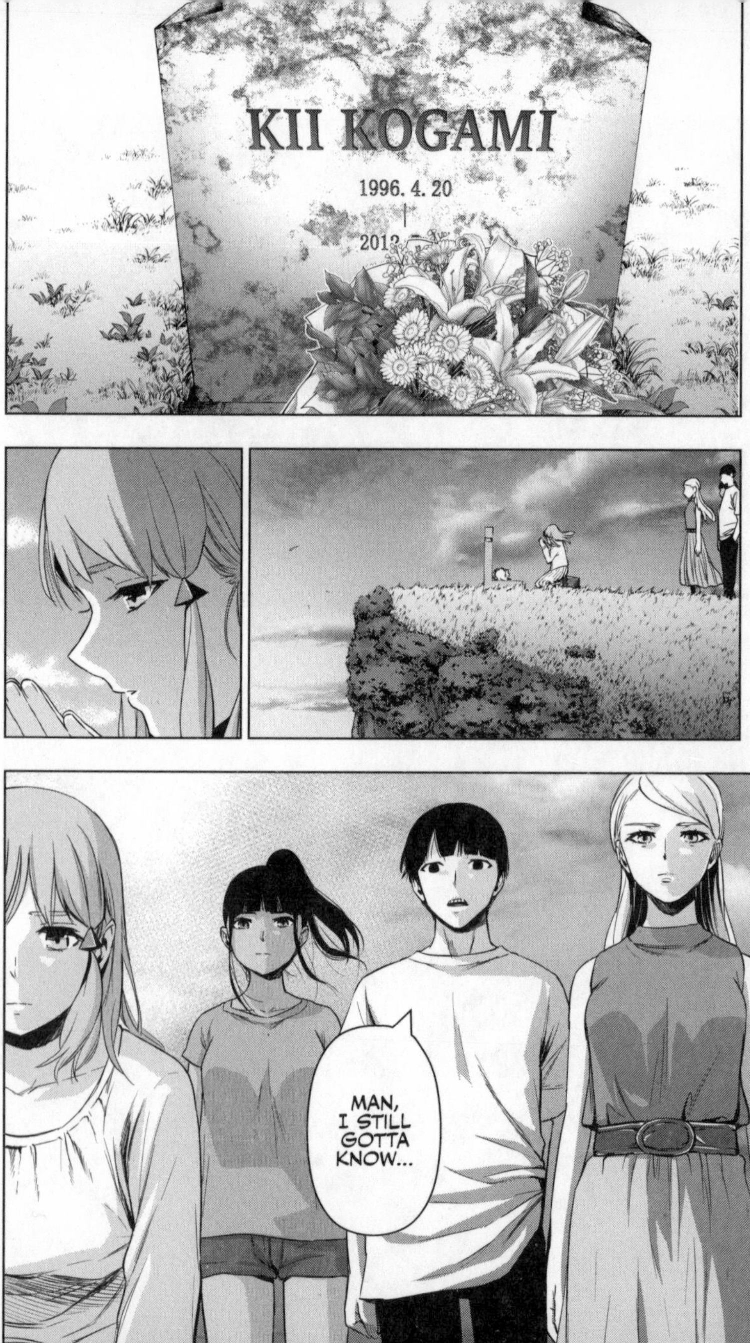
KII KOGAMI
1996. 4. 20
MAN, I STILL GOTTA KNOW...

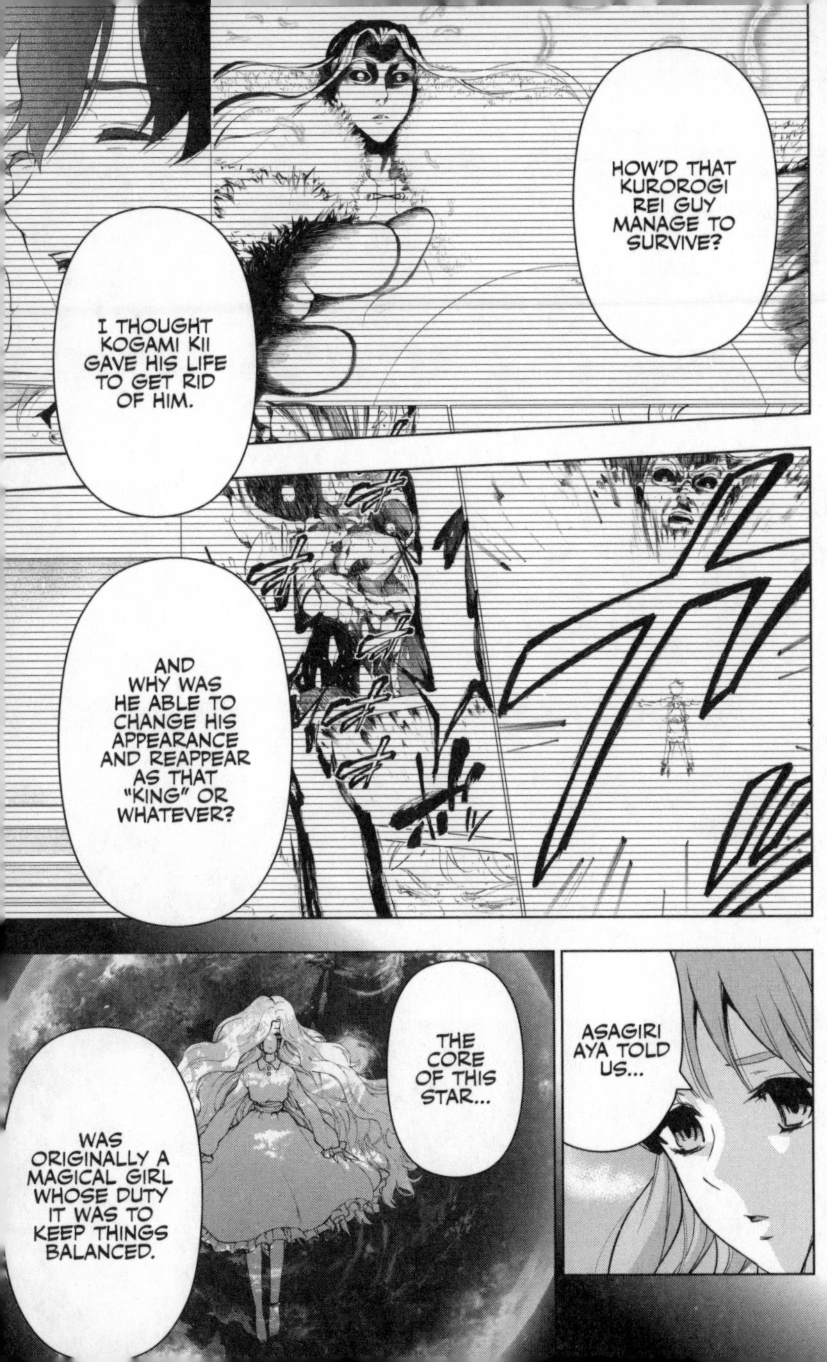
HOW'D THAT KUROROGI REI GUY MANAGE TO SURVIVE?
I THOUGHT KOGAMI KII GAVE HIS LIFE TO GET RID OF HIM.
AND WHY WAS HE ABLE TO CHANGE HIS APPEARANCE AND REAPPEAR AS THAT "KING" OR WHATEVER?
ASAGIRI AYA TOLD US...
THE CORE OF THIS STAR...
WAS ORIGINALLY A MAGICAL GIRL WHOSE DUTY IT WAS TO KEEP THINGS BALANCED.

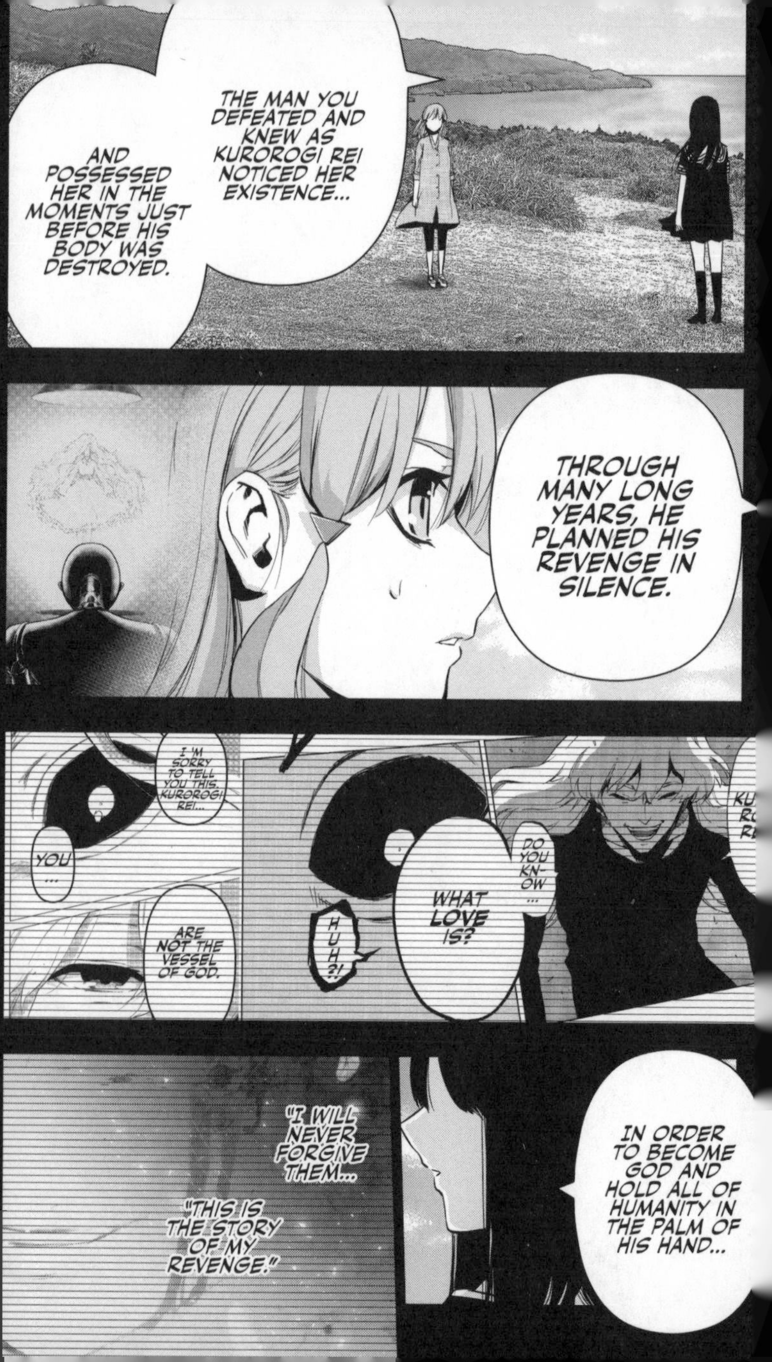
THE MAN YOU DEFEATED AND KNEW AS KUROROGI REI NOTICED HER EXISTENCE...
AND POSSESSED HER IN THE MOMENTS JUST BEFORE HIS BODY WAS DESTROYED.
THROUGH MANY LONG YEARS, HE PLANNED HIS REVENGE IN SILENCE.
DO YOU KNOW...
WHAT LOVE IS?
HUH?!
I'M SORRY TO TELL YOU THIS, KUROROGI REI...
YOU...
ARE NOT THE VESSEL OF GOD.
IN ORDER TO BECOME GOD AND HOLD ALL OF HUMANITY IN THE PALM OF HIS HAND...
"I WILL NEVER FORGIVE THEM...
"THIS IS THE STORY OF MY REVENGE."

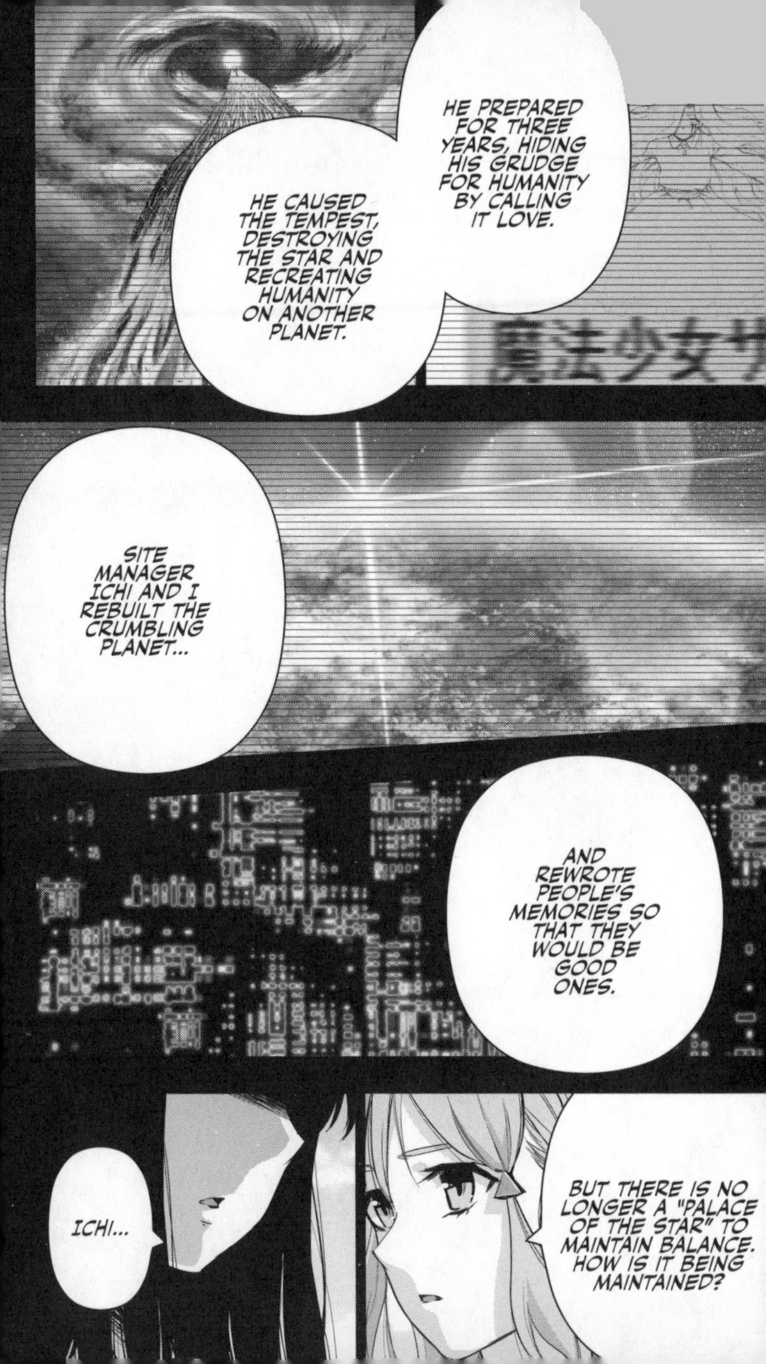
HE PREPARED FOR THREE YEARS, HIDING HIS GRUDGE FOR HUMANITY BY CALLING IT LOVE.
HE CAUSED THE TEMPEST, DESTROYING THE STAR AND RECREATING HUMANITY ON ANOTHER PLANET.
SITE MANAGER ICHI AND I REBUILT THE CRUMBLING PLANET...
AND REWROTE PEOPLE'S MEMORIES SO THAT THEY WOULD BE GOOD ONES.
BUT THERE IS NO LONGER A "PALACE OF THE STAR" TO MAINTAIN BALANCE. HOW IS IT BEING MAINTAINED?
ICHI...

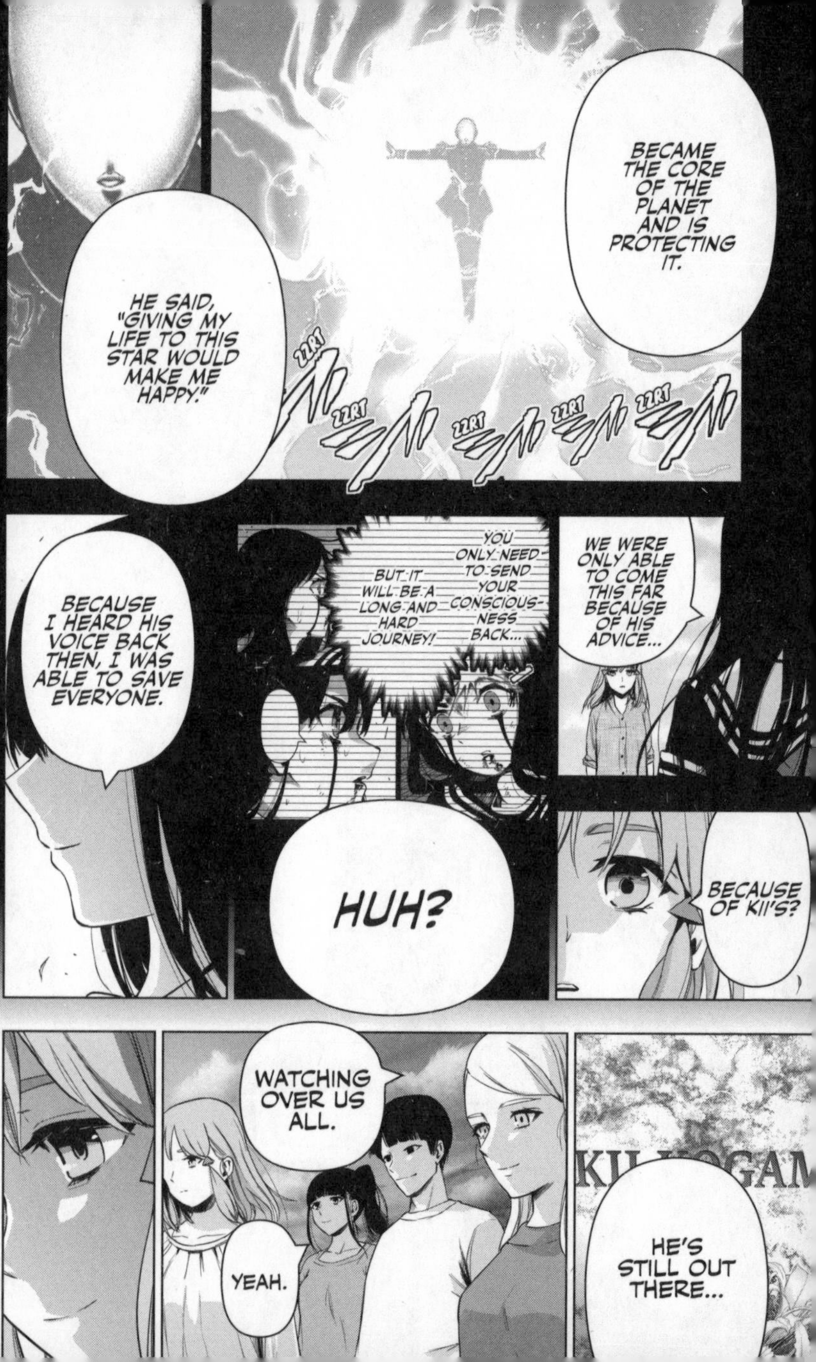
BECAME THE CORE OF THE PLANET AND IS PROTECTING IT.
ZZRT
ZZRT
ZZRT
ZZRT
ZZRT
HE SAID, "GIVING MY LIFE TO THIS STAR WOULD MAKE ME HAPPY."
WE WERE ONLY ABLE TO COME THIS FAR BECAUSE OF HIS ADVICE...
BECAUSE OF KII'S?
YOU ONLY NEED TO SEND YOUR CONSCIOUSNESS BACK...
BUT IT WILL BE A LONG AND HARD JOURNEY!
HUH?
BECAUSE I HEARD HIS VOICE BACK THEN, I WAS ABLE TO SAVE EVERYONE.
HE'S STILL OUT THERE...
WATCHING OVER US ALL.
YEAH.

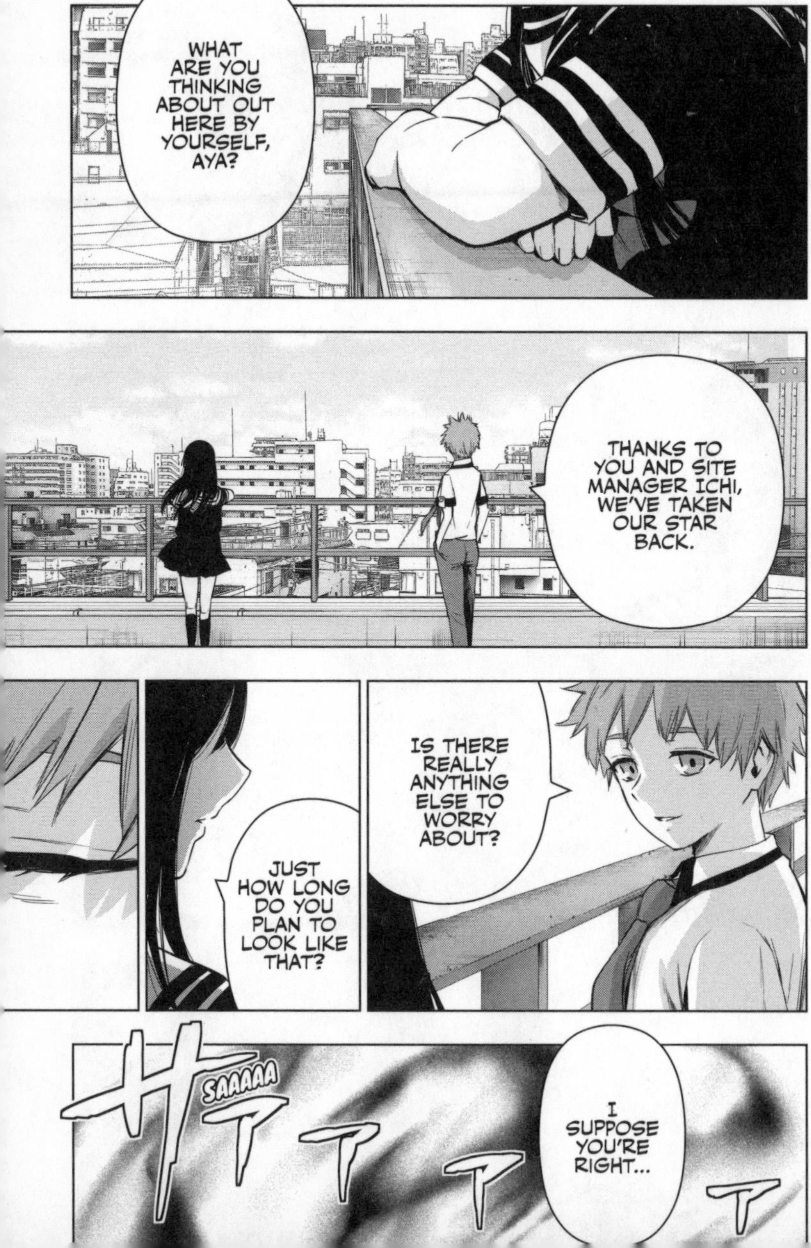
WHAT ARE YOU THINKING ABOUT OUT HERE BY YOURSELF, AYA?
THANKS TO YOU AND SITE MANAGER ICHI, WE'VE TAKEN OUR STAR BACK.
IS THERE REALLY ANYTHING ELSE TO WORRY ABOUT?
JUST HOW LONG DO YOU PLAN TO LOOK LIKE THAT?
I SUPPOSE YOU'RE RIGHT...
SAAAAA

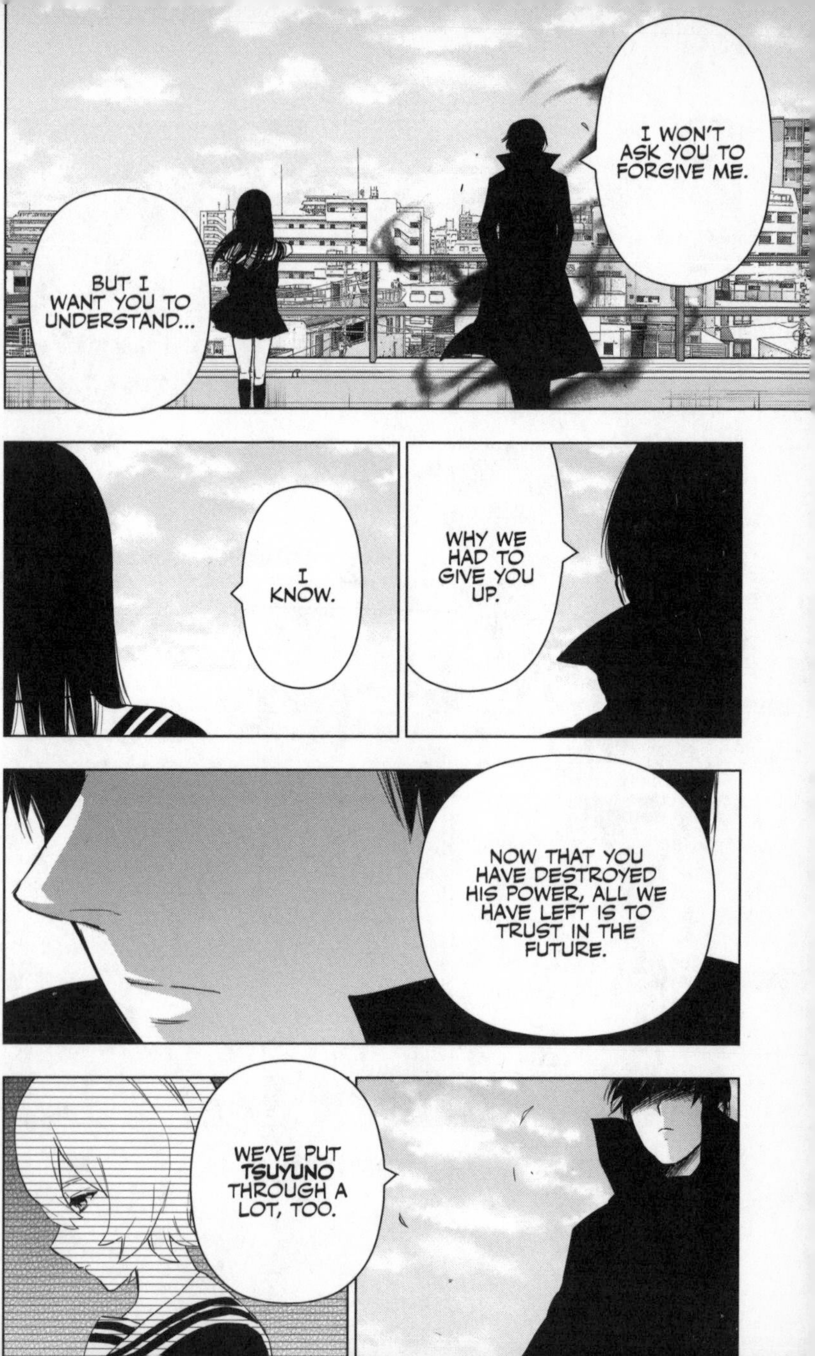
I WON'T ASK YOU TO FORGIVE ME.
BUT I WANT YOU TO UNDERSTAND...
WHY WE HAD TO GIVE YOU UP.
I KNOW.
NOW THAT YOU HAVE DESTROYED HIS POWER, ALL WE HAVE LEFT IS TO TRUST IN THE FUTURE.
WE'VE PUT TSUYUNO THROUGH A LOT, TOO.

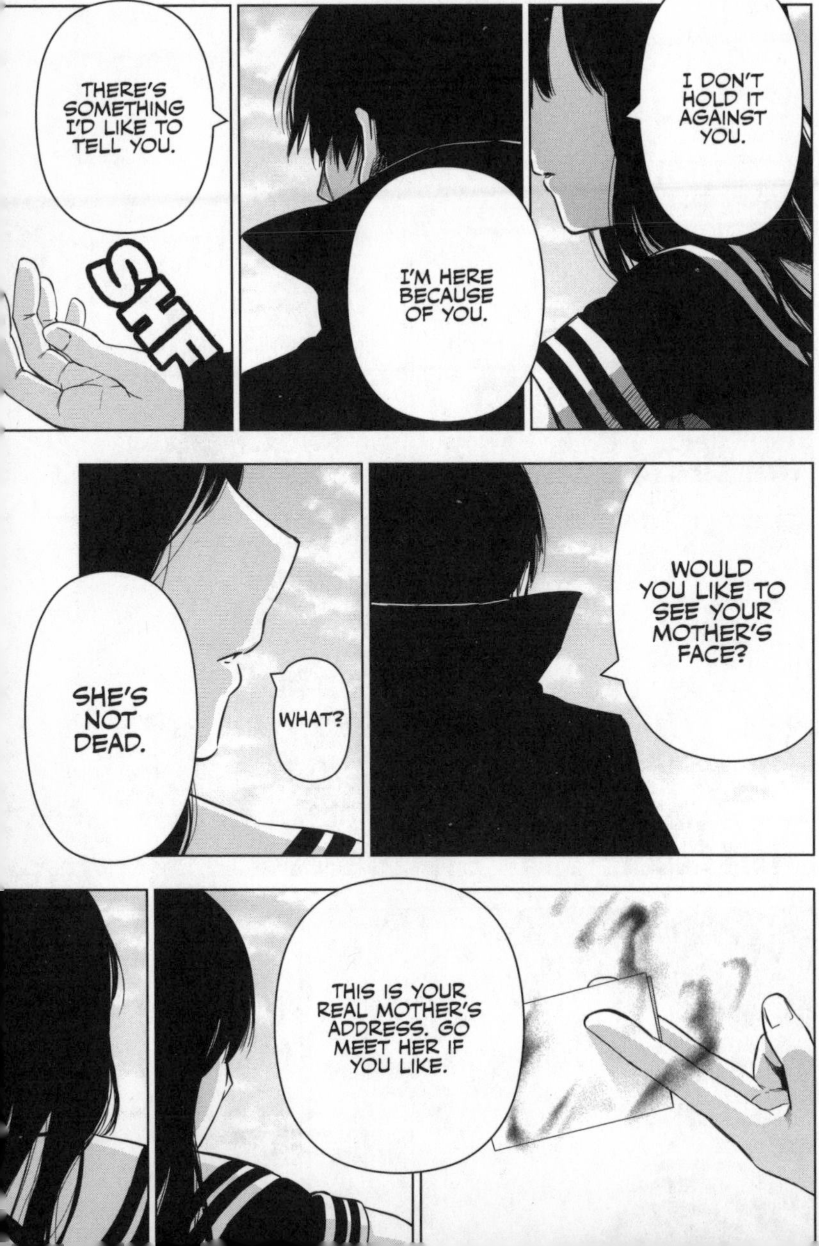
I DON'T HOLD IT AGAINST YOU.
I'M HERE BECAUSE OF YOU.
THERE'S SOMETHING I'D LIKE TO TELL YOU.
SHF
WOULD YOU LIKE TO SEE YOUR MOTHER'S FACE?
WHAT?
SHE'S NOT DEAD.
THIS IS YOUR REAL MOTHER'S ADDRESS. GO MEET HER IF YOU LIKE.

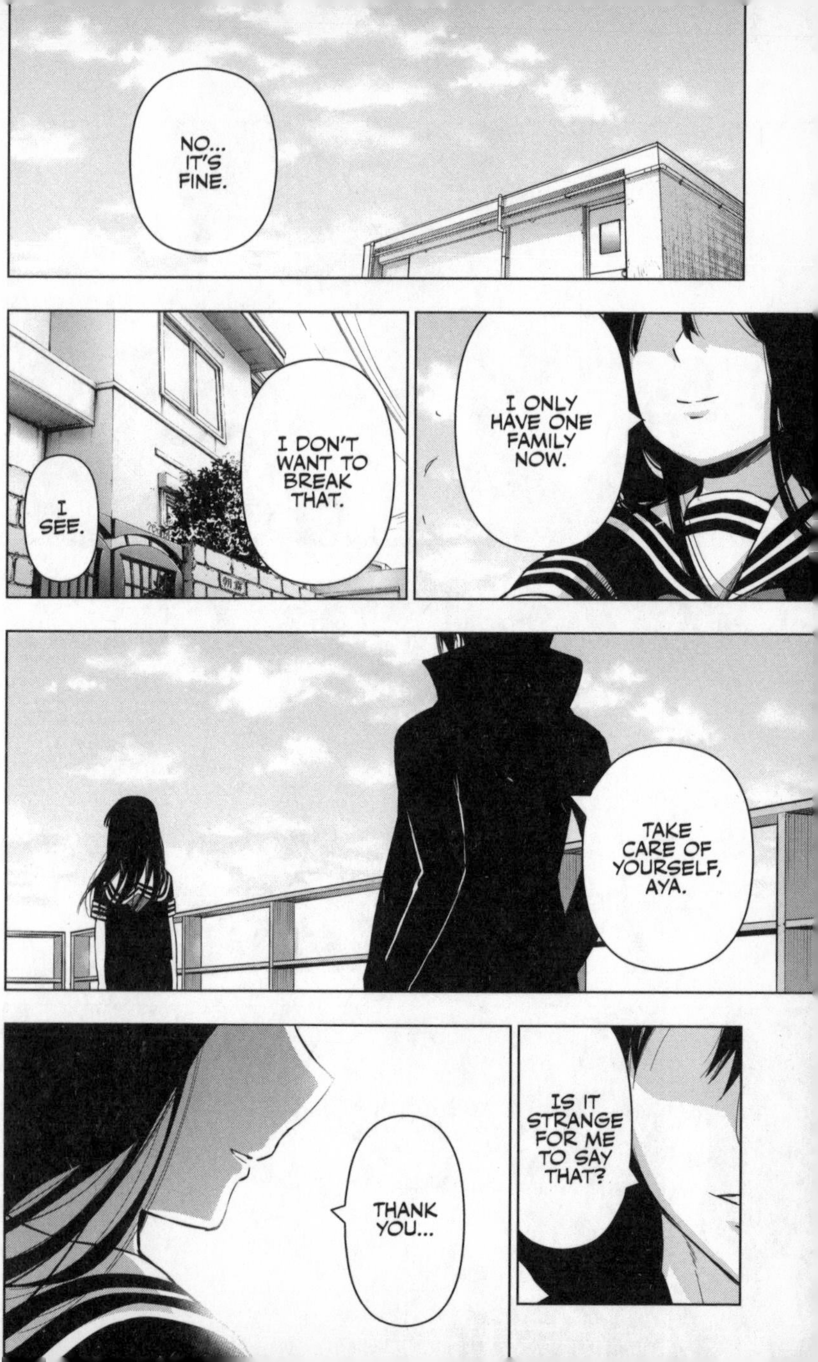
NO... IT'S FINE.
I ONLY HAVE ONE FAMILY NOW.
I DON'T WANT TO BREAK THAT.
I SEE.
TAKE CARE OF YOURSELF, AYA.
IS IT STRANGE FOR ME TO SAY THAT?
THANK YOU...

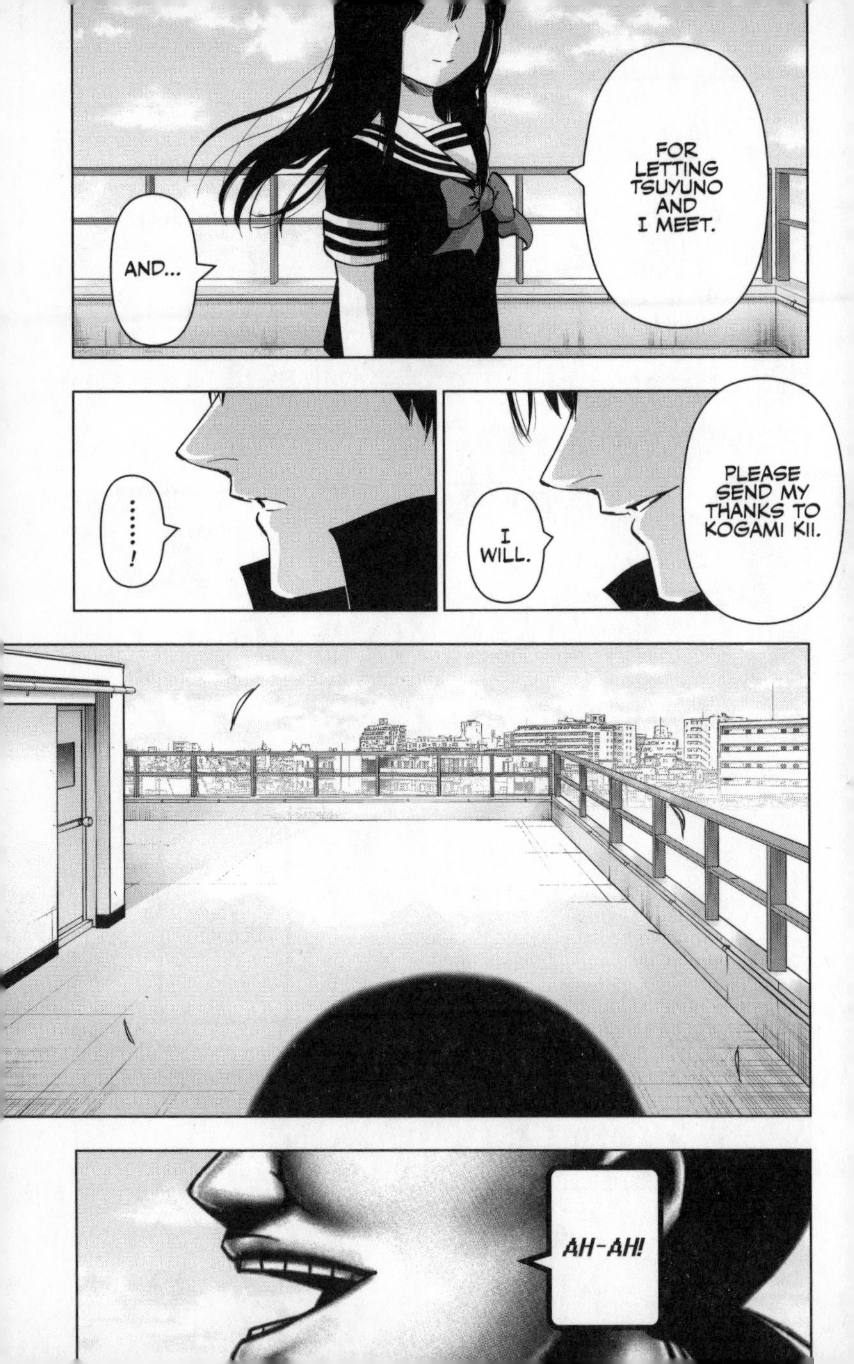
FOR LETTING TSUYUNO AND I MEET.
AND...
PLEASE SEND MY THANKS TO KOGAMI KII.
I WILL.
......!
AH-AH!

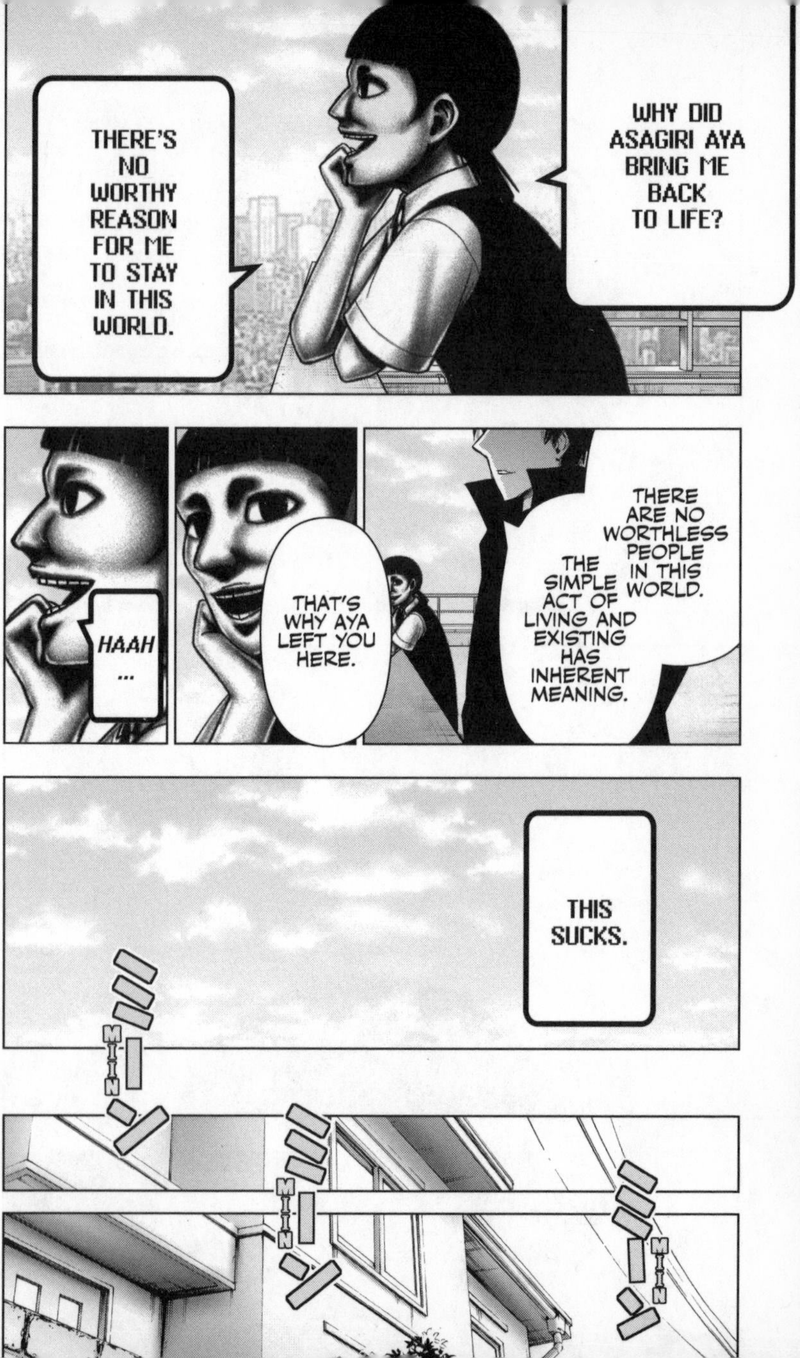
WHY DID ASAGIRI AYA BRING ME BACK TO LIFE?
THERE'S NO WORTHY REASON FOR ME TO STAY IN THIS WORLD.
THERE ARE NO WORTHLESS PEOPLE IN THIS WORLD.
THE SIMPLE ACT OF LIVING AND EXISTING HAS INHERENT MEANING.
THAT'S WHY AYA LEFT YOU HERE.
HAAH ...
THIS SUCKS.
MIIN
MIIN
MIIN
MIIN

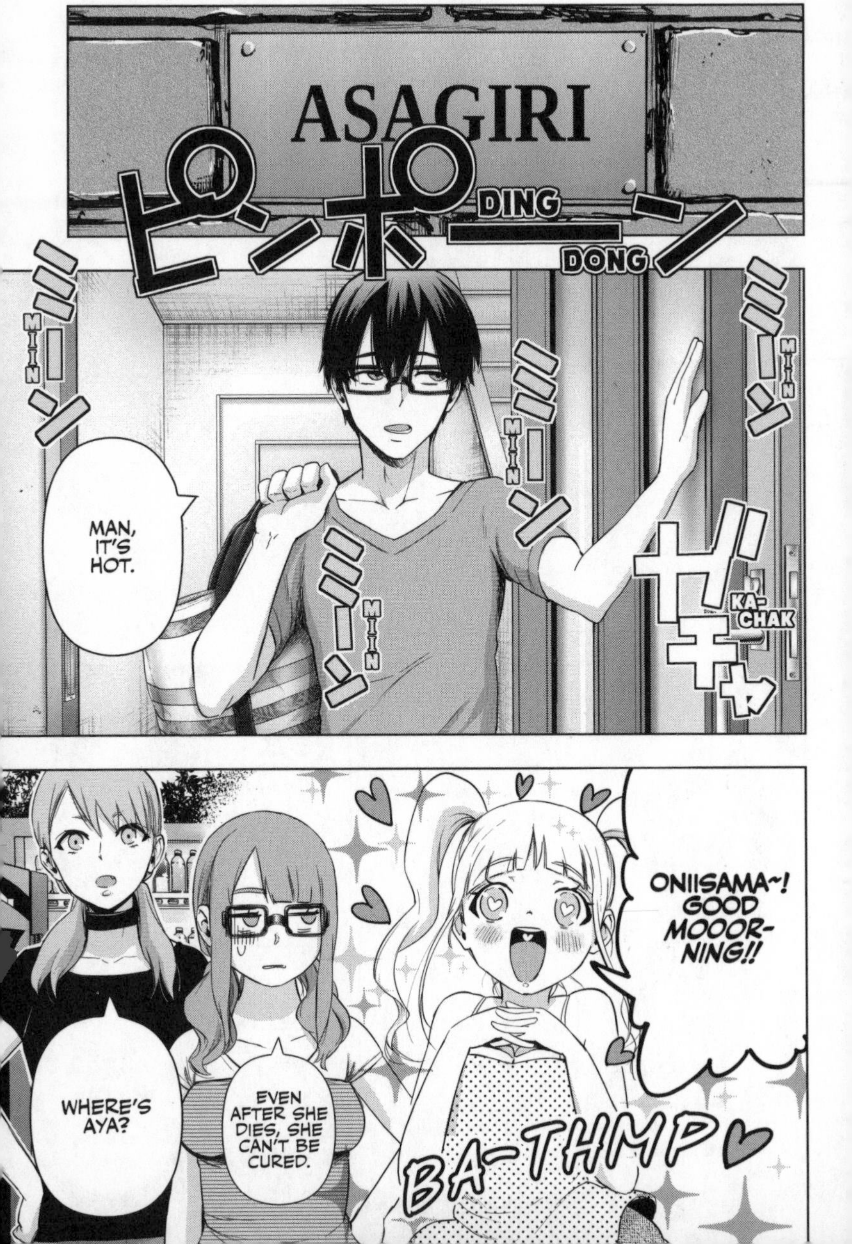
ASAGIRI
ピンポーン
DING DONG
ミーン
MIIN
ミーン
MIIN
ガチャ
KA-CHAK
ミーン
MIIN
MAN, IT'S HOT.
ミーン
MIIN
ONIISAMA~! GOOD MOOORNING!!
BA-THMP
EVEN AFTER SHE DIES, SHE CAN'T BE CURED.
WHERE'S AYA?

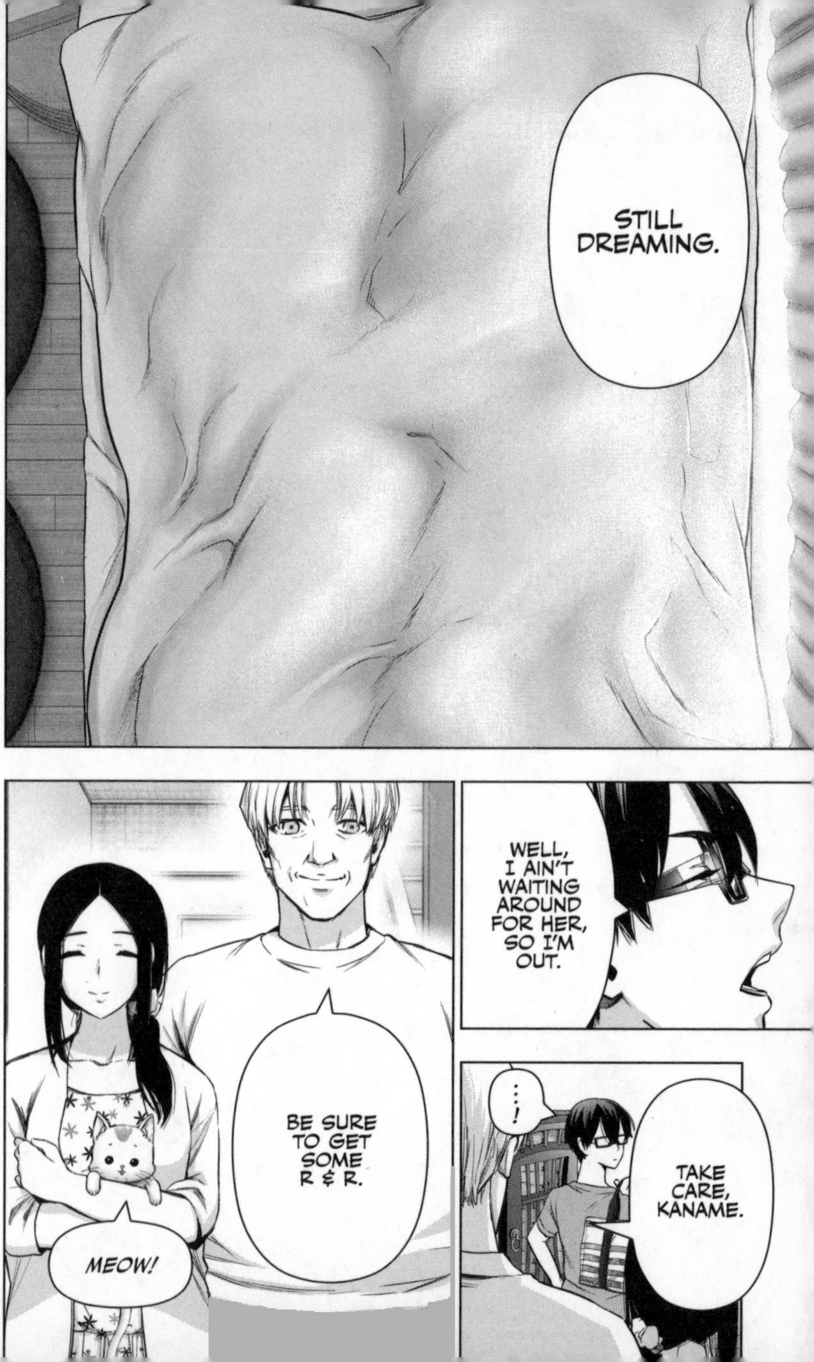
STILL DREAMING.
WELL, I AIN'T WAITING AROUND FOR HER, SO I'M OUT.
TAKE CARE, KANAME.
...!
BE SURE TO GET SOME R & R.
MEOW!

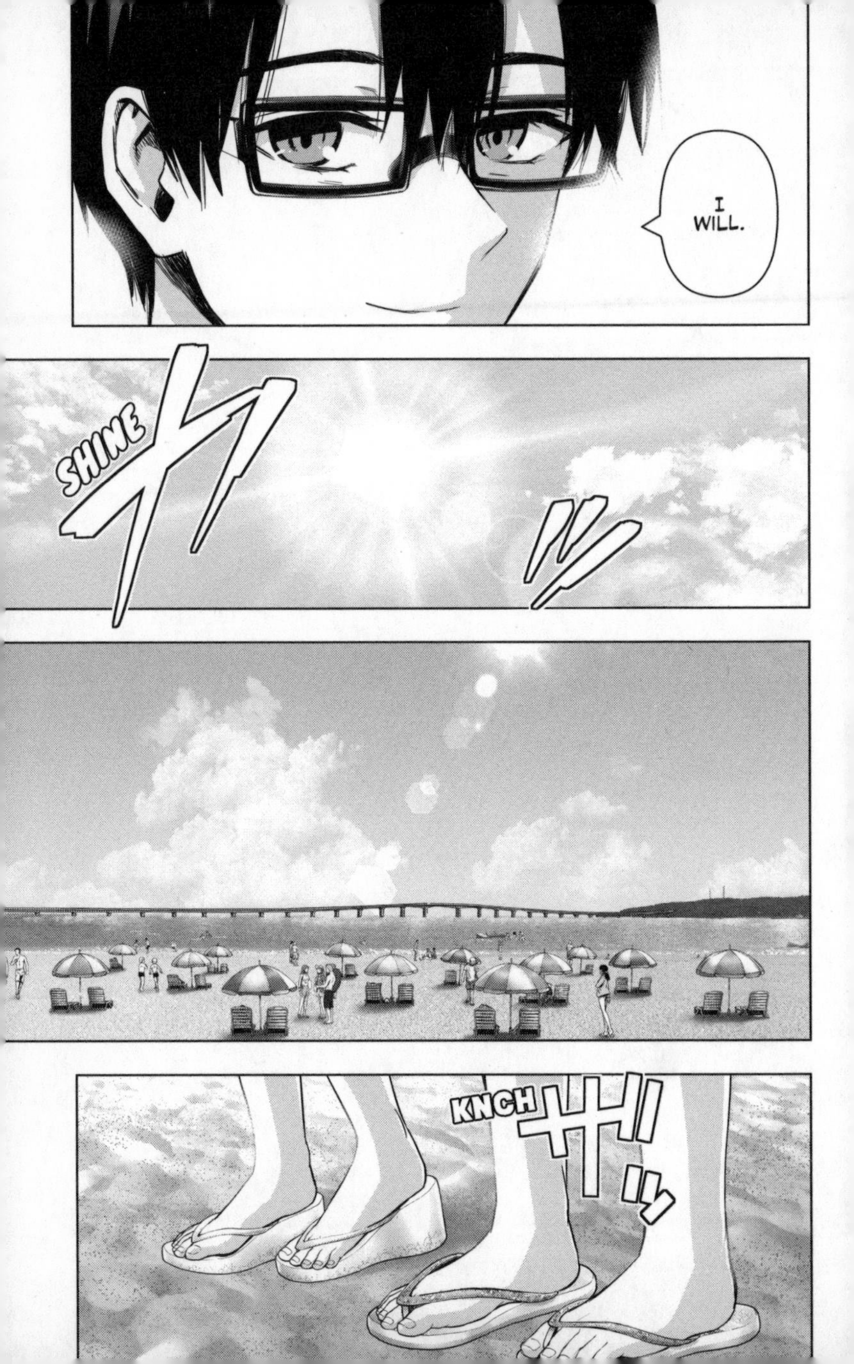
I WILL.
SHINE
KNCH

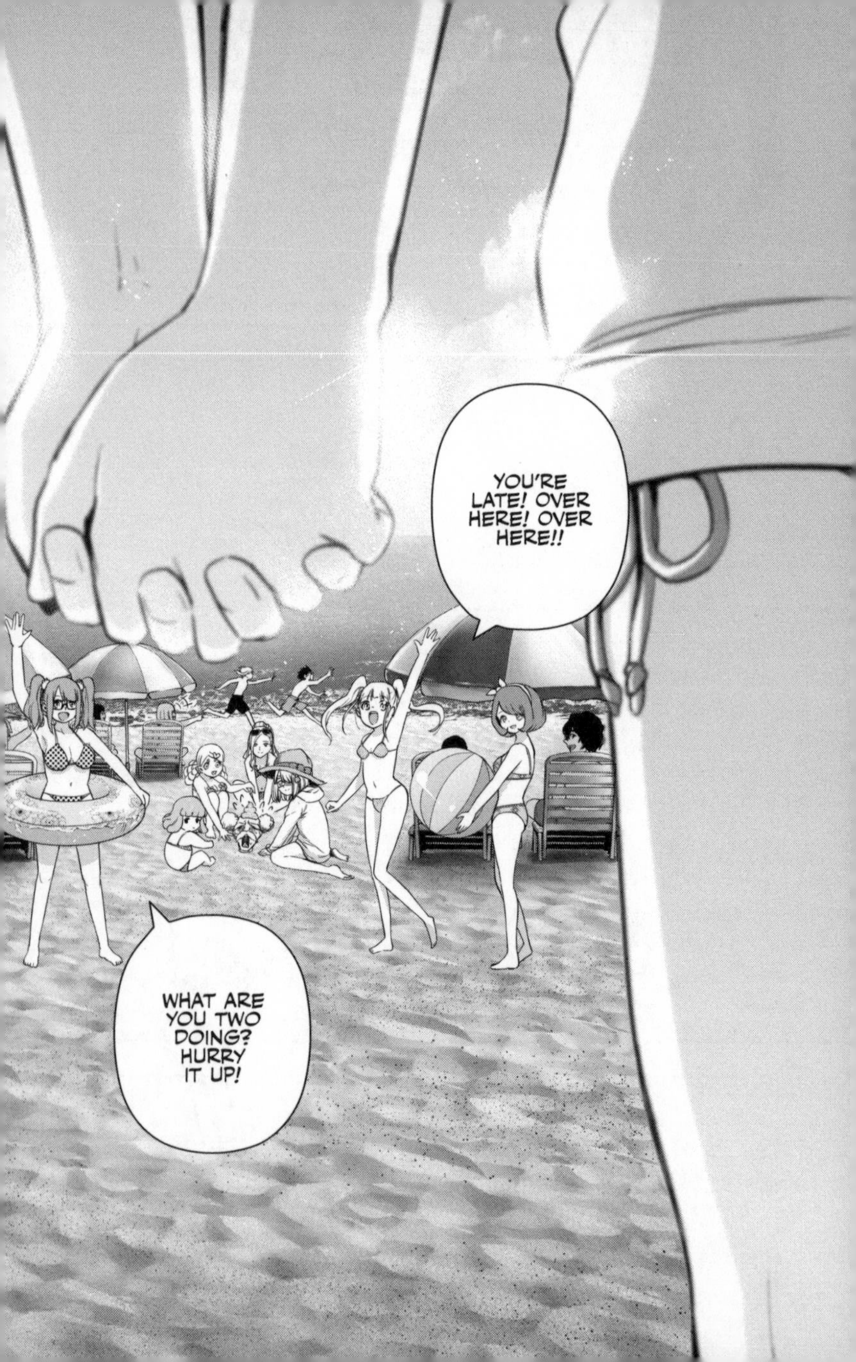
YOU'RE LATE! OVER HERE! OVER HERE!!
WHAT ARE YOU TWO DOING? HURRY IT UP!

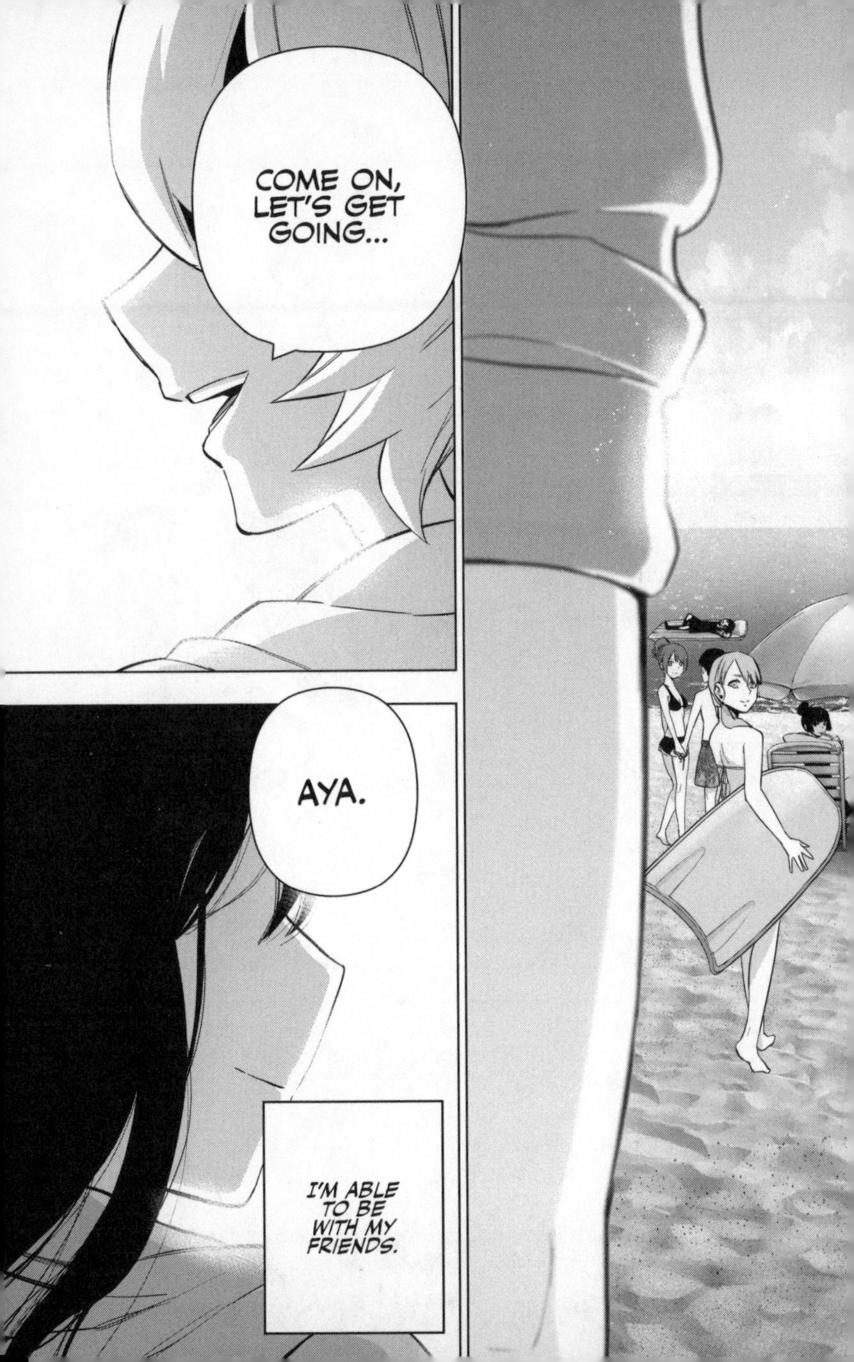
COME ON, LET'S GET GOING...
AYA.
I'M ABLE TO BE WITH MY FRIENDS.

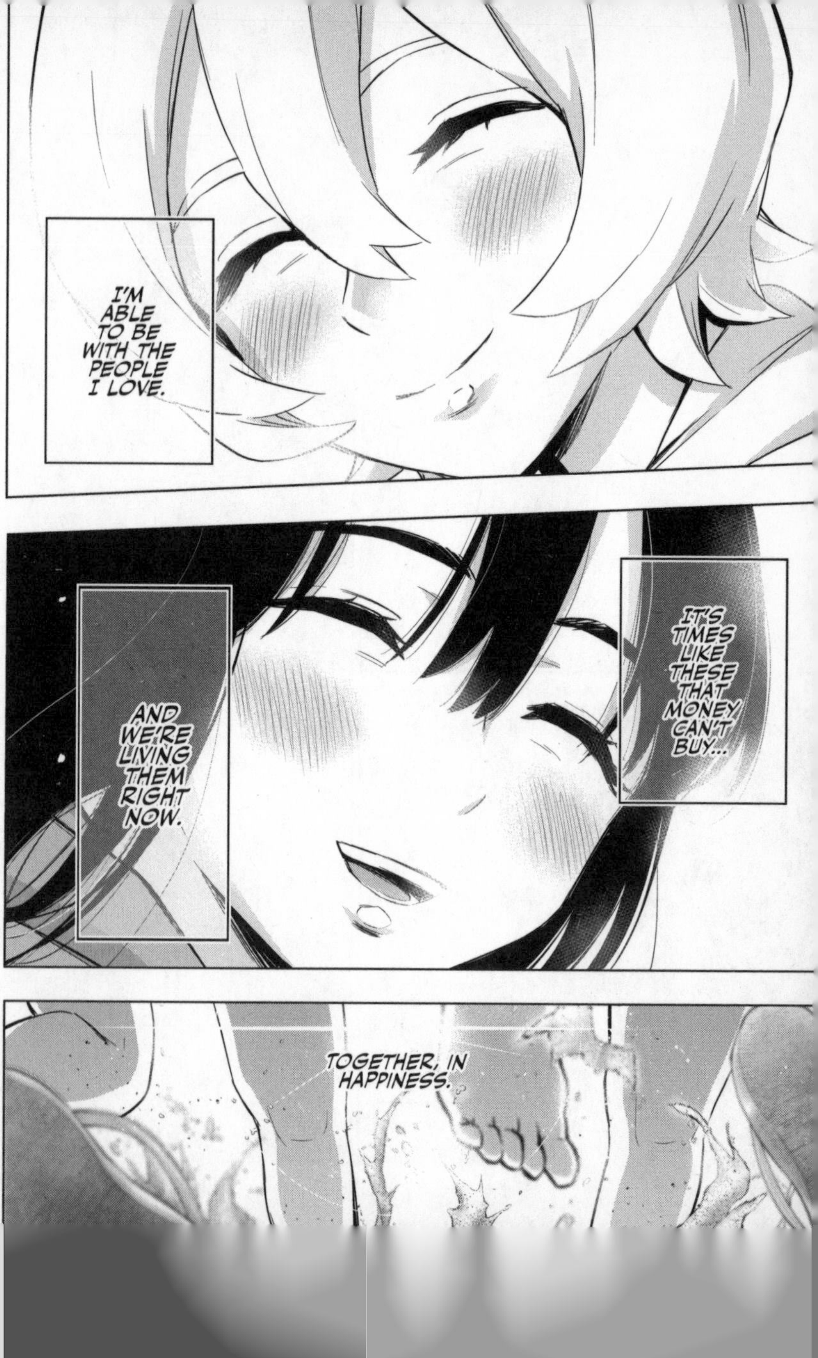
I'M ABLE TO BE WITH THE PEOPLE I LOVE.
IT'S TIMES LIKE THESE THAT MONEY CAN'T BUY...
AND WE'RE LIVING THEM RIGHT NOW.
TOGETHER, IN HAPPINESS.

Complete

AFTERWORD

It's finished!

How did you all like Magical Girl SITE?

I'm pretty sure I managed to draw up everything inside of me that I wanted to get out.

My original theme focused on unfortunate girls finding ways to earn their happiness. With a theme like that, a happy ending was really my only option.

As I worked, I kept telling myself, "It's going to have a happy ending! A happy ending! It will have a happy ending!"

Though the story has changed a bit, what began as Magical Girl Apocalypse ended as Magical Girl SITE, and now the magical girl saga has come to its end.

So what will I do for my next project?

Should I do a fantasy? Perhaps a slapstick love comedy? I'm not really sure what it will turn out to be at the moment, but I would be thrilled if you all would read it when the time comes.

For all of you who have read this from the very beginning, thank you so much! I hope we meet again sometime soon!

Kentaro Sato

SEVEN ~~SEAS~~ PRESENTS

MAGICAL GIRL SITE

story and art by KENTARO SATO

VOLUME 16

TRANSLATION
Wesley Bridges

ADAPTATION
Sam Mitchell

LETTERING AND RETOUCH
Christa Miesner

COVER DESIGN
Kris Aubin

PROOFREADER
B. Lana Guggenheim

EDITOR
Jenn Grunigen

PRINT MANAGER
Rhiannon Rasmussen-Silverstein

PRODUCTION MANAGER
Lissa Pattillo

MANAGING EDITOR
Julie Davis

ASSOCIATE PUBLISHER
Adam Arnold

PUBLISHER
Jason DeAngelis

MAHO SYOJYO SITE Volume 16
© Kentaro Sato 2019
Originally published in Japan in 2019 by Akita Publishing Co., Ltd.
English translation rights arranged with Akita Publishing Co., Ltd. through
TOHAN CORPORATION, Tokyo.

Seven Seas press and purchase enquiries can be sent to Marketing Manager
Lianne Sentar at press@gomanga.com. Information regarding the distribution
and purchase of digital editions is available from Digital Manager CK Russell
at digital@gomanga.com.

Seven Seas and the Seven Seas logo are trademarks of
Seven Seas Entertainment. All rights reserved.

ISBN: 978-1-64827-903-4

Printed in Canada

First Printing: November 2021

10 9 8 7 6 5 4 3 2 1

FOLLOW US ONLINE: www.sevenseasentertainment.com

READING DIRECTIONS

This book reads from **right to left**, Japanese style.
If this is your ~~first time~~
reading from ~~right to left~~
take it from t~~here~~
numbered dia~~gram~~
first, but you'~~ll~~

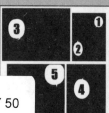